BOUND FOR AMERICA

The Transportation of
British Convicts to the Colonies
1718–1775

A. ROGER EKIRCH

CLARENDON PRESS · OXFORD

This book has been printed digitally and produced in a standard specification
in order to ensure its continuing availability

OXFORD
UNIVERSITY PRESS

Great Clarendon Street, Oxford OX2 6DP

Oxford University Press is a department of the University of Oxford.
It furthers the University's objective of excellence in research, scholarship,
and education by publishing worldwide in

Oxford New York

Auckland   Cape Town   Dar es Salaam   Hong Kong   Karachi
Kuala Lumpur   Madrid   Melbourne   Mexico City   Nairobi
New Delhi   Shanghai   Taipei   Toronto
With offices in
Argentina   Austria   Brazil   Chile   Czech Republic   France   Greece
Guatemala   Hungary   Italy   Japan   South Korea   Poland   Portugal
Singapore   Switzerland   Thailand   Turkey   Ukraine   Vietnam

Oxford is a registered trade mark of Oxford University Press
in the UK and in certain other countries

Published in the United States
by Oxford University Press Inc., New York

ISBN 978-0-19-820211-0

Printed and bound in Great Britain by CPI Antony Rowe,
Chippenham and Eastbourne

FOR ALICE

PREFACE

I became drawn to transportation, as the penalty of banishment was euphemistically called, while scanning the pages of that venerable early American newspaper, the *Pennsylvania Gazette*. Although never finding the information that I was hunting for, I did stumble upon Benjamin Franklin's celebrated polemic instructing Americans to send Mother England rattlesnakes in return for convicted felons. His bitterly sarcastic indictment propelled me to dig further, and I shortly discovered that transportation had much to say about eighteenth-century crime and society, on both sides of the Atlantic Ocean.

In the course of my research, I came to rely upon the resources of many institutions. I am grateful to the Public Record Office (at both Chancery Lane and Kew); the Scottish Record Office; the British Library; the Guildhall Records Office in London; the Bodleian Library of Oxford University; the record offices of Coventry, Cumbria, Derbyshire, Devon, Gloucestershire, and Leicestershire; the Brecknock Museum; and, most of all, the Cambridge University Library. I owe a particular debt to Christine J. Fenn and Janice MacDonald of the UL's Rare Books Department for assisting my work. In the United States, I wish to thank the Maryland Hall of Records; the Maryland Historical Society; the Library of Congress; Alderman Library of the University of Virginia; the Virginia State Library; the Colonial Williamsburg Research Center; the William L. Clements Library of the University of Michigan; and the Massachusetts Historical Society. Special thanks are expressed to Dorothy F. McCombs, Sharon D. Alls, and their fellow-librarians at Newman Library at Virginia Polytechnic Institute and State University.

Support for this study came from several sources, to whom I am very grateful: Virginia Tech, the National Endowment for the Humanities, and the American Philosophical Society. My largest debts are to Paul Mellon, the Managers of the Mellon Research Fund, and the Faculty of History at Cambridge University. This book was in its infancy when I received a year-long appointment at Cambridge as Paul Mellon Research Fellow in American History.

This good fortune aided my research immeasurably, not just because of the university's proximity to sources in London but also because of the assistance I received from local historians. My partners in crime, Joanna Innes and Peter King, were always willing to lend a hand or read an early draft, as were several specialists in American history: Roy Clayton, John A. Thompson, Betty C. Wood, William R. Brock, and Mark D. Kaplanoff. David and Margaret Reynolds helped me in innumerable ways. In addition, I became a Fellow Commoner of Peterhouse. For the many kindnesses I received there, I am deeply grateful to the Master, Lord Dacre (Hugh Trevor-Roper), and the Fellows of the College. Edward Norman, Paul Hopkins, Harold James, and Martin Golding were ever generous in their friendship. I should also like to thank Michael and Beatrice Hurst, whose unstinting good cheer made my visits to Oxford especially pleasant.

A number of people gave me their advice after reading either parts or all of earlier versions of the manuscript. Philip D. Morgan and Robert J. Brugger contributed their time and criticism on frequent occasions. Besides sharing his insights and research, John Beattie was an enormous source of encouragement. He has my fond appreciation. I also benefited from the comments of James Bacon, Paul G. E. Clemens, James S. Cockburn, Stephen J. Davies, Kenneth Morgan, Paul F. Paskoff, Marcus Rediker, Michael Ryder, and Shane White. Jack Greene, as ever, provided warm support, and John Russell-Wood furnished some delightfully droll counsel. For showing me portions of their unpublished research, I am indebted to Mollie Gillen, Farley Grubb, Peter C. Hoffer, John H. Langbein, Peter Linebaugh, Magalys Perez, Gary P. Secor, and Lida Stout. John Treadway kindly provided me with copies of some materials I missed at the Public Record Office.

Colleagues at Virginia Tech offered assistance at various times: Linda Arnold, Frederic J. Baumgartner, Richard F. Hirsh, Charles M. Reed, George Green Shackelford, Crandall A. Shifflett, and Joseph L. Wieczynski. I am grateful to Lisa Donis, Patty S. Mills, and Debbie Rhea for their accomplished typing. The Graphic Arts staff and, most particularly, Cathy Gorman were responsible for the figures and maps. For permission to draw upon portions of the book that earlier appeared in their journals, I thank the editors of the *American Historical Review,* the *Journal of British Studies,* and the *William and Mary Quarterly.* Ivon Asquith, Robert Faber, and Dorothy McLean of the Oxford University Press have been splendid editors. I very much appreciate their efforts on my behalf. My father has always been a wonderful source of inspiration, and my mother offered unfailing moral support. During research forays to Washington, DC, my sister and her husband, Caryl and George Williams, along with Morgan and Grayson, provided welcome hospitality. Most important, my final thanks are reserved for Alice, whose affection and good humour were invaluable. This book is dedicated to her, with love.

A.R.E.

Blacksburg, Virginia
August 1986

NB: All dates are rendered in new style, with the new year beginning on 1 January. Quotations are in the original spelling, except that abbreviations have been expanded and punctuation added where necessary. For the sake of convenience, the term 'Britain' is normally meant to include the whole of Ireland as well as England and Scotland (i.e. the British Isles rather than just the United Kingdom), and 'England' is normally meant to include Wales, as a reflection of the political realities of the time. Except where specially noted, references to monetary values in Britain are to British sterling and those to monetary values in America are to the common currency of the colony.

CONTENTS

MAPS AND FIGURES

ILLUSTRATIONS

TABLES

ABBREVIATIONS

Account of the Ordinary of Newgate	*The Ordinary of Newgate, His Account of the Behaviour, Confession and Dying Words, of the Malefactors who were Executed at Tyburn* (London, 1720–72)
AHR	*American Historical Review*
Cal. HO Papers	Joseph Redington and R. A. Roberts, eds., *Calendar of Home Office Papers of the Reign of George III,* 4 vols. (1878–99; reprint edn., Nendeln, Liechtenstein, 1967)
CGP	Cheston-Galloway Papers, Maryland Historical Society, Baltimore
CW	Colonial Williamsburg Inc., Research Center, Williamsburg
DCBL	Duncan Campbell Business Letter Book, Mitchell Library, Sydney, Australia
DCPL	Duncan Campbell Private Letter Book, Mitchell Library, Sydney, Australia
DNB	Leslie Stephen and Sidney Lee, eds., *Dictionary of National Biography,* 63 vols. (London, 1885–1900)
GLC	Landing Certificates, 1718–1736, Guildhall Records Office, London (Library of Congress photocopies, Washington, DC)
Hening's *Statutes*	William Waller Hening, ed., *The Statutes at Large; Being a Collection of All the Laws of Virginia from the First Session of the Legislature in the Year 1619,* 13 vols. (Richmond and Philadelphia, 1809–23)
HJ	*Historical Journal*
HPL	Harry Piper Letter Book, Alderman Library, University of Virginia, Charlottesville
Irish Statutes	*The Statutes at Large, Passed in the Parliaments, Held in Ireland* . . . 20 vols. (Dublin, 1786–1801)
JHB	H. R. McIlwaine and J. P. Kennedy, eds., *Journals of the House of Burgesses of Virginia,* 13 vols. (Richmond, 1905–15)
JHC	*Journals of the House of Commons,* 155 vols. (London, 1547–1900)

JHCI	*Journals of the House of Commons of the Kingdom of Ireland,* 19 vols. (Dublin, 1796–1800)
LJC	H. R. McIlwaine, ed., *Legislative Journals of the Council of Colonial Virginia, 1680–1776,* 3 vols. (Richmond, 1918–19)
Md. Archives	William Hand Browne *et al.,* eds., *Archives of Maryland* (Baltimore, 1883–)
Md. Gaz.	*Maryland Gazette* (Annapolis)
MHM	*Maryland Historical Magazine*
MHR	Maryland Hall of Records, Annapolis
MHS	Maryland Historical Society, Baltimore
Old Bailey Sessions Papers	*The Proceedings on the King's Commissions of the Peace, Oyer and Terminer, and Gaol Delivery for the City of London; and also Gaol Delivery for the County of Middlesex, Held at Justice-Hall in the Old Bailey* (London, 1718–77)
Pa. Gaz.	*Pennsylvania Gazette* (Philadelphia)
PP	*Past and Present*
PRO	Public Record Office, London
C	Chancery
CO	Colonial Office
HCA	High Court of Admiralty
HO	Home Office
PC	Privy Council
SP	State Papers, Domestic
T	Treasury
WO	War Office
SRO	Scottish Record Office, Edinburgh
GD	Gifts and Deposits
JC	High Court of Justiciary
RH	Register House
Va. Gaz.	*Virginia Gazette* (Williamsburg)
VMHB	*Virginia Magazine of History and Biography*
VSL	Virginia State Library, Richmond
WMQ	*William and Mary Quarterly*

It is much easier to extirpate than to amend Mankind.

SIR WILLIAM BLACKSTONE

Oh England, sweet England,
I fear I'll ne'er see you more,
And if I do its ten thousand to twenty.
For my fingers they are rotting, and my bones they are sore.
I wander about right down to death's door.
But if I can just live,
To see seven years more,
I will soon bid farewell to Virginny.

'VIRGINNY'

INTRODUCTION

A primary duty of civil society, as Edmund Burke reminded listeners shortly before the bloodbath of the French Revolution, is the protection of life and property from criminal violence. In Western culture, we have relied upon varying weapons to preserve social peace. For many years, death, torture, and other spectacles of harsh vengeance constituted favourite remedies, bolstered by lesser sanctions like fining, whipping, and pillorying. In more recent times, with the rise of hard labour and prolonged imprisonment, governments have often tried to segregate criminals from the social mainstream; less common have been efforts aimed at rehabilitation and returning reformed offenders to the normal rhythms of daily life. Still some societies, like eighteenth-century Britain, have sought to remove their malefactors altogether, by banishing them to distant continents.

Britain's policy of transporting criminals to her American colonies did not begin in the eighteenth century. As early as 1597, Parliament gave magistrates the power to exile rogues and vagabonds 'beyond the seas', and in 1615 James I authorized pardons for condemned felons on condition of banishment to the New World. But not until Parliament's passage a century later of the 1718 Transportation Act did Britain systematically adopt foreign exile as a punishment for serious crime. At an expence unprecedented for the country's criminal justice system, politicians, magistrates, and merchants transformed transportation from a sporadic, haphazard practice into a highly institutionalized procedure. Hundreds of felons were annually shipped from all parts of the British Isles to a handful of colonies 3,000 miles away and sold as servants.

By providing an intermediate penalty between capital punishment and lesser sanctions like whipping and branding, transportation became Britain's primary remedy for rising crime, a critical problem in the eyes of courts and government officials. During the course of the eighteenth-century, some 50,000 convicts were transported, including over two-thirds of all felons convicted at the Old Bailey, London's chief criminal court. And yet, despite its importance, transportation has never received much scholarly attention. All but ignoring it, some studies have assumed that punishment in England underwent a smooth transition from public spectacles of physical suffering to long terms of imprisonment.[1] Just a few works, particularly Abbot Emerson Smith's *Colonists in Bondage* and Richard B. Morris's *Government and Labor in Early America,* have given transportation to the colonies more than passing scrutiny. Though pioneering achievements, both studies, besides being brief and descriptive in their treatment, were published fully forty years ago.[2] Otherwise, only transportation to Australia, extending from 1787 until the mid-nineteenth century, has inspired a significant body of historical research, even though banishment by then constituted a less common punishment than it had in the days of transportation to America. With the exception of John Beattie's masterful new book, *Crime and the Courts in England, 1660–1800,* scant consideration has been paid to transportation's earlier role in Britain's criminal justice system, or to how the convict trade to the colonies was organized and controlled.[3] Further, historians have neglected the place that transported felons occupied as servants in early American society. Next to African slaves, they constituted the largest body of immigrants ever compelled to go to America. What kind of life did they lead? What sort of work did they do? Were they integrated into provincial communities or treated like social outcasts?

Transportation marked a profound transition in the history of British criminal justice. Unlike most non-capital punishments in

[1] See e.g. Pieter Spierenburg, *The Spectacle of Suffering: Executions and the Evolution of Repression: From a Preindustrial Metropolis to the European Experience* (Cambridge, 1984); Michael Ignatieff, *A Just Measure of Pain: The Penitentiary in the Industrial Revolution, 1750–1850* (New York, 1978). In a chapter on eighteenth-century punishment, Ignatieff mentions transportation briefly but concludes that the 'system of punishment' in England was 'heavily reliant . . . upon public ritual rather than confinement' (p. 42).
[2] Abbot Emerson Smith, *Colonists in Bondage: White Servitude and Convict Labor in America, 1607–1776* (Chapel Hill, NC, 1947), pp. 89–135; Richard B. Morris, *Government and Labor in Early America* (New York, 1946), pp. 323–37. See also Wilfrid Oldham, 'The Administration of the System of Transportation of British Convicts, 1763–1793' (Ph.D. diss., University of London, 1933); Frederick Hall Schmidt, 'British Convict Servant Labor in Colonial Virginia' (Ph.D. diss., College of William and Mary, 1976); and, for an anecdotal account, Peter Wilson Coldham, ed., *Bonded Passengers to America* (Baltimore, 1983), I.
[3] J. M. Beattie, *Crime and the Courts in England, 1660–1800* (Princeton, NJ, 1986). For an analysis of a single firm, see Kenneth Morgan, 'The Organization of the Convict Trade to Maryland: Stevenson, Randolph & Cheston, 1768–1775', *WMQ* 3rd Ser., XLII (1985), 201–27.

those days, it did not return criminals to the social mainstream. Its overriding purpose was neither rehabilitation nor deterrence, but ridding Britain of dangerous offenders. At a time when men and women felt their lives and property to be threatened daily by crime, sentencing convicted criminals to foreign exile carried enormous appeal. 'Sending annually abroad certain people, who only hurt society at home' was how a writer in 1766 described the aim of government policy.[1] Significantly, not only did transportation promise to alleviate the criminal menace without increased reliance on the death penalty, but it also afforded a remedy that did not place traditional British freedoms in jeopardy. Imprisonment at hard labour, a punishment employed elsewhere in Europe, might have isolated offenders from society, but, in the eyes of the public, it was associated with penal servitude and state tyranny. The widespread use of such a penalty, by sacrificing constitutional liberties for the sake of social peace, was vigorously opposed. By virtue of transportation, Britain was able to avoid a massive corrections system and the creation of a coercive force to staff it.

So long as the rights and liberties of Britons were not endangered at home, what happened to convicts abroad mattered little. As soon as they were safely consigned to merchants, authorities assumed no responsibility for their welfare. Parliament enacted laws to prevent their early return home but took no steps to regulate their treatment either at sea or in the colonies. Once vessels left British shores, private profit rather than penal policy shaped the character of transportation. The quality of care aboard ships, the ports to which they sailed, and the marketing of convicts as servants were determined by merchants and shipmasters. Likewise, in the Chesapeake colonies, where most transports were sent, they were left at the mercy of planters who kept the daily demands of their estates, not the needs of their servants, uppermost in mind.

For Britain's criminals, America scarcely seemed a land of opportunity. Although the bulk of them—young males without skilled trades—had been outcasts of a sort long before being banished, very few were eager to leave their homelands. Not only did they feel strong bonds of loyalty to hearth and kin, but once in the Chesapeake, transported felons encountered widespread exploitation. Tobacco planters, unlike their cousins across the Atlantic,

[1] John Callander, ed., *Terra Australis Cognita: or, Voyages to the Terra Australis* . . . (Edinburgh, 1766), I. 20.

felt few qualms about putting freeborn Englishmen to hard labour or, if need be, shackling them in chains. Neither the status of convicts as servants nor their living conditions were altogether different from those of slaves, and opportunities for achieving a settled social life were arguably worse. A few transports managed to form families and forge meaningful ties with other workers, but the typical convict endured a dreary fate. Fighting and heavy drinking became common antidotes to the drudgery of his existence. Did transported convicts turn once again to crime? The same features that rendered them an exploitable source of labour—being young, male, and poor—also made them potentially threatening. What happened once America began receiving large portions of Britain's most dangerous citizenry? In the colonies, there were dire forecasts of crime and social upheaval, and numerous provinces vainly attempted to halt the convict trade to their ports. Indeed, according to the claims of previous historians, colonial fears were often justified. One authority has written that 'such crimes as larceny and other offenses against property, in which convict servants participated to no inconsiderable degree, mounted rapidly', while another has argued, 'There can be no doubt that the convicts vastly increased the amount of lawlessness and crime in those colonies where they lived.'[1]

But Britain's crime problem, in fact, was not exported across the Atlantic. Surviving court records show that in areas where convicts were imported in large numbers they committed very few offences. The vast majority of colonial offenders came from more 'respectable' segments of the population, including not just other labourers but planters and gentlemen, too. Could the American experience have helped transported felons to escape their criminal pasts? Since most had been banished for crimes against property, perhaps opportunities for thieving were less available in the colonies. Then, also, America's environment might have provided destitute men and women with unprecedented economic opportunity, thereby making crime less necessary. Once freed from the rigours of servitude, convicts may have moved gradually into the mainstream of colonial life, as depicted by Daniel Defoe in *Moll Flanders* and the *Life of Colonel Jack*. A major objective of this study is to examine the ability of the colonies to assimilate the

---

[1] Morris, *Government and Labor*, pp. 468–9; Smith, *Colonists in Bondage*, p. 129.

'abandoned outcasts of the *British* Nation'.[1] Because convicts were newcomers starting at the bottom of white society, their progress affords an invaluable measure of opportunity in early America. One point deserves special emphasis. A basic assumption guiding this study is that Britain's convicts cannot be understood by resorting to facile stereotypes. Most convicts were neither petty thieves nor the members of a criminal underclass. While driven to crime by economic necessity, the majority were reasonably serious malefactors. I have not sought to romanticize their lives, but I *have* tried to convey something of their world, often through the experiences of individual men and women. Although there are plenty of statistical generalizations to be found in the pages of this book, I have also relied upon records of a more personal nature. In addition to convict petitions and runaway advertisements, two bodies of evidence were especially informative: the *Old Bailey Sessions Papers,* pamphlets that chronicled trials taking place at the Old Bailey, and the *Accounts of the Ordinary of Newgate,* tracts published in the wake of executions at Tyburn in London that contained, among other things, confessions dictated by the condemned and their short biographies penned by prison chaplains. From these narratives, which recent studies have shown to be essentially accurate,[2] I was able to amass a quantity of material relating to the social origins of convicts, the reasons they were drawn to crime, and the conditions under which they were transported. Some of this literature opens a rare window on their years in America and on the shadowy activities of those apprehended for returning home early. No other sources provide such an opportunity for recapturing the lives and distant voices of Britain's convicts.

In great measure, then, this book represents their story, told whenever possible in their words. Although it aims to present a comprehensive account of transportation during the period of its heyday, the chief focus of the study is on the people that were

[1] 'Philanthropos', *Md. Gaz.* 20 Aug. 1767.
[2] John H. Langbein, 'Shaping the Eighteenth-Century Criminal Trial: A View from the Ryder Sources', *University of Chicago Law Review,* L (1983), 3–26; P. Linebaugh, 'The Ordinary of Newgate and His *Account*', in J. S. Cockburn, ed., *Crime in England, 1550–1800* (Princeton, NJ, 1977), pp. 246–69; Michael Harris, 'Trials and Criminal Biographies: A Case Study in Distribution', in Robin Myers and Michael Harris, eds., *Sale and Distribution of Books from 1700* (Oxford, 1982), pp. 1–36.

exiled. Long shrouded in obscurity, they have much to tell us about the origins of crime and the treatment of lawbreakers in the Anglo-American world. The history of these cast-offs and how they fared on twin sides of the Atlantic offers a unique perspective on crime and society in the eighteenth century.

PROLOGUE

America excited noble aspirations in early explorers and visionaries. Natural abundance and vast stretches of primitive wilderness fuelled nearly as many dreams of utopian perfection as schemes for instant riches. Even before Europeans first followed their imaginations across the Atlantic, the New World inspired men's loftier instincts. No one in those days better appreciated America's potential than Richard Hakluyt. An Elizabethan clergyman who revelled in the adventures of English seadogs, Hakluyt never tired of promoting British imperialism; he deeply believed that England and the world would both benefit from overseas expansion. In return for English liberty and relief from Spanish tyranny, colonizing distant continents promised a steady supply of untapped riches. If his writings smacked of whimsy and bombast, no one could doubt his patriotism.

Nor could anyone question Hakluyt's compassion. Other than Catholic Spain, England's prime menace in the late sixteenth century lay in the troubled reaches of her countryside. Spiralling population growth and widespread unemployment had spawned droves of thieving beggars and a crisis of frightening dimensions. If early death, either on the gibbet or in the workhouse, offered one solution to domestic strife, a more humane remedy, argued Hakluyt, was to enlist petty criminals in the cause of British colonization. Once 'condempned for certen yeres in the western parts', they might 'be raised againe, and doe their countrie goodd service' by performing such useful chores as felling timber, mining precious minerals, and raising sugar cane. They would keep their lives, and England their labour.[1]

Perhaps he set his hopes too high or underestimated the darker side of man's soul, for England's first permanent colony fell far short of Hakluyt's expectations. Virginia brought neither gold and silver to Britain nor freedom to the wilderness. By virtue of its unhealthy environment and heavy reliance on tobacco cultivation,

---

[1] Richard Hakluyt, *A Discourse Concerning Western Planting,* ed. Charles Deane, Collections of the Maine Historical Society, 2nd Ser. (Cambridge, Mass., 1877), p. 37; Edmund S. Morgan, *American Slavery, American Freedom: The Ordeal of Colonial Virginia* (New York, 1975), pp. 14–31.

the colony did bring numerous indentured servants to an early death; otherwise it failed to resolve England's demographic crisis. And though a few thousand criminals and other malcontents were banished during the latter half of the seventeenth century, rarely did British officials display much enthusiasm for transporting larger numbers. Colonial apprehensions and mercantilist opposition to expelling British labourers conspired to defeat the prison without walls that Hakluyt had envisioned. Of course, by the last decades of the seventeenth century masterless men no longer posed such a threat to national tranquility, and visions of social turmoil loomed less large in English minds. Crime remained a common source of fear, but with the restoration of royal authority in 1660, brighter economic fortunes, and slowed population growth, the mother country entered an era of greater social and political peace. Though manufacturers could not promise full employment, England could better afford to resolve problems of law and order safely at home. Or so men hoped.[1]

---

[1] Smith, *Colonists in Bondage*, pp. 89–109; J. A. Sharpe, *Crime in Seventeenth-Century England: A County Study* (Cambridge, 1983), pp. 215–16, and *Crime in Early Modern England, 1550–1750* (London, 1984), pp. 59–60, 183–4; Beattie, *Crime and the Courts in England*, pp. 470–83; E. A. Wrigley and R. S. Schofield, *The Population History of England, 1547–1871: A Reconstruction* (London, 1981), pp. 161–2, 402–3, 408; Keith Wrightson, *English Society, 1580–1680* (London, 1982), pp. 142–8.

PART ONE: JUSTICE

1

BANISHING VICE

I

Although a dizzying spirit of material improvement swept England during the eighteenth century, life was often hard and cruel. Few families were left unscathed by poverty, violence, or the scourge of disease. In the midst of fabulous riches and flourishing trade, thousands languished in squalour and filth, made worse at times by rising prices and falling wages, and later in the century by a rapid upsurge in population. After levelling off during the second half of the seventeenth century, the number of England's inhabitants nearly doubled over the following hundred years. Death came easily. As J. H. Plumb has written, 'The wheel turned, some were crushed, some favoured. Life was cheap enough. Boys were urged to fight. Dogs baited bulls and bears. Cocks slaughtered each other for trivial wagers. Bare-fisted boxers fought the clock round and maimed each other for a few guineas.' Hogarth, not Gainsborough, captured the mood of the age.[1]

Almost no problem preyed more seriously upon public fears than crime. Not since the masterless men of over a century ago had lawlessness once again seemed such a menace to life and property. Although it remains unclear to what degree crime was increasing over the eighteenth century, whether it was rising at a faster rate than population, certainly there were periods of high criminal activity. Moreover, England's propertied classes believed that crime was becoming more prevalent, particularly thefts and other property offences. This was partly because of the greater publicity accorded to crime by the country's expanding newspaper trade, but also because the propertied grew anxious about threats to their mounting wealth posed by the growing masses of poor inhabiting London and other major cities. Unemployed labourers, uprooted from the traditional rural order by advances in commercial agriculture, vainly flocked to urban centres in search of work. Not only were

[1] Plumb, *Men and Centuries* (Boston, 1963), p. 9; Wrigley and Schofield, *Population History of England*, pp. 161-2, 402-3, 408.

many of them without means of subsistence, but they were also no longer bound by the paternalistic authority of the master or landlord. 'A miserable Prospect in a civilized Country,' complained a person in 1722, 'to see lawless Gangs of *Banditti*, Out-laws, and Felons, robbing and plundering their Fellow-Citizens, in Defiance of all Law'. Horace Walpole, himself the victim of a robbery in Hyde Park, bemoaned, 'One is forced to travel, even at noon, as if one was going to battle.'[1] Within London, bands of thieves roamed the streets. Named after such daring figures as Jack Hall, Isaac Rag, and James Valentine Carrick, gangs committed especially serious offences, such as robbery and horse-theft.[2] Meanwhile, parts of the countryside became plagued by teams of criminals utilizing a network of ale-houses and flashpubs. So widespread were the operations of one notorious gang that in 1764 its chief nemesis, Alderman John Hewitt of Coventry, calculated that 'this family confederacy' contained 'at least one hundred' members 'dispersed in different parties' throughout Britain. 'Their house in Northumberland', he wrote to the Earl of Halifax, was 'a kind of garrison, and the repository of the stolen property and cattle from all parts of the Kingdom'.[3]

[1] *An Account of the Endeavours That have been Used to Suppress Gaming-Houses* ... (London, 1722), p. 20; Walpole quoted in Leon Radzinowicz, *A History of English Criminal Law and its Administration from 1750* (London, 1948-68), I. 28; Beattie, *Crime and the Courts in England, passim*; Sharpe, *Crime in Seventeenth-Century England*, pp. 215-16; David Philips, ' "A New Engine of Power and Authority": The Institutionalization of Law-Enforcement in England, 1780-1830', in V. A. C. Gatrell, Bruce Lenman, and Geoffrey Parker, eds., *Crime and the Law: The Social History of Crime in Western Europe Since 1500* (London, 1980), p. 178.

[2] Gerald Howson, *Thief-Taker General: The Rise and Fall of Jonathan Wild* (London, 1970); John L. McMullan, *The Canting Crew: London's Criminal Underworld, 1550-1700* (New Brunswick, NJ, 1984). For contemporary references to gangs and their reputed stomping grounds, see e.g. *Account of Endeavours to Suppress Gaming-Houses*, p. 20; Lord Townshend to [?], 8 Oct. 1728, PC 1/4/86, PRO; Lord Carteret to Chairman of Middlesex Quarter Sessions, 26 Sept. 1744, SP 36/64/310-11, PRO; Westminster and Middlesex Justices of the Peace to Townshend, [1720s], SP 35/67/8; 'Methods to prevent Robbery', [1759?], SP 36/144/146.

[3] Hewitt to Halifax, 22 Nov. 1764, in [John Hewitt], *A Journal of the Proceedings of J. Hewitt* ... (n.p., 1790), p. 207; Hewitt to Halifax, 17 July 1763, SP 44/139/252-6; Douglas Hay, 'Crime, Authority and the Criminal Law: Staffordshire, 1750-1800' (Ph.D. diss., University of Warwick, 1975), pp. 157-76. For additional references to country gangs, see e.g. Mr Pope to Col. Negus, 21 Feb. 1725, SP 35/55/61; Sir John Shelley to Lord [?], 5 May 1729, SP 36/11/120; Philo Georgius to [Duke of Newcastle], 2 Mar. [1730?], SP 36/22/155-6; J. Lenthal to [?], 7 Oct. 1738, SP 44/131/37-9; Newcastle to Recorder of Chester, 10 Apr. 1739, SP 44/131/118; [?] to Lord Justices of Ireland, May 1754, SP 36/127/31; Sir William

Crime grew especially worrisome when times were hardest, since probably the great bulk of offences was committed, not by professional thieves, but by the needy poor. 'The immediate general cause of most Villanies', wrote the clergyman Francis Hare in 1731, 'is certainly the extreme Misery and Poverty great Numbers are reduced to'. In many places, a close relationship existed between criminal prosecutions at court and the rising price of basic foodstuffs like bread. For numerous working people, much of the weekly budget was devoted to food, particularly with the growth in manufacturing and wage labour by the eighteenth century, so that rising prices could prove disastrous. In urban areas, crime also escalated during peacetime, most visibly in the immediate aftermath of England's wars with France and Spain. The end of foreign conflict spurred widespread joblessness, as large numbers of workers in war-related industries found themselves unemployed, along with thousands of soldiers and sailors hardened by the brutality of military service. 'At the conclusion of a war', lamented Sir Stephen Janssen, 'we turn adrift so many thousand Men, great Numbers fall heedlessly to thieving as soon as their Pockets are empty'.[1]

Not just poverty, but wealth too was to blame. As centres of England's commercial revolution, London, Bristol, Liverpool, and other cities afforded rich fields for thieves. Besides offering them an anonymous setting in which to commit their crimes, urban thoroughfares abounded with new stores and warehouses, attracting scores of burglars and shop-lifters. The extension of commerce into the countryside and increased traffic on roads and waterways furnished added targets, especially for armed robbers. According to the 1788 editor of Hawkins's *Pleas of the Crown*, England's 'increase of commerce, opulence, and luxury' created a 'variety of

---

Maynard to Sec. Pitt, 19 Mar. 1760, SP 36/145/69; Andrew Knapp and William Baldwin, eds., *The Newgate Calendar* ... (London, 1824-28), II. 33; Derek Barlow, *Dick Turpin and the Gregory Gang* (Chichester, 1973); John G. Rule, 'The Manifold Causes of Rural Crime: Sheep-Stealing in England, c 1740-1840', in John Rule, ed., *Outside the Law: Studies in Crime and Order, 1650-1850* (Exeter, 1982), pp. 114-15.

[1] Francis Hare, *A Sermon Preached to the Societies for the Reformation of Manners* ... (London, 1731), p. 30; Janssen quoted in J. M. Beattie, 'The Pattern of Crime in England, 1660-1800', *PP* 62 (1974), 94; Beattie, *Crime and the Courts in England*, pp. 199-237; Douglas Hay, 'War, Dearth and Theft in the Eighteenth Century: The Record of the English Courts', *PP* 95 (1982), 117-60. Cf. Peter John Ryland King, 'Crime, Law and Society in Essex, 1740-1820' (Ph.D. diss., University of Cambridge, 1984), pp. 59-73.

temptations to fraud and rapine'. 'It appears to me wonderful,'
wrote a German visitor to London, 'that the crowds of poor
wretches who continuously fill the streets of the metropolis, excited
by the luxurious and effeminate life of the great, have not some
time or another entered into a general conspiracy to plunder them'.[1]
If harsh times brought rising crime, never had opportunities for
larceny been so great. Dire poverty always carries the potential for
lawlessness, but permitting want to spread amidst spectacular
wealth is asking for trouble.

The need to preserve social peace must have seemed unusually
grave when Parliament met during the winter months of 1717-18.
In the wake of the coronation of George I, urban disturbances had
grown so alarming that legislators passed the Riot Act of 1715,
which allowed demonstrators to be charged with a capital offence
if they failed to disperse when ordered to do so. That same year,
James Stuart the Pretender and his Scottish supporters had
embarked upon a bloody challenge to Hanoverian supremacy.
Although the rebellion was quashed and hundreds of prisoners
either executed or exiled to the colonies, recurring violence on the
part of London crowds and rumours of new Jacobite plots
kept Whig politicians continually on edge. A succession of stiff
Parliamentary acts, as well as the suspension of Habeas Corpus,
signalled the height of their alarm.[2] To make matters worse, the
arrival of peace in 1713 after twelve years of war with France had
sparked a sudden upsurge in serious crime. Military demobilization
set loose thousands of toughened young men in the London area
with a need for employment and a taste for hard living. If all else
failed, a dose of larceny promised to satisfy both. 'Desperate' was
Daniel Defoe's term for scores of seamen 'thrown on the public
without present subsistence'. In the parishes of Surrey belonging
to the metropolis of London, John Beattie has found that in 1714-
15 the rate of prosecution was 'close to being the highest of the

[1] Editor quoted in Douglas Hay, 'Property, Authority and the Criminal Law', in
Douglas Hay *et al.*, eds., *Albion's Fatal Tree: Crime and Society in Eighteenth-Century
England* (New York, 1975), p. 20; Johann Wilhelm von Archenholz quoted in
Radzinowicz, *History of English Criminal Law*, I. 711. See also P. Colquhoun, *A
Treatise on the Police of the Metropolis* . . . (London, 1800), *passim*; Beattie, 'Pattern
of Crime in England', pp. 92-3.
[2] Nicholas Rogers, 'Popular Protest in Early Hanoverian London', *PP* 79 (1978),
70-100.

eighteenth century'. Surrey records are incomplete for the next several years, but alarm in the capital remained widespread. In 1718, the City Marshal remarked, 'It is the general complaint of the taverns, the coffee-houses, the shop-keepers and others, that their customers are afraid when it is dark to come to their houses and shops for fear that their hats and wigs should be snitched from their heads or their swords taken from their sides, or that they may be blinded, knocked down, cut or stabbed'.[1]

Crown officers commanded few weapons to stem the rising crime wave that swept London and its environs. Agencies of law enforcement were notoriously ill-equipped. Unlike France and other absolutist monarchies in Europe, England lacked professional police on either the national or the county level. The country's long-standing commitment to protecting popular liberties hindered the development of a coercive bureaucracy. Much like the traditional fear Englishmen had of standing armies, the prospect of a full-time police force engendered widespread alarm. Consequently, London and other urban areas depended heavily upon amateur guardians like constables and watchmen who laboured under an onerous workload. 'The Liberties of a free people,' the philosopher William Paley remarked, 'and still more the jealousy with which these liberties are watched, and by which they are maintained, permit not those precautions and restraints, that inspection, scrutiny, and control, which are exercised with success in arbitrary governments.'[2]

Then, too, existing methods of punishment for convicted felons were limited. Government authorities looked to the death penalty as one means to ensure social peace, and by the early eighteenth century Parliament had made numerous crimes capital offences. Capital punishment, it was hoped, would help to compensate for inadequate agencies of law enforcement. If an amateur constabulary could not deter criminals, or later apprehend them, then the terror of the gallows might keep them honest.[3] On the other hand, use

---

[1] Defoe quoted in Beattie, 'Pattern of Crime in England', p. 94; Beattie, *Crime and the Courts in England*, pp. 214–16; City Marshall quoted in M. Dorothy George, *London Life in the 18th Century* (New York, 1965), pp. 10–11.

[2] Paley quoted in Philips, 'Law-Enforcement in England', pp. 161–2; John Brewer, 'An Ungovernable People? Law and Disorder in Stuart and Hanoverian England', *History Today*, XXX (1980), 22; Radzinowicz, *History of English Criminal Law*, I. 25–8; John H. Langbein, '*Albion's* Fatal Flaws', *PP* 98 (1983), 115–16.

[3] Radzinowicz, *History of English Criminal Law*, I. 27–8; Langbein, '*Albion's* Fatal Flaws', pp. 115–16.

of the death penalty for serious offences was partially limited by the fact that courts widely ignored the reading requirement for benefit of clergy, the privilege that literate offenders had traditionally invoked to escape hanging for some crimes. Eligibility for clergyable felonies was possible for most first-offenders, and in 1706 Parliament eliminated the literacy requirement once and for all. Non-capital forms of punishment included whipping, pillorying, and brief terms of imprisonment, which some courts seem to have experimented with after being permitted in 1706 to incarcerate clergied felons for a period of six months to two years. In sentencing malefactors, courts were forced to choose from among a range of often unsatisfactory alternatives: the harsh finality of the death penalty, branding with either a hot or cold iron as a condition of clergy, a short term of imprisonment, corporal punishment, or a lighter penalty. None held out much chance of reform in the offender or, except perhaps for the death penalty, any hope of deterrence, which was thought to be the prime purpose of most punishments in those days. In large urban areas, England no longer resembled a traditional, face-to-face society, and such public rituals as whippings and pilloryings, designed to shame and deter offenders, were losing their original rationale. Transients and other anonymous onlookers filled the crowds that gathered for such spectacles, not the victim's friends and neighbours as they did in more tightly-knit communities. Moreover, the calculated effect of these punishments was often lost upon the crowds themselves. Criminals did not always behave penitently, and even public executions were becoming known for their festive, carnival atmosphere. '*Some* have been so fool-hardy,' a person complained in 1701, 'as to go fearless and ranting to the Gallows, not in the least concerned at the approach of Death'. The writer Bernard Mandeville bemoaned the public perception that there was nothing to a hanging but an 'awry Neck and a wet pair of Breeches'.[1]

By the early eighteenth century, lawmakers had spent decades tinkering with England's system of punitive justice. Efforts at experimentation had repeatedly failed to bolster the nation's penal

---

[1] J. R., *Hanging, Not Punishment Enough, for Murtherers, High-way Men, and House-Breakers* . . . (London, 1701), p. 14; Mandeville, *An Enquiry into the Causes of the Frequent Executions at Tyburn* . . ., (1725; reprint edn., Millwood, NY, 1975), p. 37; Beattie, *Crime and the Courts in England*, pp. 450–500; Ignatieff, *Just Measure of Pain*, p. 23.

armoury. In many minds there was a growing sense that not just new punishments but new objectives in penal policy would have to be devised if lawlessness was to be effectively combated. Parliamentary dissatisfaction finally crested during the early turbulence of George I's reign, as members of the emergent Whig oligarchy searched anxiously for solutions to prevailing levels of crime and ways to restore order. Not surprisingly, perhaps, they adopted much the same remedy used after the uprising of 1715 to dispose of several hundred Jacobites. The fruit of their labours was the Transportation Act of 1718.

The act had been introduced into the House of Commons in late 1717 by William Thomson, a 39 year-old member from Ipswich and the Solicitor-General. Because Thomson also had served as the Recorder of London for the past three years and thus sat at the Old Bailey, he knew well the problem of mounting crime. Conditions being worst in the capital probably explains the inclusion of all the members from London, Middlesex, and Surrey on a committee appointed to consider the bill. Other than squabbles over wording with the House of Lords, the bill occasioned little apparent debate and was approved in early spring. Promising relief from 'robbery, burglary, and other felonies', its provisions were reasonably straightforward. No longer would transportation be confined solely to the pardoning process and acts of executive clemency, as it had been in past years. Petty larcenists and offenders convicted of clergyable, i.e. what were in practice non-capital, felonies could now be banished directly to America for seven years, and receivers of stolen goods banished for fourteen. Capital felons meanwhile remained eligible for royal mercy upon condition of transportation for either fourteen years or life. In addition, returning early from exile became a capital offence.[1]

Equally noteworthy, government authorities completely over-hauled the internal mechanics of transportation. Such was the makeshift nature of the system before 1718 that either convicts received the privilege of arranging their own passage or, more

---

[1] 'An act for the further preventing robbery, burglary, and other felonies, and for the more effectual transportation of felons . . .', 1718, 4 George I, c. 11; Minutes, 23 Dec. 1717, 20, 27 Jan. 1718, *JHC* XXXVIII. 667, 675, 691; House of Lords Minutes, 1718, in *The Manuscripts of the House of Lords*, New Ser. (London, 1977), XII. 506-8; Beattie, *Crime and the Courts in England*, p. 503. Henceforth, clergyable felonies will be referred to as non-capital felonies. For Thomson, see *DNB*, s.v. 'Thompson, Sir William'; Howson, *Thief-Taker General*, pp. 92-3.

commonly, courts consigned occasional batches of transports to English merchants eager to profit from the American servant trade. That happy arrangement began to founder when contractors developed a preference for only able-bodied males to sell as indentured servants. With passage of the new act, the Treasury began to subsidize transportation by paying merchants three pounds for every convict successfully shipped to the colonies, a major advance over the haphazard methods of past years. Though the subsidy only applied to felons from London, Middlesex, Buckinghamshire, and the Home Counties, courts elsewhere were expected to contract with merchants for the removal of local offenders.[1]

Transportation called for an unprecedented commitment of government resources. Never before had authorities been prepared to spend such large amounts of money or to become so actively involved in efforts to curb crime. Expenditures in the past had been limited to such modest matters as gaol construction, prisoner maintenance, and constables' expences. Maybe the country's 'financial revolution' made transportation possible. Government revenues over the previous twenty years had rapidly increased, so that exporting large numbers of felons across the Atlantic had now become more feasible.[2]

But if new revenues made transportation possible, another circumstance made its adoption seem imperative. England had lost control over its criminals. At a time of severe crisis, transportation offered numerous advantages over other punishments. To some degree, it gave greater hope of rehabilitation, much as Richard Hakluyt had dreamt. Though crime was primarily attributed to human frailty and criminals were viewed as the dregs of society, addicted to practically every kind of vice, prevailing opinion in the early eighteenth century attached some weight to the impact of environment upon criminal behaviour. Whether or not most Englishmen agreed with the sentiment expressed in the Transportation Act that 'idle persons' who 'want employment' may be 'tempted to become thieves', there was the hope that criminals might benefit as servants from the discipline of honest work, especially in the stark American wilderness

[1] 4 George I, c. 11; William Thomson to Lord [?], 2 Mar. 1736, SP 36/38/162; Smith, *Colonists in Bondage*, pp. 99–114.
[2] Beattie, *Crime and the Courts in England*, p. 504.

away from their confederates.[1] America, in turn, would profit from an injection of English labour to help colonists remedy their 'great want of servants', in the words of the preamble to the act. And it was further hoped that the prospect of an ocean crossing followed by servile labour in a distant continent might be sufficiently terrifying to keep potential lawbreakers on an honest course. The preamble pointedly observed that past punishments had 'not proved effectual to deter wicked and evil-disposed persons'.[2]

Each of these goals played a role. Still, the principal value of this punishment lay elsewhere. By punishing offenders abroad and removing them from public view, transportation could not have been chiefly intended as a deterrent. Nor was its primary objective filling America's need for able bodies; during this time, after all, economic thinking discouraged sending strong, young men to the colonies, so that domestic manufacturers could instead profit from their labour. Furthermore, the fact that transportation in past years had aroused colonial apprehensions must have been well known in government circles. As for prospects for human redemption, reclaiming lost souls was at most a secondary goal of penal policy. What needs to be stressed instead is that, unlike most non-capital punishments, transportation did not return criminals to the social mainstream. Its most compelling advantage, in the eyes of policymakers, lay in expelling from British shores significant quantities of threatening offenders whose ways would not be mended by more mild penalties. 'The intent of the Law', William Thomson later remarked, 'being to prevent their doing further mischiefs which they generally doe if in their power by being at large'. 'Those who merit transportation', noted another person, 'are bad subjects, and, if allowed scope, might essentially injure society'. Whatever the combined utility of other, less certain benefits, expulsion guaranteed swift deliverance from hundreds, potentially thousands, who had forfeited their right to remain members of civil society. 'Transported out of the way', the novelist and magistrate Henry Fielding later wrote.[3]

---

[1] 4 George I, c. 11; Joyce Oldham Appleby, *Economic Thought and Ideology in Seventeenth-Century England* (Princeton, NJ, 1978), pp. 141–4; Morgan, *American Slavery, American Freedom*, pp. 320–2. See also Sir John Fielding to Earl of Suffolk, 1 Feb. 1773, SP 37/10/11.

[2] 4 George I, c. 11.

[3] Report of Thomson, 6 Apr. 1737, SP 36/40/229; 'Candidus', *London Magazine*,

Significantly, transportation afforded lawmakers a means of ridding England of criminals without heavy reliance upon the hangman's noose. 'Draining the Nation of its offensive Rubbish, without taking away their Lives' was how a 1731 pamphleteer put it.[1] In past years, transportation pardons had been available to capital offenders, but by placing transportation on a firmer footing, the Act of 1718 made executive clemency a more realistic alternative to the death penalty. Then, too, transportation offered a means of removing criminals without threatening traditional English liberties. Prolonged imprisonment at hard labour might have rid society of numerous malefactors, but, in addition to the heavy cost of prisons and the danger of escapes, prison construction would have raised fears of excessive state power. Although felons and vagrants were occasionally incarcerated in workhouses, there was always the apprehension that a future tyrant could use a strong corrections system, staffed by a salaried bureaucracy, to subjugate the nation. Further, subjecting prisoners to hard labour, though considered a possible means of rehabilitation and though widely used on the Continent, smacked to many of slavery. 'Their being constantly seen in so sad a condition', a pamphleteer commented at the start of the century, 'would draw too great an Odium on the Government'. 'Such a punishment is not calculated for this *meridian of liberty*', a penal reformer later observed. In 1733, a writer noted the sentiment that 'ill Consequences' would result from imprisoning 'freeborn' Englishmen at hard labour, 'which in Time' could affect the people's 'Liberties', while another person similarly observed the view that the 'English are free, and should never be Slaves; they should not be accustomed to the sight of Chains which are the badges of Slavery'. Transportation, to be sure, threatened to impose involuntary servitude, but in a foreign land three thousand miles away, a prospect more palatable to the English public. Not only was America a primitive wilderness where all manner of licence seemed more common, including slavery and other varieties of

1776, p. 424; Fielding quoted in Beattie, 'Pattern of Crime in England', p. 93; Appleby, *Economic Thought and Ideology*, pp. 135-57. See also Herman Merivale, *Lectures on Colonization and Colonies* (1861; reprint edn., New York, 1967), p. 370. For evidence of colonial anxiety, see Smith, *Colonists in Bondage*, pp. 103-9. The pamphleteer 'J. R.' noted in 1701 that American planters were 'beginning already . . . to grow weary of *Those* they have' (*Hanging, Not Punishment Enough*, p. 18).

[1] George Ollyffe, *An Essay Humbly Offer'd for an Act of Parliament to Prevent Capital Crimes* (London, [1731]), pp. 11-12.

forced labour, but Englishmen would be spared a corrections system and the spectacle of manacled prisoners toiling like slaves. 'Punctilious' gentlemen 'disdain that *Englishmen* should be Slaves on *English* Land', a correspondent in the *Gentleman's Magazine* pointed out, 'and rather chuse *America* for the Theatre of our Shame'.[1] Out of sight, out of mind. Liberty would not be sacrificed for the sake of social peace, not, at least, in England. For a country threatened by mounting crime but dedicated to protecting popular freedoms, no other punishment could promise so much.

II

Transportation commanded widespread appeal. Though single magistrates lacked authority to banish offenders, quarter sessions and especially assize courts relied heavily upon the penalty. In 1720, a person claimed the the 'Correction of the Hangman' had already grown 'out of date since the Transportation Act', as had 'Whipping at the Carts Arse' and 'Burning in the Hand'. At the Old Bailey, offenders had started receiving the sentence immediately after passage of the act. During the April session in 1718, twenty-seven of fifty-one felons were ordered transported. From then until 1769, more than two-thirds of all Old Bailey felons (69.5 per cent) were banished to America. By contrast, only one in every six or seven received the death penalty (15.5 per cent).[2] Elsewhere, variations in sentencing existed from one county to the next, but for non-capital

---

[1] J. R., *Hanging, Not Punishment Enough*, pp. 16–17; Jonas Hanway, *The Defects of Police* . . . (London, 1775), p. 221; Eboranos [Thomas Robe], *Some Considerations for Rendering the Punishment of Criminals more Effectual* . . . (1733, reprinted in his *A Collection of Political Tracts* [London, 1735]), p. 48; 'Extract from an Essay on Punishment of Felony, etc. . . .', 1751, SP 36/117/382; 'Verus', *Gentleman's Magazine*, London, 1738, p. 288; Radzinowicz, *History of English Criminal Law*, I. 33, 422–3; Langbein, '*Albion's* Fatal Flaws', pp. 115–16. See also Mandeville, *Enquiry into the Causes of Frequent Executions*, p. 53. W. E. H. Lecky observed, 'English opinion in the eighteenth century allowed the execution of criminals to be treated as a popular amusement, but at the same time revolted against the continental custom of compelling chained prisoners to work in public, as utterly inconsistent with English liberty'. Quoted in Radzinowicz, *History of English Criminal Law*, I. 423. For the limited use of hard labour and houses of correction, see Beattie, *Crime and the Courts in England*, pp. 492–500.

[2] Alexander Smith, *A Compleat History of the Lives and Robberies of the Most Notorious Highway-men, Foot-pads, Shop-lifts and Cheats* (London, 1719–20), III. 339. Of 16,704 felons, 11,615 were sentenced to transportation, 2,593 received the death penalty, and 2,496 were given lesser punishments. *Old Bailey Sessions Papers*, 1718–69.

property offences, the most common variety of crime, recent studies indicate that banishment became the leading punishment over such lesser penalties as branding, whipping, and imprisonment. Figures for the mid-eighteenth century reveal that Surrey courts ordered over half of non-capital property offenders for transportation. In Essex during roughly the same period, most grand larcenists and housebreakers drew sentences of tranportation, as did nearly three-quarters of grand larcenists in Staffordshire during the third quarter of the century.[1]

Over the course of the eighteenth century, the number of transports rose, at least those from London, Middlesex, Buckinghamshire, and the Home Counties, if we may judge from records kept by the English Treasury from 1718 to 1772. During the first half of that period, 1718-45, 7,622 felons were transported, in contrast to 10,133 transported from 1745 to 1772. To a minor degree, this increase may have reflected the multiplying number of offences for which criminals could be banished. Between 1720 and 1765, Parliament passed sixteen acts establishing transportation as a penalty for crimes ranging from perjury to poaching.[2] Population growth and rising crime rates, however, generally inflated transportation levels. As shown in Figure 1, the number of transports grew with particular rapidity during peacetime. The aftermath of war brought not only normalized shipping but unemployment and economic distress. On the other hand, comparatively small numbers were transported during the War of the Austrian Succession, 1743-48, and the Seven Years War, 1755-63.

[1] J. M. Beattie, 'Crime and the Courts in Surrey, 1736-1753', in Cockburn, ed., *Crime in England*, p. 178; King, 'Crime, Law and Society in Essex', p. 342. The figures given on p. 487 of Douglas Hay's 'Crime, Authority and the Criminal Law' have been adjusted to include only non-capital offenders. The procedure whereby convicted felons received transportation sentences was described by the assize judge Dudley Ryder: 'The method is when a clergyable felony is found, the prisoner is asked by a clerk of arms [*sic*; arraigns] why judgement of death shall not be passed against him; the prisoner falls on his knees and begs transportation, and then no sentence of death is pronounced, but transportation or whipping.' Quoted in Langbein, 'Shaping the Eighteenth-Century Criminal Trial', p. 28 n. 103.

[2] Eris O'Brien, *The Foundation of Australia* (London, 1937), p. 86. The Home Counties comprised Essex, Hertfordshire, Kent, Sussex, and Surrey. In so far as the Treasury paid subsidies to merchants for the transportation of felons from London and nearby counties, it kept reasonably accurate records of their numbers. The original records can be found in Treasury Money Books in the Public Record Office, which I have used in conjunction with Marion and Jack Kaminkow, eds., *Original Lists of Emigrants in Bondage from London to the American Colonies, 1719-1744* (Baltimore, 1967), pp. 180-203, and Coldham, ed., *Bonded Passengers,*

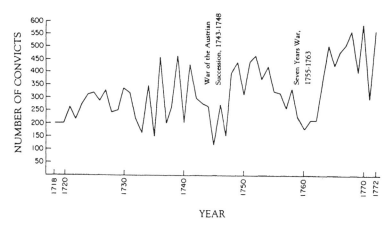

YEAR

FIG. 1. Convicts Transported fom London, Middlesex, Buckinghamshire, and the Home Counties, 1718–1772

Well over 30,000 convicts boarded ships in England for transportation to America from the beginning of the trade in 1718 to its end in 1775. Approximately 19,000 were transported from London, Middlesex, Buckinghamshire, and the Home Counties, if to Treasury figures for the period up to 1772 we add between 1,200 and 1,300 that were probably transported after 1772.[1] In the view of Duncan Campbell, a London merchant who traded in transports, roughly the same number of convicts were sentenced to transportation by courts in '*other parts* of the Kingdom' as in those counties and London. If one assumes that by 'Kingdom' Campbell meant England, convict totals between 1769 and 1776 lend credence to his estimate; 45.9 per cent of transports from England originated

I. pp. 172–7. Figures for convicts sentenced to transportation by assize and quarter sessions courts from 1750 to 1772 in the counties comprising the Midland assize circuit also reflect the impact of war. The average number of persons annually transpoited during those years was 46. During just the Seven Years War, it was 41, and from 1760 to 1762, only 28. John Howard, *An Account of the Principal Lazarettos in Europe* (Warrington, 1789), p. 253. To a slight degree, the decline in transports during wartime also may have reflected the fact that felons sometimes had the chance to serve in the military rather than be transported.

[1] The Treasury ceased paying subsidies in 1772, so I have had to estimate the number of felons from London and nearby counties who were transported from then until the trade ended in mid-1775. My computation is based on an annual average of 513 convicts given for the years 1769–76 in Howard, *Account of the Principal Lazarettos*, pp. 246–7.

outside London and nearby counties. The whole body of English transports consequently may have exceeded 36,000.[1] The English were not alone in the British Isles in trying to purge society of threatening offenders. Authorities in Scotland and Ireland also transported criminals to America, though variations existed among all three judicial systems. Ireland resorted to transportation beginning in the 1660s, though at the time restricting it only to reprieved felons. Statutes enacted by the Irish Parliament first extended transportation to non-capital felons in the early eighteenth century; courts could similarly banish vagrants by virtue of an act passed in 1707.[2] Extant court reports, though not abundant, indicate that assize and quarter sessions courts regularly sentenced both non-capital felons and vagrants to seven-year stays in America. Probably typical of sentencing practices was the April 1767 quarter session at Tholsel. Of fourteen defendants the court found guilty,

[1] Campbell to Evan Nepean, 29 Jan. 1787, CO 201/2/209, PRO. Although Buckinghamshire was included in Campbell's estimate in addition to London, Middlesex, and the Home Counties, I have counted it in my 1769-76 calculation as a county outside the environs of London since it lay in the Norfolk assize circuit. During those years, Buckinghamshire courts sentenced only 54 felons to transportation. Howard, *Account of the Principal Lazarettos*, pp. 246-7. Though transportation ended in 1775, totals include figures until mid-1776 because courts continued to sentence criminals to transportation during the early stages of the American Revolution.
  Probably the geographic origins of convicts during the period 1769-76 were roughly the same as those in earlier decades, at least in so far as the proportion of the English population represented by London, Middlesex, and the Home Counties remained fairly constant throughout the eighteenth century. Phyllis Deane and W. A. Cole, *British Economic Growth, 1688-1959: Trends and Structure* (Cambridge, 1967), p. 103.
  Such was transportation's popularity that public-minded men occasionally invoked it as a panacea for England's other great social ills, poverty and unemployment. The founding of Georgia as a debtor colony in the 1730s reflected this impulse, as did later efforts. Proposals were advanced for shipping abroad any one of several varieties of eighteenth-century poor: beggars, vagrants, or merely the long-term unemployed. In addition to the problem of expence, traditional opposition in Britain to the loss of potential manpower helped to defeat these plans. See e.g. *Account of Endeavours to Suppress Gaming-Houses*, p. 20; Joshua Gee, *The Trade and Navigation of Great-Britain Considered* (1738; reprint edn., New York, 1969), pp. 87-8; *Serious Thoughts in Regard to the Publick Disorders . . .* (London, [1751]), pp. 23-4; *Pa. Gaz.* 19 Oct. 1752; Saunders Welch to Lord [?], 18 Feb. 1754, SP 36/153/28; Callander, ed., *Terra Australis Cognita*, I. 21; Curtis P. Nettles, *The Roots of American Civilization: A History of American Colonial Life* (New York, 1938), p. 403.
[2] Smith, *Colonists in Bondage*, p. 134; Audrey Lockhart, 'Some Aspects of Emigration from Ireland to the North American Colonies between 1660 and 1775' (M. Litt. thesis, Trinity College, Dublin, 1971), pp. 80-4.

it sentenced two robbers to the death penalty and ordered twelve lesser felons for transportation.[1] From 1737 to 1743, according to a parliamentary report, Ireland transported 1,938 men and women, or an average of about 277 a year. Of the 1,938, though, it is likely that higher than average numbers, perhaps as many as 400 annually, were transported in 1740 and 1741 due to the increased levels of lawlessness that famine probably produced in those years. If we allow for that imbalance and estimate that in an ordinary year closer to 227 people, rather than 277, were transported, then more than 13,000 may have been expelled over the entire period from 1718 to 1775.[2]

In Scotland, courts had routinely banished criminals as early as the mid-seventeenth century. While some offenders were specifically ordered 'beyond the seas' or to 'his Majesty's plantations in America', most were merely banished 'furth of the Kingdom', largely because Scotland lacked legal claim to the colonies before its union with England in 1707. In later years, though Parliament's act in 1718 exempted Scotland, magistrates increasingly seem to have followed the lead of English courts. By the mid-eighteenth century, banishment to America had become 'one of the ordinary and established punishments' of the land. A local attorney in 1767 affirmed, 'In many cases it is absolutely necessary for the Safety of the State, and the good order of Society, that the Country should be rid of certain Criminals'.[3]

---

[1] *Belfast News-Letter*, 21 Apr. 1767. See also, e.g., ibid., 12 Apr. 1765, 5 Dec. 1766, 4 Sept. 1767, 5 Feb., 18 Mar. 1768, 14 Mar., 26 May, 12 Sept. 1769, 2 Nov. 1770; Lockhart, 'Emigration from Ireland', pp. 171-4; David Noel Doyle, *Ireland, Irishmen and Revolutionary America, 1760-1820* (Dublin, 1981), p. 64.

[2] In the mid-eighteenth century, the size of the Irish population did not grow dramatically. It rose from around 3,015,000 in 1731 to 3,530,000 in 1771. Deane and Cole, *British Economic Growth*, p. 6. My estimate of the total number of Irish transports represents a modification of the number given in my article, 'Bound for America: A Profile of British Convicts Transported to the Colonies, 1718-1775', *WMQ*, 3rd Ser., XLII (1985), pp. 186-7. The figure of 1,938 transports was compiled from totals for individual cities and counties. Minutes, 9 Feb. 1744, *JHCI* VII. 562-614. The combined totals given in 'A General abstract of the number of convict felons and vagabonds' on pp. 561-2 are inaccurate and not to be trusted.

[3] 'Information for Duncan Kennedy . . .', by Robert Blair, 2 Feb. 1767, JC 3/35, SRO; 'Information for John Gray . . .', 2 Feb. 1767, JC 3/34/628-9,634-5; David Hume, *Commentaries on the Law of Scotland, Respecting the Description and Punishment of Crimes* (Edinburgh, 1797), II. 101-19; Earl of Hay to [?], 21 Oct. 1725, SP 54/16/53.

Under Scottish law, courts reserved transportation mainly for capital offenders, usually on condition that they be banished for life. Moreover, defendants awaiting trial possessed the right to petition to be transported and thereby avoid further judicial proceedings and a possibly harsher punishment if convicted. Nearly always these requests were granted, particularly if victims of the crimes assented to the petitions. In Scotland's complex judicial system, authority to order transportation was held by various courts, including hereditary jurisdictions such as Argyllshire until 1747 when the Heritable Jurisdiction Act vested their powers in royal courts.[1] Perpetrators of the most serious crimes were tried by the High Court of Justiciary, Scotland's supreme royal court, which sat in Edinburgh and on circuit. From 1718 to 1775 this court, sitting in Edinburgh, prosecuted 395 felons whose sentences can be determined. Nearly half of them (181) either successfully petitioned or were ordered for transportation to America, in contrast to ninety-three who received the death penalty. Scotland's small population (about one-fifth of England's in 1751) and the High Court's comparatively small number of capital prosecutions meant that far fewer criminals were exiled from the country than from either England or Ireland. When lesser jurisdictions in Scotland and the Justiciary's three circuit courts are taken into account, it appears that close to 700 Scottish criminals were transported from 1718 to 1775.[2]

What was the total number of British convicts transported to America? Traditional estimates that put the figure at close to 30,000 are too conservative. If we consider that there were nearly 700

---

[1] 'Information for Gray', 2 Feb. 1767, JC 3/34/630–1; Stephen J. Davies, 'The Courts and the Scottish Legal System, 1600–1747: The Case of Stirlingshire', in Gatrell, Lenman, and Parker, eds., *Crime and the Law*, pp. 120–54.

[2] High Court figures are missing for the years 1722–25. Books of Adjournal, 1718–75, JC 3/8–39. For how I arrived at a total figure see my article, 'The Transportation of Scottish Criminals to America during the Eighteenth Century', *Journal of British Studies*, XXIV (1985), 370–1. The calculation does not include political prisoners transported during the eighteenth century, of whom there were over 1,200. Smith, *Colonists in Bondage*, 197–203. In David Dobson, comp., *Directory of Scots Banished to the American Plantations, 1650–1775* (Baltimore, 1984), there are 437 criminals identified as having been ordered for transportation from 1718 to 1775. Unfortunately, Dobson does not furnish adequate information on the judicial records that he consulted, making it impossible, on the basis of this figure, to estimate more accurately the total number of transports during those years.

transports from Scotland, more than 13,000 from Ireland, and at least 36,000 from England, we find that Britain probably banished some 50,000 people. Convicts represented as much as a quarter of all British emigrants to colonial America during the eighteenth century.[1]

III

Lewis Gunner, a gamekeeper in the small market-town of Alton in eastern Hampshire, was one of the first men in his neighbourhood condemned to die under the Waltham Black Act of 1723. Charged with maliciously firing his pistol inside a public house, Gunner, a notorious troublemaker and gang chieftain, was convicted in July 1729 at the Winchester assizes. Such a harsh sentence, however, deeply troubled the presiding judge, Sir John Fortescue, so that when upwards of fifty Alton residents petitioned for Gunner's life, he happily urged that the crown grant a pardon upon condition of transportation for fourteen years. In that way, mercy would be served and the 'quiet' of the 'Neighbourhood' insured, as Gunner's own supporters had desired.

Freed on bail and armed with two loaded pistols, Gunner heartily repaid his well-wishers. Before long, his gang had wounded an assistant constable, fired at a woman in front of her home, and mutilated all the cattle and horses belonging to a local farmer. In the meantime, the gang forced villagers to sign petitions to gain Gunner a free pardon by which to escape his forthcoming trip to America. Not only did the petitions attract numerous signatures, but local authorities dared not arrest him. 'Should He succeed and obtain his Freedom, which

---

[1] For the commonly accepted figure of 30,000 convicts, see Smith, *Colonists in Bondage*, pp. 116–17. Smith underestimated the number of English convicts, and he apparently did not include in his calculation convicts from Ireland and Scotland that are mentioned briefly on pp. 133–5. See also Morgan, 'Convict Trade to Maryland', p. 202; Schmidt, 'Convict Labor in Virginia', p. 71 n. 22. My immigration estimate was formed in conjunction with figures supplied in R. C. Simmons, *The American Colonies: From Settlements to Independence* (New York, 1976), p. 182.

God forbid . . . ,' predicted one Alton resident, 'We shall be glad to purchase our Safety on his Terms.'[1]

*

Symptomatic of Georgian England was the country's infamous 'Bloody Code'. At a time when property offences, in the popular mind, were rising, public officials continued to rely upon the terror of capital punishment in an attempt to bolster Britain's habitually weak agencies of law enforcement. Public hangings at Tyburn and rotting corpses adorning village greens bore stark testimony to a criminal code that, estimated William Blackstone, contained 160 capital offences by 1769. 'Our possessions are paled up with new edicts every day,' a contemporary noted, 'and hung round with gibbets to scare every invader.'[2]

According to popular lore, the severe nature of British justice meant that petty offenders filled the ranks of convicts transported to America. Saved from the grips of the executioner were beggars, prostitutes, and small-time thieves. Fairly typical we might conclude was the young woman who was banished by a London court in September 1771. Pregnant and famished, she had committed a felony by stealing a basin filled with soup.[3] On the other hand, although most transports were non-capital felons banished by virtue of the Transportation Act for a period of seven years, a good many of them were serious criminals. Non-capital felonies included crimes ranging from bigamy and buying stolen fish to manslaughter and assault with intent to rob, but the predominant offence for which felons were transported was grand larceny. In counties comprising the Norfolk assize circuit, for example, assize and quarter sessions courts between 1750 and 1772 sentenced 566 offenders to transportation. Grand larcenists numbered 523 (92.4 per cent). The crime was defined as the theft

---

[1] Georgius to [Newcastle], 2 Mar. [1730?], SP 36/22/155-6; Petition of Alton Inhabitants to Fortescue, 12 Sept. 1729, SP 36/15/71; Report of Justice Fortescue, 12 Sept. 1729, SP 36/15/68; Petition of Southampton Inhabitants to Newcastle, 4 Mar. [1730?], SP 36/22/158; Daniel Defoe, *A Tour Thro' the Whole Island of Great Britain* . . . (1724-26; reprint edn., London, 1968), I. 142. For the notorious Waltham Black Act and its numerous capital provisions, see E. P. Thompson, *Whigs and Hunters: The Origins of the Black Act* (London, 1975), and pp. 225-7 for information on Gunner.

[2] 'The Vicar of Wakefield', *London Magazine*, 1766, p. 199; William Blackstone, *Commentaries on the Laws of England* (Oxford, 1769), IV. 18.

[3] Purdie & Dixon's *Va. Gaz.* 2 Jan. 1772.

of goods valued at a shilling and above, not including thefts exceeding 4s. from shops or those exceeding 39s. from homes. In Surrey, according to John Beattie, about one-half of the goods mentioned in grand larceny indictments were each worth five or more shillings, and over one-fifth of them were each worth over two pounds. Besides money, stolen goods typically included clothing, food, furniture, and jewellery. For an unskilled labourer, whose daily income did not much exceed a shilling, the loss of property worth that sum or more to a thief did not represent a trifling crime.[1]

Additionally, most non-capital criminals who were not common offenders escaped being transported because of the discretionary nature of Britain's legal system. Though outwardly harsh, it permitted a surprising degree of flexibility, popular participation, and human compassion at all levels of judicial administration. Many non-capital offenders, in fact, were never formally tried, because victims of crimes were responsible for bringing prosecutions. Unless offenders seemed particularly threatening, victims frequently chose not to prosecute due to the trouble and the fees associated with court proceedings. 'What Encouragement is there for a Man, whose House is Broke open and Robbed perhaps of 30 or 40 Shillings worth of Goods', the essayist Timothy Nourse wondered, 'to throw 5 or 10 Pounds after it, to have him Tried, and perhaps Acquitted'? Further, according to J. A. Sharpe, communities possessed a 'number of methods of resolving conflicts, or of bringing sanctions against a delinquent, which were seen as offering less disruptive, perhaps more effective, and certainly cheaper remedies against certain offenders than did formal prosecution'. Such individuals might be sent to a house of correction or a local manor court, bound over to keep the peace, exhorted by the parish priest,

---

[1] Howard, *Account of the Principal Lazarettos*, p. 252; Langbein, 'Shaping the Fighteenth-Century Criminal Trial', p. 40; Beattie, *Crime and the Courts in England*, p. 184; W. A. Speck, *Stability and Strife: England, 1714-1760* (Cambridge, Mass., 1977), pp. 56-7. Although petty larceny, the theft of property worth less than a shilling, was a transportable offence, courts imposed corporal punishment in such cases unless a sudden rash of thefts plagued the community. According to the magistrate and novelist Henry Fielding, transporting petty larcenists had 'such an Appearance of extreme Severity, that few Judges' were 'willing to inflict such a Punishment'. Fielding, *A Proposal for Making an Effectual Provision for the Poor. . .* (London, 1753), p. 72; Beattie, 'Crime and the Courts in Surrey', pp. 177-9. Vagrants could also be sentenced to transportation, but this was not a very widespread practice. Communication from Joanna Innes, 17 Mar. 1984.

or ostracized by the community. Among persons that were instead tried at assizes and quarter sessions, most were probably 'persistent offenders' or 'outsiders who attracted an unusually hostile response'.[1]

If prosecuted and brought to trial, non-capital criminals still enjoyed a good chance of escaping transportation, especially those who impressed courts as objects of mercy rather than hardened offenders. In filing bills of indictment, prosecutors could choose to 'downvalue' the worth of stolen goods or 'downcharge' offences to ones that were not transportable. Grand juries, for their part, had the option of either finding true bills or throwing the bills out by marking them 'ignoramus'. In addition, many trial juries, if they chose not to acquit defendants, instead returned so-called 'partial verdicts' by finding them guilty of lesser crimes than the offences with which they were charged.[2] Once guilt was established, judges, too, could show mercy by sentencing offenders to punishments other than transportation, even when offenders were convicted of transportable offences. In 1737, William Thomson observed of

---

[1] Nourse, *Campania Foelix. Or, a Discourse of the Benefits and Improvements of Husbandry* (1700; reprint edn., New York, 1982), p. 290; Sharpe, 'The History of Crime in Late Medieval and Early Modern England: A Review of the Field', *Social History*, VII (1982), 195, and *Crime in Seventeenth-Century England*, p. 181. Similarly, Michael Ignatieff has remarked that prosecuted crime represented a 'small part of those disputes, conflicts, thefts, assaults too damaging, too threatening, too morally outrageous to be handled within the family, the work unit, the neighborhood, the street'. 'State, Civil Society, and Total Institutions: A Critique of Recent Social Histories of Punishment', *Crime and Justice: An Annual Review of Research*, III (1981), 186. See also Sharpe, *Crime in Early Modern England*, pp. 47-8, 77-93; King, 'Crime, Law and Society in Essex', pp. 149-92, 254-90; Langbein, 'Shaping the Eighteenth-Century Criminal Trial', pp. 47-50; J. M. Beattie, 'Towards a Study of Crime in 18th-Century England: A Note on Indictments', in Paul Fritz and David Williams, eds., *The Triumph of Culture: Eighteenth-Century Perspecitves* (Toronto, 1972), pp. 302-7, and 'Judicial Records and the Measurement of Crime in Eighteenth-Century England', in Louis A. Knafla, ed., *Crime and Criminal Justice in Europe and Canada* (Waterloo, Ontario, 1981), pp. 131-5; Bruce Lenman and Geoffrey Parker, 'The State, the Community and the Criminal Law in Early Modern Europe', in Gatrell, Lenman, and Parker, eds., *Crime and the Law*, pp. 18-23. Not until the 1750s were 'poor' prosecutors reimbursed for their costs, though only in felony cases resulting in convictions. Philips, 'Law-Enforcement in England', p. 179. For how justices of the peace dealt with minor offenders by not binding them over for trial at quarter sessions or the assizes, see Elizabeth Silverthorne, ed., *Deposition Book of Richard Wyatt, JP, 1767-1776* (Guilford, 1978); Elizabeth Crittal, ed., *The Justicing Notebook of William Hunt, 1744-1749* (Devizes, 1982); Norma Landau, *The Justices of the Peace, 1679-1760* (Berkeley, Calif., 1984), pp. 173-84.

[2] Langbein, 'Shaping the Eighteenth-Century Criminal Trial', pp. 50-5; King, 'Crime, Law and Society in Essex', pp. 301-4.

proceedings at the Old Bailey, 'If the Court find at the tryal any thing to render the prisoners objects of mercy they usually change the sentence from transportation to burning in the hand or whipping'. Conversely, in 1741 a judge remarked that a convicted thief in Surrey was not 'an Object of mercy and therefore I ordered him, instead of being burnt in the hand, to be Transported for Seven Years'.[1] In short, many opportunities existed by which non-capital offenders were able to avoid being sentenced to transportation. Those who failed to receive mercy at some stage of the judicial process were reasonably threatening criminals.

In Ireland, probably the pattern was similar, with one exception. In addition to other offenders, Irish courts banished large numbers of 'vagabonds'. These were generally vagrants associated in the common mind with petty crime, begging, and prostitution. Of 1,938 transports between 1737 and 1743, surviving records list offences for 990. Within this group, 531 were vagabonds and 459 were felons. Grand larcenists predominated among the latter. Of 208 felons between 1737 and 1743 whose precise crimes can be determined, 187 were guilty of grand larceny (89.9 per cent), 19 of petty larceny (9.1 per cent), and 2 of other infractions (1.0 per cent). As in England, non-capital property offences made up a large portion of transportable crimes.[2]

Sentencing in Scotland was different inasmuch as transportation was chiefly employed to punish capital offenders. Though the death penalty was normally reserved for the most heinous criminals, transportable offences sometimes included serious acts of violence. Of the 181 men and women banished to America by the High Court of Justiciary in Edinburgh from 1718 to 1775, 22 were charged with murder or infanticide, 10 with robbery, and 3 with rape. Among the others were horse thieves, kidnappers, and counterfeiters. The court showed special leniency to defendants

---

[1] Report of Thomson, 6 Apr. 1737, SP 36/40/229; Report of Fortescue, 26 Oct. 1741, SP 36/57/56. See also Report of Justice Raymond, 10 May 1728, SP 36/6/194–5; Report of Fortescue, 29 Aug. 1732, SP 36/28/64; Report of Justice Niccoll, 12 June 1771, SP 37/8/95. At the Old Bailey from 1718 until the early 1730s, a system also prevailed whereby judges sometimes altered transportation sentences during subsequent court sessions, i.e. after the original trials had taken place. See Report of Thomson, 18 July 1735, SP 36/35/141; Beattie, *Crime and the Courts in England*, pp. 510-11.

[2] Minutes, 9 Feb. 1744, *JHCI* VII. 561-614; John H. Langbein, *Torture and the Law of Proof: Europe and England in the Ancien Regime* (Chicago, 1977), pp. 34-5.

who petitioned for banishment before their cases came to trial. A person in Edinburgh noted in 1763 how 'great Criminals, who fear the Consequence of a Trial' often petitioned to be transported. Sometimes, however, the court proved willing to forgo the death penalty even after guilt had been established. 'It is generally the same Crime,' commented an attorney, 'to which the punishment of Death and the punishment of Transportation are applied, but differently applied according to the different Circumstances and degrees of guilt'.[1]

There were British transports, other than those from Scotland, who had committed such capital felonies as murder, highway robbery, and burglary. However notorious England's 'Bloody Code', courts and crown officials commonly circumvented the formal severity of statute law. Many capital offenders escaped the gallows by being banished instead. These were 'steadily winnowed', as John H. Langbein has remarked, from the pool of capital felons 'through the pre-trial, trial, and post-verdict phases of the criminal procedure'.

[1] Petition of William Dunbar, 24 Aug. 1763, HO 104/1, PRO; 'Information for Gray', 2 Feb. 1767, JC 3/34/631-2; Books of Adjournal, 1718-75, JC 3/8-39. Sentencing in the Highlands represented something of an exception to this pattern, at least where hereditary jurisdictions until 1747 retained the authority to banish criminals. Clan chiefs handled transportation arrangements in their localities as they saw fit. Not only were criminals occasionally permitted to escape from imprisonment because of 'Clan-Interest' or 'Clannish Terror', as the traveller Edward Burt described, but chiefs also sold innocent tenants to awaiting merchants under the guise that they had been ordered for transportation. 'It has been whispered,' Burt affirmed, 'their Crimes were only asking their Dues, and such-like Offences; and, I have been well assured, they have been threatened with hanging, or at least perpetual Imprisonment, to intimidate and force them to sign a Contract for their banishment.' [Edward Burt], *Letters From a Gentleman in the North of Scotland . . .* (London, 1754), I. 54–5. Probably the most notorious instance whereby tenants were disguised as criminals took place in 1739. Under the orders of two lairds on the Isle of Skye, Sir Alexander MacDonald and Norman MacLeod, over 100 men, women, and children were kidnapped one evening from their homes on Skye and several neighbouring islands. As one of the victims later recounted, they were 'all guarded and Delivered as Criminals and a good deal of them were at the Same time bound and tied'. The plan was to ship the prisoners to either New England or Pennsylvania, where they would be sold as servants, but when the vessel stopped to take on supplies at Donaghadie, in Northern Ireland, they escaped across the surrounding countryside. The hoax was uncovered and the tenants freed by an official inquiry, but neither MacDonald nor MacLeod was ever prosecuted. In fact, in 1741, MacLeod was elected to Parliament as a member from Inverness-shire. Deposition of John Johnston, 7 Nov. 1739, SP 63/402/137. See also the accompanying depositions and letters in SP 63/402/129-43; W. C. Mackenzie, *The Western Isles: Their History, Traditions and Place-Names* (Paisley, 1932), pp. 45–9.

In a sample of 200 felons, for instance, who appeared at the Old Bailey, roughly half could have been charged with a capital offence. Yet, of that number, only nine were eventually executed. Convicted criminals who offered some chance of rehabilitation but posed a potential menace were exiled to the colonies.[1] Juries especially showed little enthusiasm for the death penalty, particularly since transportation offered a ready alternative. As in the case of non-capital offenders, jurors frequently returned partial verdicts in capital trials, what Blackstone referred to as a 'kind of pious perjury'. In Surrey, juries between 1736 and 1753 awarded partial verdicts to 149 (45.4 per cent) of 328 offenders in capital property cases. Punishments included whipping and imprisonment, but most of the recipients, as many as 128 men and women, received seven-year transportation sentences. Generally juries only favoured the death penalty for particularly serious criminals who offered no prospect of mending their ways, persons whose moral degeneration was thought to be irreversible.[2]

Judges also exercised a vital hand in the sentencing process, just as they did when presiding at non-capital trials. Offenders convicted of capital crimes remained eligible for royal clemency, normally extended on a judge's recommendation that the offender be transported for fourteen years or life. Whenever condemned criminals petitioned the king to be transported, a secretary of state typically consulted the trial judge. Normally his advice, not royal whimsy, determined the final sentence—'a most noble and Excellent principle', wrote Justice Fortescue in 1740, 'not to be found with any other Prince in Europe'.[3]

Transportation pardons constituted an important element in the

[1] Langbein, 'Shaping the Eighteenth-Century Criminal Trial', p. 47.

[2] Blackstone, *Commentaries on the Laws*, IV. 239; Beattie, 'Crime and the Courts in Surrey', pp. 179–80; J. M. Beattie, 'Administering Justice without Police: Criminal Trial Procedure in Eighteenth-Century England', in Rita Donelan, ed., *The Maintenance of Order in Society* (Ottawa, 1982), p. 17; Beattie, *Crime and the Courts in England*, p. 225. See also King, 'Crime, Law and Society in Essex', pp. 301–4; Langbein, '*Albion's* Fatal Flaws', p. 106.

[3] Fortescue to [?], 11 Apr. 1740, SP 36/50/300; [?] to Fortescue, 8 Apr. 1740, SP 36/50/288. For several analyses of the pardon process, see Peter King, 'Decision-Makers and Decision-Making in the English Criminal Law, 1750–1800', *HJ* XXVII (1984), 38–51; Beattie, *Crime and the Courts in England*, pp. 430–49; Langbein, '*Albion's* Fatal Flaws', pp. 109–14. Cf. Douglas Hay's provocative argument that pardons represented an attempt by England's governing élite to foster the illusion that the legal system was merciful and fair. 'Property, Authority and the Criminal Law', in Hay *et al.*, eds., *Albion's Fatal Tree*, pp. 42–9.

sentencing of capital criminals. In the long run, they may have strengthened the death penalty by making it more tolerable to the public. John Beattie has written, 'If every prisoner who was guilty on the evidence of committing a capital offence had actually been hanged, . . . so many would have been executed every year that public acceptance of the law might well have been threatened'. But the immediate impact of pardons, as Beattie notes, was to introduce a welcome degree of compassion. Because transportation represented an attractive alternative to the death penalty, judges were more willing to recommend clemency than they had been in the decades preceding the Transportation Act. In Surrey, for instance, the percentage of condemned felons that were executed fell from roughly between 50 and 60 per cent in the late seventeenth century to about 45 per cent during the second quarter of the eighteenth century. 'Before that Act took Place,' a person remarked in 1733, 'the Execution of Criminals encreased every Year, but since, it has proportionably lessened'.[1]

Equally important, transportation pardons, much like partial verdicts returned by juries, meant that large numbers of capital felons were banished. As shown in Table 1, 1,121 felons at the Old Bailey between 1749 and 1771 were sentenced to death. Although 678 (60.5 per cent) met their appointed fate, 401 (35.8 per cent) obtained transportation pardons. The remaining 42 (3.8 per cent) either died in gaol or received free pardons setting them at liberty. The 443 felons who escaped hanging included 111 highwaymen, 90 housebreakers, 68 horse thieves, and 9 murderers. Meanwhile, on the Norfolk and the Midland assize circuits, less than 30 per cent of all capital felons were executed, with most of the others ordered instead for transportation.[2] In Scotland and Ireland, capital offenders received transportation pardons for crimes ranging from cattle theft to murder. Scottish courts, however, recommended fewer defendants for executive clemency than did some British tribunals, probably because capital offenders already enjoyed opportunities to be ordered for transportation. From 1768 to 1775,

[1] Beattie, 'Crime and the Courts in Surrey', p. 170; Eboranos, *Considerations for Rendering the Punishment of Criminals more Effectual*, p. 43; Beattie, *Crime and the Courts in England*, p. 518.
[2] Howard, *Account of the Principal Lazarettos*, pp. 252–3. Blackstone estimated that judges recommended one-half of all capital felons for royal mercy. *Commentaries on the Laws*, IV. 19.

Table 1. Old Bailey Offenders Condemned to Death, Executed, and Pardoned, 1749–1771 (percentages in parentheses)

Offence	Condemned to death	Executed	Pardoned[a]
Defrauding creditors	3 (100.0)	3 (100.0)	— —
Coining	11 (100.0)	10 (90.9)	1 (9.1)
Murder	81 (100.0)	72 (88.9)	9 (11.1)
Forgery	95 (100.0)	71 (74.7)	24 (25.3)
Returning from transportation	31 (100.0)	22 (71.0)	9 (29.0)
Highway robbery	362 (100.0)	251 (69.3)	111 (30.7)
Housebreaking	208 (100.0)	118 (56.7)	90 (43.3)
Horse-stealing	90 (100.0)	22 (24.4)	68 (75.6)
Other[b]	240 (100.0)	109 (45.4)	131 (54.6)
Total	1,121 (100.0)	678 (60.5)	443 (39.5)

Notes: a. 401 offenders who received transportation pardons and 42 offenders who died in gaol or received free pardons.

b. Shop-lifting, riot, and twelve other crimes.

Source: John Howard, *An Account of the Principal Lazarettos in Europe* (Warrington, 1789), p. 255.

for example, only 16 of 45 criminals (35.6 per cent) sentenced to death in Scotland were ultimately pardoned.[1]

The extent to which royal mercy ensured that significant numbers of capital felons joined lesser offenders in exile, even after juries had deemed them unworthy of partial verdicts, may be seen from records that have survived for some convicts transported to Maryland. Several counties in the colony methodically kept lists of arriving transports, and of those listed there were 2,050 men and women with identifiable sentences. Of that number, 393 or nearly one-fifth were the recipients of transportation pardons for fourteen years or life.[2]

Judges sifted a multitude of considerations in determining a capital convict's eligibility for transportation. Their decisions reflected priorities common to eighteenth-century courts, and judicial reports consequently throw considerable light on the criminal justice system. Judges occasionally commented upon such matters as rehabilitation

[1] Lockhart, 'Emigration from Ireland', pp. 171-4; Howard, *Account of the Principal Lazarettos*, p. 248.

[2] Kent County Bonds and Indentures, 1719-44, Queen Anne's County Land Records, 1727-50, Baltimore County Convict Record, 1770-74, Anne Arundel County Convict Record, 1771-75, MHR.

and the proper grounds for royal mercy. Their observations provide a unique view of transportation and its day-to-day role in government penal policy. What reasons, in their view, qualified capital convicts for transportation? Of course, the pardon process remained susceptible to corruption and the pleas of special interests, especially since executive clemency was the most coveted gift British justice could bestow. Pardons routinely required the payment of clerks' fees and other charges, and some officials solicited special bonuses for their influence. The bribe of twelve pounds demanded in 1720 by a Westminster justice of the peace was perhaps a typical sum in such instances, though the friends of Luke Ryley, a London felon, reportedly offered as much as a thousand pounds in an unsuccessful bid to prevent his execution. More fortunate was William Parsons (otherwise known as 'Robbing Parsons'), the son of a Nottinghamshire baronet. Sentenced in March 1749 to hang for forgery, Parsons obtained a transportation pardon through the aid of his brother-in-law, a Kent justice of the peace.[1]

Influence-peddling on the part of rich and powerful men pervaded public life. What is surprising is that it did not exert a greater impact upon judicial recommendations to the crown. In marginal cases, judges may have been swayed by considerations of social position and class, but enlisting powerful connections on behalf of hardened offenders did not always ensure success. As a judge explained in the matter of a habitual horse thief, 'I had strong Applications made to me at the assizes to reprieve him for Transportation, But under the Circumstances of his Case (there having been so many Indictments against him), I did not think, that I could in Justice comply with the Request.' No more receptive to such entreaties was the Recorder of London, William Thomson. Responsible for recommending clemency for city felons, Thomson staunchly opposed special considerations for undeserving offenders. 'If His Majesty should be induced, by the applicacon of persons

---

[1] Information of Ann Williams and David Roberts, 18 July 1720, SP 35/22/24b; *London Magazine*, 1744, p. 515. Connections could not save Parsons a second time, however, when later he was apprehended for returning early from transportation. *A Genuine . . . Account of the Life and Transactions of W. Parsons, Esq. . . .* (London, 1751), p. 6. See also Thomas Blencowe to Mr Wilmot, 9 Aug. 1720, in J. Charles Cox, *Three Centuries of Derbyshire Annals . . .* (London, 1890), II. 51-2; James Borthwick to John Drummond, 23 Sept. 1732, GD 24/1/464/E/248-9, SRO; 'Account of Fees paid in passing the Pardon of William Murray Esq.', Dec. 1746, SP 36/90/277; Thomas Giles and Thomas Cornwell to Halifax, 26 Mar. 1763, SP 44/87/176-7; Lord Warwick to Lord [?], 5 June 1771, *Cal. HO Papers*, III. 262-3.

who know the Relations of Highwaymen to grant His mercy . . .', he warned in 1726, 'it may prove of very dangerous consequence'.[1] Exceptions, to be sure, occurred, but more influential than upper-class intrigue was often the sheer weight of public opinion that communities marshalled to rescue condemned men from the gallows. Just as they affected earlier stages of the course of justice, localities continued to play a role. Even after juries rendered their verdicts, capital cases excited intense interest among neighbourhood residents. If the convicted man was an object of sympathy, juries themselves might urge judges to press for mercy. At the same time, judges might be petitioned by any number of community leaders and inhabitants, including victims of criminal acts, whose pleas for mercy sometimes influenced judicial recommendations most of all.[2]

Advocates of condemned men could appeal directly to Whitehall, though never with much success unless a judge's report bolstered their pleas. Among the most energetic petitioners were MPs eager to woo local electors by saving the lives of popular figures. A loyal government supporter from the borough of Launceston, Humphrey Morice, twice appealed in 1767 on behalf of William Pearse, condemned for plundering a shipwreck. Noting that 'the people of this neighbourhood are now more anxious than ever' to have Pearse saved, Morice wrote to the Earl of Shelburne, then secretary of state, that he need not explain 'the situation one is in with voters of boroughs just before a general election'. For his part, Shelburne reminded Morice of the gravity of the crime and noted that it was 'His Majesty's invariable rule to pay the greatest regard to the opinion of the judges', which in Pearse's case was strongly opposed to mercy. The trial judge, in fact, had already declared in court that 'no importunities whatsoever' could 'induce him to reprieve the criminal'.[3]

[1] Report of Justice Bathurst, 21 Aug. 1754, SP 36/128/33; Report of Thomson, 28 Jan. 1726, SP 35/61/16. See also, e.g., *Account of the Ordinary of Newgate*, 8 Aug. 1750, p. 71; Knapp and Baldwin, eds., *Newgate Calendar*, I. 274; Langbein, '*Albion's* Fatal Flaws', pp. 112–13.

[2] See e.g. Report of Thomson, 30 Mar. 1732, SP 36/26/152; Duke of Richmond to Lord [?], 15 Feb. 1737, SP 36/40/86; Hanbury Williams to Lord [?], 5 Aug. 1738, SP 36/46/54; Reports of Fortescue, 26 Mar. 1739, SP 36/47/154, 3 Sept. 1739, SP 36/48/143; Charles Clarke to Newcastle, 12 May 1747, SP 36/97/59; Report of Justice Barnett, 25 May 1750, SP 36/113/77; Report of Justice Wynne, 3 June 1762, *Cal. HO Papers*, I. 225; Report of Justice Smythe, 17 Aug. 1765, ibid. I. 661; Thomas Miller to Suffolk, 25 Oct. 1773, SP 54/46/249.

[3] Morice to Lord [Shelburne], 31 Aug. 1767, Morice to [Shelburne], 4 Sept. 1767, Shelburne to Morice, 30 Sept. 1767, Report of Justice Yates, 21 Sept. 1767, *Cal.*

More important was a range of other considerations affecting judicial reports and royal pardons. Judges, for one thing, frequently lent a compassionate ear to defendants willing to impeach criminal accomplices. So long as their testimony stood a good chance of producing successful convictions, transportation pardons were easily obtained. In Ireland after the murderer John M'Mahon turned king's evidence in 1772 against three sidekicks, they were hanged and he was transported for life.[1] On the other hand, pardons were difficult to procure during serious outbreaks of crime. In the midst of mounting lawlessness, the need for 'exemplary punishment' became all the more urgent. 'Surely when there is a Necessity of making public Examples of Executions,' the Westminster magistrate Sir John Fielding wrote in 1773, 'Wisdom Policy and Humanity dictate that the most abandoned dangerous and incorrigible Offenders should be pointed out for this melancholy Purpose'.[2] Convictions for certain crimes were also less likely to produce transportation pardons. Execution rates varied considerably among Old Bailey defendants sentenced to death between 1749 and 1771 (see Table 1). While more than three-quarters of all horse thieves received executive clemency, convicted murderers enjoyed less success. Forgery, coining, and defrauding creditors, all offences that directly endangered trade and manufacturing in addition to the well-being of the community, also resulted in fewer pardons. At a time of expanding economic prospects, courts proved anxious to protect Britain's steady commercial growth.[3]

Judges also tried to gauge the potential of criminal offenders for rehabilitation. Gender was a factor in so far as courts typically thought females less depraved than males. Important, too, was a defendant's character and criminal history. Judges looked fa-

---

HO Papers, II. 184–5, 187–8, 251. See also William Carr to Newcastle, 22 Aug. 1727, SP 36/3/11–12; [?] to Fortescue, 8 Apr. 1740, SP 36/50/288–9; George Townshend to Lord [?], 29 Oct. 1751, SP 36/117/181–2.

[1] Purdie & Dixon's *Va. Gaz.* 30 July 1772. See also, e.g., Thomson to Lord [?], 25 Sept. 1732, SP 36/28/150; Charles Horskene to Newcastle, 19 Jan. 1754, SP 36/125/105–6; Report of Bathurst, 21 Aug. 1754, SP 36/128/33; William Burke to John Holms, 29 Aug. 1766, *Cal. HO Papers*, II. 71.

[2] Report of Justices Pollen and Poore, 3 Oct. 1765, *Cal. HO Papers*, I. 662; Fielding to Suffolk, 1 Feb. 1773, SP 37/10/11. See also, e.g., Report of Lord Chief Baron Parker, 9 Aug. 1749, SP 36/111/48; Miller to Suffolk, 25 Oct. 1773, SP 54/46/248–9.

[3] Beattie, 'Crime and the Courts in Surrey', p. 181; Hay, 'Property, Authority and the Criminal Law', pp. 17–22.

vourably upon reputed first offenders along with defendants who either came from reputable families or could produce strong character witnesses. 'No Instance I believe can be produced, at least of late Years,' a London barrister observed in 1751, 'where any Man has actually suffered at Tyburn for the first Offence, except in the Case of Murder'.[1] An offender's reasons for committing a criminal act figured in judicial evaluations. Since prevailing attitudes attached some weight to crime's social and economic roots, pleas of poverty occasionally gained pardons. 'Theft, in case of hunger,' remarked Blackstone, 'is far more worthy of compassion, than when committed through avarice or to supply one in luxurious excesses'.[2]

A related factor was age. Felons in their teens, who could blame the excesses of youthful intemperance, stood a better chance of obtaining pardons than did more 'hardened villains', whose lives held out no hope of amendment. Courts often viewed young offenders as unwitting dupes seduced into committing criminal acts by older, more cunning compatriots. When two burglars in 1735 received death sentences at Kingston assizes, the judge recommended a pardon for only one, Thomas Richardson, a 'young man . . . drawn in by the other' who was 'an old offender'. Similarly, in 1754 clemency was urged for one of two women convicted of a Bristol robbery because she was 'a Young unexperienced Country Girl not more than Nineteen Years of Age'.[3] Only in isolated cases

[1] Joshua Fitzsimmonds, *Free and Candid Disquisitions, on the Nature and Execution of the Laws of England* . . . (London, 1751), p. 41. See also, e.g., Report of Thomson, 1 May 1732, SP 36/26/318; Report of Justice [Trevor?], 25 May [1733], SP 36/29/225; Justice Denton to Lord [?], 5 Sept. 1734, SP 36/32/228; Report of Justice [Wilkes?], 3 May 1738, SP 36/45/269; Report of Justice Denison, 29 May 1750, SP 36/113/87; Reports of Justice Adams, 4 July 1761, 22 Aug. 1763, *Cal. HO Papers*, I. 108, 353; Report of Justice Eardley, 9 Apr. 1766, ibid. II. 115; Beattie, *Crime and the Courts in England*, pp. 430-49.

[2] Blackstone quoted in King, 'Decision-Makers and Decision-Making', p. 42. See also, e.g., Report of Bathurst, 23 Mar. 1763, *Cal. HO Papers*, I. 353; Report of Justice Perrott, 14 July 1764, ibid. I. 487; Langbein, '*Albion's* Fatal Flaws', pp. 111-12.

[3] Report of Justice Reeve, 24 Oct. 1735, SP 36/36/177; Report of Recorder Foster, 30 Sept. 1754, SP 36/128/120-1. See also, e.g., Report of Justice Eyre, 20 Aug. 1731, SP 36/24/32; Report of Thomson, 1 May 1732, SP 36/26/318; Report of [Trevor?], 25 May [1733], SP 36/29/225; Denton to [?], 5 Sept. 1734, SP 36/32/228; Reports of [Wilkes?], 3 May 1738, SP 36/45/269, 12 Aug. 1738, SP 36/46/74-5, 24 Feb. 1749, SP 36/110/84-5; Report of Foster, 11 Apr. 1740, SP 36/50/299; Report of Justice Clive, 26 Oct. 1748, SP 36/108/67; Reports of Parker, 9 Aug. 1749, SP 36/111/47, 9 Feb. 1750, SP 36/112/41; N. Ball to Lord [?], [20?] Mar. 1754, SP 36/126/37; Report of Justice Legge, 1 Apr. 1755, SP 36/130/2-3;

might courts have thought young defendants best able to withstand the rigours of transportation, first in crossing the Atlantic and later in adjusting to life in the American wilderness.[1] Also unlikely is the possibility that judges thought such criminals best suited for the colonies' labour needs. None of those considerations ever figured in recommendations for clemency. Instead, the principal premiss guiding judges was their conviction that rehabilitation remained a possibility for youthful felons. Offenders, who by their gender, behaviour, upbringing, or age gave some hope of reformation, could escape the gallows. Their crimes were sufficiently grave to warrant banishment for fourteen years or even life, and transportation seemingly offered an environment less conducive to idleness and sin. There remained a chance that old habits might be broken and new virtues nurtured.

While criminals on the hangman's list hoped to find refuge in America, many other felons struggled to escape being transported. Some were recipients of transportation pardons trying to press their luck; most, however, were non-capital offenders anxious to avoid seven years in exile. Unsuccessful in receiving a light sentence at an earlier stage of the legal process, they petitioned for penalties less severe than transportation, or for free pardons setting them at liberty. How often petitions were granted by the crown is difficult to determine, though from 1761 to 1770 as many as 284 persons originally sentenced to transportation were ultimately successful.[2] Much like the frequent extension of transportation pardons, the granting of these petitions not only introduced a greater measure of mercy into the legal system, but it also affected the compostion of criminals transported to America.

As, too, in the case of transportation pardons, success or failure depended upon a written evaluation by the trial judge, who in turn based his decision upon many of the criteria that informed recommendations for capital felons. Age, sex, and character were

Report of Recorder *et al.* of Exeter, 6 Nov. 1764, *Cal. HO Papers*, I. 487; Report of Justice Yates, 15 Apr. 1765, ibid. I. 660.

[1] Judges did not express this concern, though for the suggestive comments of others, see [?] Jeffreys to Walter Carey, 10 Sept. 1738, SP 36/46/120; Ball to [?], [20?] Mar. 1754, SP 36/126/37; Recommendation regarding William Harris, 'Cases of Convicts', [1757?], SP 36/138/229.

[2] Criminal Pardons, 1761–70, *Cal. HO Papers*, I. 109–15, 226–31, 354–8, 487–94, 662–9, II. 116–24, 252–63, 410–19, 566–73, III. 149–58.

usual factors in the commutation of transportation sentences. Judges, however, sometimes weighed additional considerations. Serious illness and physical disabilities kept some convicts at home. Fairly typical was Lord Mansfield's request for a free pardon for John Thorne, a Wiltshire labourer. Convicted of highway robbery but pardoned on condition of transportation, Thorne had been struck blind soon after his arrest.[1] Then, also, the infirmities of old age aroused the sympathy of courts. In July 1727, Justice Alexander Denton requested pardons for two convicts imprisoned in Dorset and Southampton. Not only were both in a 'Starving and deplorable Condition', but, 'by reason of their Old Age', there was 'no likelyhood', he explained, 'of their being Transported'.[2]

The transportation of offenders invariably aroused community concern. Both in petitions to Whitehall and in meetings with court officers, residents vented their opinions when local felons were scheduled for exile. While judges bore the responsibility for recommending clemency, communities stood to gain or lose the most by their recommendations, and few issues excited such sharp passions within counties. For one thing, transportation could produce hardships for localities beyond paying the fees required by merchants. Banishing local breadwinners in some cases threw families onto parish poor rolls, creating new burdens that communities were reluctant to assume. Economic distress as much as humanitarian concern prompted more than a few churchwardens and other officials to favour convict petitions for lesser punishments or free pardons. 'They frequently choose rather to continue a pilfering Fellow among them', observed Sir Michael Foster, 'than to take the Burden of Wife and Children.' Determined to keep at least one community to its word, the king agreed in 1774 to pardon William Butcher of Boxhill parish only after his friends entered a £500 recognizance guaranteeing his good behaviour and constant residence in the parish. By doing so, the Earl of Rochford, then

---

[1] Report of Justice Mansfield, 20 Dec. 1759, SP 36/144/95. See also, e.g., Robert Tracy to [?], 6 May 1755, SP 36/130/142. This is not to say that disabled convicts were not transported. In June 1764, for instance, 13 of 69 Newgate transports were so 'indisposed' that they had to be conveyed to the dock in carts. *London Magazine*, 1764, p. 325.

[2] Report of Denton, 10 July 1727, SP 36/2/22. See also, e.g., [?] to Recorder of London, [June 1727], SP 36/1/65.

secretary of state, remarked, 'they will prove to His Majesty that they think he may be reclaimed'.[1]

Most judges proved hesitant to honour local pleas unless they were supported by mitigating circumstances. Equally important, in their eyes, was the likelihood that convicts would be assured trades after being pardoned, particularly since probation facilities did not exist in those days. Gainful employment was necessary to combat the twin dangers of poverty and idleness. An assize judge suggested a free pardon for Joseph Hall of Essex partly on the grounds that a local broadweaver had agreed to employ Hall as an apprentice— 'a more Effectual means to Reform him than Transportation', the judge assured the king in his report. In 1735, William Thomson was against clemency for a thief whose unsavoury reputation, he predicted, would inhibit others from offering employment. 'After being Convicted of Theft in this manner,' Thomson bluntly warned, 'he cannot expect to be employed againe so as to maintaine his family in an honest way.' Transportation, he asserted, remained the proper solution.[2]

Communities, of course, rarely endorsed pardon petitions without first weighing all the consequences. Just as transportation occasionally brought unwelcome financial strains, it also rid localities of menacing offenders. Felons who seemed least threatening attracted the greatest sympathy and support. Thus, Benjamin Rand of Hammersmith received the warm assistance of local friends. Petitioners on his behalf strongly affirmed that Rand, a disabled soldier sentenced to transportation for theft, had a pregnant wife, and, moreover, had 'always behaved himself as a Good and Civil Neighbour among us'. In 1751, Drayton residents petitioned on behalf of a Shropshire woman, long known for her 'good behaviour', so that she might 'dwell amongst her neighbours again'. In contrast,

[1] Foster to [?], 5 Apr. 1760, SP 36/145/105; Earl of Rochford to Earl of Ashburnham, 17 Aug. 1774, *Cal. HO Papers*, IV. 238. See also, e.g., Petition of Benjamin Rand and Hammersmith Inhabitants to Queen, [1729], SP 36/15/47; Petition of St John Wappin Parishioners to King, [1735], SP 36/35/111; Report of Thomson, 18 July 1735, SP 36/35/141; Petition of Aldeburgh Parishioners to [?], 7 Apr. 1740, SP 36/50/278; Petition of Drayton Inhabitants to Sir Martin Wright, [1751], SP 36/116/306.

[2] Report of Eyre, 20 Aug. 1731, SP 36/24/32-3; Report of Thomson, 18 July 1735, SP 36/35/141; Langbein, '*Albion's* Fatal Flaws', p. 111. See also, e.g., Thomson to [?], 16 June 1732, SP 36/27/34; Report of Thomson, 12 Aug. 1732, SP 36/27/294; Report of Recorder Eyre, 19 Nov. 1767, Reports of Justice Hawkins, 21 Mar., 1 Oct. 1768, *Cal. HO Papers*, II. 252, 405, 410.

the Derbyshire apprentice John Williams, prosecuted for theft by his master, encountered stout opposition to his pardon application after he had threatened his master with revenge; and memorialists to the king opposed a pardon for Thomas Jones because they feared 'his iniquitous Practices in being sett at large'. A judge in 1732 opposed pardoning a thief because he had a 'very ill Caracter' from local 'Gentlemen' and had been guilty of 'many crimes'. 'Transportation', he urged, was 'a suitable punishment'. Equally notorious was a Maidstone criminal whose transportation sentence provoked a loud burst of applause from the people assembled at court. 'The Outrages He has committed', remarked one person, 'have been so enormous, that if He is not totally removed, Nobody can be safe.'[1]

If the ranks of transported convicts did not normally include Britain's most dangerous criminals, for whom the death penalty was reserved, neither were they filled with many beggars, petty thieves, and prostitutes. The principal exception consisted of large numbers of Irish vagrants. Otherwise, grand larcenists made up the majority of transports. Furthermore, due to the discretionary nature of British justice, more than a few convicts were capital felons and the beneficiaries of either partial verdicts or executive clemency. For example, of the 517 property offenders sentenced to transportation in Surrey from 1736 to 1753, 128 men and women (24.8 per cent) had received partial verdicts, whereas another 92 (17.8 per cent) had obtained transportation pardons. In short, as many as 220 Surrey convicts (42.6 per cent) ordered for transportation were in some sense capital offenders.[2]

In some capital cases, it must be·emphasized that transports had committed major crimes prior to the offences for which they were sentenced by courts. While first-time capital offenders stood the best chance of escaping the gallows, courts could not always

---

[1] Petition of Rand and Hammersmith Inhabitants to Queen, [1729], SP 36/15/47; Petition of Drayton Inhabitants to Wright, [1751], SP 36/116/306; Francis De la Balle *et al.* to King, [1744?], SP 36/64/446; Report of Fortescue, 24 Aug. 1732, SP 36/28/64; Thomas Winborne *et al.* to Lord [?], 23 July 1735, SP 36/35/152-3; Report of Thomson, 18 July 1735, SP 36/35/141; P. [Cromp?] to Lord Sydney, 17 Jan. 1785, HO 42/6/38. See also, e.g., Thomas Martin to [?], 18 Aug. 1732, SP 36/28/8; Petition of Corn Traders to Newcastle, [1743?], SP 36/62/277; Petition of Corn Traders to Duke of Bedford, 24 Aug. 1750, SP 36/114/138; Thomas Lane to Earl of [Holdernesse?], 22 Mar. 1760, SP 36/145/85-6.

[2] Beattie, 'Crime and the Courts in Surrey', pp. 178, 180.

be aware of past convictions in order to punish recidivists more severely. The transmission of criminal intelligence between different legal jurisdictions was costly and inconvenient. Moreover, quite a few transports probably had committed crimes that were never prosecuted, especially if we consider Britain's inefficient system of law enforcement. The police magistrate Patrick Colquhoun estimated that no more than a tenth of crimes committed in London at the end of the eighteenth century resulted in indictments. Among London convicts ordered for transportation in early 1772, Alexander Clubb had reputedly committed upwards of twenty-five highway robberies in Kent, while Robert Day had stolen some sixty horses. Similarly, the London robbery for which John Grimes was transported was but the 'first Crime' he 'was known to be guilty of'. Previously, he had committed numerous offences throughout England and Ireland as the member of a gang of robbers and pickpockets.[1]

In addition to more routine opportunities courts and communities possessed to exercise discretion, the pardon process played a particularly crucial role in determining the composition of British transports. Whereas royal mercy granted to condemned criminals was meant to ensure that transported convicts embodied the least serious capital offenders, the extension of free pardons and lesser punishments meant that transports also included the most serious non-capital offenders. Those who were judged by courts and communities to pose a threat to social peace were cast for the colonies. But then, transportation was intended to serve British, not colonial, needs. Despite Parliament's reference in the Transportation Act to America's want of servants, clearly judges, juries, and high crown officials never gave genuine consideration to labour shortages in banishing men and women to America. Along with ridding Britain of large numbers of non-capital offenders, transportation extended a measure of mercy to capital felons who, in the minds of courts and crown officials, gave some hope of rehabilitation but

---

[1] Beattie, 'Pattern of Crime in England', p. 54; Fred Shelley, ed., 'The Departing Confessions of Three Rogues, 1765', *MHM* LII (1957), 343; Purdie and Dixon's *Va. Gaz.* 16 July 1772. See also King, 'Crime, Law and Society in Essex', pp. 29-30. Not until the 1770s, through the efforts of Sir John Fielding, was an attempt made to collect and disseminate criminal information on a national scale. See John Styles, 'Sir John Fielding and the Problem of Criminal Investigation in Eighteenth-Century England', *Transactions of the Royal Historical Society*, 5th Ser., XXXIII (1983), 127-49.

whose crimes were alarming enough to warrant banishment for fourteen or more years. Whether or not rehabilitation succeeded, all would be safely removed from the ranks of society. As a resident of the village of Alton remarked after urging that a notorious troublemaker be transported, 'We were in Hopes that we should then have been ridd of Him, and the Fears, which he had put us all in'. Transportation offered a much-needed alternative to existing punishments without putting the public at serious risk — not, at least, the British public.[1]

---

[1] Georgius to [Newcastle], 2 Mar. [1730?], SP 36/22/155. The author of a parody of Jonathan Swift's *Gulliver's Travels* quipped: 'It must be observed to the Honour of the *Lilliputians*, who have in all Ages been famous for their Politicks, that they have the Art of of civilizing their remote Dominions without doing much Injury to their Native Country; for when any of their People have forfeited the Rights of Society, by Robberies, Seditions, or any other Crimes, which make it not safe to suffer them to live, and yet are esteemed scarce heinous enough to be punished with Death, they send them to some distant Colony for a certain Number of Years proportionate to their Crimes. Of these Mr. Gulliver during his Stay, saw ten thousand conveyed from the Prisons of *Mildendo* in close Lighters to Ships that lay at Anchor in the River to carry them to *Columbia*, where they were disposed among the Inhabitants, undoubtedly very much to the Propagation of Knowledge and Virtue, and no less to the Honour of their Native Country.' 'Debates in the Senate of Magna Lilliputia', *Gentleman's Magazine*, 1738, p. 286.

2

NATIVE SONS

I

After the death penalty, transportation was Britain's most severe sanction. By forfeiting the right to remain within the bounds of civil society, convicts truly became outcasts. How different were these exiles from their fellow countrymen? Previous studies have provided little information on their social and geographic origins. Where in England and the rest of Britain did most convicts come from? What were their ages, sex, and occupations? Did they represent a cross-section of the population or a narrow segment? Rather than moving in the mainstream of eighteenth-century society, were many already down and out before being expelled from British shores?

Widespread reliance by courts upon transportation made for an arguably more geographically diverse population than any other set of British emigrants to the New World. Transported felons came from every corner of the British Isles, from the Cornish cliffs to the Scottish Highlands, though with variations from one area to another depending on population density, rates and types of crime, and the sentencing practices of local courts. The smallest proportion of convicts, as we have seen, came from Scotand. Although its inhabitants formed nearly 12 per cent of the population of the British Isles, Scotland probably provided less than 2 per cent of all transported felons over the course of the eighteenth century. Scots were occasionally tried in English courts, but the number sentenced must have been minute, judging from the fact that of 1,126 felons hanged at Tyburn in London during the first half of the century whose origins can be determined, only thirty were native Scots.[1]

A much larger proportion of transports was Irish. If vagabonds are included as well as felons, Irish courts may have furnished slightly more than a quarter of all transports, almost the same

---

[1] Deane and Cole, *British Economic Growth*, p. 6; Peter Linebaugh, 'Tyburn: A Study of Crime and the Labouring Poor in London during the First Half of the Eighteenth Century' (Ph.D. diss., University of Warwick, 1975), p. 332.

proportion that Ireland's population constituted in the entire British population. From 1737 to 1743, according to a parliamentary report, practically half of Irish transports were sentenced in the province of Leinster, which contained about one-third of the Irish population in 1744. With the city of Dublin within its bounds, Leinster accounted for 904 (46.7 per cent) of 1,938 men and women transported to the colonies. Munster sent 553 (28.5 per cent); Connaught, 145 (7.5 per cent); and Ulster, 336 (17.3 per cent).[1] Many Irish criminals also ended up in English courts. By the early eighteenth century, swarms of emigrants eager for work were crossing the Irish Sea, many of whom turned to crime. In addition, London reputedly served as a magnet to criminals on the run from Irish authorities. 'To prevent these desperadoes coming here', the high constable Saunders Welch asserted in 1754, 'will be the prevention of many Robberies.' Of the persons hanged at Tyburn, Irish criminals made up nearly 15 per cent.[2]

The majority of transports were native Englishmen sentenced by English courts. A large number of these sentences originated in London and nearby counties, where crime rates were higher than in more rural areas. From 1769 to 1776, for instance, English courts annually ordered an average of 933 convicts for transportation. Of these, as many as 505 received their sentences in London, Middlesex, and the Home Counties, an area encompassing only about 22 per cent of the English population.[3] A sizable number of London convicts were newcomers from other parts of England as well as from Ireland. Inasmuch as London's growth during the eighteenth century was fuelled by a steady stream of migrants, one inhabitant claimed in 1757 that upwards of 'two thirds of the grown persons at any time in London come from distant parts'. The exact percentage of non-natives among transported convicts is impossible to determine, but only 40.8 per cent of the felons hanged at Tyburn

---

[1] Deane and Cole, *British Economic Growth*, p. 6; Stuart Daultrey, David Dickson, and Cormac Ó Gráda, 'Eighteenth-Century Irish Population: New Perspectives from Old Sources', *Journal of Economic History*, XLI (1981), p. 624; Minutes, 9 Feb. 1744, *JHCI* VII. 561–614.

[2] Welch to [?], 18 Feb. 1754, SP 36/153/27; Linebaugh, 'Tyburn', p. 332. See also George, *London Life*, pp. 119–21.

[3] Howard, *Account of the Principal Lazarettos*, pp. 246–7. The population estimate for London, Middlesex, and the Home Counties is taken from the 1781 'b' estimates in Deane and Cole, *British Economic Growth*, p. 103.

were native Londoners, while nearly as many, 38.5 per cent, came from elsewhere in England.[1] Outside the environs of London, convicts were sentenced to transportation by courts in practically every county, ranging from tiny Radnor in Wales, where justices between 1769 and 1776 ordered only two felons for exile, to Somerset, where officials banished 269 over that same period. Map 1 indicates the distribution of transports among the seven assize circuits of England. The largest proportion of convicts outside the London area (12.8 per cent) originated in the six counties that made up the Western assize circuit: Cornwall, Devon, Dorset, Hampshire, Wiltshire, and Somerset. The smallest proportion (1.7 per cent) came from the region of Cheshire and Wales. Otherwise, the Oxford circuit furnished 10.9 per cent; the Northern circuit, 8.5 per cent; the Midland circuit, 6.5 per cent; and the Norfolk circuit, 5.6 per cent. Differing population sizes largely explain the variations, but other circumstances, such as London's high rate of crime, also played a role, that only intensive study of local courts and criminal offences could describe with precision. Thus, while the six counties of the Northern circuit provided less than 10 per cent of transports, these counties possessed nearly 21 per cent of the country's population.[2]

What personal characteristics did transports share? Were they ordinary members of society or the representatives of one segment? The most obvious fact is that a large majority were male. A census for the colony of Maryland in 1755 reveals that of 1,981 transports, 1,574 (79.5 per cent) consisted of men and boys. In close accord are figures drawn from lists of felons brought into four Maryland counties at different times. As shown in Table 2, males strongly predominated, numbering 1,693 (81.6 per cent) of 2,074 convicts. This proportion does not seem to have changed significantly over time. Combined totals for the counties of Kent and Queen Anne's during the first half of the century indicate that males made up 83

[1] George Burrington quoted in Speck, *Stability and Strife*, p. 66; E. A. Wrigley, 'A Simple Model of London's Importance in Changing English Society and Economy, 1650-1750', *PP* 37 (1967), 44-70; Linebaugh, 'Tyburn', p. 332.

[2] Wales and Cheshire did not technically constitute an assize circuit; instead, great sessions courts were their principal tribunals. Howard, *Account of the Principal Lazarettos*, pp. 246-7. The population estimate for the Northern circuit counties (Cumberland, Durham, Northumberland, Westmorland, Lancashire, and Yorkshire) is taken from the 1781 'b' estimates in Deane and Cole, *British Economic Growth*, p. 103.

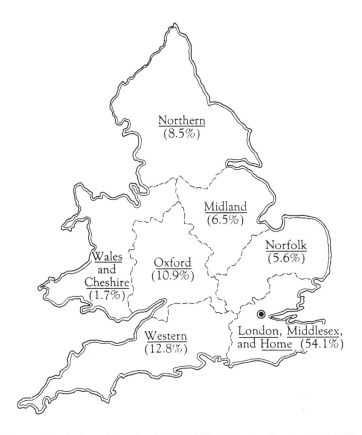

Map 1. Distribution of Convicts in English/Welsh Assize Circuits, 1769–1776

per cent of transports. They composed 81 per cent of the convicts sent into Baltimore and Anne Arundel counties during the early 1770s. Males were especially prepondcrant among capital felons pardoned for fourteen years or life. Among the 393 capital transports who could be found in county records were 342 men (87 per cent) and only 51 women. In contrast, non-capital convicts included 1,331 men (80.3 per cent) and 326 women.[1] Such high

[1] 'An Account of the Number of Souls in the Province of Maryland, in the Year 1755', *Gentleman's Magazine*, 1764, p. 261. Actually, the proportion of males ordered for transportation in Britain was probably slightly higher than figures for convicts received in the colonies suggest, for men seem to have suffered from a

Table 2. Sex of Convicts Imported into Maryland Counties (percentages in parentheses)

County	Years	Male	Female	Total
Kent	1719–1744	333 (82.8)	69 (17.2)	402 (100.0)
Queen Anne's	1727–1750	207 (83.1)	42 (16.9)	249 (100.0)
Baltimore	1770–1774	475 (82.8)	99 (17.3)	574 (100.1)
Anne Arundel	1771–1775	678 (79.9)	171 (20.1)	849 (100.0)
Total		1,693 (81.6)	381 (18.4)	2,074 (100.0)

Sources: Kent County Bonds and Indentures, 1719–44, Queen Anne's County Land Records, 1727–50, Baltimore County Convict Record, 1770–74, Anne Arundel County Convict Record, 1771–75, Maryland Hall of Records, Annapolis.

proportions of male offenders reflected the degree to which most crime in Britain, especially serious crime, was committed by men. Then, too, courts treated women more leniently and were less likely to order them to be transported. Not only did female offenders have a better chance of being acquitted, but, as a rule, judges and juries favoured banishment over lesser punishments only for those who constituted a clear menace. Of the defendants convicted of non-capital larceny at the Surrey assizes from 1736 to 1753, only 39.6 per cent of the women, in contrast to 62.5 per cent of the men, were transported.[1]

Most convicts, in addition, were young. The typical transport seems to have been in his early twenties, though there were striking exceptions. The captain of a convict vessel arriving in Maryland in 1773 reported that 'one man died but it was with old age [for] he was 84 years old'. Conversely, during the mid-1750s London courts banished numerous boys no more than 12 to 16 years of age for picking pockets and for shop-lifting. 'There was no less than 300 of these wretched Boys,' estimated Sir John Fielding, 'ragged as Colts, abandoned, Strangers to Beds, and who lay about under Bulks and in ruinous empty Houses.'[2] Precise information on the

higher mortality rate in the passage across the Atlantic. On the other hand, mortality rates declined during the century, so that differences in mortality would have had a less pronounced impact on sex ratios by the late colonial period. See below, Chapter 4, p. 104 n. 1.

[1] J. M. Beattie, 'The Criminality of Women in Eighteenth-Century England', *Journal of Social History*, VIII (1975), pp. 82–95. For the basis of the percentages, see Beattie, 'Crime and the Courts in Surrey', pp. 182–3.

[2] Capt. Simon Bressett to James Cheston, 10 Dec. 1773, CGP, Box 13; Sir John Fielding, *An Account of the Origins and Effects of a Police ...* (London, 1758), pp. 19-20.

Table 3. Age of Convicts Aboard the *Gilbert Frigate*, 1721, and the *Jonathan*, 1724 (percentages in parentheses)

Age	Convicts
10–14	1 (0.7)
15–19	24 (15.7)
20–24	58 (37.9)
25–29	32 (20.9)
30–34	13 (8.5)
35–39	11 (7.2)
40–44	5 (3.3)
45–49	2 (1.3)
50–54	3 (2.0)
55–59	3 (2.0)
60+	1 (0.7)
Total	153 (100.2)

Source: Certificates for the *Gilbert Frigate*, 18 May 1721, and the *Jonathan*, 27 July 1724, Landing Certificates, 1718–36, Guildhall Records Office, London (Library of Congress photocopies, Washington, DC).

ages of transports is scarce. The 1755 Maryland census merely differentiated between adults and children under 16, the latter forming 4.4 per cent of the colony's convicts. Fortunately, landing certificates filed for two convict vessels in the early 1720s provide a breakdown of ages that is probably close to the mark. As shown in Table 3, of a combined total of 153 felons shipped aboard the *Gilbert Frigate* and the *Jonathan* from London to Annapolis, Maryland, as many as 83 (54.3 per cent) were under 25 years of age, 14 (9.2 per cent) were 40 years or older, and only one individual was in his sixties. On the other hand, just one transport was under 15. The bulk, 74.5 per cent, ranged from 15 to 29 years of age, a bracket containing about one-quarter of England's population at the beginning of the eighteenth century. Transported convicts, on average, were probably not much younger than other British criminals. A recent study has shown that of more than 1,600 individuals prosecuted for property crimes on the Home assize circuit between 1782 and 1787, just over 65 per cent were aged between 15 and 29, with 1.6 per cent younger than 15.[1] While youth constituted a criterion for partial verdicts and transportation pardons, it permitted some felons to escape transportation altogether

[1] 'Account of Number of Souls in Maryland', *Gentleman's Magazine*, 1764, p. 261; Wrigley and Schofield, *Population History of England*, p. 218; King, 'Decision-Makers and Decision-Making', pp. 35–6. The landing certificates, of course, would not have included elderly transports who died in transit aboard ship.

by receiving free pardons or alternative forms of punishment.
And though elderly offenders were occasionally reprieved from
transportation, such cases were infrequent.
Due to their youth, it is likely that most convicts were single.
During the mid-eighteenth century, the average age at first marriage
in England was around 27 for men and slightly over 25 for women.
If we also consider older convicts who were single by choice,
perhaps 6 of every 10 convicts were single at the time of being
transported.[1]

II

Crime in eighteenth-century Britain never became the preserve of
any single social class. Bully-boy gangs of young aristocrats like
the Macaronis and the Mohawks provided a periodic reminder that
vagrants and street ruffians were not always to blame for rising
lawlessness. Transported convicts represented a broad spectrum of
occupations, ranging from soldiers and silversmiths to coopers
and chimney sweeps; one was a former cook for the Duke of
Northumberland. An Irish convict styled himself a metal refiner,
chemist, and doctor, while a woman from Wales was reputedly
'capable of any Business'.[2] A handful of transports came from
well-to-do backgrounds. One gentleman of fortune, John Eyre,
boasted a net worth of £30,000. Transported to Virginia in 1772,
he had been convicted at the Old Bailey for pilfering eleven quires
of common writing paper. Also affluent was a thief transported
that same year for stealing several silver spoons; besides a yearly
stipend of £200, his estate included £4,000 in ready cash.[3] Other
transports were known for their 'polite' manners and 'genteel'
bearing, though few fell from such lofty heights as Henry Justice.
A Middle Temple barrister, Justice was sentenced in May 1736 at
the Old Bailey to seven years transportation. No petty felon, he
had smuggled rare books out of both the library of Trinity College,
Cambridge, and the main university library. He appealed for
clemency partly on the strength of his background, but the court

---

[1] For the basis of these estimates, see Wrigley and Schofield, *Population History
of England*, pp. 255, 260-2.
[2] Purdie & Dixon's *Va. Gaz.*, 'Elizabeth Lewellin', 26 May 1772; *Va. Gaz.*, 'Hugh
Dean', 4 July 1751; *Md. Gaz.*, 'Hugh Clark', 12 Nov. 1767.
[3] Purdie & Dixon's *Va. Gaz.* 30 Jan., 11 June 1772. See also *Va. Gaz.* 26 Nov.
1736; Rind's *Va. Gaz.* 13 July 1769; Purdie & Dixon's *Va. Gaz.* 11 Apr. 1771; *Genuine
Account of W. Parsons*, p. 7; *London Magazine*, 1764, p. 325.

testily declared that Justice's offence was 'greatly aggravated by his Education, his fortune, and the Profession he was of'.[1]

Still, the callings of most transports were those of the lower orders. Despite the scarcity of source materials, some idea of their occupations can be gleaned from information on the male felons put aboard the *Gilbert Frigate* and the *Jonathan* in London. As indicated in Table 4, nearly half, forty-eight of ninety-eight, possessed no identifiable skill and were presumably labourers. Sixteen of these were minors and perhaps too young to have acquired a trade; thirty-two were older and probably never had an opportunity to learn one. Twenty-one of the remaining fifty had low-skilled occupations such as weaving and fishing; twenty-seven were tradesmen and craftsmen such as barbers, perukers, carpenters, tailors, and shoemakers; and two, an attorney and a miller, enjoyed relatively lucrative occupations. As might be expected, not one of the ninety-eight was a member of Britain's aristocracy or landed gentry.[2]

[1] *Pa. Gaz.*, 'John Murphy', 28 Aug. 1760; *Md. Gaz.*, 'Arundale Carnes', 11 Sept. 1766, 'Thomas Jones', 15 Sept. 1774; *Va. Gaz.* 26 Nov. 1736.

[2] The number of men with trades listed in the certificates may, in fact, be exaggerated, since 'fictitious handicrafts' were sometimes attributed to transports to increase sales. Smith, *Colonists in Bondage*, p. 221. Transports also tended to claim skills they did not possess in order to avoid field labour as servants. See below, Chapter 5, p. 148. Moreover, some transports with stated trades probably were only apprentices, rather than journeymen or masters, while still others may have been unemployed. Beattie, *Crime and the Courts in England*, p. 249. On the point that the absence of stated occupations probably meant that individuals did not have skilled callings, see David W. Galenson's discussion with regard to indentured servants in his *White Servitude in Colonial America: An Economic Analysis* (Cambridge, 1981), pp. 45-7, 61, 75-8. Though occupations for working women were not given in the certificates and in general are less easily identified, there is no reason to doubt that most female offenders came from the lower orders. See Beattie, 'Criminality of Women', pp. 99-109.

Sales of transports as servants also suggest that most of them were at best low-skilled. Duncan Campbell, who traded in convicts on the eve of the Revolution, claimed that he sold 'common Male Convicts, not Artificers', in the colonies 'on an Average, for 10 Pounds apiece', whereas 'those who were of useful Trades, such as Carpenters and Blacksmiths, from Fifteen to Twenty-five Pounds'. On another occasion, he estimated that 'about 14 Guineas' (£14. 14s.) was the 'usual charge' for a convict wishing to buy his freedom in America, providing he was not a 'Tradesman'. Roughly similar was the observation of a colonist in Maryland in 1767 that 'Common Labourers sell at £12 Sterling, and Tradesmen, from £18 to £50 Sterling per Head'. Testimony of Duncan Campbell, 1 Apr. 1779, *JHC* XXXVII. 310; Campbell to Perigrin Crust, 13 Sept. 1774, DCPL, p. 312; 'Philanthropos', *Md. Gaz.* 20 Aug. 1767. On the basis of sales figures for 338 male convicts sold in Maryland by the Bristol firm of Stevenson, Randolph, & Cheston between 1767 and 1775, only 74 (21.9%) retailed for £15 or more apiece. Sixty-nine (20.4%)

Table 4. Occupations of Male Convicts (percentages in parentheses)

Occupational group	*Gilbert Frigate/Jonathan* convicts	Nottingham convicts
Unskilled labourers[a]	48 (49.0)	36 (65.5)
Low-skilled labourers	21 (21.4)	13 (23.6)
Skilled craftsmen and tradesmen	27 (27.6)	6 (10.9)
Wealthy tradesmen and professionals	2 (2.0)	— —
Landed society	— —	— —
Total	98 (100.0)	55 (100.0)

Note: a. Labourers and not given.

Sources: Certificates for the *Gilbert Frigate*, 18 May 1721, and the *Jonathan*, 27 July 1724, Guildhall Landing Certificates, 1718–36; K. Tweedale Meaby, *Nottinghamshire: Extracts from the County Records of the Eighteenth Century* (Nottingham, 1947), pp. 353–8.

Convicts aboard the *Gilbert Frigate* and the *Jonathan* likely included a sizable proportion of men from London. The evidence that most transports held either unskilled or low-skilled occupations receives stronger confirmation from records for fifty-five male convicts sentenced to transportation in the more rural setting of Nottinghamshire, an East Midlands county with agricultural as well as industrial and commercial interests. Tried between 1723 and 1775, these convicts included as many as thirty-six labourers and individuals without specific callings, plus thirteen men with low-skilled occupations. Just six of the fifty-five were craftsmen and tradesmen. These and the above findings roughly parallel the scanty information available for criminals as a whole. Surviving records for the 1780s indicate that half of male property offenders tried at Surrey assizes were without a trade that required some sort of skill and training, while in the more rural county of Sussex the proportion of unskilled was as high as two-thirds.[1]

fetched between £3 and £10, and 195 (57.7%) between £11 and £14. See below, Chapter 4, Table 10. Compared to what these transports cost, Campbell's price estimates actually may have been a bit too low, with regard not just to common labourers and tradesmen but also to women. Whereas Campbell claimed that he sold women for £8 or £9, most of those in Maryland cost between £9 and £10. (All prices above are in sterling.)

[1] Beattie, *Crime and the Courts in England*, pp. 249–51. See also King, 'Crime, Law and Society in Essex', pp. 128–30. One minor difference that might have made transports slightly less skilled is the fact that offenders sentenced to transportation

Young, male, single, and minimally skilled, a majority of convicts belonged to that segment of society most vulnerable to economic dislocation. Britain's working poor led lives filled with uncertainty. Regular employment depended upon the harvest, the weather, the seasons, the fluctuations of foreign markets, and upon the general health of the economy. 'Either the badness of the seasons, or the badness of men, has put most of the necessaries of life almost out of the reach of the poor', commented a writer in the *London Magazine*. It is no coincidence that most offences committed by convicts were crimes against property, or that levels of crime rose whenever economic conditions sharply deteriorated. At those times, anywhere from 20 to 45 per cent of England's population may have lacked the means to buy sufficient bread or otherwise feed themselves. Even when economic prospects were generally good, 10 per cent suffered from such destitution. 'Great Numbers that happen to be out of Employment, and have no possible Way of recommending themselves to any Service,' noted the economist Joshua Gee, 'are forced to starve, or fall into the Practice of picking Pockets, Thieving, or other wicked Courses, to supply their immediate Necessities'.[1]

The number of offences committed by the typical felon sentenced to transportation is impossible to calculate, but probably many of them were multiple offenders. Though they did not identify themselves as full-time felons, such criminals were prone to steal so long as their circumstances remained urgent, and they were able to elude arrest because of Britain's weak system of law enforcement. A weaver's apprentice, John Meff, later recalled committing a series of thefts because his 'Business' was not 'sufficient to maintain' his wife and children. Gee believed most malefactors 'run from one Evil to another till at last they come under the Sentance of Felons, *viz.* Transportation or the Gallows'. Then, too, non-recidivists,

---

stood a better chance of receiving a free pardon or lesser penalty if they had a steady means of employment. See above, Chapter 1, p. 42.

[1] Anon., *London Magazine*, 1766, p. 424; Gee, *Trade and Navigation of Great-Britain*, p. 87; Hay 'War, Dearth and Theft', p. 132. Poor offenders were also more likely to be brought to court by prosecutors. As Joanna Innes has remarked, 'The poorer the thief, the less likely he or she, if caught, to have the means to placate the potential prosecutor.' 'Social Problems: Poverty and Marginality in Eighteenth-Century England' (Unpublished paper presented at a conference on 'The Social World of Britain and America, 1600–1820', Williamsburg, Va., 4–7 Sept. 1985), p. 101. See also King, 'Crime, Law and Society in Essex', p. 127.

guilty of single larcenies, often never came to trial, but were instead punished informally in their communities.[1] For some criminals, breaking the law virtually became a profession. Though sometimes drawn to thieving, like other offenders, by necessity, crime for them constituted a more regular source of income. On occasion, it also represented less an act of desperation than an easy means of ready money. Born in London to reputable parents, Jeffe Walden, for instance, had been apprenticed to a butcher after receiving several years of schooling. By his own account, he could 'have lived very well, and maintained' himself 'by following' his 'own Trade'. Over the years Walden committed a series of burglaries and robberies, some netting him and his accomplice several hundred pounds. He was transported at the age of 26. The thief Thomas Butler, who enjoyed a decent upbringing and was apprenticed as a youth to a shoemaker, turned to street robberies and pickpocketing, for which he, too, was transported. Similarly, the robber Robert Artlett had probably committed numerous crimes before his execution at Winchester in March 1773. Members of his family included a mother who had been transported, a brother under sentence of transportation, and a father and grandfather who had already lost their lives on the gallows, also at Winchester for robbery.[2]

Often belonging to organized gangs, such felons committed particularly serious offences like horse-theft and highway robbery that demanded skill and planning. A successful highway robbery, for instance, normally required pinpoint scheduling, trusted lookouts, several armed men, and a shopowner to receive the stolen merchandise. Gangs necessarily employed a network of informants, receivers, and quasi-legitimate contacts. In London by mid-century, many criminals had set up store in the squalour of 'old ruinous Buildings' on the city's outskirts. 'Not one fourth' of the inhabitants, estimated Saunders Welch, 'could obtain a just Character of

---

[1] Gee, *Trade and Navigation of Great-Britain*, p. 87; *Select Trials . . . at the Sessions-House in the Old Bailey . . .* (London, 1742), I. 71. See also Barbara A. Hanawalt, *Crime and Conflict in English Communities, 1300–1348* (Cambridge, Mass., 1979), pp. 216–17; and above, Chapter 1, pp. 29–30.

[2] *Account of the Ordinary of Newgate*, 7 Apr. 1742, pp. 11–14, 11 Oct. 1752, pp. 135–7; Rind's *Va. Gaz.* 20 May 1773. See also, e.g., *Account of the Ordinary of Newgate*, 8 June 1744, pp. 3–4, 23 Mar. 1752, p. 48, 16 Apr. 1753, pp. 40–3, 4 June 1770, p. 43; *The Newgate Calendar* (New York, 1962), pp. 7–17.

Honesty and Industry, the rest composed of rotten whores, Pick pockets, pilferers and others of more desperate denomination'.[1]

Gang life reflected not a mature underclass but a nascent criminal subculture. Membership remained fluid and the lives of thieves frequently intersected with those of more respectable citizens. None the less, criminal gangs shared an increasingly distinct existence, personified most sharply perhaps by their everyday use of 'cant', the so-called language of thieves. Containing a rich and varied vocabulary, 'cant' was a special body of street slang employed chiefly for the purpose of secrecy. Its terms suggest a well-defined jargon as well as a division of labour common within gangs, ranging from 'millkens' (burglars) and 'vulcans' (picklock experts) to 'knowing fellows' (highwaymen's scouts and spies) and 'faytors' (forgers of documents). Some expressions, such as 'Mill his Nobb' (break his head) and 'Chive his Muns' (cut his face), lent graphic testimony to the grim realities of gang life. Being 'down for my Scragg' signified being hanged, whereas being 'legged' meant being transported. Neither romantic revolutionaries nor ordinary crooks, numerous gang members were tough, often violently determined men and women accustomed to alternating bouts of poverty and quick wealth. Scarcely surprising was the comment of one London resident: 'It will be to the Advantage of Society in generall [that] such offenders should be transported.'[2]

III

At a London inn one summer day in 1766, Elizabeth Martin shared a pint of wine with a servant named Briant Borough.

[1] Welch to [?], 18 Feb. 1754, SP 36/153/27. How prevalent organized crime actually was in eighteenth-century Britain remains a difficult question, but see Beattie, *Crime and the Courts in England*, pp. 252–63; Sharpe, *Crime in Early Modern England*, pp. 105–8, 111–20; McMullan, *Canting Crew*; Hay, 'War, Dearth and Theft', pp. 134–5; Howson, *Thief-Taker General*, *passim*; Thompson, *Whigs and Hunters*, p. 195; John Styles, 'Criminal Records', *HJ* XX (1977), 981; Sharpe, 'History of Crime in Late Medieval and Early Modern England', pp. 199–200.

[2] Howson, *Thief-Taker General*, p. 24; *The Discoveries of John Poulter . . .* (London, 1761), pp. 42–3; Thomas Lane to [Holdernesse?], 22 Mar. 1760, SP 36/145/85–6. For the transportation of gang members, see e.g. [?] Pope to Negus, 21 Feb. 1725, SP 35/55/61a; Sir John Shelley to Lord [?], 5 May 1729, SP 36/11/120; Report of Thomson, 25 Sept. 1732, SP 36/28/150; J. Lenthal to [Newcastle], 7 Oct. 1738, SP 44/131/37–8; *London Magazine*, 1751, p. 43; Fielding, *Origins and Effects of a Police*, p. 19; Knapp and Baldwin, eds., *Newgate Calendar*, II. 125; Barlow, *Dick Turpin*, pp. 98, 114, 208, 228–9, 236–7, 242, 252–3, 319–20, 327–9.

Amid the chatter, she prodded Borough to know how she
could be transported, adding that her husband was set for the
colonies and that she longed to join him. Borough, after a
hearty laugh, urged that she pay for passage abroad. An
onlooker jested that a brief visit to a nearby goldsmith's shop
might accomplish her aim. Hardly a week had passed before
Martin found herself standing before an Old Bailey judge for
stealing a silver spoon out of a Knight Street tavern. Offering
no defence, she was swiftly convicted of grand larceny. The
judge, however, proved merciful. Perhaps because she was a
woman and a first offender, a fine and a smart whipping were
Martin's only punishment.[1]

*

The typical malefactor cast for transportation, then, was a young
male labourer driven to crime by economic necessity, though at
least some felons were members of organized gangs. Convicts in
several respects resembled another, larger body of emigrants
that periodically embarked for the colonies from British ports—
indentured servants. Comprising about half of all British emigrants
to colonial America during the eighteenth century, they, too, mostly
consisted of labouring men in their twenties who travelled to the
colonies by themselves, not with families. For many of them,
America seemingly offered a means of employment not available
either in the countryside or in large cities like London and Bristol.
Jobless workers, having trekked to urban areas looking for new
opportunities, decided to indenture themselves to ship captains
bound across the Atlantic. Ironically, some urban newcomers, less
willing to leave family and home for prolonged periods, instead
turned to crime, only to find themselves ordered for transportation.
Daniel Defoe believed it would be 'a much wiser Course' for
England's poor to embark as indentured servants rather 'than to
turn Thieves, and worse, and then be sent over by Force'. A person
commented in 1758 that if migrants to London 'cannot get such
employment as they expected or chuse to follow, many of them
will not go home again to be laughed at . . . but enlist for soldiers,

[1] *Old Bailey Sessions Papers*, 3–8 Sept. 1766, pp. 308–9.

go to the plantations etc. if they are well enclined; otherwise they probably commence theives or pickpockets'.[1]

Despite the similarities they shared, there were also important differences between convicts and indentured servants. Largely because of growing colonial demand for skilled labour, men who were indentured by shipmasters increasingly came from better backgrounds than did convicts. The proportion of unskilled labourers among indentured servants declined during the century, by the 1770s forming only 15 per cent of male servants embarking from London.[2] Furthermore, transportation and contract servitude represented very different paths to the colonies. Like ordinary emigrants, indentured servants, in choosing to cross the Atlantic, shared a more hopeful vision of America. They wagered their lives that the promise of the New World would outweigh its dangers. New-found opportunities would help to replace lost friends, family, and country. Very different was the outlook shared by convicts cast for transportation. Inasmuch as they were wards of the government, freedom of choice had nothing to do with their departure from Britain. Most transports, unlike indentured servants, were deeply reluctant to leave their homeland. Though many of them might have journeyed to cities in search of work, their ties to hearth and kin were more enduring. Guilty of crimes against society, convicts none the less felt stronger bonds of attachment.

There were, of course, exceptions. For capital felons, the advantages of transportation were manifest. Confronted by the alternative of hanging, large numbers of condemned criminals anxiously applied to the crown for transportation pardons. As Defoe's Moll Flanders concluded, 'I Had now a certainty of Life indeed, but with the hard Condition of being ordered for Transportation, which indeed was a hard Condition in it self, but

---

[1] Defoe, *Tour Thro' Great Britain*, III. 748; J. Massie quoted in George, *London Life*, p. 355 n. 2. For indentured servants, see Galenson, *White Servitude*; James Horn, 'Servant Emigration to the Chesapeake in the Seventeenth Century', in Thad W. Tate and David L. Ammerman, eds., *The Chesapeake in the Seventeenth Century: Essays on Anglo-American Society* (Chapel Hill, NC, 1979), pp. 51–95; David Souden, ' "Rogues, Whores and Vagabonds"'? Indentured Servant Emigrants to North America and the Case of Mid-Seventeenth-Century Bristol', *Social History*, III (1978), 23–41; Richard S. Dunn, 'Servants and Slaves: The Recruitment and Employment of Labor', in Jack P. Greene and J. R. Pole, eds., *Colonial British America: Essays in the New History of the Early Modern Era* (Baltimore, 1984), pp. 159–72.

[2] Galenson, *White Servitude*, pp. 62, 139, *passim*.

not when comparatively considered'.[1] Only a few capital prisoners thought otherwise. In 1751, a London street robber, Philip Gibson, stubbornly refused clemency on the grounds 'that if he lived he would only be a burthen to himself' and his friends. Robert Webber, having even less to live for, promised to disclose details of recent crimes only if the king approved his execution. Convicted at Maidstone assizes of robbery, Webber had been driven to 'utter Want' by 'Losses in Trade'. He now found himself seriously ill and entirely deserted by friends and his pregnant wife. 'Death', he wrote to the Earl of Shelburne, 'is all I require'.[2]

No matter how bleak their prospects, the vast majority of condemned prisoners preferred to face life's hardships. If granted mercy, they resigned themselves to transportation as best they could. In fact, according to at least some felons like John Meff, who pledged himself to 'lead an honest and regular Course of Life', transportation offered a chance to begin life anew. It would assure 'an Opportunity . . .', echoed a Surrey highwayman, 'of becomeing a Usefull Member of the Community'. 'To repair the Breach now made in his Character, and to gain a Livelyhood, with Reputation and Honesty' was the hope of Robert Scott, an Edinburgh convict charged in 1765 with forgery.[3]

Otherwise, transportation appealed to felons who stood to lose the least by leaving Britain. Probably some, like Edward Newbee, appreciated the chance to escape burdensome legal obligations. In 1750, creditors urgently tried to delay Newbee's departure long enough for him to repay a £400 debt. For other criminals, particularly those who still lived in tightly-knit communities, the public shame caused by their crimes provided incentive. In Yorkshire, a woman convicted of pickpocketing asked to be banished

[1] Daniel Defoe, *The Fortunes and Misfortunes of the Famous Moll Flanders . . .*, ed. G. A. Starr (London, 1971), p. 293.

[2] *London Magazine*, 1751, p. 427; *Md. Gaz.* 27 Nov. 1766; Webber to Shelburne, 11 Aug. 1766, *Cal. HO Papers*, II. 66. See also *The Third Charge of Sir Daniel Dolins* . . . (London, 1726), pp. 12–13; [D. Barrington], *Observations upon the Statutes, Chiefly the More Ancient* . . . (London, 1766), p. 352.

[3] *Select Trials at the Old Bailey* (1742), I. 71; Petition of Joseph Chambers to King, n.d., SP 36/150/38; Petition of Robert Scott, 27 July 1765, JC 3/34/99. See also Arundell Coke to Lord [?], 15 Mar. 1721, SP 35/30/58; James Cranston to Lord Justice Clerk, 14 Sept. 1723, SP 35/45/35; Petition of James Owen to King, n.d, SP 35/67/32; Petition of John Pryor to King, n.d., SP 35/67/39; Petition of William James to King, [1750?], SP 36/115/168; Petition of John Low to King, 18 Apr. 1755, SP 36/130/79; Petition of Alexander Russell to King, n.d., SP 36/149/53.

rather than face the ignominy of a public whipping. Indeed, depending upon the degree of neighbourly wrath, felons not uncommonly faced considerable personal danger. Even before his conviction, Martin FitzGerald, a notorious coin thief, was severely beaten in 1734 by a vengeful mob and dragged several times through a horse pond.[1]

Among Scottish offenders petitioning for banishment, fear of scorn and ridicule was the reason that they cited most frequently. Some of their pleas must have been genuine, though many petitioners doubtless opted for transportation to avoid the gallows. At the High Court of Justiciary in Edinburgh between 1736 and 1775, 108 men and women previously indicted for committing capital crimes asked to be banished to America before their cases came to trial. Of the ninety-two who explained their motives, twenty-three stated that they wished to avoid the trouble and anguish of a trial that might end in conviction and a harsher sentence; having to suffer an extended period of pre-trial imprisonment was cited by seven; only two expressed the hope that banishment would help reform their characters; and eleven gave some combination of reasons. However, as many as forty-nine (53.3 per cent) declared that they could no longer live comfortably in their communities, whether or not their trials ended in acquittal. Fairly common was the petition of Christian Scott, accused in 1762 of murdering an infant. 'After the Imputation of such a Crime', pleaded Scott, 'it would be highly disagreeable for her to return to her former place of residence and appear among her acquaintances.'[2]

Transportation's most obvious appeal lay in its promise of deliverance, not just from the death penalty but also from personal hardship and scornful neighbours. By removing criminals to an entirely new continent, it permitted them some measure of escape from the past, especially those guilty of the most serious offences. Foreign exile did not, however, generate much appeal in its own right. Among convicted felons, probably only naïve daredevils or hardnosed adventurers genuinely viewed banishment with detachment. Undeterred by new worlds and unencumbered by friends and

[1] Bedford to Recorder of London, 28 Sept. 1750, SP 44/85/237-8; North Riding Quarter Sessions, 2 Oct. 1744, in J. C. Atkinson, ed., *The North Riding Record Society* ... (London, 1890), VIII. 248; Petition of Martin FitzGerald to King, [1734], SP 36/31/135; Beattie, *Crime and the Courts in England*, pp. 133-5.

[2] Petition of Christian Scott, 6 Aug. 1762, JC 3/33/75; Books of Adjournal, 1736-75, JC 3/19-39.

family, they alone expressed scarce regrets over impending years in exile. Few felons displayed the nonchalance of Bampflyde-Moore Carew, a seasoned European traveller, who informed an Exeter court that transportation 'would save him Five Pounds for his Passage, as he was very desirous of seeing' America. Nor could most afford the brave optimism of a 14 year-old boy, who when ordered for transportation along with a friend, told his weeping comrade, 'Damn you Jack, never mind it; we shall be only transported, and have the pleasure of seeing foreign parts, carriage paid.'[1]

In the end, transportation represented a harsh prospect. Though a writer in 1766 claimed that it 'seldom falls on those who have much to lose',[2] banishment was a curse that large numbers of men and women feverishly sought to avoid, particularly non-capital offenders for whom it did not represent an act of clemency. Besides petitioning for free pardons, such criminals commonly requested that other punishments be substituted in transportation's place. Often they asked to be whipped,[3] or to serve either in the army or navy.[4] A few, when opportunities arose, allowed their bodies to be

[1] Boy quoted in J. Hewitt, 'A Comparative View of the Ancient and Present Laws', in [Hewitt], *Journal of J. Hewitt*, p. 63; Carew quoted in C. H. Wilkinson, ed., *The King of the Beggars, Bampflyde-Moore Carew* (Oxford, 1931), p. 149, but see also ibid., p. 241.

[2] Callander, ed., *Terra Australis Cognita*, I. 20.

[3] See e.g. Petition of John [Mikell?] to Mr Delafay, 26 June 1723, SP 35/43/160; Petition of Edward Dickinson to Newcastle, 9 Sept. 1725, SP 35/58/14; Petition of John Broome to Newcastle, n.d., SP 36/1/64; Petition of John Bulney to Sir William Bilkers, [1733], Petition of Elizabeth Howard to Sir Robert Baylys, n.d., Petition of Anne Bowers to Sir Francis Forbes, n.d., Petition of John Wilson to Sir John Eyles, n.d., Petition of James Barton to [Seirj?] Raby, n.d., Petition of Thomas Sharp to Sir Richard Brocas, n.d., Petition of John Balm to Sir Edward Bellamy *et al.*, n.d., Miscellaneous Manuscripts, Guildhall Records Office, London; Petition of Edmund Stone to Lawrence Carter, 1 Apr. 1734, SP 36/31/126; Petition of William Turbutt to King, [1745], SP 44/132/373-4; Petition of James Wilson to Newcastle, 31 July 1745, SP 36/66/374; Petition of Elizabeth Percivale to Lords Justices, 8 Aug. 1745, SP 36/67/58; Petition of John Brimley, Jr., to King, [1747], SP 36/97/46; Petition of Robert Harwood to Newcastle, n.d., SP 36/150/60; Petition of William Chaney to Newcastle, n.d., SP 36/150/115.

[4] See e.g. Petition of John Forby to King, 30 Mar. 1734, SP 36/31/114; Petition of Thomas Richardson to Queen, [1735], SP 36/35/236-7; Petition of George Watton to Sir Charles Wagar, n.d., SP 36/50/130; Petition of John Anderson to King, [1740], SP 36/50/136; Petition of Francis Grammont to Earl of Northampton, 1742, SP 36/59/262; Petition of Joseph Baker to Newcastle, 17 Mar. 1746, SP 44/133/114-15; 'Cases of Convicts', [1757?], SP 36/138/229; Petition of John Cooper to Pitt, [1758], SP 36/139/237; Petition of John Smith to Pitt, 28 June 1758, SP 36/139/281; Charles Gore *et al.* to [?], 23 July 1759, SP 36/142/185; Petition

used for medical research. In 1721, six prisoners volunteered to undergo a smallpox experiment in exchange for free pardons. Similarly, ten years later, Charles Ray, a prisoner in Newgate, offered to let doctors remove his ear drum rather than be transported.[1]

Among other fears, the grinding labour required of American servants fuelled widespread dread. Use by convicts of such terms as 'bondage' and 'slavery' to describe their fates reflected profound apprehension over the heavy demands placed upon colonial workers. At least a degree of truth existed in Defoe's characterization of Moll Flanders's Lancashire husband: 'He had a kind of Horror upon his Mind in his being sent over to the Plantations as *Romans* sent condemned Slaves to Work in the Mines'. James Brown, a Londoner convicted of grand larceny, later recalled that he was 'terrified and affrighted . . . at the Labour the People transported undergo Abroad'. Similarly, another reason why the robber Robert Webber pleaded to be hanged rather than given a transportation pardon was that he 'had rather die than live under Bondage for so many Years'. Such was the wish of a London malefactor after hearing that he would be transported to the West Indies 'to work there at the sugar works with the negroes'. He pleaded that 'he had rather bear strangling for a minute, than to make sugar all his life-time'.[2]

Elderly and infirm convicts, some already dangerously weakened by the dank squalour of Newgate and other gaols, feared they would never survive transportation. Besides the hard lives most of them faced in the colonies, there were dangers posed by crossing the Atlantic under foul and cramped conditions. Protesting that he was 'a very weakly man', John Greene was 'sure' he 'must dye in

of Samuel Gibbeson to Pitt, 13 Sept. 1758, SP 36/143/78; Petition of Thomas Landrekin and Joseph Chapman to King, 2 Nov. 1770, SP 37/7/238; Petition of Edmund Rupe and William Appleton to Earl of Harrington, n.d., SP 36/149/8; Petition of Michael Vernon to Lords Justices, n.d., SP 36/149/85.

[1] Townshend to Recorder of London, 31 Aug. 1721, SP 44/79A/434; *Pa. Gaz.* 3 June 1731.

[2] *Md. Gaz.* 27 Nov. 1766; Petition of Elizabeth Canning to King, 26 June 1754, SP 36/127/157; Defoe, *Moll Flanders*, ed. Starr, p. 301; *Account of the Ordinary of Newgate*, 1 June 1752, p. 80; 'Philanthropos', *London Magazine*, 1768, p. 640. See also, e.g., Petition of Grammont to Northampton, 1742, SP 36/59/262; 'Answers for Mr. Hays . . .', by Patrick Haldone, 20 June 1744, JC 3/24/593; Wilkinson, ed., *King of the Beggars*, p. 241; William Eddis, *Letters from America*, ed. Aubrey C. Land (Cambridge, Mass., 1969), p. 40.

going over'. Just as pessimistic, John Wilson, alias 'Half Hanged Smith', was 66 years old, nearly blind, and still suffering from battle wounds received at Vigo during a naval engagement against the Spanish, whereas Peter Delafountan, the recipient of a transportation pardon, asked to be banished to Holland where he had friends and family. 'Brought almost to Death's Door' in prison, he implored the king in 1751 that transportation would cause 'the certain Loss of that Life Your Majesty is pleased to prolong'. In the case of Jonathan Hudson, a London thief purported to be insane, his father feared that 'he must perish abroad, for want of help in his Crazed Condition'.[1]

The prospect of being shipped to America did little to ease prevailing alarm. Though long fabled for economic plenty and vast stretches of abundant wilderness, the New World still generated fears of barbarism and isolation. 'Virginny', in the words of a convict ballad, was a 'cold shameful place'.[2] In all likelihood, few transports had previously visited the colonies,[3] and probably no greater number possessed American relations.[4] Instead, America remained for many the 'Remotest Corner of the World', a primitive land on the outer margins of the British empire. The thief Mary Stanford, believing that 'living in foreign Parts was worse than a disgraceful and shameful Death at Home', pleaded to be hanged rather than transported.[5] Although transportation for some convicts afforded an escape from social ostracism, most offenders, even

---

[1] Greene to Townshend, n.d., SP 36/46/79; Petition of John Wilson to Eyles, n.d., Misc. Guildhall MSS; Delafountan to King, 28 Oct. 1751, SP 36/117/214; Petition of George Hudson to Newcastle, n.d., SP 36/149/18. See also, e.g., Petition of Broome to Newcastle, n.d., SP 36/1/63; Charles Ray to Queen, 16 June 1731, SP 36/23/167; Petition of Stone to Carter, 1 Apr. 1734, SP 36/31/126; Petition of Elizabeth Harris to Duke of Mountague, [June 1744], SP 36/64/169; Petition of James Wilson to Newcastle, n.d., SP 36/79/133; Petition of Broome to Eyles *et al.*, n.d., Misc. Guildhall MSS.

[2] I am indebted to Michael Sewell for referring me to a recent recording of 'Virginny' on the album *Crown of Horn* by Martin Carthy.

[3] Probably most previous visitors had been sailors. See e.g. *Pa. Gaz.*, 'William Callahan', 29 Aug. 1765; *Md. Gaz.*, 'James Reed', 11 Dec. 1766; Rind's *Va. Gaz.*, 'William Sims', 13 Dec. 1770.

[4] For references to colonial relatives, see Petition of Edward Beezley to King, n.d., SP 36/150/153; Petition of James Dawes to King, n.d., SP 36/159/143; *Md. Gaz.*, 'John Tongue', 29 Mar. 1764, 'William Newcomb', 19 Mar. 1767, 'Thomas Moore', 17 Aug. 1769, 'William Hall', 13 June 1776; Rind's *Va. Gaz.*, 'Philip Vaughan', 1 June 1769.

[5] Petition of Coke to [?], 15 Mar. 1721, SP 35/30/58; *Account of the Ordinary of Newgate*, 3 Aug. 1726, p. 4.

migrant labourers, shared priorities rooted in place and community. No matter how bleak their economic horizons, local connections and familiar surroundings were very important. References in petitions to 'nativity' and 'home' bespoke a deep reluctance to abandon much of what gave meaning to their lives. Particularly in rural areas, Robert Malcolmson has noted, labouring people had a 'closely defined sense of place: a place—both its landscape and its people—that was known in minute detail; a place that was richly associated with its own distinctive memories, relics, folklore, legends and customary practices'. Transports faced the prospect of being banished not just from their communities, but from the British Isles. The London thief Elizabeth Howard asked to be whipped rather than transported 'out of her Native Isle'. To be a 'useful Man in the Country to which he belongs' was the desire of John Broughton, a 22 year-old convict in Norwich. 'Oh England, sweet England,' lamented the ballad 'Virginny', 'I fear I'll ne'er see you more'.[1]

Blood ties were especially strong, even for persons who were single. Banishment for any number of years threatened to prevent men and women from once again seeing their families. Even if death did not first intervene, passage home across the Atlantic was never assured. Very few criminals found themselves in the position of the Boswell family of Hertfordshire; among the twenty convicts ordered for transportation in October 1740 were fully five Boswells, including Charles, Sr., and Charles, Jr. More common was the plight of Eleanor Connor, for whom never seeing her children again, 'should she be transported into a strange Country', was 'next to Death itself'.[2] Equally unfortunate, transportation frequently

---

[1] Petition of Mary Nolloth to King, n.d., SP 36/117/292; Petition of Elizabeth Chambers to Baron Thomson, n.d., Petition of Howard to Baylys, n.d., Misc. Guildhall MSS; Malcolmson, *Life and Labour in England, 1700–1780* (New York, 1981), p. 94; Petition of John Broughton to King, 8 Oct. 1734, SP 36/33/14. See also, e.g., Petition of Joseph Addison to Queen, 4 Aug. 1732, SP 36/27/251; Petition of Catherine Floyd to King, 18 Sept. 1739, SP 36/48/152; Petition of John Martin to King, 16 June 1749, SP 36/110/246; Petition of Thomas Bavin to Newcastle, 15 July 1749, SP 36/110/285; Petition of Ann Cokeley to Lords Justices, n.d., SP 36/150/123; Petition of Balm to Bellamy *et al.*, n.d., Petition of Barton to Raby, n.d., Misc. Guildhall MSS; Wilkinson, ed., *King of the Beggars*, p. 241; *Liberty Regain'd: Set Forth in the Remarkable Life and Actions of W*** S***, Esq. . . .* (London, 1755), pp. 7, 17, 19.

[2] Hertfordshire Quarter Sessions, 6 Oct. 1740, in William Le Hardy, ed., *Hertfordshire County Records: Calendar to the Sessions Books . . .* (Hertford, 1931), VII. 280; Petition of Eleanor Connor to Archbishop of Canterbury, [1748?], SP 36/109/45.

removed breadwinners responsible for their family's welfare. The most common plea made in petitions by convicts trying to remain in Britain was that their departure would create unavoidable hardship for their families. At best they would be thrown upon county authorities for poor relief, at worst they would perish.[1] No doubt a calculated degree of self-serving figured in such appeals, since, by making them, some criminals hoped to enlist the support of penurious communities. But the piercing note of alarm sounded so persistently in convict petitions suggests that often their fears for family members were real. Banished for fourteen years, the Irish felon Mary Brown despaired that 'her Absence' would deprive her five youngsters 'not only of Education but of the Common Necessarys of Life'. They would, she declared, 'be equall Sufferers by her Transportation as if she had actualy been Executed'. In Surrey, Thomas Atwood feared the certain indigence of his mother,

---

[1] See e.g. Petition of John Foorde to King, [15? Apr.1719], SP 35/16/24; Petition of Richard Paxford to James Craggs, [1718-21], SP 35/19/68; Petition of [Mikell?] to Delafay, 26 June 1723, SP 35/43/160; Petition of Mary Earland to Newcastle, 17 Nov. 1724, SP 35/53/62; Petition of Dickinson to Newcastle, 9 Sept. 1725, SP 35/58/14; Petition of Broome to Newcastle, n.d., SP 36/1/64; Petition of George Dewing to King, [6 Apr. 1728], SP 36/6/252; Petition of John Fountain to King, May 1729, SP 36/11/226; Petition of Ann Pritchett to Newcastle, [1730], SP 36/20/47; Petition of Addison to Queen, 4 Aug. 1732, SP 36/27/251; Petition of John Harvey to Queen, [1732], SP 36/28/143; Petition of Emanuel Greetham to King, [8 Feb. 1734], SP 36/31/36; Petition of Stone to Carter, 1 Apr. 1734, SP 36/31/126; Petition of Stephen Collard to Queen, 8 Dec. 1736, SP 36/39/308; Petition of Anthony Warren to Newcastle, 21 Dec. 1737, SP 36/44/134; Petition of James Green to Harrington, [1738?], SP 36/46/76; Petition of Floyd to King, 18 Sept. 1739, SP 36/48/152; Petition of John Harman to Lords Justices, [1740], SP 36/52/50; Petition of William Anderson to Lords Justices, 16 Sept. 1740, SP 36/52/158; Petition of William Rogers to Lords Justices, 12 Aug. 1741, SP 36/56/210; Petition of Richard West to King, Dec. 1742, SP 36/59/247; Petition of James Wilson to Newcastle, 31 July 1745, SP 36/66/374; Petition of Thomas Powell to Lords Justices, [Dec. 1745], SP 36/78/342; Petition of William Wilkes to King, 1 Dec. 1748, SP 36/108/208; Petition of William Miles to Newcastle, [23 Jan. 1750], SP 36/112/40; Petition of Richard Lighthouse to Lord Foley, [1751], SP 36/116/54; Petition of James Peele to Newcastle, [1752], SP 36/118/119; Petition of Mary Jenkins to Countess of Yarmouth, 25 Nov. 1753, SP 36/124/108; Foster to [?], 5 Apr. 1760, SP 36/145/105; Petition of Thomas Palmer to King, n.d., SP 36/149/1; Petition of William Osbourn to King, n.d., SP 36/149/32; Petition of Wilks to Archbishop of Canterbury, n.d., SP 36/149/102; Petition of Chaney to Newcastle, n.d., SP 36/150/115; Petition of William Bland to Secretaries of State, [12 June 1771], SP 37/8/95; Petition of Barton to Raby, n.d., Petition of John Wilson to Eyles, n.d., Petition of Bowers to Forbes *et al.*, n.d., Petition of Mary Tracey to Thomson, n.d., Petition of John Lord to Simon Urlwin, n.d., Misc. Guild-hall MSS.

wife, and small child, who all depended 'on his Single Labour'. Ordered for seven years transportation, he had originally stolen a sheep because of the 'Cryes of his familey for Bread, at a tyme, when he had it not to give them'.[1]

Not that family bonds were inviolable. Criminals occasionally preyed upon their own relations, and families periodically disowned dissolute sons and daughters. One set of parents reputedly took the drastic step of moving to America, 'where they might be free from the constant dismal Accounts' of their 'irreclaimable Son', William Howard; in time, however, Howard dauntlessly followed them to South Carolina after having first been transported to Virginia for housebreaking.[2] Families also seized upon transportation as an opportunity to rid themselves of trying relations. At least, some convicts thought so. According to Sarah Marchant, banished for stealing several sheets, her husband's family lent decisive support to her courtroom prosecution in trying to dissolve her marriage. Edward Powlitt charged his father-in-law 'with being the chief Instrument of his being sent away'. Though John Jettea's brother-in-law claimed no credit for Jettea's exile, neither was he upset by the prospect. 'I was glad to see him [gone],' he later recalled, 'he having been very troublesome to me'. Slightly different was the claim of Benjamin Rand, a soldier found guilty of stealing money from his father to procure a discharge from the army. Sentenced to transportation, Rand accused his uncle of instigating his prosecution so that he might 'better secure' the family 'Estate'.[3]

Still, the families of most convicts remained warmly supportive. Far from trying to speed the departure of close relations, many households tirelessly submitted petitions attempting to block their transportation. If all else failed, some families tried to remain together in exile. Thus, John Totterdale's lover publicly affirmed that 'if he should happen to be Transported, she would go with him at all Events', and David Douglas, a Scottish horse thief,

---

[1] Petition of Mary and Daniel Brown to King, n.d., SP 36/149/6; Petition of Thomas Atwood to King, [Sept. 1730], SP 36/20/272.

[2] *Account of the Ordinary of Newgate*, 2 Oct. 1734, p. 8.

[3] Petition of Sarah Marchant to King, [Sept. 1754], SP 36/128/112; *Account of the Ordinary of Newgate*, 1 Feb. 1725, p. 5; *Old Bailey Sessions Papers*, 21–6 Feb. 1753, p. 107; Petition of Rand and Hammersmith Inhabitants to Queen, [1729], SP 36/15/47. See also Petition of Elizabeth Upton to King, [1754], SP 44/134/302-3.

declared in 1766 that he 'would most willingly banish himself and
family for Life'. Edward Robinson, a sheep-stealer, possessed a
wife and seven children who hoped to 'transport themselves a Long
with him' if they could raise enough money—'he Being', as a set
of friends wrote to the Earl of Powis, 'their whole Dependance for
a Support'.[1] Courts could do little to interfere with such schemes
as long as convicts and their families took separate paths across
the Atlantic. Only rarely were criminals allowed to transport
themselves or were close relations given permission to travel aboard
convict vessels. Even when the former servant Mary Featherstone
in 1730 gave birth in a Cambridge gaol to an illegitimate son, she
was not allowed, upon being sentenced to transportation for larceny,
to carry her child abroad.[2]

Well before being expelled from British shores, convicts had become
down and out. Young, male, and minimally skilled, most did not
inhabit the middle ranks of eighteenth-century society. Belonging
to the lower orders, they invariably fell victim to rough times, a
disproportionately large number in the squalour of London slums.
To judge from their backgrounds and behaviour, they were neither
harmless wastrels nor the members of a criminal underclass. If
most were driven to crime out of economic hardship, many had
also committed reasonably serious offences, in some cases on
repeated occasions. More than a few lived in a harsh, at times
violent world that placed a premium on strength and daring. On
the other hand, theirs was also a world that stressed the importance
of family and place. For persons who owned few material goods,
family ties were particularly critical, critical enough for some to
resort to crime when times turned hard. Thus in 1769, the convict
John Creamer, being 'out of work', stole nine guineas from a

---

[1] *Account of the Ordinary of Newgate*, 5 Oct. 1737, p. 9; Petition of David
Douglas to King, 10 Oct. 1766, HO 104/1/55; Thomas Whitmore *et al.* to Earl of
Powis, 21 Apr. 1760, SP 36/145/119. See also Petition of Solmon Jacob to
Holdernesse, 10 Sept. 1754, SP 36/128/88. In an early scene in the *Beggar's Opera*,
the character Polly asks Mac, her lover, 'Were you sentenced to transportation,
sure my dear, you could not leave me behind you-could you?' To which, he
responds, 'Is there any power, any force, that could tear me from thee? You might
sooner tear a pension out of the hands of a courtier, a fee from a lawyer, a pretty
women from a look-glass' (act 1, sc. 1).

[2] Hertfordshire Quarter Sessions, 4 Oct. 1730, in Le Hardy, ed., *Hertfordshire
County Records*, VII. 230. For the unusual case of a woman accompanying her
convict-husband aboard a vessel from Exeter, see T 47/10/72-73, PRO.

London home in order to support his 'young family'.[1] No wonder such men were reluctant to leave Britain; no wonder, too, that Britain was loath for them to remain.

[1] *Account of the Ordinary of Newgate*, 5 Aug., 14 Oct. 1772, p. 13.

3

THE ROUGH TRADE

I

Ordering felons for exile represented only a preliminary phase in the transportation process. In the months that followed trials, convicts needed to be assembled and shipped across the Atlantic without putting vessels, crews, and cargoes in jeopardy. With so many criminals at hand, government officials could not afford to adopt the haphazard methods relied upon in the past. Before 1718, either convicts were carried in irregular shipments by merchants or they transported themselves. Despite the small numbers involved, neither approach worked well. Many merchants refused to transport women because they proved difficult to market in the colonies, while prisoners given the right to arrange their own passage frequently remained in Britain. As the preamble to the Transportation Act noted, 'Many of the offenders to whom royal mercy hath been extended, upon condition of transporting themselves . . ., have often neglected to perform the said condition, but returned to their former wickedness'.[1]

No clearer sign existed of government commitment to transportation than the decision to assign a contract for the regular removal of convicts. Beginning in August 1718, the Treasury awarded Jonathan Forward, a 33 year-old London merchant, the lucrative sum of £3 for every convict transported from London and seven nearby counties. Recommended for the contract by the Solicitor-General, William Thomson, Forward not only had experience in the Atlantic slave trade, but in 1717 he had transported 131 convicts to Maryland and in July 1718 had shipped another forty. Further, Thomson observed, 'It would be of great service to the public to have them carried away every year', and 'no one else is ready to take

---

[1] 4 George I, c. 11; Thomson to [?], 2 Mar. 1736, SP 36/38/162; Smith, *Colonists in Bondage*, pp. 97-109; Beattie, *Crime and the Courts in England*, pp. 479-83. Shortly before passage of the Transportation Act, government authorities took a preliminary step to improve shipping arrangements. In early 1717, the Treasury paid the merchant Francis March £108 to transport fifty-four felons aboard three vessels to Jamaica. Treasury Order, 6 Mar. 1717, in William A. Shaw, ed., *Calendar of Treasury Books* (London, 1904-57), XXXI. 171-2.

them at so low a rate'. Thomson also believed that by expelling large numbers of felons, the 'government' would 'save considerably in rewards' commonly offered for the capture of 'highwaymen and house breakers'. 'This is really cheap', he concluded of the agreement.[1] Over the next decade, the subsidy rose, at Forward's strong urging, to £4 (1721) for London prisoners and to £4 (1719) and later to £5 (1722) for county prisoners. In 1727, £5 became the fee for all convicts taken from London and nearby counties, which remained the standard allowance until 1772 when the subsidy ended. Crown payments between 1718 and 1772 totalled more than £86,000 and funded the transportation of nearly 18,000 felons.[2]

In return, Forward and succeeding contractors signed bonds guaranteeing that convicts would be transported regardless of age, physical condition, or sex. The normal penalty was £40 for each convict not shipped within two months. While he was Recorder of London, Thomson claimed to 'read over carefully the names in every bond that is given by the merchant for transportation, and see with my own eyes, that every thing is right'. The system's merits seemingly justified the heavy government costs, for as Thomson wrote in 1736, 'The merchant is esteemed an Officer with a publick trust, and if he should willfully missbehave does not only forfeite his bond but is liable to publick censure. And it has been found by experience that he is carefull in the performance of his duty, the felons being carried directly from the Gaol to the Ship, and confined there in a proper manner.' In addition, shipmasters were required, upon arriving in the colonies, to procure customs certificates confirming the safe delivery of their cargoes.[3]

Occasionally, convicts petitioned for the right to arrange their own passage, as in past years. Often of higher social standing, they sought to avoid being cast with the common run of criminal offenders. In 1729, for example, Thomas Gawdey, the relation of 'several worthy inhabitants', hoped that 'his friends might be allowed to

---

[1] Thomson to [?], 9 July 1718, in Joseph Redington, ed., *Calendar of Treasury Papers* (1868–89; reprint edn., Nendeln, Liechtenstein, 1974), V. 389; Treasury Minute, 7 Aug. 1718, in Shaw, ed., *Calendar of Treasury Books*, XXXII. 90; Coldham, ed., *Bonded Passengers*, I. 35–7, 138; Appeals Report, 4 July 1724, in Carroll T. Bond, ed., *Proceedings of the Maryland Court of Appeals, 1695–1729*, American Legal Records, I (Washington, DC, 1933), p. 436.

[2] The convict total was compiled from Treasury Money Books in the PRO and from lists of voyages in Kaminkow and Kaminkow, eds., *Lists of Emigrants in Bondage*, pp. 180–203, and Coldham, ed., *Bonded Passengers*, I. 172–7.

[3] Thomson to [?], 12 Oct. 1727, SP 36/3/145–6, 2 Mar. 1736, SP 36/38/162.

transport him'.[1] Due, however, to the danger that large numbers might secretly remain in Britain, authorities rarely honoured such requests. Moreover, self-exile threatened to diminish whatever value transportation had as a deterrent. According to Thomson, frequent applications for such a privilege 'would almost change the terror of the punishment if it were known that it could be easily obtained'. As a consequence, not even George Vaughan, the celebrated brother of Lord Lisburne, was allowed private passage after having been convicted of highway robbery.[2] Only following the Seven Years War did the crown adopt a more lenient attitude, but never was the privilege of self-passage granted in any one year to more than a handful of offenders. It was also normally extended as a pardon.[3]

During the course of the eighteenth century, English merchants shipped convicts from numerous ports. Most of them, such as Plymouth, Exeter, Bideford, and Barnstaple, lay in the South-west. But two ports in particular, London and Bristol, came to dominate the trade. Although records are sparse for the early decades of transportation, shipping returns for the colony of Maryland[4] plainly show that from 1746 to 1775 the overwhelming number of convicts imported from England came from those two ports. Whereas 56.2 per cent originated in London and 35.8 per cent in Bristol, just 8 per

---

[1] Philip Floyd to Duke of [?], 2 Sept. 1729, SP 36/15/13. See also, e.g., John and Elizabeth Robinson to Duke of Montagu, 5 June 1732, SP 36/27/13; J. Brudenell to Lord [?], 28 Sept. 1732, SP 36/28/163; E. Vaughan to Duke of [?], 4 Mar. 1736, SP 36/38/164; Petition of Mary Jones to King, n.d., SP 36/150/53; Petition of John Beezley to Newcastle, n.d., SP 36/150/155.

[2] Thomson to [?], 19 June 1732, SP 36/27/43; Thomson to [?], 2 Mar. 1736, SP 36/38/162; *Va. Gaz.* 26 Nov. 1736. See also Thomson to [?], 16 June 1732, SP 36/27/34; J. Willes to [?], 10 Apr. 1734, SP 36/31/139.

[3] See e.g. the pardons listed in *Cal. HO Papers*, I. 229, II. 123-4, 262, 412, 572, III. 149, 151, 154-5, 378-9, 610, IV. 137-8, 141, 145, 278, 281, 283-4, 293-4.

[4] Maryland during the mid-eighteenth century had four naval districts (North Potomac, Patuxent, Chester, and Pocomoke) containing a total of six ports of entry for clearing vessels through customs: Annapolis, St. Marys, Oxford, Chestertown, and unnamed locations on the Patuxent and Wicomico Rivers. Lester J. Cappon, ed., *Atlas of Early American History: The Revolutionary Era, 1760-1790* (Princeton, NJ, 1976), p. 40. For the period 1746-75, shipping returns do not exist for St. Marys and the Wicomico River site, and those for Oxford, Chestertown, and the Patuxent River site cover only a few years. Returns for Annapolis, while not entirely complete, are far superior. Annapolis was clearly the busiest port of entry for vessels with convicts, as may be seen from the much smaller number of convicts entering at Oxford, Chestertown, and the Patuxent River site during the years for which records have survived. All these returns have been supplemented, when possible, with notices of convict arrivals that sometimes appeared in the *Maryland Gazette*.

Table 5. English Ports of Embarkation for Convicts Transported to Maryland, 1746–1775 (percentages in parentheses)

Years	London	Bristol	Other[a]	Total
1746–1755	1,322 (61.3)	405 (18.8)	431 (20.0)	2,158 (100.1)
1756–1765	1,261 (48.2)	1,170 (44.8)	183 (7.0)	2,614 (100.0)
1766–1775	2,656 (58.4)	1,764 (38.8)	131 (2.9)	4,551 (100.1)
Total	5,239 (56.2)	3,339 (35.8)	745 (8.0)	9,323 (100.0)

Note: a. Barnstaple, Bideford, Liverpool, Newcastle, and Plymouth.

Source: Maryland Shipping Returns, 1746–75, Maryland Historical Society, Baltimore, and Maryland Hall of Records, Annapolis.

cent boarded vessels elsewhere (see Table 5). London, of course, was England's greatest commercial centre. Even by 1760, despite the growing importance of northern ports like Liverpool, Whitehaven, Sunderland, and Newcastle, it accounted for 73 per cent of English exports. Bristol, which Defoe early in the century proclaimed the 'greatest, the richest, and the best Port of Trade in Great Britain, London only excepted', only became a serious competitor in the convict trade beginning in the late 1750s. It rose to importance largely at the expence of other ports, principally Barnstaple and Bideford, whose commerce generally was being engrossed by the 'metropolis of the west', with its extensive marketing system and affluent merchant community.[1] From 1746 to 1755, just 18.8 per cent of the English convicts imported into Maryland boarded vessels in Bristol; however, during the next two decades 41 per cent sailed from there. Conversely, from 1746 to 1755, 20 per cent of Maryland-bound convicts originated in ports other than Bristol and London, but by 1756–65 only 7 per cent came from other ports, and by 1766–75 the number had fallen to 2.9 per cent.

The greater part of the convict trade was concentrated in the hands of a few merchant companies. Usually, in order to amass capital and minimize risk, these consisted of several partners, though single traders controlled some companies. In London, which offered the special lure of the Treasury subsidy, several firms captured the market for the bulk of the century. Jonathan Forward, operating out of his Cheapside house on Fenchurch Street, dominated the trade for twenty years. In 1739, Andrew Reid, a friend of the Secretary

---

[1] Defoe, *Tour Thro' Great Britain*, II. 435; W. E. Minchinton, 'Bristol-Metropolis of the West in the Eighteenth Century', *Transactions of the Royal Historical Society*, 5th Ser., IV (1954), 70; Speck, *Stability and Strife*, p. 125.

to the Treasury, was placed on the government's payroll, though Forward continued to transport felons from provincial gaols until the late 1740s. Reid had several partners, including James and Andrew Armour of London and John Stewart, a Scotsman. During the 1750s, Stewart and the Armours held the Treasury contract. Thereafter, Stewart was joined by fellow Scot Duncan Campbell. Their company served until 1772 as the government's final contractor. Other London merchants, though not government beneficiaries, trafficked in convicts on a smaller scale. Their cargoes came from counties and towns outside the environs of the capital. Of thirty-four identifiable London firms involved in the trade to Maryland from 1746 to 1775, twenty-four never sponsored more than a single voyage. As indicated in Table 6, these carried 1,545 felons to the colony. At the other end of the trading spectrum stood John Stewart's company, Stewart & Armour, which from 1749 to 1759 transported 1,147 felons over a span of thirteen voyages. In Bristol, still fewer merchants controlled the malefactor market. Eight companies from 1746 to 1775 transported felons to Maryland, with only four of these each sponsoring more than a single voyage. Two firms, Sedgely & Co. (1749–68) and Stevenson, Randolph, & Cheston (1768–75), accounted for nearly 90 per cent of the total trade. Together, they shipped 2,954 felons over the course of forty-seven voyages.[1]

From the little known about contractors in London and Bristol, they formed a heterogeneous group, including not just Englishmen and Scots but, at least in one case, a member of the Portuguese Jewish colony in London, Moses Israel Fonesca. One merchant, himself a carrier of convicts, claimed that they belonged to the 'lowest' class of traders. Unlike some leading slave merchants in Bristol and Liverpool, they were not men of high social or political standing in their communities, nor do they seem to have descended from established mercantile families. That does not mean, however, that their origins were altogether humble, for few if any of them ever served as shipmasters, a not uncommon avenue of mobility for self-made men in the slave trade. Families of respectable means probably produced most of the big contractors, for whom trans-

---

[1] Schmidt, 'Convict Labor in Virginia', pp. 33–9; Smith, *Colonists in Bondage*, pp. 113–15; Maryland Shipping Returns, 1746–75, MHS and MHR.

Table 6. Number of Convicts Transported by London and Bristol Firms to Maryland, 1746–1775 (percentages in parentheses)

Number of shipments per merchant firm	London		Bristol	
	Merchant firm	Number of convicts	Merchant firm	Number of convicts
1	24 (70.6)	1,545 (29.8)	4 (50.0)	140 (4.2)
2	5 (14.7)	711 (13.7)	2 (25.0)	245 (7.3)
3	2 (5.9)	696 (13.4)	— —	— —
4	— —	— —	— —	— —
5–9	1 (2.9)	279 (5.4)	— —	— —
10–19	2 (5.9)	1,956 (37.7)	1 (12.5)	1,201 (36.0)
20+	— —	— —	1 (12.5)	1,753 (52.5)
Total	34 (100.0)	5,187 (100.0)	8 (100.0)	3,339 (100.0)

Source: Maryland Shipping Returns, 1746–75.

portation offered an attractive opportunity to augment their modest fortunes.[1]

Large companies did not deal solely in convicts. Some participated in the indentured servant trade, so that servants and convicts were at times transported on the same ships. In addition, convict vessels frequently contained varying quantities of dry goods, and on return trips brought colonial exports like tobacco, wheat, and pig iron back to Britain. A few merchants, at one time or another, were also slave traders, including not only Jonathan Forward but also Samuel Sedgley of Bristol and James Gildart of Liverpool.[2] The convict trade, however, was the predominant branch of commerce for large firms. Between 1746 and 1775, four companies in London and Bristol each sponsored ten or more voyages to Maryland, in which a total of 4,910 convicts were transported. During that period, the same companies carried to Maryland only 233 indentured servants and five slaves, nearly all of them aboard vessels with convicts. Although firms may have carried large numbers of servants and slaves to other provinces, there is no evidence to suggest that that happened.

---

[1] John Stewart quoted in Coldham, ed., *Bonded Passengers*, I. 144; Schmidt, 'Convict Labor in Virginia', p. 40; James A. Rawley, *The Transatlantic Slave Trade: A History* (New York, 1981), pp. 183–4, 210. For the absence of former shipmasters, see e.g. the Md. Shipping Returns, 1746–75, in which none of the principal traders to Maryland were previously listed as captains of vessels.

[2] Md. Shipping Returns, 1746–75; Coldham, ed., *Bonded Passengers*, I. 52.

Records of Stevenson, Randolph, & Cheston, for example, indicate
that its ships sailed only to Maryland.[1]

Such a high degree of specialization suggests how lucrative trans-
portaton was for firms. Some merchants, to be sure, shied away
from carrying convicts; one person even claimed that 'few people'
were 'caring for so perilous an exercise'. And, like contractors in the
slave and indentured servant trades, those involved in transportation
were always vulnerable to mishaps at sea, losses due to shipboard
mortality, shifting conditions in the colonial labour market, and
slow remittances. Further, convict traders were required to transport
felons regardless of their market value—a disadvantage not suffered
by merchants in the servant and slave trades. The Virginia factor
for a firm in Whitehaven noted this important difference when he
upbraided his employers for sending 'Indifferent' indentured servants that were not 'Tradesmen' but were instead 'as Infamous as
the Convicts', including one servant who was 'an Idiot'. 'Convicts I
know you are obliged to take,' he complained, 'but the Idiot . . . was
a 4 year Servant'.[2]

On the other hand, at least in comparison with the slave trade,
the capitalization required by transportation was modest. Besides
outlays for one or more vessels and equipment, operating costs
included seamen's wages, provisions, and insurance and port
charges, but convict voyages were far shorter nor were there expences associated with maintaining agents or factories in Africa. In
1767, the firm of Stevenson & Cheston began with only £1,500 and
a vessel valued at £1,000, the *Isabella*. The folowing year, with the
addition of William Randolph as a third partner, the firm's capitalization rose to £9,000, but, then, Stevenson, Randolph, & Cheston immediately became the largest trader of convicts in Bristol,

---

[1] Md. Shipping Returns, 1746-75; CGP. The high priority given to convicts by
Stevenson, Randolph, & Cheston is suggested in a letter from William Stevenson in
Bristol to James Cheston in Maryland: 'I have shipped Mess. Price and Withered
chief part of the Goods they ordered, some of them We are obliged to leave behind
as all the Convicts will be aboard today and the wind is fair and the Goods cannot
be down by the Trows till tomorrow, but We could not think of detaining the Vessel
as it might totally ruin the Voyage.' Stevenson to Cheston, 12 Sept. 1768, CGP, Box
9.

[2] John Stewart quoted in Coldham, ed., *Bonded Passengers*, I. 144; Harry Piper to
Dixon & Littledale, 24 Oct. 1767, 28 June 1768, HPL, pp. 21, 43. By the 1760s, slow
remittances in the colonies posed a special problem. Because of poor prices for
tobacco and a general shortage of money, local factors often had a difficult time
collecting debts incurred by their customers. For a more detailed discussion, see
Morgan, 'Convict Trade to Maryland', pp. 223-5.

with several vessels at its command. Moreover, major firms were guaranteed a steady supply of men and women to sell as servants, for whom they did not have to expend capital but instead reaped government fees. Because of such sales, one contemporary complained that contractors 'ought to Pay instead of Receiving a Consideration for the Passage'.[1]

Certainly there were large profits to be made. On three voyages in 1772, for instance, Duncan Campbell transported 348 convicts to Virginia at an estimated cost of £2,001. 12*s*. 9*d*. Though there were other expences, such as his crew's wages and the upkeep of his ships, and though he subsequently lost money on return cargoes of tobacco due to a sudden collapse in prices during the credit crisis of 1772–73, Campbell sold the transported felons for as much as £2,957. 9*s*. This return did not include fees that Campbell had customarily received as government contractor, since payment of the subsidy had just been discontinued. Had it not been, he would have received an additional £1,740 for the three voyages. Meanwhile, Stevenson, Randolph, & Cheston earned an estimated profit of roughly 26 per cent from sixteen trips from Bristol to Maryland, not including fees paid by localities for the removal of their transports. Recent studies of the British slave trade during the second half of the eighteenth century have concluded that merchants earned profits of less than 10 per cent. With good reason William Stevenson could write to James Cheston in 1769 that their business 'if properly managed will in a few years make Us very genteel fortunes. The Sales of the Convicts run up amazingly in a little time.' About the same time, a factor in the Virginia trade echoed that by convicts 'the most is made'.[2]

---

[1] [Lord Baltimore], Observations on the Memorial of John Stewart, [1757], *Md. Archives*, LV. 769; 'Memorandum of an Agreement . . . Between William Stevenson of the City of Bristol Merchant of the one part and James Cheston of the same City of the other part', 3 Aug. 1767, Stevenson to Cheston, 5 Aug 1768, CGP, Boxes 18, 9; Roger Anstey, *The Atlantic Slave Trade and British Abolition, 1760–1810* (London, 1975), pp. 5–6, 44–5.

[2] Stevenson to Cheston, 30 Dec. 1769, CGP, Box 9; Piper to Dixon & Littledale, 28 June 1768, HPL, p. 43; Duncan Campbell, 'A State of the Contract for Felons . . .', 15 Feb. 1774, T 1/500; Smith, *Colonists in Bondage*, pp. 122–3; Scott Fassbach, 'The Convict Trade to the Late Eighteenth Century Chesapeake' (Unpublished seminar paper, Johns Hopkins University, 1981), pp. 28–31; Anstey, *Atlantic Slave Trade*, pp. 46–7; Rawley, *Transatlantic Slave Trade*, p. 265. See also Horatio Sharpe to Joshua Sharpe, 27 May 1757, *Md. Archives*, IX. 5; Henry Laurens to George Appleby, 10 Mar. 1774, in Philip M. Hamer and George C. Rogers, Jr., eds., *The Papers of Henry Laurens* (Columbia, SC, 1968-) IX. 347. By the late colonial

Profits for enterprising merchants in London and Bristol were enhanced by their ability to attract transportation contracts from elsewhere in the kingdom. While traders in other ports dabbled in shipping felons, London and Bristol each served as a funnel for convicts drawn from nearly half the counties in England. As shown in Map 2, the country became bisected north to south into two major trading zones: London controlled most of the eastern traffic and Bristol most of the western, including that of Wales. Large firms in both cities could guarantee local officials fixed schedules and several shipments per year. Further, despite the often great distances felons needed to be marched, carted, or ferried, each port had access by land and water to a dense hinterland containing large numbers of convicts. Probably for that reason, the rapidly growing port of Liverpool was not a major convict entrepôt, despite its prominence after mid-century in the slave trade and the fact that by 1750 it ranked second only to London in the value and volume of its trade with America. Though blessed with a booming population, excellent dock and harbour facilities, and a diverse commercial base,[1] Liverpool was removed from areas with the heaviest concentrations of felons needing to be shipped. Because of its north-western location, there was never much opportunity to assemble sufficiently large numbers.

In the Transportation Act, Parliament had first authorized provincial courts to contract with merchants for the removal of convicts. Financial costs for localities were not negligible. Just as Treasury subsidies represented a significant expence for the crown, counties and towns regularly demonstrated their commitment to transportation by shouldering a heavy share of the cost, and not without some hardship. So financially pressed were Warwick officials that in 1730 they petitioned the Treasury for funds but were told that the

period, indentured servants probably fetched higher sums than transports because they were more highly skilled; even then, government fees in all likelihood made transportation the more profitable trade. For a discussion of the profitability of the indentured servant trade, see Sharon Vineberg Salinger, 'Labor and Indentured Servants in Colonial Pennsylvania' (Ph.D. diss., University of California, Los Angeles, 1980), pp. 85–90; Farley Ward Grubb, 'Immigration and Servitude in the Colony and Commonwealth of Pennsylvania: A Quantitative and Economic Analysis' (Ph.D. diss., University of Chicago, 1984), *passim.*

[1] Paul G. E. Clemens, 'The Rise of Liverpool, 1665–1750', *Economic History Review*, 2nd Ser., XXIX (1976), pp. 211–25; P. J. Corfield, *The Impact of English Towns, 1700–1800* (Oxford, 1982), pp. 41–2.

MAP 2. London and Bristol Trade Zones, and Other Ports of Embarkation for English Convicts

Sources: Transportation Bonds and Contracts listed in chapter footnotes and in the bibliography; Kent County Bonds and Indentures, 1719-44, Queen Anne's County Land Records, 1727-50, Baltimore County Convict Record, 1770-74, Anne Arundel County Convict Record, 1771-75, Maryland Hall of Records, Annapolis. The trade zone border represents a rough approximation since information was not available for some counties and since a few of those in the middle of the country occasionally sent transports to both London and Bristol.

crown could not provide subsidies beyond those already being paid. Besides hefty merchant commissions that localities assumed, there were occasional fees paid to clerks for transportation certificates plus fees charged by gaolers for conveying felons safely to awaiting contractors. Even Middlesex, the Home Counties, and Buckinghamshire had to pay these incidental charges, not to mention poor relief payments for convict families and the normal costs associated with subsisting and guarding felons while they remained in gaol. Hertfordshire in 1736 needed to levy a special tax to raise £174 for conveying its convicts to London.[1] Some idea of transportation's financial impact on localities can be gained by looking at the western county of Gloucestershire. From 1727 to 1773, assize and quarter sessions courts ordered 642 felons for transportation, a number somewhat higher than that of most counties but, then, so too was the county's population, about 200,000 by mid-century. Direct costs, including only fees charged by merchants, gaolers, and clerks, amounted to roughly £4,230 or £6. 11s. per convict. Put another way, transportation charges, other than gaol expences for prisoners and poor relief for their families, comprised more than 9 per cent of Gloucestershire's entire budget of £46,584 from 1727 to 1773, which, among other things, also covered official salaries and local improvements.[2]

In the provinces, several pounds per convict was the normal fee set by contractors, though sometimes during wartime rates were raised because of added dangers to shipping. Distance from major ports increased fees when merchants, not local justices, paid the travel expences of gaolers. In 1770, for instance, the London merchant Jonathan Forward Sydenham charged Derbyshire justices a fee of only £2 in contrast to the £6 he received from officials in Yorkshire's North Riding. Occasionally, the nature of the cargo affected rates. Young males, for instance, with marketable skills as servants offered merchants higher profits than women. 'What we

[1] 4 George I, c. 11; Treasury Order, 18 Nov. 1730, in William A. Shaw, ed., *Calendar of Treasury Books and Papers* (London, 1897–1903), I. 472; Hertfordshire Quarter Sessions, 12 July 1736, in Le Hardy, ed., *Hertfordshire County Records*, VII. 260. For local fees, see also Transportation Records, 1720–72, Derbyshire Record Office, Matlock; Quarter Sessions Bonds and Orders, 1720–83, Leicestershire Record Office, Leicester; Transportation Records, 1741–66, City Record Office, Coventry; K. William-Jones, ed., *A Calendar of the Merioneth Quarter Sessions Rolls*, I, *1733–1765* (Aberystwyth, 1965); W. H. Stevenson et al., eds., *Records of the Borough of Nottingham* . . . (Nottingham, 1947), VII; J. Perry, ed., 'The Transportation of Felons to America, 1717–1775: Some North Riding Quarter Sessions Records', *North Yorkshire County Record Office Journal*, VIII (1981), 75–86; Oldham, 'Transportation of British Convicts', p. 48.

[2] Treasurers' Books, 1727–73, Gloucestershire Record Office, Gloucester. The population estimate is taken from the 1751 estimate in Deane and Cole, *British Economic Growth*, p. 103.

shall take . . .', noted a firm in 1751, 'will depend some what on the Age, Constitution, and Trades of the Persons to be Transported'. Physical size could be a consideration because of cramped quarters aboard ships. 'If he be either old or large', a Liverpool merchant wrote to a Derbyshire official in 1743, 'I cannot take him under £5.' Traders never could refuse to carry less appealing felons, but they could always make it worth their while by raising fees.[1]

Of course, counties and towns might try to lower fees by appealing to rival contractors. Beginning in the mid-1740s, the two London firms Reid & Armour and Sydenham & Hodgson avidly competed for the franchise to transport felons from the city of Coventry. Whereas the larger contractor, Reid & Armour, had traditionally received £4. 4s. per felon, by March 1751 they were promising to give 'as low terms as any other Person'. Equally, they urged, 'You have the Advantage of haveing a Certainty with us, as our Contract for those of Newgate and the Neighbouring Counties obliges us to send Four or five Ships yearly.' In the end, Coventry authorities, who described transportation costs as 'a heavy affair upon our poor Small Jurisdiction', supplied felons to both companies that year at a rate of only £3. 3s.[2]

Most localities, however, wielded little leverage in negotiating favourable contracts, for open bidding between merchants was not common. London and nearby counties remained a closed market to anyone but government contractors. When Jonathan Forward lost his subsidy in 1739, Treasury officials plainly warned that 'if he . . . intermeddles in such transportations' they would not honour his charges.[3] The Bristol trade, meanwhile, was in most years monopolized by a single firm, except for occasional interlopers. In 1768, the prospect loomed of open conflict between William Randolph,

---

[1] Armour & Stewart to James Birch, 18 Apr. 1751, Coventry Transportation Records; William Pole to Clerk of Peace, 22 Aug. 1743, in Cox, *Derbyshire Annals*, II. 52; Merchant Contracts, 1723–72, Derbyshire Transportation Records; Transportation Contract, 23 Aug. 1770, in Perry, ed., 'North Riding Quarter Sessions Records', p. 84. See also [?] to Sydenham & Hodgson, 26 Sept. 1751, Coventry Transportation Records.

[2] William Currie to Birch, 14 Mar. 1751, Birch to [Currie], 14 Mar. 1751, Sydenham & Hodgson to William Wood, 21 Sept. 1745, Sydenham & Hodgson to Birch, 2 Nov. 1745, 22 Dec. 1748, Sydenham & Hodgson to Mr Wheately, 7 Dec. 1745, 11 Apr. 1747, Bills of Receipt, 1742, 1745, 26 Apr., 1 Oct. 1751, Coventry Transportation Records.

[3] Treasury Order, 12 Apr. 1739, in Shaw, ed., *Calendar of Treasury Books and Papers*, IV. 20.

formerly of the firm Sedgley & Co., and an upstart firm founded by William Stevenson and his stepbrother James Cheston. Rather than compete against each other, however, the combatants established a partnership that dominated the Bristol trade until the American Revolution. As Stevenson wrote to Cheston shortly before the alliance was forged, 'If we were to Join Him there would be no competition in the business and the convicts will all fall into our hands.' By the following year, Stevenson reported, 'We have secured all the Goals round about'.[1]

Nor could counties and towns afford indefinite delays in negotiating the disposal of felons. Besides the costs of imprisonment that communities shouldered, provincial gaols, built for short stays not long prison terms, were notoriously unhealthy. Cold, damp quarters, abysmal sanitation, and rampant malnutrition created ideal conditions for infection and pestilence. Smallpox and 'gaol fever', an especially virulent form of typhus spread by lice, brought early death to numerous prisoners. In Surrey between 1736 and 1753, upwards of thirty-five persons awaiting trial in the county gaol for property offences probably perished from gaol fever. At Newgate, so great was the danger of contagion that doctors routinely refused to enter the prison, nor was it uncommon for 10 per cent of the inmate population to die in a single year. 'The goal distemper renders Newgate almost as fatal to their lives as Tyburn', claimed a London newspaper in 1773.[2] Then, too, convicts were always prone to escape. After twenty-one felons broke out of York Castle in 1731, it took the keeper two years at a cost of £150 to retrieve just seventeen of the prisoners. Later that decade, Oxford's gaol suffered repeated assaults by a gang of more than forty criminals intent on rescuing fourteen comrades. Local justices, understandably, remained anxious to rid their counties of cargoes that were just as dangerous as they were perishable.[3]

---

[1] Stevenson to Cheston, 5 Aug. 1768, 17 Aug. 1769, CGP, Box 9. For much the same reason, the new firm was in a stronger position to negotiate fees paid to gaolers for bringing felons to Bristol. 'We have already reaped some advantage', Stevenson wrote to Cheston, 'as instead of giving 2 Guineas a head for the Convicts, some We give nothing at all, a few We get Money from and a few others We only give a Guinea.' Stevenson to Cheston, 12 Sept. 1768, ibid.

[2] Rind's *Va. Gaz.* 13 May 1773; Beattie, 'Crime and the Courts in Surrey', p. 162; Beattie, *Crime and the Courts in England*, pp. 298–309; W. J. Sheehan, 'Finding Solace in Eighteenth-Century Newgate', in Cockburn, ed., *Crime in England*, pp. 229–30.

[3] Deposition and Petition of Richard Woodhouse, 22 Apr. 1734, in Perry, ed.,

II

In Ireland, trading arrangements operated on a smaller scale. During a typical year, probably between 200 and 300 felons and vagabonds sailed from Irish ports. In so far as most prisoners came from the province of Leinster, Dublin handled the bulk of the trade, just as it did a great part of the indentured servant trade to America. From 1730 to 1774, at least fifty-three vessels with convicts cleared Dublin harbour for the colonies.[1] Ireland's three other provinces, Ulster, Connaught, and Munster, probably boarded their prisoners elsewhere. Surviving records, though sparse, suggest that each province relied upon its own ports: Newry in Ulster, Galway in Connaught, and Cork, Limerick, and Waterford in Munster. Of 104 convicts, for instance, transported on three vessels from Dublin in the early 1740s, only two came from outside Leinster. Within Leinster itself, the remaining 102 convicts represented a broad geographic spectrum, originating from as many as seven counties.[2]

In Dublin, the structure of transportation was decentralized. More so than in London or Bristol, no one firm dominated the trade. From 1737 to 1743, for example, the County of the City of Dublin contracted with local merchants for the removal of 384 convicts. Nineteen different firms participated, and, of those, fourteen carried convicts only once. The largest trader was Joseph Weld, who received four separate contracts accounting for less than a quarter of Dublin transports.[3] Not that Weld did not do his best to monopolize trading arrangements. In 1739, he and a partner petitioned authorities for the transportation franchise for both Dublin and Cork. Though they invested £1,500 in shipping and equipment, their effort failed, as did, that same year, a rival firm's more brazen attempt to corner the entire Irish trade by securing a contract from the Irish House of Commons. Perhaps due to pressure from other merchants,

---

'North Riding Quarter Sessions Records', pp. 72–4; Lenthal to [?], 7 Oct. 1738, SP 44/131/37–9.

[1] Lockhart, 'Emigration from Ireland', pp. 181–207.

[2] Shipping Lists, 1742, 1743, *JHCI* VII. 627–30; Lockhart, 'Emigration from Ireland', pp. 185, 191, 195, 204, 207; Voyages of the *Endeavour*, 1755, and the *Enterprise*, 1756, Md. Shipping Returns, 1746–75; R. J. Dickson, *Ulster Emigration to Colonial America, 1718–1775* (London, 1966), pp. 83–5.

[3] County of the City of Dublin 'Abstract of presentments for money . . .', 1737–43, *JHCI* VII. 568–9.

government officials were inclined to keep transportation in as many hands as possible.[1] For that reason and because there were fewer Irish transports, the trade never became as specialized as it did in England. Convicts were shipped not only with servants, as was occasionally done in England, but also with ordinary passengers. Before embarking, in fact, convicts sometimes were indentured as servants, probably to create a more pleasing impression upon their arrival in America and to evade import duties and other restrictions upon the convict trade that colonies routinely tried to impose. Individuals identified as convicts in Dublin newspapers were not infrequently listed later as 'servants' or 'passengers' in colonial shipping returns. Thus, the *Two Friends* left Dublin in October 1741 with a cargo of convicts, according to Faulkner's *Dublin Journal*, but upon its arrival in Virginia the vessel reportedly contained forty-three 'passengers'. Two years later, the *George* arrived in Virginia with seventy 'servants', despite an earlier report, again in Faulkner's *Dublin Journal*, that it sailed with over sixty convicts.[2]

Commissions charged by Irish merchants commonly fell short of fees collected in England. Although counties, by virtue of a 1729 statute, were supposed to allot up to £6 per prisoner, rather than just £2 as stipulated in previous years, the market was too competitive for merchants always to receive the maximum allowance. Moreover, gaolers responsible for conveying convicts to awaiting contractors frequently demanded as much as half of every payment, though legally permitted to charge no more than £1 per person. As John Langley, a Dublin merchant, testified before the House of Commons in 1744, the 'most he ever got for transporting any of the . . . convicts was three pounds a man', although he was 'credibly informed . . . there were presented on the several Counties . . . five or six pounds a man'.[3]

Transportation costs for localities were not inconsiderable. Though merchants, in contrast to English contractors, shipped fewer convicts, and at reduced commissions, gaolers' fees added sig-

---

[1] Minutes, 15 Dec. 1739, *JHCI* VII. 129.

[2] *Pa. Gaz.* 16 Sept. 1736, 25 July 1754; Lockhart, 'Emigration from Ireland', pp. 81, 91, 181–207; Dickson, *Ulster Emigration*, pp. 82–4.

[3] Depositions of John Langley *et al.*, 9 Feb. 1744, *JHCI* VII. 558–9; 'An Act for the more effectual transporting Felons and Vagabonds', 1725, 'An Act . . . for the more effectual transporting Felons, Vagabonds, and others', 1729, *Irish Statutes* (Dublin, 1786–1801), III. 290, 388.

nificantly to the fiscal woes of local officials. After all, Ireland's population totalled about half that of England, and it was less able to shoulder new financial burdens. The expence of transporting just 1,938 felons and vagabonds between 1737 and 1743 ran to approximately £8,500, or £4. 7s. 8d. per passenger. If fees were roughly the same throughout the century (except before 1729 when the sum paid per transport was £2), then local authorities may have expended over £50,000, since we have already estimated that Ireland transported more than 13,000 convicts.[1]

If Ireland's transportation network was decentralized, trading arrangements in Scotland were even more haphazard. Because there were so few convicts to be transported and because Scottish authorities were reluctant to subsidize their removal, prisoners were not consigned to contractors to be carried to the colonies and sold as servants. Instead, they remained confined in tolbooths until they could arrange private passage abroad. Once arrangements had been finalized, ship captains filed bonds with local authorities guaranteeing the safe delivery of their passengers. Thus, Alexander Karr in 1764 was remanded to the Edinburgh tolbooth until 'any merchant Shipmaster or other person' who could 'find Sufficient Caution and Surety' agreed to 'transport and land him' in one of 'his majestys plantations'. Unless prisoners were fortunate enough to afford the price of passage, they were forced to sign servant indentures with captains. Fairly typical were Robert Thomson who indentured himself in 1740 with John MacIntosh, a merchant travelling to Jamaica, and Janet Anderson who in 1754 sold her services to a merchant destined for Maryland.[2]

Although such traders profited from the sale of indentured servants, they did not receive fees from local authorities. This

---

[1] 'Abstract of the number of convict felons and vagabonds', 9 Feb. 1744, *JHCI* VII. 561–2.

[2] Sentence of Banishment against Alexander Karr, 14 Feb. 1764, JC 3/33/442; Petition of Robert Thomson, 27 Jan. 1740, JC 3/23/163–4; Petition of Janet Anderson, 12 June 1754, JC 3/29/563–4. See also, e.g., Earl of Hay to [?], 21 Oct. 1729, SP 54/16/53; 'Answers for Mr. Hays. . .', by Patrick Haldone, 20 June 1744, JC 3/24/593; Remission for Peter Taylor, 21 Dec. 1750, JC 3/27/468; Petition of John Donaldson, 11 Aug. 1753, JC 3/29/271; Petition of John Macfarlane and James Young, June 1754, JC 3/29/567; Petition of Ronald McDonald, 10 Feb. 1755, JC 3/30/258; Petition of Alexander Shand, 22 July 1760, JC 3/32/314–15; and assorted cases in John Imrie, ed., *The Justiciary Records of Argyll and the Isles, 1664–1772* (Edinburgh, 1969), II. esp. 382, 384. By the 1760s, recipients of transportation pardons in Scotland were normally allowed to transport themselves. See Criminal Pardons, 1762–72, in *Cal. HO Papers*, I. 256, 380, II. 285, III. 385, 614.

circumstance, coupled with the comparatively sparse numbers of men and women banished to America, meant that Scotland's trade remained small and irregular. Convicts were conveyed not in large gangs but as individuals contracted to sail out of any one of several ports. Only during the final years of transportation were trading arrangements placed on a firmer footing. In 1766, Parliament extended to Scotland the provisions of the original Transportation Act of 1718, thereby opening the door to full-fledged contractors with the right to receive fees and to sell convicts for a full seven years. The new act pointedly noted that the 'effectual transportation of offenders' from Scotland was 'often disappointed'. A Scottish attorney commented at the time, 'The purpose of the Statute was not to bestow the power of Transportation upon any Judge who had it not before, But merely to render more Effectual those Sentences which should be pronounced by any Competent Court.'[1] In 1771, the Glasgow trader and future police magistrate Patrick Colquhoun received the entire Scottish commission. Though he reserved the privilege to transport felons from different ports, Colquhoun mostly shipped his vessels out of Glasgow. Landing certificates for Scottish convicts carried to Virginia and Maryland from 1771 to 1775 list ports of origin for sixty felons, some of whom were tried as far away as Aberdeen, Jedburgh, and Inverary. Fifty of that number embarked at Glasgow and ten at nearby Greenock.[2]

III

'Going to Hell in a Cradle' was how one prisoner described the journey. Ordered for transportation at the Worcester assizes in the summer of 1734, eight men and a woman were placed in a small boat bound down the Severn River for Bristol. There they would have boarded a ship for the colonies, but within a mile of the Bristol Avon disaster struck. With the wind blowing

[1] 'Information for Kennedy', by Blair, 2 Feb. 1767, JC 3/35; 'An Act to extend an act . . . intituled, An act for the further preventing robbery, burglary, and other felonies, and for the more effectual transportation of felons . . .', 1766, 6 George III, c. 32.

[2] Colquhoun to John Davidson, 30 Nov. 1770, GD 214/726/2; Landing Certificates, 1771–75, Transportation Papers, JC 27; Sentence of Banishment against Thomas Young, 11 July 1771, JC 3/37. In 1773, for unknown reasons, Parliament repealed the 1766 act, but transportation arrangements remained in Colquhoun's hands. 'An Act for . . . repealing and amending Several of the laws now in being . . .', 1773, 13 George III, c. 54.

furiously, one of the convicts, amidst the constant cursings of his companions, dropped a massive ballast stone onto the vessel's bottom, thereby tearing a deep hole in a wooden plank. Crying out, 'The Boat is almost full of water', he forced the captain to run the vessel aground. The crew survived, but the 'three greatest Rogues', reported a later account, all drowned.[1]

*

Before transports were assembled for shipping, they first languished in gaol. Close, nauseating confinement marked their final months in Britain. Periods of incarceration varied among localities. Transports in the vicinity of London and Bristol endured relatively brief terms after their trials; confined to prisons or nearby gaols, they probably waited on average two months before contracts were signed, bonds filed, and vessels were boarded. Merchants normally contracted for convicts in April after the winter assizes, but ships sailed at other times during the year, such as following summer assize sessions. Large firms, such as Reid & Armour in London and Stevenson, Randolph, & Cheston in Bristol, undertook several voyages each year.[2] A different fate awaited convicts in outlying areas where court officials moved less swiftly. Counties removed from major ports faced the difficult chore of conveying felons overland or by water to awaiting vessels. Though anxious to rid themselves of troublesome malefactors, many localities arranged for their removal no more than once or twice a year. In the North Riding of Yorkshire, where officials usually authorized a single shipment every summer or early autumn, transports stayed in gaol on average three and a half months before the signing of a contract. Capital felons who received transportation pardons at later assize sessions typically remained imprisoned for five months. In neither instance did these prison terms include the many days spent in gaol either before cases came to trial (an average of nearly four months in the North Riding) or after a contract was concluded; two months could still elapse before prisoners were carried to ports and finally put to sea.[3] Unexpected postponements also could arise, for merchants

---

[1] *Pa. Gaz.* 12 Dec. 1734.

[2] Testimony of Campbell, 1 Apr. 1779, *JHC* XXXVII. 311; Fassbach, 'Convict Trade to the Chesapeake', pp. 7-8.

[3] These calculations are based on the gaol terms from 1754 to 1774 of 53 non-capital felons and 35 capital felons. See the list of transported felons in Perry, ed., 'North Riding Quarter Sessions Records', pp. 89-117.

allowed only a few days for loading their vessels. If prisoners did not arrive on schedule, they again had to be incarcerated until new plans were made. 'You must bring them Exactly at the 10th Instant or before,' Jonathan Forward wrote to a Derbyshire official in early October 1724, 'for if in case you should faile that time I shall not be ready to take them on severall months'.[1] Then, too, courts, contractors, and crown officials sometimes failed to process the mass of paperwork that transportation required. In addition to bonds filed by merchants, there were contracts, court orders, and royal pardons. A few days' delay could be disastrous, such as in 1740 when Martha Williams was threatened with an added six months in gaol after a local court adjourned before authorization had arrived for her transportation. Wiltshire prisoners in the late 1720s were not transported for several years because the Western assize clerk demanded his customary fees for processing their pardons. 'Nothing will be done', the keeper of the Wiltshire gaol was told, unless he paid 'a Guinea for each Persons Certificate'.[2]

Convicts in Ireland experienced many of the same delays, particularly during the first decades of the century. Before government fees rose, some merchants remained reluctant to carry transports. In 1729, a committee appointed by the Irish House of Commons found that transports made up nearly 120 of 160 persons confined in Dublin's Newgate prison. The 'miserable Fullness of this Gaol', the committee concluded, arose chiefly from the 'Difficulties of Transportation'.[3] Prisoners in Scotland, before the Act of 1766, faced especially long periods of confinement, since trading arrangements there were less organized. Responsible for their own passage, transports endured indefinite stays until proper bargains

[1] Forward to John Greatorex, 1 Oct. 1724, Derbyshire Transportation Records. See also Sydenham & Hodgson to Wheately, 7 Dec. 1745, Sydenham & Hodgson to Birch, 2 Feb. 1748, Armour & Stewart to Birch, 25 Aug. 1752, Coventry Transportation Records; Campbell to Keeper of Oakham Gaol, 12 May 1772, Campbell to Philip Detitten, 23 Dec. 1773, DCPL, pp. 26, 220.

[2] Petition of Robert Thorpe to Newcastle, [1730], SP 44/127/99–100; Henry [Faur?] to Andrew Stone, 24 Apr. 1740, SP 36/50/339; Thomson to Lord [?], 17 Aug. 1730, SP 36/20/45. See also, e.g., Nicholas Paxton to [?], 5 Dec. 1723, SP 35/47/7; Coldham, ed., *Bonded Passengers*, VI. vii-viii.

[3] 'Report from the Committee appointed to enquire into the State of the Gaols and Prisons of this Kingdom', 24 Nov. 1729, *JHCI* III, Appendix, p. ccclxxxviii. See also *Some Reasons Humbly Offer'd, Why the Castration of Persons Found Guilty of Robbery and Theft . . .* (Dublin, 1725), p. 2; 'An Act for the more effectual transporting Felons and Vagabonds', 1725, *Irish Statutes*, III. 289; 'An Act . . . for the more effectual transporting Felons, Vagabonds, and others', 1729, ibid., p. 388.

could be struck with ship captains. The departure of vessels for the colonies was frequently erratic. As Defoe observed in the mid-1720s of commerce with America, 'No Town in *Scotland* has yet done any Thing considerable in it but *Glasgow*.' Thus, Robert Purdie, after being convicted in October 1749 at Inverness, was ordered that if he could not be transported from there, he was to be transferred from sheriff to sheriff until 'brought to the Port or Place' where shipping could be arranged. Even in Glasgow, despite its heavy involvement in the Chesapeake tobacco trade, shipping could be seasonal and difficult to schedule. Walter Denny, a 'miserable' and 'starving' prisoner in the Glasgow tolbooth, despaired in July 1735 that no 'outward bound Ships' would again sail 'till the next Spring'.[1]

Scheduling became more problematic when passage was not prepaid and merchants refused to indenture prisoners as servants. Women faced special hardships. Merchants feared they would be difficult to market in the colonies since they were considered less suited to either skilled or heavy labour and liable to become pregnant. The Aberdeen prisoner Janet Jameison complained in 1734 that 'no merchants, either at Montrose or Glasgow, that traded to America' would 'undertake to Transport her, unless she could pay her passage'. Old and infirm prisoners encountered as few opportunities for transportation. Convicted at Stirling in May 1729, William Lauder agonized after three years' confinement that merchants would never transport him, as he was elderly and 'not fit for any Service in the Plantations'. Helen Mortimer similarly feared a lifetime of 'perpetual Imprisonment'. Jailed for two years in Aberdeen, she suffered from 'Histerick fits and several other Dangerous Diseases'. Not only was she too weak and destitute to transport herself, but 'no merchant nor shipmaster' would 'Transport her'.[2]

---

[1] Defoe, *Tour Thro' Great Britain*, III. 746; Northern Circuit Court Order, 16 Oct. 1749, JC 11/14; Petition of Walter Denny, 1 July 1735, JC 3/19/716-17; Jacob M. Price, 'The Rise of Glasgow in the Chesapeake Tobacco Trade, 1707-1775', *WMQ*, 3rd Ser., XI (1954), 179-99. See also [James Campbell] to Sir James Campbell, 7 Apr. 1729, GD 14/10/1/281-82. As late as 1767, a person noted that 'in Scotland there are but few ports which have any trade to the plantations, and still fewer which have so Constant and regular a Communication as to afford opportunity of transporting persons'. 'Information for Kennedy', by Blair, 2 Feb. 1767, JC 3/35.

[2] Petition of Janet Jameison, Jan. 1734, JC 3/18/757; Petition of William Lauder, July 1732, JC 3/18/394-5; Petition of Helen Mortimer, 17 Aug. 1759, JC 3/32/198-9. See also, e.g., Petition of Anne Mar, 6 Feb. 1760, JC 3/32/247; Petition of Jean Davidson, 3 Aug. 1732, JC 3/18/412-14. Courts sometimes responded sympathetically to such prisoners by banishing them from Scotland but permitting their residence elsewhere in Britain.

No matter where convicts awaited transportation, gaol conditions were atrocious. Plagued by disease and filth, prisons embodied the most squalid features of eighteenth-century life. They also suffered from severe overcrowding, a problem only made worse by the temporary incarceration of great numbers of transports. Designed to confine, not to correct, malefactors, prisons bore a fearsome reputation. Newgate in London was England's most infamous structure. Called a 'tomb for the living', it provided temporary quarters for at least a third of all convicts transported to the colonies. Situated near the Old Bailey, it often contained twice the number of prisoners it could comfortably quarter. Except for well-to-do inmates who paid several pounds a week for private rooms, bare floors covered with rags and straw sometimes afforded the only beds.[1] Gaols outside London ranged from castle dungeons to brick strongrooms. In Durham, turnkeys placed transports every evening into a pit called the 'Great Hole'. Chained to a stone floor, they slept on matted straw 'almost worn to dust'. Plymouth convicts occasionally resided in the 'Clink', a dank chamber measuring 8 by 17 feet. For light and air, prisoners took turns pressed up against a small opening in the door. 'No yard, no water', and 'no sewer' typified their accommodations. Such was the distress of one prisoner awaiting transportation that he 'had much rather have been hanged than confined' in his cell. In many counties, transports did not even receive the customary weekly allowance of 2s. 6d. for food. Unless provisioned by friends or family, begging from prison visitors or other inmates afforded the only alternative to starvation.[2] Conditions outside England were hardly much better. Most Scottish tolbooths were miserable hovels—'old buildings, dirty and offensive, without courtyards and also generally without water', according to the reformer John Howard. Irish prisons may have been worse. Investigators of Dublin's Newgate prison in 1729 discovered numerous naked convicts on the verge of death from cold and hunger; many had gone as many as four days together without food.[3]

---

[1] Beattie, *Crime and the Courts in England*, pp. 298-309; Sheehan, 'Eighteenth-Century Newgate', pp. 229-45.

[2] John Howard, *The State of the Prisons in England and Wales* (Warrington, 1777), pp. 417, 380, *passim*. See also Ignatieff, *Just Measure of Pain*, pp. 29-43.

[3] Howard quoted in Joy Cameron, *Prisons and Punishment in Scotland: From the Middle Ages to the Present* (Edinburgh, 1983), p. 50; Gaol Committee Report, 24 Nov. 1729, *JHCI* III, Appendix, p. ccclxxxviii; Henry Grey Graham, *The Social Life of Scotland in the Eighteenth Century* (London, 1937), pp. 502-5.

Greedy gaolers aggravated prison life. Dependent upon fees for income, they extorted frequent sums from prisoners. Gaol rates for food and drink were exorbitant, not to mention the heavy bribes exacted for special privileges. After months of near-starvation, John Christie, an Edinburgh prisoner, was forced to pay £5 in 'prison dues' just to be able to leave the tolbooth to be transported. The keeper 'assumed a power to himself,' Christie complained, 'of Commuting' his 'Sentence of Banishment, into perpetual Imprisonment, or rather indeed Capitall punishment'.[1]

Surrounded by filth and disease, large numbers of prisoners spent their final weeks vainly seeking pardons to escape both imprisonment and transportation. Marshalling friends and family, they barraged crown officials with plaintive memorials. Others sought temporary respites in order to settle last-minute affairs. A Reading convict requested time to collect £300 in outstanding debts, whereas another prisoner bemoaned that he had made 'no Provision att all, for so long and dismal a Journey'.[2] Many, too, probably fell victim to the numbing monotony of prison life, punctuated only by card games, occasional visitors, and excessive drinking for the few who could afford liquor. Less popular were religious services; chapel in Newgate was poorly attended and freely disrupted. Still, some inmates attempted to make the best of their lot. In 1737, two horse-stealers imprisoned in London sent circular letters throughout England to former victims of their crimes. Anxious to earn some travelling money, they promised to divulge the location of every stolen horse for 5s. per steed. No less ambitious, the thief Mary Young, alias Jenny Diver, spent her months in Newgate as a fence for stolen goods. At the time of her departure for the colonies, she possessed 'as many Goods of one Sort or other, as would almost have loaded a Waggon'. William Riddlesden, while awaiting transportation, gave lessons in how to forge banknotes, whereas a transport in Maidstone took the opportunity to extort £19 from a fellow inmate.[3]

---

[1] Petition of John Christie, [1734?], JC 3/19/173-4. See also, e.g., the Petition of Samuel Gibbeson to William Pitt, 13 Sept. 1758, SP 36/143/78; 'An Act for better preventing the Severities and unjust Exactions practised by Gaolers . . . ', 1763, *Irish Statutes*, V. 116; Ignatieff, *Just Measure of Pain*, pp. 36-8.

[2] Petition of John Martin to Newcastle, 16 June 1749, SP 36/110/248; Petition of William Orpwood to Lords Regents, [1742?], SP 36/59/265.

[3] *Account of the Ordinary of Newgate*, 18 Mar. 1741, p. 7; Sheehan, 'Eighteenth-Century Newgate', pp. 234-45; *Va. Gaz.* 28 Jan. 1737; Howson, *Thief-Taker General*, p. 136; *Genuine Account of W. Parsons*, p. 7.

Few prisoners, however, accepted their fate as exiles. Before embarking for the colonies, they continually struggled to escape from confinement. Gaol breaks by transports remained common throughout the century, from larger prisons as well as from small provincial lockups. In 1758, all the transports in Newgate nearly absconded after a few ringleaders sawed through eight iron bars. So worried were Coventry officials at one point that they applied to the Secretary of War for armed troops to guard the city gaol.[1] Conveying prisoners to ports for embarkation was doubly hazardous. Travel by open roads inevitably exposed turnkeys to attacks from gangs eager to rescue their comrades. Prisoners also found ways of breaking their chains. John Simmons, while being carted one evening from Reading to London, managed to cut his manacles, jump from the wagon into a nearby thicket, and escape undetected. Three years later, he was retaken in London, after first stabbing several Covent Garden watchmen in a ferocious clash.[2]

Most escapes never succeeded, and transports finally found themselves carried onto ships for the colonies. When that day came, the boarding ritual in major ports was much the same everywhere. Whether in London, Bristol, or Dublin, they filed in chains through city streets to the docks. In London, Newgate prisoners were put aboard lighters near Blackfriars for waiting ships downriver; others from across the Thames in Southwark boarded lighters at Blackwall.[3] Though criminals in common, not all were common criminals.

[1] *Gentleman's Magazine*, 1758, p. 285; Hewitt to Halifax, 17 July 1763, SP 44/139/252-6. See also, e.g., 'An Act for the more effectual transporting Felons and Vagabonds', 1725, *Irish Statutes*, III. 289; Thomson to [?], 12 Oct. 1727, SP 36/3/145; Petition of Edward Collyer to King, Apr. 1734, SP 36/31/175; J. Evelyn *et al.* to Lords of Treasury, 12 Oct. 1738, SP 36/46/177; Newcastle to Sec. of War, 10 Apr. 1739, SP 44/131/119; Report of Baron Adams, 6 Oct. 1757, SP 36/138/60-1; Sydenham & Hodgson to Wheately, 7 Dec. 1745, Coventry Transportation Records; *Old Bailey Sessions Papers*, 7-12 Dec. 1743, p. 40, 7-14 July 1773, p. 319, 11-16 Jan. 1775, pp. 83-4; *The Whole Genuine Proceedings at the Assize of Peace, Oyer and Terminer, for the County of Kent . . .*, 11-14 Mar. 1766, pp. 16-17; *Pa. Gaz.* 9 Apr. 1730, 29 Nov. 1753; *Va. Gaz.* 5 Dec. 1751; *Belfast News-Letter*, 13 Oct. 1767, 20 Dec. 1768; [Burt], *Letters From the North of Scotland*, I. 53-4; Howard, *State of the Prisons*, pp. 417, 426; Deposition of Richard Woodhouse, 22 Apr. 1734, in Perry, ed., 'North Riding Quarter Sessions Records', p. 72.

[2] *Old Bailey Sessions Papers*, 30-1 May 1745, pp. 150-2. See also, e.g., Cecill Wray *et al.* to Lord [?], 14 Oct. 1724, SP 35/53/16; Quarter Sessions Minutes, 1736, in J. P. M. Fowle, ed., *Wiltshire Quarter Sessions and Assizes, 1736* (London, 1955), p. 21; [Birch] to Andrew Reid, 17 Aug. 1745, Coventry Transportation Records.

[3] See e.g. *London Magazine*, 1732, p. 368, 1736, p. 47, 1739, p. 48, 1748, p. 40; *Va. Gaz.* 5 Dec. 1751; Rind's *Va. Gaz.* 5 Jan. 1769; *Annual Register*, London, 1766,

The greater part travelled to the docks on foot or horseback, but well-to-do felons paid for the privilege of arriving in hackney coaches. In June 1736, for example, five convicts rode in coaches to the Thames: James Russet, a butcher; George Bird, a bailiff; two attornies, William Wreathcocke and Henry Justice; and the infamous 'Lord Vaughan'.[1] Coaches permitted a small number to avoid the public shame of convict coffles as they wound their way through city streets; however, they could not always protect prisoners from the fury of crowd justice. Urban mobs met coaches and coffles alike with torrents of abuse and showers of stones and mud. Particularly obnoxious prisoners received the angriest receptions. Cries of 'Hang the Dog, Hang the Dog' greeted the murderer Daniel Bishop in 1752 as he was guided on horseback through Bristol streets crammed with thousands of enraged onlookers. Five other prisoners were thrown from their horses. Pelted repeatedly with dirt, Bishop cockily kept his composure but barely escaped with his life. The following year in London, a notorious perjurer nearly had his carriage overturned, though constables had taken pains to convey him in the dead of night.[2]

Doubtless such spectacles, besides magnifying the shame and terror of many transports, vividly testified to their unhappy fate as outcasts. Having survived months of imprisonment, they departed amidst catcalls and cries for vengeance. They still faced untold weeks in transit and long years in exile, but the terms of their punishment had commenced well before their vessels made their way out to sea.

*

Justice for John Jettea came swiftly. On the same Wednesday in October 1746 that he stole a guinea out of Thomas Morgan's pawn shop, Jettea was sentenced at the Old Bailey to seven years transportation. After a spell in Newgate, he was led in chains with other convicts to Blackfriars stairs. Before boarding the lighter, however, Jettea was first blessed with a visitor—not

p. 134; *Belfast-Newsletter*, 3 Oct. 1764, 25 June 1765, 23 Sept. 1766; Dickson, *Ulster Emigration*, p. 83.

[1] *Va. Gaz.* 26 Nov. 1736. While this seems to have been a customary privilege, in June 1764 the *London Magazine* reported that none of the 69 transports taken from Newgate were 'allowed to go to Blackwall in coaches', though one of them was reputedly worth £1,500 (p. 325).

[2] *Pa. Gaz.* 6 Aug. 1752, 26 July 1753.

one of his five children or two wives, but Samuel Boulton, for many years his landlord. Boulton arrived on purpose to see Jettea off. 'Mr. Jettea,' he declared, 'I am sorry to see you transported.' Buoyed, Jettea returned the favour by extending a handshake. 'Not so familiar as that,' Boulton cried, 'I think it is ten thousand pities you was not hanged!' Jettea, bound by a collar about his neck, swore furiously that he'd 'stick' Boulton if he could. The landlord escaped unharmed, but not before Jettea first hurled a gin bottle as he boarded the lighter.[1]

[1] *Old Bailey Sessions Papers*, 21–6 Feb. 1753, p. 107.

PART TWO: PENANCE

4

RITES OF PASSAGE

I

The role of the British government in transportation ended once traders filled their holds. After courts ordered felons for exile, ocean-going merchants saw that Britain's cast-offs crossed the Atlantic. Parliament enacted trade regulations, but these measures were designed solely to hold merchants to their bargains. By requiring bonds and landing certificates and by threatening heavy fines, officials hoped to make certain that transports reached American shores. 'It being the wish of Government to have them out off [*sic*] the Country', an Englishman later observed, authorities cared little for 'what became of them provided they never came here again'.[1]

Shipboard conditions during the six to eight weeks at sea rested in the hands of merchants and shipmasters. In the absence of government supervision, the care given to transports varied enormously. According to the London merchant John Stewart, the 'transporting of criminals' was left to the 'most corruptible class' of traders. He once described his former partner, Andrew Reid, as a 'person against whom almost every species of complaint was made'.[2] On the other hand, contractors sometimes manifested genuine sympathy for the well-being of transports. 'As I am grieved so many healthy young People die in the Voyage,' Reid himself wrote in 1742, 'I would do all in my power to prevent it'. More important, traders had a vital stake in the safe passage of transports, for, besides government fees, profits depended upon successful servant sales in America. Most merchants, to be sure, tried to limit expences, often by restricting water and provisions, which were costly and used up cargo space; and financial incentives were less strong than they were in the Atlantic slave trade. Not only did slaves fetch higher prices, but sales constituted the principal source

---

[1] [?], 'In Holy Writ . . .', [1785?], HO 42/7; 4 George I, c. 11; 'An act for the further preventing robbery, burglary, and other felonies, and for the more effectual transportation of felons', 1720, 6 George I, c. 23.

[2] Stewart quoted in Coldham, ed., *Bonded Passengers*, I. 144.

of a slave trader's income. Keeping convicts healthy, however, still made sound economic sense. 'Bringing them in healthy', observed a contractor in 1774, 'has saved us a large Sum of Money'.[1] Vessels consisted mostly of 'ships', 'snows', and 'brigantines'. Since most were less than 200 tons, they were not among Britain's largest commercial vessels.[2] Between 1746 and 1775, 182 vessels carried convicts to Maryland whose tonnage is given in surviving shipping returns. As indicated in Table 7, only six were 250 or more tons, while 118 fell in the middle range of 100 to 199 tons, also

Table 7. Tonnage of Convict Ships Entering Maryland, 1746–1775 (percentages in parentheses)

Tonnage	Ships
0–49	1 (0.6)
50–99	29 (15.9)
100–149	82 (45.1)
150–199	36 (19.8)
200–249	28 (15.4)
250–299	5 (2.8)
300–349	1 (0.6)
350–399	— —
Total	182 (100.2)

Source: Maryland Shipping Returns, 1746–75.

the size of most vessels in the English slave trade. At least a few ships, in fact, were former slavers. Jonathan Forward claimed that his 'Guinea ship', the *Eagle*, was 'most suitable' for convicts.[3] In age, these vessels were well weathered by years plying the Atlantic.

[1] Reid to Birch, 8 Sept. 1742, Coventry Transportation Records; Cheston to Stevenson and Randolph, 23 Dec. 1774, CGP, Box 8. See also Stevenson to Cheston, 3 Jan. 1769, CGP, Box 9.

[2] Tonnage figures cited throughout this chapter are 'registered' tons. They understate a ship's 'measured' tonnage by about one-third. For a discussion of the problems associated with tonnage measurements, see John J. McCusker, 'Colonial Tonnage Measurement: Five Philadelphia Merchant Ships as a Sample', *Journal of Economic History*, XXVII (1967), 82–91; Gary M. Walton, 'Colonial Tonnage Measurement: a Comment', ibid., 392–7; Christopher J. French, 'Eighteenth-Century Shipping Tonnage Measurements', ibid., XXXIII (1973), 434–43.

[3] Forward quoted in Coldham, ed., *Bonded Passengers*, I. 38; Herbert S. Klein, *The Middle Passage: Comparative Studies in the Atlantic Slave Trade* (Princeton, NJ, 1978), pp. 158–9. See also Coldham, ed., *Bonded Passengers*, I. 52. The term 'ship' applied to three-masted, square-rigged vessels, but hereafter it will be used in its generic context. Brigantines were two-masted and square-rigged, while snows were two-masted but differently rigged.

Among those listed in Maryland returns, the average age was 7.8 years. Though owned by British firms, a majority were constructed outside Britain, mostly in Maryland and New England. The growing importance of colonial shipping can be seen from the fact that American-built vessels accounted for 57.7 per cent of the voyages bringing convicts to Maryland. Most other ships were constructed in Britain (32 per cent), apart from a few prizes seized from the French during wartime.

Vessels carried sizable numbers on single voyages. From 1746 to 1775, 182 ships are known to have transported 9,423 convicts to Maryland. As shown in Table 8, of 7,315 men and women aboard ships that carried only convicts, more than half arrived in groups of more than 90 passengers. Batches tended to be smaller aboard vessels that carried both convicts and indentured servants, but quantities remained ample. Of 2,108 convicts in that category, 1,248 reached Maryland in shipboard contingents exceeding 60 men and women.

Table 8. Number of Convicts per Ship Entering Maryland, 1746–1775 (percentages in parentheses)

Number of passengers per ship	Ships with convicts		Ships with convicts and servants	
	Number of shipments	Number of convicts	Number of shipments	Number of convicts[a]
1–30	37 (31.4)	381 (5.2)	21 (32.8)	156 (7.4)
31–60	21 (17.8)	957 (13.1)	23 (35.9)	704 (33.4)
61–90	28 (23.7)	2,163 (29.6)	11 (17.2)	531 (25.2)
91–120	18 (15.3)	1,877 (25.7)	9 (14.1)	717 (34.0)
121–150	11 (9.3)	1,414 (19.3)	— —	— —
150+	3 (2.5)	523 (7.2)	— —	— —
Total	118 (100.0)	7,315 (100.1)	64 (100.0)	2,108 (100.0)

Note: a. Does not include 839 servants transported with convicts on the same vessels.

Source: Maryland Shipping Returns, 1746–75.

Much like African slaves, convicts found themselves chained below deck in damp quarters with little light or fresh air. Periodically, they were permitted topside, but only in small shifts of several prisoners each. Otherwise, conditions remained cramped.[1] According

---

[1] See e.g. *Account of the Ordinary of Newgate*, 24 Sept. 1722, p. 6; Wilkinson, ed., *King of the Beggars*, p. 241; William Green, *The Sufferings of William Green* . . . (London, [1775?]), p. 5; George Salmon to George Moore, 20 Dec. 1783, Woolsey

to tonnage figures, convicts enjoyed more room on trans-Atlantic voyages than did slaves, but less room than indentured servants. Aboard ships entering Maryland ports, there were on average 60 convicts per 100 tons burden, in contrast to 181 slaves and 43 indentured servants.[1] A visitor to one of John Stewart's vessels, after viewing a transport, exclaimed: 'All the states of horror I ever had an idea of are much short of what I saw this poor man in; chained to a board in a hole not above sixteen feet long, more than fifty with him; a collar and padlock about his neck, and chained to five of the most dreadful creatures I ever looked on'.[2]

Provisions on vessels were barely sufficient, with each convict receiving a diet high in carbohydrates. Starchy foods are likely to have served the same purpose as they did in the slave trade; as one person said of beans fed to slaves, 'It is a proper fattening food for captives.' According to information compiled by Francis Place, the typical weekly ration given to a convict included 1.2 pounds of beef and pork, 13.3 ounces of cheese, 4.7 pounds of bread, half a quart of peas, 1.7 quarts of oatmeal, 1.3 ounces of molasses, half a gill of gin, and 5.3 gallons of water. The diet would have provided

---

& Salmon Letterbook, p. 509, Library of Congress, Washington, DC. See also [James Revel], *A Sorrowfull Account of a Transported Felon, That Suffered Fourteen Years Transportation at Virginia, in America* ... (n.p., n.d.), p. 3. The date of Revel's chapbook is unknown, though John Melville Jennings has suggested that it was published during the third quarter of the seventeenth century. Jennings, ed., 'The Poor Unhappy Transported Felons Sorrowful Account of His Fourteen Years Transportation at Virginia in America', *VMHB* LVI (1948), 182. For several reasons, I believe that it was published after 1718. First, Jennings states that Revel at one point mentions residing in Rappahannock County, which ceased to exist in 1692 after it was divided into Richmond and Essex. Jennings, however, bases this conjecture upon a printed copy of Revel's account; in a manuscript version at the Library of Congress, the reference seems to be to 'Rappahannock Country'. This would make sense of Revel's claim to have lived in Wicomico, which was never in the county of Rappahannock. Second, Revel mentions that felons were banished for either seven or fourteen years, which was characteristic of transportation only after 1718. Third, he states that his Virginia master owned as many as eighteen slaves, which would have been much more plausible during the eighteenth century.

[1] In these calculations, only vessels not carrying additional imports were considered. They included 20 ships with 1,809 British convicts, 13 ships with 2,188 African slaves, and 95 ships with 4,562 British servants. Ships carrying both convicts and servants were not counted, nor were ships with fewer than 10 passengers in order to eliminate the odd circumstance in which a large vessel might have carried just a few people. Md. Shipping Returns, 1746-75.

[2] Quoted in Basil Sollers, 'Transported Convict Laborers in Maryland during the Colonial Period', *MHM* II (1907), 41 n. 1.

only about twelve hundred calories a day, and likely it was not administered faithfully. A Scottish felon later recalled that ship provisions were 'very bad, especially Water', whereas James White's daily meal consisted only of a pint and a half of water and a quantity of salt meat. It was not unknown for shipmasters in the indentured servant trade to embezzle provisions, and there is no reason to suspect those aboard convict vessels of any greater honesty.[1] Shipmasters bore ultimate responsibility for the quality of care. Merchants could prescribe standards, but masters exercised autonomy aboard vessels. Fearful of potential uprisings, many of them applied strict discipline. It was usual for transports with unruly tempers to travel in double irons, and some were whipped and beaten.[2] At least a few captains, such as Edward Brockett of the *Rappahannock Merchant*, were totally unfit. During a voyage in 1725, Brockett frequently stayed drunk, squandered large quantities of provisions, and nearly wrecked the ship before it arrived in Virginia. Irish captains, reluctant to cross the Atlantic, earned a black reputation for dumping transports on European shores. Convicts that were not freed were either sold as servants or pressed into foreign armies.[3]

The very worst excesses were revealed during the voyage of the *Justitia* in 1743. Under the command of Barnet Bond, the vessel

[1] James Barbot quoted in Rawley, *Transatlantic Slave Trade*, p. 298; James Borthwick to [John Drummond], 7 Aug. 1733, GD 24/1/464/N-0/545; *Account of the Ordinary of Newgate*, 6 Nov. 1723, p. 3; 'Transportation of Felons', 1740, Additional MSS, 27826/27, British Library, London; Smith, *Colonists in Bondage*, p. 214. Caloric values were obtained from Audrey H. Ensminger et al., *Foods and Nutrition Encyclopedia* (Clovis, Calif., 1983), I. The National Academy of Sciences in the United States recommends 3,000 calories a day for young men, whereas during the Seven Years War British regulars and provincial troops serving in America were supposed to receive daily rations containing between 2,200 and 3,000 calories. See Fred Anderson, *A People's Army: Massachusetts Soldiers and Society in the Seven Years War* (Chapel Hill, NC, 1984), pp. 84–85. Transported convicts, of course, received less physical exercise than did soldiers, but their caloric intake was still quite low, particularly when we consider their uncomfortably cold quarters aboard ship.

[2] See e.g. *Old Bailey Sessions Papers*, 13–15 Oct. 1725, p. 6; *Account of the Ordinary of Newgate*, 3 Nov. 1725, p. 4; *The Life and Actions of James Dalton . . .* (London, [1730]), p. 25; Purdie's *Va. Gaz.* 21 July 1775; Whitfield J. Bell, Jr., 'Adam Cunningham's Atlantic Crossing, 1728', *MHM* L (1955), 196–7.

[3] 'Answers of Jonathan Forward', 5 July 1726, George Tilley to Forward, 15 July, 2 Aug. 1725, C 11/1223/28, PRO; [?] to Duke of Dorset, Aug. 1733, SP 36/30/115; *Pa. Gaz.* 10 Nov. 1743; 'An Act for the more effectual Transportation of Felons and Vagabonds', 1743, *Irish Statutes*, IV. 204.

carried some 170 felons from London to Maryland. Besides extorting money and keelhauling disobedient prisoners, Bond set stringent water rations. Despite ample reserves of water on board, he allotted each transport only one pint a day. Some started to drink their own urine, and by the end of the voyage nearly fifty of them had died. Bond, who openly claimed their money and clothing, declared himself 'Heir of all the Felons that should happen to dye under his Care'.[1]

Not all transports fell victim to bad sailing conditions. A few received special treatment, often as the manservants, cooks, or mistresses of captains.[2] Wealthier convicts brought private provisions or purchased them on board. A prisoner on the *Honour* possessed 'two Caggs of Geneva' and 'fifty pound of Bisket' besides cheese and butter; the transport William Parsons carried a large chest of clothes on ship. Then, too, the Atlantic crossing, like other phases of transportation, occasioned bribes and personal favours. Before the thief Maurice Salisbury was transported from Bideford, a local gentleman made certain that he was 'sent Abroad with a Master of a Ship' that would 'use him as kindly' as possible. Well-to-do transports frequently paid for special accommodation, including in some cases the captain's private quarters.[3] Wealth, however, never guaranteed safe treatment and could even expose transports to personal abuse. Private goods were stolen by fellow prisoners and by unscrupulous masters and crews.[4] Moreover, all convicts, regardless of social position, faced other hazards. During both the War of the Austrian Succession and the Seven Years War, vessels fell prey to enemy navies.[5] In peacetime, pirates posed an occasional menace, as did fierce storms; several ships sank in gales,

[1] Depositions of James Corrie *et al.*, 24–31 Mar. 1744, HCA 1/57/86–96, PRO; Coldham, ed., *Bonded Passengers*, I. 65–9, 71–2.

[2] See e.g. *Account of the Ordinary of Newgate*, 18 Sept. 1727, p. 3; Petition of Thomas Ashby to King, [1743], SP 36/60/190; Campbell to John Paterson, 6 June 1771, DCPL, p. 93.

[3] *Life of James Dalton*, p. 25; *Genuine Account of W. Parsons*, p. 7; *Account of the Ordinary of Newgate*, 1 June 1752, p. 74. See also, e.g., Borthwick to [Drummond], 7 Aug. 1733, GD 24/1/464/N-0/545; *Va. Gaz.* 26 Nov. 1736; *Account of the Ordinary of Newgate*, 18 Mar. 1741, p. 7; Stevenson and Randolph to Cheston, 25 Sept. 1773, CGP, Box 12.

[4] See e.g. *Life of James Dalton*, p. 25.

[5] Depositions of William Briscoe and James Pitcarne, 16 Oct. 1745, SP 36/72/7,9; 'Extract of a letter from Capt. James Dobbins . . .', 7 Mar. 1746, *Va. Gaz.* 29 May 1746; *Md. Gaz.* 6 Aug. 1761; Petition of John Harvey to Newcastle, n.d., SP 36/150/163.

and others were severely damaged. In 1768, the Snow *Rodney* with ninety-two transports was forced to head for the West Indies after encountering a series of storms off the American coast. By the time she finally arrived in Antigua, eleven convicts had perished, numerous others were gravely ill from lying for weeks in flooded holds, and many had been reduced to eating leather shoes for their only food.[1]

As in prison, disease posed a constant threat. Poor provisions, contaminated water, damp lower decks, cold temperatures, not to mention the unhealthy condition of transports when first taken from British gaols, were largely responsible. Cramped quarters seemingly made conditions worse. The governor of Maryland in 1767 wondered whether the 'Crowding too great a Number of the poor Wretches into a small Compass may not be the means of destroying some of them'. The Virginia factor for a small Whitehaven firm wrote to his employers after the arrival of a vessel with convicts and servants, 'If ever you should send Servants here again, [I] would not advise so many, for there was not room upon deck to muster them, and besides the danger of Distempers'.[2] Apart from the normal problem of seasickness, such maladies as gaol fever, smallpox, and dysentery at times claimed over one-third of the transports on a single trip. During the voyage of the *Owners Goodwill* in 1721, 19 of 50 convicts perished after leaving London. Five years later, as many as 48 died among the 108 aboard the *Rappahannock* bound for Virginia. Crew members were also at risk. The master of the *Isabella* informed James Cheston after a voyage in 1772, 'The doctor at present is the worst of any on board'. Cheston himself complained of the 'Sickness which our Ships are generally infected with'. In the autumn of 1773 after the arrival of a vessel, he wrote to his Bristol partners, 'I never Saw the Disorder any thing so inveterate before; Those who have recovered having had 3 or 4 Relapses. Indeed the Mate, Second Mate, Doctor and one of the hands are now more like Ghosts than living men.'[3]

[1] *Pa. Gaz.* 10 Mar. 1768. See also Certificate for the *Eagle*, 20 Mar. 1719, GLC; *Select Trials at the Old Bailey* (1742), I. 71; *Pa. Gaz.* 27 Apr. 1749, 12 Apr. 1753; Perry, ed., 'North Riding Quarter Sessions Records', pp. 67-8; Purdie & Dixon's *Va. Gaz.* 16 Nov. 1769.

[2] Horatio Sharpe to Hugh Hamersley, 27 July 1767, *Md. Archives*, XIV. 412; Piper to Dixon & Littledale, 24 Oct. 1767, HPL, p. 21.

[3] Capt. Thomas Spencer to Cheston, 26 Nov. 1772, Cheston to Stevenson and Randolph, October 1773, CGP, Boxes 11, 8; Certificates for the *Owners Goodwill*, 1 Nov. 1721, and the *Rappahannock*, 13 Aug. 1726, GLC.

Mortality rates improved during the century. Landing certificates listing deaths have survived for 3,599 men and women transported from London to the colonies from 1719 to 1736. Apparently the certificates included only deaths occurring at sea, not those occurring afterwards while convicts were waiting to be disembarked and sold. As shown in Table 9, they reveal that a minimum of 10.7 per cent of the convicts died over the course of thirty-eight voyages. Duncan Campbell, who traded convicts from London up until the American Revolution, reasoned that 10 per cent during the crossing was considered a 'moderate Loss', and that more than 14 per cent of transports perished between the time when they were jailed in Britain and their landing in America. This view has been adopted by Abbot Emerson Smith, who has written that 10 or 15 per cent 'commonly died during the voyage'.[1] Still, figures for the Bristol firm Stevenson, Randolph, & Cheston suggest that the overwhelming majority of convicts by the final years of transportation survived the crossing. Though the firm's shipments were always threatened with disease, during twelve trips from Bristol to Maryland between 1770 and 1775 only 23 (2.3 per cent) of 990 convicts died in transit. If to this number are added 18 who died shortly after arriving in Maryland, the rate of mortality rises to just 4.1 per cent. To some degree, of course, these lower rates, in contrast to those suffered by convicts aboard vessels from London, might have stemmed from the quicker sailing time between Bristol and the colonies. Bristol vessels had a shorter, more direct route, and they were not threatened by the stiff easterly winds that sometimes held up outbound ships in the Thames. With less time at sea, their cargoes were not as vulnerable to disease and shortages of food and water.

For the most part, however, the Bristol figures suggest that conditions improved over time, in which respect transportation

---

[1] Testimony of Duncan Campbell, 15 Apr. 1778, *JHC* XXXVI. 927; Smith, *Colonists in Bondage*, pp. 118, 125-6. Two other studies have arrived at a mortality rate in the range of 14%, but by relying solely on the Guildhall Landing Certificates. Schimdt, 'Convict Labor in Virginia', p. 62; Peter Wilson Coldham, 'Transportation of English Felons', *National Genealogical Society Quarterly*, LXIII (1975), 174. Campbell estimated that proportionally half as many women died as men because of 'their Sobriety' and 'their Constitutions being less impaired'. However, figures drawn from the Guildhall Landing Certificates suggest a smaller difference in mortality rates between the sexes. For eighteen voyages between 1719 and 1736 in which deaths were differentiated by gender, the mortality rate was 15.5% for men and 12.7% for women. Testimony of Campbell, 1 Apr. 1779, *JHC* XXXVII. 311; GLC.

Table 9. Passage Mortality in the Convict Trade

Origin	Years	Voyages	Convicts	Died	Mortality
London	1719–1736	38	3,599	385	10.7%[a]
Bristol	1770–1775	12[b]	990	23	2.3%

Notes: a. Some certificates listed no deaths. The figure of 10.7% is based on the assumption that this omission reflected the absence of any deaths in transit. If, however, the absence of recorded deaths was merely a clerical omission and those voyages are discounted, the adjusted mortality rate rises to 14.9% for a total of 2,581 convicts transported over the course of 27 voyages.

   b. Mortality figures for Stevenson, Randolph, & Cheston were only available for these voyages, though the firm sponsored others.

Sources: Guildhall Landing Certificates, 1718–36; Cheston-Galloway Papers, Maryland Historical Society, Baltimore.

resembled the slave trade, which also experienced declining mortality rates during the eighteenth century. In the English slave trade by the second half of the century, passage mortality fell to between 7 and 10 per cent, a marked improvement over earlier rates, before ultimately falling to less than 5 per cent by the late 1790s. Mortality rates for slaves may have remained higher than those for convicts partly due to the slightly greater time it took slavers to cross the Atlantic, an extra one or two weeks. Africans may also have suffered from poorer health and greater disorientation at the time of enslavement. Furthermore, space was more cramped aboard slavers, though recent studies have generally discounted the effect of overcrowding, or 'tightpacking', upon slave mortality.[1]

---

[1] Anstey, *Atlantic Slave Trade*, pp. 30-1, 414-15; Klein, *Middle Passage*, pp. 229-36; Rawley, *Transatlantic Slave Trade*, pp. 289-306. The German passenger trade probably experienced lower mortality rates. On the basis of fourteen voyages that brought 1,566 Germans to Pennsylvania between 1727 and 1805, Farley Ward Grubb has calculated that the passage mortality was 3.8%. In contrast to transported convicts, though, the Germans included 382 children, who had a passage mortality 'almost three times the adult rate'. Moreover, the true mortality figure was doubtless lower for both adults and children, for Grubb's sample excludes voyages with no mortality, 'of which there were many'. 'Morbidity and Mortality on the North Atlantic Passage: Evidence from Eighteenth-Century German Immigration to Pennsylvania', *Journal of Interdisciplinary History*, forthcoming; 'Immigration and Servitude in Pennsylvania', pp. 69-71. In later years, among convicts transported to Australia, the mortality rate aboard ships was even lower, only 1.8%, despite the extended length of the voyage. L. L. Robson, *The Convict Settlers of Australia*,

While various factors, including improvements in shipping, medicine, and hygiene, accounted for declining mortality rates in the slave trade, it is difficult to know how many of the same factors lowered mortality rates among convicts. A development that probably occurred too late to have played a role was the adoption of copper sheathing, a costly innovation that began to be used in the slave trade in the 1770s. In giving better protection to the hull, copper sheathing helped to lower slave mortality by increasing sailing speed.[1] On the other hand, there was greater specialization in the size of convict vessels, another important factor behind lower mortality rates in the slave trade. Both trades increasingly used vessels of from 100 to 199 tons, once that was found to be the optimal range for shipping speed and efficiency. By 1766–75, 70 per cent of the English vessels transporting convicts to Maryland were from 100 to 199 tons, whereas 57.4 per cent had been in that category in 1746–55. A trader remarked in 1763 that 'ships must be provided for that end of a construction so far peculiar as to be fit only for the Guinea trade, whose burden is given up to fast sailing and accomodations'.[2]

Another measure that eventually lowered convict mortality rates was Parliament's decision to accelerate the process by which capital felons received transportation pardons, thereby reducing the amount of time they spent confined in disease-ridden gaols. By virtue of a 1767 statute, pardons were extended shortly after sentencing, rather than after a customary delay of several months.[3] Further, gaol conditions themselves became somewhat better after mid-century due to heightened sensitivity to the dangers posed by disease, particularly in the wake of the notorious 'Black Session' at the Old Bailey when in the spring of 1750 more than fifty people at the court died after contracting gaol fever from prisoners. From then

an Enquiry into the Origins and Character of the Convicts Transported to New South Wales and Van Diemen's Land, 1787–1852 (Carlton, Victoria, 1965), p. 9.

[1] Gareth Rees, 'Copper Sheathing, An Example of Technical Diffusion in the English Merchant Fleet', *Journal of Transport History*, New Ser., I (1971), 85–94; Rawley, *Transatlantic Slave Trade*, pp. 256–7.

[2] Stewart quoted in Coldham, *Bonded Passengers*, I. 54; Klein, *Middle Passage*, pp. 158–9; Md. Shipping Returns, 1746–75. The average age of Maryland-bound vessels also dropped during these decades, from 11.1 years in 1746–55 to 5.7 years by 1766–75.

[3] 'An act for the more speedy and effectual transportation of offenders', 1767, 8 George III, c. 15.

on, efforts were occasionally made to improve sanitation and air circulation within gaols.[1]

Also important was the experience that merchants gradually accumulated over the years. In addition to relying upon more-specialized ships, they took various steps to reduce deaths, though these fell short of markedly improving the quality of provisions and lodging. Early on, some traders recognized the need to keep transports healthy before boarding. In 1742, the London merchant Andrew Reid wrote to an official in Coventry:

As my ship falls down on the 18th, your Convicts will be here just time enough on the 17th. As I find by experience that carrying them to any of the Goals about Town, though but for a few Days, is of great Detriment to their Healths, I beg I may be informed exactly where, and about what Hour they will arrive, that some body may attend to conduct them directly on board. It would be very agreeable as well as serviceable to me, and an Act of great humanity to the Prisoners, and their fellow Passengers, to have them Shaved, and their Bodies as well Cloaths washed as clean as possible before they set out . . . . Nothing contributes more to make a Ship sickly than nastiness, which you will easily imagine has a very bad Effect where one hundred unclean Creatures are cooped up between a Ship's Decks.

The trader Duncan Campbell made certain that, once on board, convicts were clothed 'as good as can be had at the prices'. Women were fitted out with gowns, shifts, petticoats, yarn hose, and linen handkerchiefs to cover their heads; men with canvas frocks and trousers, shirts, cotton waistcoats, yarn hose, and caps.[2]

Several companies tried to make the design of vessels more healthy, in some cases perhaps because colonies started passing quarantine laws by the 1760s that threatened shipmasters with fines if they landed diseased convicts. Virginia and Maryland both passed legislation in 1766, though Virginia's law was eventually disallowed by the crown, as was a similar statute in 1772. To increase the flow

---

[1] Beattie, *Crime and the Courts in England*, pp. 304-9.

[2] Reid to Birch, 8 Sept. 1742, Coventry Transportation Records; Campbell to James Bare, 8 Dec. 1773, 9 July, 5 Nov. 1772, 20 Apr., 19 July 1774, 13 Apr., 14 July 1775, DCBL, pp. 203, 35, 74, 241, 272, 370-1, 397. Not that all merchants were so scrupulous. The Virginia factor Harry Piper was forced to write to his Whitehaven employers after the arrival of a vessel in 1767, 'The Women this year were very Naked, their Cloaths especially their Gowns are very Scanty and sorry and many of them had no Handkerchiefs, the weather has been Cold, they must have suffered.' Piper to Dixon & Littledale, 24 Oct. 1767, HPL, p. 21.

of air on lower decks, Sedgley & Co. of Bristol installed a ventilator, whereas others, like Stevenson, Randolph, & Cheston, added gratings and portals. Ventilators, William Stevenson feared, pumped 'in such a torrent of fresh and cold air, when perhaps they [i.e. the convicts] are in a sweat'. 'The Guinea Men', he observed, 'do not carry them', so that slaves instead could be allowed a 'more equal and moderate current of air'. One of Stevenson's partners, James Cheston, urged for the sake of safety that copper rather than iron boilers be used to prepare the convicts' food. 'Experiments' should be made, he counselled in 1773, 'even almost at any expence'. The firm also began hiring doctors for its voyages, evidently to some advantage. 'The Doctor of the *William*', wrote Cheston, 'is one of the cleverest fellows I ever Saw on Board of a Servant Ship. I have such an Opinion of him, that I think it would be of great advantage to us, to give him an Annual Sum for coming out in the Spring and fall ships'. However, he also noted, 'Every other of the Ships Doctors I have seen are good for Nothing'.[1]

James Cheston was exceptional. Virtually all merchants had a stake in lowered mortality rates, but Cheston brought an uncommon degree of compassion to the convict trade. At one point, because of moral qualms, he considered withdrawing from trading convicts altogether, thereby forcing Stevenson to write: 'You would find the Trade would not be worth carrying on without the convicts, some difficultys no doubt must arise in every kind of Business, and a sickly Ship is a disagreeable circumstance. We can but do all in our power to prevent it'. Otherwise, transportation remained a branch of commerce wedded to carrying human cargoes at minimal expence. Despite declining mortality rates, sizable numbers never reached American shores, whether from disease, mistreatment, or mishaps at sea. Perhaps as many as 5,000 men and women perished from the beginning of the trade to its end. While Cheston represented one extreme in the world of contractors and ship captains, Barnet Bond, master of the *Justitia*, represented the other. After his disastrous voyage in 1743, he was prosecuted by Andrew Reid, the ship's owner, and barely escaped conviction at the Old Bailey on four charges of murder.[2]

[1] Stevenson to Cheston, 9 Apr. 1768, Cheston to Stevenson and Randolph, Oct. 1773, 23 Dec. 1774, CGP, Boxes 9, 8; Oldham, 'Transportation of British Convicts', pp. 69–71; Sharpe to Hamersley, 27 July 1767, *Md. Archives*, XIV. 413.

[2] Stevenson to Cheston, 3 Jan. 1769, CGP, Box 9; Coldham, ed., *Bonded Passengers*, I. 71–2.

Not that transports acquiesced in the face of shipboard conditions. Determined to remain in Britain, some escaped by jumping overboard before vessels reached open water. The Scottish convict Gabriel Cunningham absconded while his ship was still docked at Leith, whereas Anthony Thompson in 1730 'swam away at Graves End', the site on the lower Thames where outward-bound ships from London awaited customs inspection.[1] More than a few convicts also rebelled against captains and their crews. Brutality doubtless triggered some uprisings, but physical mistreatment only fuelled deeper yearnings to escape agonizing years in exile. Just as convicts often tried to flee before their departures from British ports, so too did they plot insurrections once aboard ship. In April 1752, a vessel had not even left its London moorings when fifty prisoners staged a brief mutiny that sentinels alertly suppressed.[2]

On at least six occasions, uprisings met with greater success. Either transports captured vessels long enough to reach land and fashion escapes, or they took control completely, often with bloody consequences for masters and crews. Forty Irish convicts in late 1735 ran their vessel aground off Nova Scotia, murdered the entire ship's company, and ran off among local Indians and French settlers. A black servant boy was found with his throat cut from ear to ear. Transports from Liverpool in 1751 shot the vessel's captain, imprisoned the crew, and escaped after reaching the coast of North Carolina. When a cabin boy at one point tried to summon help from a nearby sloop, the mutineers drove a spike through his jaw. The very same year, another captain was slain before sailors finally quelled the rebellion.[3]

About a dozen uprisings were sufficiently large to attract contemporary notice, with reports sometimes appearing in news-

---

[1] Certificate for the *Forward Galley*, 12 June 1730, GLC; Petition for Gabriell Cunningham, [July 1732], JC 3/18/375-6. See also Pardon for Joseph Green, 10 Aug. 1763, SP 44/87/205-6.

[2] *Pa. Gaz.* 2 July 1752.

[3] *Pa. Gaz.* 2 Sept. 1736, 11 Apr. 1751; *Va. Gaz.* 5 Dec. 1751. See also *American Weekly Mercury*, Philadelphia, 13 Apr. 1721, 18 Mar. 1724; *Old Bailey Sessions Papers*, 7-12 Sept. 1722, p. 3; John Gouraud to Robert Trevor, 18 Sept. 1741, in *Buckinghamshire Manuscripts*, Historical Manuscripts Commission, Fourteenth Report, Appendix, Part IX (London, 1895), p. 77; 'Extract of a letter from a Gentleman in Waterford . . .', 18 Oct. 1766, Purdie & Dixon's *Va. Gaz.* 12 Feb. 1767; *Pa. Gaz.* 10 Feb. 1773.

papers.[1] It is impossible to gauge how many abortive mutinies may never have been publicized. A person in 1723 wrote of the 'Attempts which Transport Fellons have frequently made'. Certainly the prospect of violence excited merchants' fears. As early as 1719, Jonathan Forward urged authorities to enact stiff penalties for unruly prisoners, including capital punishment for those that escaped. Some years later, one of his American factors remarked that Forward gave 'great encouragement to supercargo and factors because of the great danger to the ship's company when felons are transported and attempt to regain their liberty'. Andrew Reid, noting that transportation was 'always attended with very great risk', claimed that 'an extraordinary number of seamen' was 'necessary to prevent the felons rising upon them'. Their wages, he lamented, were 'always very great by reason of the nature of such a cargo'.[2]

Most transports nevertheless remained in custody. Bound by chains and confronted by guards, they hatched imaginary plots that never materialized. Typical perhaps was Henry Sims who secretly planned to seize the ship's captain and make his escape onto the Isle of Wight. 'But', he later recalled, 'as a strict watch was kept on him, it was not possible ... to carry this plan into execution'.[3] In the end, Sims, like thousands of others, arrived safely in the colonies. If he had better known what lay ahead, he might have been less willing to bide his time.

*

Lewis Davis, a periwigmaker from St. Bartholomew the Less,

[1] Besides those cited above, see William Blewitt to Charles Delafaye, 16 Oct. 1723, SP 35/45/98; Thomson to Lord [?], 18 Apr. 1724, SP 35/49/21; *Va. Gaz.* 24 June 1737; *Md. Gaz.* 23 Aug. 1764; *Pa. Gaz.* 10 Mar. 1768; *Old Bailey Sessions Papers*, 12-17 Jan. 1769, p. 107.

[2] *Account of the Ordinary of Newgate*, 6 Nov. 1723, p. 3; Factor and Reid quoted in Coldham, ed., *Bonded Passengers*, I. 41, 49; ibid., p. 139. See also Stewart quoted in ibid., p. 144. In 1768, London sailors boarded the ship *Middleton* while convicts were being readied for a voyage to Maryland. Before being dispersed, the sailors threatened to wreck the ship and 'intimated their Desire of turning the Felons on Shore' unless members of the ship's crew were paid an increased wage of 37s. per month. Jonathan Forward Sydenham to Shelburne, 24 Aug. 1768, SP 44/232/40-1. The new wage would have been substantially higher than that which most other seamen received. A sailor on an East Indiaman was paid 23s. per month, while the crew member of a slave ship received about 28s. Anstey, *Atlantic Slave Trade*, pp. 13-14.

[3] Quoted in *The Malefactor's Register* ... (London, [1779?]), III. 99.

1. *A Picture on the Punishment of Titus Oates* (1685), showing principal punishments before the Transportation Act.

2. William Hogarth, *Industry and Idleness*, Plate 10 (1747). Tom Idle is examined before a justice of the peace for committing a felony.

3. *Representation of the Transports going from Newgate to take water at Blackfriars* (n.d.)

4. Illustration for *The Fortunate Transport* . . . (1741), the fictional story of a young woman's tribulations as a transported convict.

5. Illustration of a servant in runaway advertisement.

6. *Portrait of, and Invitation to the Execution and Burial of Jonathan Wild, Thief-Taker* (1725). Wild, the notorious criminal, recruited returned convicts for his London gang.

was a devoted husband. In the late summer of 1742, his pregnant wife, a seamstress named Catherine, was convicted at the Old Bailey for stealing nearly seven yards of lace out of a Whitechapel shop. Following a brief spell in prison, she was placed aboard the *Forward* as a common convict bound for Maryland. Anxious for her safety, Lewis gave the captain, John Sargent, a set of silver buttons and three guineas so she could travel in comfort with the vessel's crew. He also carried on ship two trunks filled with clothing and valuables for Catherine's use in America. With great reluctance, he was then off, and the *Forward* made its way down the Thames.

The crossing was unusually rough with constant storms and high seas. Of 190 convicts, nearly half perished. Catherine Davis kept her life but little else. Once at sea, the captain lodged her with other prisoners in the ship's hold. Her child died within a fortnight of its birth, and when her own death seemed imminent, Capt. Sargent robbed her trunks of watches, handkerchiefs, and several pounds in currency. In the meantime, he refused to remove her to warmer quarters. Catherine survived the ordeal and later returned to England. But when convicted once again for stealing goods out of a London shop, she pleaded to be given any sentence other than transportation, including the death penalty. The court ordered her transported for seven years.[1]

II

Government officials never gave much thought to selecting a proper site for transported felons. Nor did officials express serious concern for their fate in America. The Transportation Act spoke of the colonies' labour shortage, and some trial judges viewed transportation as a way to remove youthful offenders from hardened accomplices. For the most part, however, authorities rarely betrayed any interest in their future prospects. In 1763, the Board of Trade was authorized to prepare a report on whether transports could be employed in the colonies in public works, but the plan was

---

[1] *Old Bailey Sessions Papers*, 9–13 Sept. 1742, pp. 34–35, 10–12 May 1744, pp. 129–30, 144; Depositions of John Johnstown and Richard Gawdon, 24 Mar. 1743, HCA 1/19/191–4. Prior to her initial conviction, Davis had been tried for an earlier theft and acquitted. *Old Bailey Sessions Papers*, 14–17 July 1742, pp. 6–7.

never pursued. Other proposals usually came from the pens of public-spirited commentators like the Revd Hugh Jones. Writing in the early 1720s, Jones advocated moving petty convicts to an unsettled stretch of Virginia where they would pose no danger to law-abiding colonists. Under the watchful care of overseers, they would be kept 'to their labour, by such methods as are used in Bridewell' (i.e. a house of correction), and in time would produce great quantities of hemp and flax for linen and naval stores cordage. The mercantilist Joshua Gee similarly proposed that convicts be settled on the frontier to grow hemp and flax. If given land, they could provide their own subsistence and form a valuable bulwark against French encroachment. At the time of the Seven Years War, the writer John Shebbeare urged that 'young criminals, which the present inattention to religious education and civil policy almost compels to steal', be sent among the Indians. There, they would marry into tribes and form a 'stronger alliance between those American nations and the English'.[1]

In proposing a frontier settlement of convicts, each of these schemes was reminiscent of Richard Hakluyt's much earlier plan for transporting English criminals. Like Hakluyt's, all three seem to have assumed not only that transportation would serve England's imperial needs but also that wayward men and women might benefit from the harsh discipline of frontier labour. Nothing, however, came of these proposals, or for that matter, of a suggestion by Jonathan Forward that a penal settlement be founded in Nova Scotia. Instead, the Transportation Act was meant to apply to 'all his Majesty's Dominions in *America*', and merchants ended up carrying transports to British provinces scattered throughout North America and the West Indies.[2] Over the course of the eighteenth century, at least eighteen different colonies received convicts at one time or another, comprising eleven mainland colonies, Bermuda, and six islands in the Caribbean.

Many provinces imported only a smattering. In the far north, fewer than 400 men and women may have been shipped to the combined area of Nova Scotia, New England, and New York. Most

[1] Jones, *The Present State of Virginia*, ed. Richard L. Morton (Chapel Hill, NC, 1956), pp. 134–5; [John Shebbeare], *Letters on the English Nation by Batista Angeloni, a Jesuit Who Resided Many Years in London* (London, 1756), I. 146; Halifax to Board of Trade, 5 Nov. 1763, CO 5/65/281; Oldham, 'Transportation of British Convicts', p. 44; Gee, *Trade and Navigation of Great-Britain*, pp. 89–92.
[2] 4 George I, c. 11; Petition of Forward to King, n.d., CO 217/37/1.

shipments were small, such as in 1747 when Charles Brackenbury, a Hull merchant, transported seven convicts to Boston.[1] A greater number went to the West Indies, though rarely in large quantities. Jamaica probably admitted the most, followed by Barbados and Antigua. Nevis, however, may have received the greatest single shipment, when the *Alexander* arrived in 1722 from London with 103 transports.[2] At least a few vessels with convicts docked in Florida after it was obtained in the Seven Years War,[3] but Georgia, despite its historic reputation as a penal colony, only received a lone shipment when local authorities in the mid-1730s admitted forty Irish convicts refused entry into Jamaica.[4] In all likelihood, fewer than 200 felons were ever transported to the Carolinas.[5]

[1] 'Convicts for Transportation', Massachusetts Historical Society, *Proceedings*, XLIX (Oct. 1915–June 1916), pp. 328–9. For New England, see also Transportation Bond for Diana Cole, 1 July 1719, GLC; *Pa. Gaz.* 3 July 1732; James Davie Butler, 'British Convicts Shipped to American Colonies', *AHR* II (1896), 22 n. l; *Malefactor's Register*, IV. 69. For New York, see Douglas Greenberg, *Crime and Law Enforcement in the Colony of New York, 1691–1776* (Ithaca, NY, 1976), pp. 29, 31–2; E. B. O'Callaghan, ed., *Calendar of Historical Manuscripts in the Office of the Secretary of State, Part II, English Manuscripts* (Albany, 1866), p. 527. For Nova Scotia, see *Pa. Gaz.* 2 Sept. 1736, 2 July 1752. For Irish convicts sent to these areas, see Lockhart, 'Emigration from Ireland', pp. 181, 192, 195.

[2] For Jamaica, see *Account of the Ordinary of Newgate*, 5 July 1721, p. 3, 8 Apr. 1723, p. 5; Sir Nicholas Lawes to Board of Trade, 10 Dec. 1722, in W. Noel Sainsbury, ed., *Calendar of State Papers, Colonial Series* (1860–; reprint edn., Nendeln, Liechtenstein, 1964–), XXXIII. 185; Robert Hunter to Board of Trade, 13 Nov. 1731, CO 137/19/110; Petition of R. Thomson, 27 Jan. 1740, JC 3/23/163–4; Holdernesse to Attorney-General, 14 Dec. 1753, SP 44/85/367–8; Bond for Alexander Sime, 28 Dec. 1754, JC 3/30/170–1; Petition of Thomas Alves, Oct. 1766, *Cal. HO Papers*, II. 112; Testimony of Duncan Campbell, 12 May 1785, Minutes of House of Commons Committee on Convicts, HO 7/1/79. For Antigua, see Landing Certificates, 19 June 1742 and 28 May 1743, Derbyshire Transportation Records; *Pa. Gaz.* 10 Mar. 1768. For Nevis, see Certificate for the *Alexander*, 26 Sept. 1722, GLC. For St Vincent, see Lud Grant to John David, 10 Dec. 1772, Transportation Papers, JC 27. For Bermuda, see George Bruere to Earl of Dartmouth, 19 Apr. 1774, CO 37/36. For further references to individual islands and to the West Indies generally, see Hay to [?], 21, 26 Oct. 1725, SP 54/16/53, 57; Kaminkow and Kaminkow, eds., *Lists of Emigrants in Bondage*, pp. 180–3, 186–7.

[3] *Belfast News-Letter*, 8 Feb. 1765; *South Carolina Gazette*, Charleston, 20 Apr. 1765; *Georgia Gazette*, Savannah, 6 June 1765; Lockhart, 'Emigration from Ireland', p. 198; *Pa. Gaz.* 19 Feb. 1767.

[4] Sarah B. Gober Temple and Kenneth Coleman, *Georgia Journeys* . . . (Athens, Ga., 1961), p. 76.

[5] Transportation Bonds, 5 May 1718, and Certificate for the *Eagle*, 20 Mar. 1719, GLC; Kaminkow and Kaminkow, eds., *Lists of Emigrants in Bondage*, pp. 184–5; Theo D. Jervey, 'The White Indentured Servants of South Carolina', *South Carolina Historical and Genealogical Magazine*, XII (1911), 170–1; Transportation Contract, 2 May 1729, in Historical Manuscripts Commission, *Report on the Records*

Merchants carried the overwhelming majority of convicts to just three colonies, situated in the heart of British North America: Virginia, Maryland, and Pennsylvania. Receiving shipments throughout the eighteenth century, they probably admitted well over 90 per cent of all transports. Pennsylvania, of the three, took in the smallest number. Exact totals are impossible to calculate, largely because very few vessels bearing convicts for Pennsylvania originated in English ports, and voyages from elsewhere are not easily identified. Between 1718 and 1744, the English Treasury paid merchants to transport some 7,542 felons from London and nearby counties. Out of 7,010 whose destinations can be determined, none went to Pennsylvania.[1] Most convicts transported there came from Ireland, for which shipping records are sparse. Notices in Dublin newspapers, however, reveal that vessels with convicts periodically sailed for Philadelphia. Of fifty-five vessels from 1730 to 1774 whose departures from Ireland were reported, particular destinations in the colonies were given for forty-nine. Nine of the vessels were said to be destined for Philadelphia.[2] Those, however, probably carried a small fraction of the total number of Pennsylvania-bound convicts. Not only do newspapers offer an incomplete guide, but Irish convicts were often disguised by merchants as indentured servants, not all of whom would have been identified as convicts in papers. The prominent Pennsylvania politician James Logan railed that 'few besides convicts' made up the colony's annual influx of Irish immigrants. 'They are put on them,' a Maryland resident observed in 1767, 'as HONEST PEOPLE, under colour of INDENTURES'. It seems likely that convicts composed at least several thousand of the more than 25,000 Irish immigrants reported to have travelled to Pennsylvania between the 1720s and the Revolution.[3] At the

of the City of Exeter (London, 1916), p. 237; 'Transportation of Felons', 1740, Additional MSS, 27826/27; *Md. Gaz.* 3 Apr. 1751; Lockhart, 'Emigration from Ireland', p. 191.

[1] The 7,010 convicts also included 52 felons from outside London and nearby counties who were transported at government expence. After 1744, destinations were not listed in Treasury Records. Kaminkow and Kaminkow, eds., *Lists of Emigrants in Bondage*, pp. 180-201; Coldham, ed., *Bonded Passengers*, I. 172-4.

[2] Two of the nine vessels also reportedly sailed to Maryland, and one to Nova Scotia. Lockhart, 'Emigration from Ireland', pp. 187, 190, 191, 192, 199, 202, 203.

[3] Logan quoted in Dickson, *Ulster Emigration*, p. 96; 'A. B.', *Md. Gaz.* 30 July 1767; Salinger, 'Indentured Servants in Pennsylvania', pp. 72-3. See also works cited above, Chapter 3, p. 84 n. 2; Cheesman A. Herrick, *White Servitude in Pennsylvania: Indentured and Redemption Labor in Colony and Commonwealth* (New York, 1969), p. 124.

same time, Delaware and New Jersey, both important parts of Philadelphia's trading nexus, received convict shipments of their own, though never as many. The New Jersey legislature complained in 1730 about merchants who 'frequently' imported 'divers Persons convicted of heinous Crimes'.[1]

The Chesapeake provinces received the great bulk of British convicts. As early as 1720, a person in Maryland noted the 'great number of convicts' entering the colony. Of the 7,010 transports shipped by government contractors from 1718 to 1744 to identifiable locations, as many as 6,815 (97.2 per cent) were sent to the Chesapeake. 'Maryland or Virginia' was the only terminus given for 768 men and women; of the remaining 6,047, some 3,341 were shipped to Maryland and 2,706 to Virginia.[2] Both provinces continued to take in large numbers of convicts until the Revolution. A visitor to Virginia in 1765 remarked that the 'number of Convicts and Indented servants' imported by the colony was 'amazing'. Soon afterwards, a contemporary estimated that Maryland had annually admitted at least 600 transports over the preceding thirty years.[3]

Shipping returns lend some precision to these claims. While unfortunate gaps exist in records for Virginia, those for Maryland, as we have seen, are reasonably good. From 1746 to 1775, Maryland received a minimum of 9,423 convicts, representing nearly 40 per cent of all persons, including slaves, servants, and ordinary immigrants, to enter the colony's ports during that period. The actual number of convicts might easily have exceeded 12,000 due to the incomplete nature of the shipping returns in addition to the fact that numbers of Irish convicts, along with some from Scotland, entered the Chesapeake as indentured servants.[4] For its part,

---

[1] 'An ACT imposing a Duty on Persons convicted of heinous Crimes . . .', 1730, in Bernard Bush, comp., *Laws of the Royal Colony of New Jersey, 1703–1745* (Trenton, 1977), p. 423; John A. Munroe, *Colonial Delaware: A History* (Millwood, NY, 1978), p. 196; Lockhart, 'Emigration from Ireland', pp. 94–5.

[2] 'Maryland in 1720', *MHM* XXIX (1934), 254; Kaminkow and Kaminkow eds., *Lists of Emigrants in Bondage*, pp. 180–201; Coldham, ed., *Bonded Passengers*, I. 172–4.

[3] 'Journal of a French Traveller in the Colonies, 1765, I', *AHR* XXVI (1920–21), 744; 'A. B.', *Md. Gaz.* 30 July 1767.

[4] Md. Shipping Returns, 1746–75; Sollers, 'Transported Convict Laborers', p. 44; Lockhart, 'Emigration from Ireland', pp. 181–207, *passim*; 'An Act to prevent the Abuses of concealing convicted Felons, and other Offenders . . .', 1728, *Md. Archives*, XXXVI. 300; John F. Watson, *Annals of Philadelphia, and Pennsylvania, in the Olden Time . . .* (Philadelphia, 1884), II. 266–7; Council Proceedings, 28 Apr. 1756, *Md. Archives*, XXXI. 118; Piper to Dixon & Littledale, 10 Aug. 1768, HPL,

Virginia probably received just as many transports. Treasury records
suggest that of convicts sailing from London between 1718 and
1744 slightly more were imported into Maryland; but even if we
assume that the entire English trade reflected such an imbalance,
Virginia seems to have received larger numbers of convicts from
Ireland than did Maryland, at least of those that can be positively
identified as convicts. Of the forty-nine Irish vessels from 1730 to
1774 that sailed with convicts to known destinations, as many as
twenty-seven sailed to Virginia, and only ten to Maryland.[1]

What, then, was the total number of convicts received in the
Chesapeake? While Maryland and Virginia may each have admitted
more than 12,000 between 1746 and 1775, we must remember that
the total number of people transported during those years exceeded
the number transported during the previous period from 1718 to
1745, if we may judge from available figures for the number of
transports from London, Middlesex, Buckinghamshire, and the
Home Counties. If we calculate that at least 24,000 convicts were
imported into the Chesapeake from 1746 to 1775, then perhaps
16,000 would be a conservative estimate for 1718-45. Whatever
the exact total, whether it lies a bit above or below 40,000, the
commonly accepted estimate of slightly more than 20,000 for the
years 1718-75 is much too low.[2]

Such large numbers were not carried to the Chesapeake because

p. 50. In addition to being incomplete for certain years, Virginia's returns generally
either listed convicts as 'passengers' or they did not record them at all, thus making
their identification very difficult. For an inventory of surviving returns, see Walter
Minchinton, Celia King, and Peter Waite, eds., *Virginia Slave-Trade Statistics,
1698-1775* (Richmond, 1984), Appendix e, pp. 200-1.

[1] Lockhart, 'Emigration from Ireland', pp. 181-207.

[2] For the traditional estimate, see Smith, *Colonists in Bondage*, p. 119; Schmidt,
'Convict Labor in Virginia', p. 71. The accuracy of my estimate for 1718-45 is
bolstered by the fact that English merchants shipped to the Chesapeake a minimum
of 6,815 convicts from London and nearby counties from 1718 to 1744. If we
include several hundred more for the single year, 1745, double the result to obtain
an estimate for all of England, and include several thousand convicts from Ireland
and Scotland, the total probably would near 18,000 convicts. By allowing for a
passage mortality rate of approximately 11%, it seems reasonable to conclude that
at least 16,000 men and women arrived in the Chesapeake between 1718 and 1745.
An estimate similar to 40,000 for the entire Chesapeake trade is reached by
doubling the figure of 19,000 convicts transported from London and nearby counties
to obtain a total for all of England. Since at least 95% of those went to the
Chesapeake, we arrive at a figure of 36,100. Even by allowing for a generous passage
mortality rate of 11% from 1718 to 1775, a total of 40,000 is likely if we include
convicts received from Ireland and Scotland.

the governments of Maryland and Virginia wanted them. Officials in both provinces opposed transportation more vocally than did many authorities elsewhere. Nor were the Chesapeake colonies specially suited to receiving large quantities of felons. In some respects, in fact, a worse location would have been hard to imagine. Both contained thousands of restive slaves and at least in Virginia's case had experienced repeated servant unrest in the second half of the seventeenth century. Masterless men, unruly servants, and the tumult of Bacon's Rebellion were part of Virginia's early experience.[1] Trading connections posed another difficulty. Since both colonies enjoyed strong commercial ties with the mother country, greater opportunities existed for escaped convicts to gain a passage home. In Scotland, the Earl of Ilay appreciated this problem when he urged that felons there be shipped to the West Indies where there was 'no intercourse' with Scotland. 'They will not there meet with any of their friends or relations,' he wrote in 1725, 'or opportunities of returning home as they would in the other places.' Similarly, Jonathan Forward endorsed Nova Scotia as a potential dumping ground partly because it provided 'a Prison in it Self' where it would be 'impossible that any' convicts 'should return from their Transportation'.[2]

But while some men feared the consequences of close trans-Atlantic ties, for most merchants they exerted great appeal. Certainly one reason traders were drawn to Virginia and Maryland was that each colony exported valuable commodities to Britain. Other provinces, such as Georgia and North Carolina, might easily have absorbed large numbers of convicts, but their fledgeling economies offered traders less in return.[3] More appealing were regular exports of tobacco and grain farther north. Equally important, of course, Virginia and Maryland experienced a common demand for white labour. The Chesapeake provinces, though heavily dependent upon slaves, annually imported hundreds of indentured servants during

[1] Morgan, *American Slavery, American Freedom*, pp. 235-70. A recent study of the convict trade mistakenly concludes that one reason convicts were transported to the Chesapeake was because their 'importation' was 'generally accepted, whereas some other colonies passed laws to restrict the traffic'. Morgan, 'Convict Trade to Maryland', p. 203.

[2] Ilay to [?], 21 Oct. 1725, SP 54/16/53; Petition of Forward to King, n.d., CO 217/37/1.

[3] See A. Roger Ekirch, *'Poor Carolina': Politics and Society in Colonial North Carolina, 1729-1776* (Chapel Hill, NC, 1981), pp. 9-18; Kenneth Coleman, *Colonial Georgia: A History* (New York, 1976), pp. 129-33.

the late colonial period. Recent studies have correctly pointed out that while skilled servants were highly valued, there was no longer a strong demand for ordinary white labourers, as there had been during the heyday of indentured servitude in the seventeenth century. But we would be wrong to conclude that planters showed no interest in unskilled servants. Provided they were cheap enough, they, too, attracted buyers. Interest was especially keen in Maryland, where, in comparison to Virginia, there were fewer slaves to meet planters' needs for unskilled labour. By 1750, Virginia's population was about 44 per cent black, whereas Maryland's was 31 per cent. It was not coincidental that Maryland imported roughly as many convicts as did its neighbour, even though Virginia's white population was more numerous, 129,581 in 1750 compared to 97,623 in Maryland.[1]

Parliament never mandated servitude in the colonies as a necessary condition of transportation, but the Transportation Act did grant contractors or their assigns 'property and interest in the service' of felons for the duration of their banishment. Various factors may have lain behind this provision, including the colonies' need for stout workers and Parliament's perception that criminals might benefit from heavy doses of hard labour. More consequential, however, were the potential profits merchants stood to reap from convict sales, thereby giving them a greater stake in transportation without putting the Treasury to additional expence. Had merchants been precluded that revenue, plus the opportunity to take on tobacco, grain, and other exports, government fees would have been considerably higher, totalling as much as £12 per convict, estimated one trader.[2] And of course, allowing merchants to sell convicts as servants promised to give colonists a greater stake as well. Given the chance of obtaining cheap white labour, planters would naturally be less averse to transportation.

In short, commercial, not penal, priorities guided the flow of convicts to America. Government authorities, wedded as they were

[1] Md. Shipping Returns, 1746-75; Galenson, *White Servitude*, pp. 62-3, 139, 157, 177, *passim*; Russell R. Menard, 'From Servants to Slaves: The Transformation of the Chesapeake Labor System', *Southern Studies*, XVI (1977), 387-8; US Bureau of Census, *Historical Statistics of the United States, Colonial Times to 1970: Part 2* (Washington, DC, 1975), p. 1168.

[2] 4 George I, c. 11; Testimony of Campbell, 12 May 1785, Minutes of House of Commons Committee on Convicts, HO 7/1/80; [Baltimore], Observations on Stewart Memorial, [1757], *Md. Archives*, LV. 769.

to the immediate task of expelling criminals from British shores, happily granted merchants free rein over other phases of transportation. The Chesapeake colonies took in large numbers of felons because it made economic sense for merchants to send them there. Safer sites, such as Nova Scotia or the Southern backcountry, never received more than a trickle. 'Here they may barter [servants] . . . for tobacco,' a former servant noted of the Chesapeake, 'upon which they have an immense return of profit.'[1]

III

Myriad inequalities pervaded transportation. British courts remained reasonably immune to entreaties from men of wealth and influence, but gaolers and merchants almost always granted their wishes. Thus as previously noted, privileged felons enjoyed benefits in British prisons, they travelled in carriages to awaiting vessels, and once on board they enjoyed choice accommodation. 'A Criminal who has money . . .', complained a writer in the *Political State*, 'may blunt the Edge of Justice, and make That his Happiness which the Law designs as his Punishment.'[2]

Wealthier transports also gained their liberty once ships docked in colonial ports. Normally payment of a sum equivalent to what the transport could have fetched as a servant was required to satisfy shipmasters, whose legal responsibility lay only in conveying transports to the colonies. 'Those that have Money', remarked a Virginia transport, 'shall have Favour showed.' In Britain, use of the convict escape-hatch was common knowledge. Awaiting transportation in 1742, a Surrey prisoner noted, 'The Captain always sells such as are not able to pay'. If convicts possessed a skill, purchase prices could be particularly steep. As Duncan Campbell explained in one felon's case, 'The Expence will depend upon his being a Tradesman.'[3] Transports lacking the full sum could still reduce the period of their service by paying a lesser

[1] Peter Williamson quoted in Coldham, *Bonded Passengers*, I. 163.
[2] *Va. Gaz.* 26 Nov. 1736.
[3] [Revel], *A Transported Felon's Account*, p. 4; Campbell to Crust, 13 Sept. 1774, DCPL, p. 312; Petition of Grammont to Northampton, 1742, SP 36/59/262. See also, e.g., *American Weekly Mercury*, 14 Feb. 1721; Campbell to Minet & [Fictor?], 6 May 1772, DCPL, p. 25; Testimony of Campbell, 1 Apr. 1779, JHC XXXVII. 310. For how two convicts bound for New York purchased their liberty with a stolen bank-note, see Knapp and Baldwin, eds., *Newgate Calendar*, I. 367.

amount. By the time the *Isabella*, for example, docked in Annapolis in December 1773, three out of ninety-one convicts on board had paid varying sums to the Bristol firm of Stevenson, Randolph, & Cheston. William Pinton and William Stone had each forfeited about £7, whereas John Hillery had given up his silver watch plus nearly £2. In return, each was sold for a reduced term of servitude.[1] Most transports could scarcely command a few shillings, much less several pounds. Whereas a lucky handful obtained some measure of freedom, transportation for the majority required an extended period of labour. Seven years was the standard length of time, though in a few cases capital felons may have been forced to serve a full fourteen years. There are no documented instances of that, but the Revd Hugh Jones observed that convicts served 'seven, and sometimes fourteen years'.[2] Sales commenced almost immediately. Once arriving vessels had cleared customs, factors for British firms took charge of local transactions. Factors included longstanding residents, though sometimes they were British natives. James Cheston, who conducted sales in Maryland for seven years until the outbreak of the Revolution, was a full-fledged partner in his Bristol firm. Similarly, Jonathan Sydenham, an agent for Jonathan Forward in Leedstown, Virginia, originally hailed from London, though he later married a local girl.[3]

To the good fortune of merchants, the arrival of convict ships generally coincided with periods of peak demand for servants. With tobacco, corn, and wheat planted in mid- to late spring and harvested from mid-summer until early autumn, labour was then at a premium. In addition, crops became available during the summer for voyages home. Contractors, whose shipping schedules normally depended upon the meeting of assize courts, transported the greatest number of convicts every spring after the winter assizes. With most vessels arriving in late spring and summer, there was considerable regularity to the convict trade, even more so than in

---

[1] Stevenson and Randolph to Cheston, 27 Sept., Sept. 1773, CGP, Box 12; Md. Shipping Returns, 1746-75.

[2] Jones, *Present State of Virginia*, ed. Morton, p. 87. See also Cable to Forward, 10 May 1727, Thomas Cable Letterbook, p. 36, MHS; 'An Act to prevent the Abuses of concealing convicted Felons, and other Offenders . . .', 1728, *Md. Archives*, XXXVI. 300; Testimony of Campbell, 12 May 1785, Minutes of House of Commons Committee on Convicts, HO 7/1/6.

[3] Morgan, 'Convict Trade to Maryland', p. 205; Schmidt, 'Convict Labor in Virginia', pp. 34-5, 85-94.

the indentured servant and slave trades to the Chesapeake. Although they also peaked in the summer due to the seasonal demand for labour, supplies of servants and slaves were obtained at various times of the year. Figure 2 indicates the number of convicts imported into Maryland in different months, in the period 1746–75. Of 9,423 convicts, over half, 5,254, came during June and July.

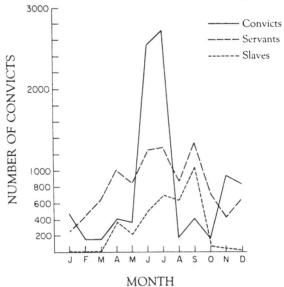

FIG. 2. Arrival by Month of Convicts, Servants, and Slaves Imported into Maryland, 1746–1775

Sources: Maryland Shipping Returns, 1746–1775. In a few instances, the returns were supplemented by shipping notices in the *Maryland Gazette*.

Scattered shipments arrived at other times during the year. Because the summer assizes also generated sizable numbers, as many as 1,799 transports were admitted in November and December, even though there was less demand then for labourers and colonial exports were in short supply for return trips. A Virginia importer of both servants and convicts told his English suppliers in November 1769, 'I hope you have dropt the thoughts of sending the *Ruby* this Winter with Servants as it now grows very late to be concerned with them Gentry.'[1]

[1] Piper to Dixon & Littledale, 25 Nov. 1769, HPL, p. 107; David O. Percy,

Within the Chesapeake, numerous trading points dotted the region's rivers and estuaries. Besides private plantations, key locations in Virginia included Leedstown, Hobb's Hole, and Fredericksburg on the Rappahannock River, and Dumfries and Alexandria on the upper Potomac. In Maryland, Baltimore and Annapolis predominated, though Port Tobacco on the lower Western Shore and the Eastern Shore ports of Oxford and Chestertown sometimes received convicts. Vessels made their way from one trading site to another. In August 1770, Cheston, having sold almost half of a convict shipment at Annapolis, had 'no Doubt but the remainder will go off as well at Baltimore'. Thomas Hodge, a Virginia factor for Stewart & Campbell of London, reported in April 1765: 'The *Tryal* is in Potomack with about 100 Convicts. The Sale will commence at Cedar point the 1st of May and will continue till the Saturday following. From thence the Ship will be moved to Alexandria about the 8th or 10th.'[1]

Some shipmasters, in order to heighten sales, made certain that convicts bathed and that men shaved their beards; occasionally, women were encouraged to wear headdresses, and men, caps. Still, as one contemporary commented, a 'peculiar smell' plagued 'all servants just coming from ships'. Another colonist, upon viewing the sale of some one hundred convicts in Williamsburg, commented: 'I never see such pasels of pore Raches in my Life, some all most naked and what had Cloths was as Black [as] Chimney Swipers, and all most Starved by the Ill [usage] in their Pasedge By the Capn, for they are used no Bater than so many negro Slaves'. The transport William Green recounted, 'A wretched crew as are was seen, Our cloths ragged, and our bodies lean.'[2]

Sales took place aboard ships, or infrequently in nearby towns.

'Agricultural Labor on an Eighteenth-Century Chesapeake Plantation' (Unpublished paper presented at the 45th Conference on Early American History, Baltimore, 13–15 Sept. 1984). See also Cable to Forward, 18 Jan. 1724, 3 July 1724, Cable Letterbook, pp. 15, 20.

[1] Cheston to Stevenson and Randolph, 22 Aug. 1770, CGP, Box 8; Thomas Hodge to [William Allason], 19 Apr. 1765, William Allason Papers, Box 4, VSL; Schmidt, 'Convict Labor in Virginia', pp. 86–98.

[2] Rind's *Va. Gaz.* 26 July 1770; William Barker, Jr., to John Palmer, 16 Dec. 1758, George Pitt Original Papers, 3, Prentis Papers, Documents, 1743–1858, Alderman Library, University of Virginia, Charlottesville; Green, *Sufferings of William Green*, p. 5. See also [Revel], *A Transported Felon's Account*, p. 4; Wilkinson, ed., *King of the Beggars*, pp. 151, 243; Dixon & Hunter's *Va. Gaz.*, 'William Pearce' and 'Ralph Emanuel', 22 Apr. 1775.

Contemporary accounts likened them to livestock auctions. '[They] are Brought in hare', a person noted, 'and sold in the same maner as horses or Cows in our market or fair'. Green recalled: 'They search us there as the dealers in horses do those animals in this country, by looking at our teeth, viewing our limbs, to see if they are sound and fit for their labour'. Buyers also enquired into the backgrounds of transports. One later remarked, 'He asked My Trade, My Name, and whence I came, And, what vile Fact had brought Me to this Shore.'[1] Even at that stage, however, a minority of transports received privileged treatment from factors and ship-masters, especially if influential families with connections to contractors in Britain had pressed for special favours. Cheston in 1773 was informed by his Bristol partners to sell the transport Henry Buckle to the Revd Dr Dunford and to 'no other master'. Dunford's brothers were 'Justices and Men of consequence in Hampshire who,' Stevenson and Randolph added, 'it is our Interest to oblige.' Likewise, a Scotsman urged in 1765 that a servant girl 'now goeing out by Capt. Robertson' be 'placed with some good family'. Banished for infanticide, the girl was a 'good natured Creature' who had 'good hands and could worke' in addition to being 'related to the very best famileys'.[2]

In disposing of transports, factors pushed for quick sales. Payment was received in cash, produce, and bills of exchange. Credit, however, was widely given. The Chesapeake economy was based upon a nexus of debt linking planters and merchants. 'For Servants we are obliged to give Credit', Harry Piper noted in 1768. So long as times remained good, merchants were strongly disposed to provide credit in order to ensure sales.[3] Unsold convicts posed special problems. If they were lodged aboard ship, delays threatened to disrupt sailing schedules. As Piper remarked, it was 'not practicable to do any thing with a Ship while the Servants are on

---

[1] Barker to Palmer, 16 Dec. 1758, Prentis Papers; Green, *Sufferings of William Green*, p. 6; [Revel], *A Transported Felon's Account*, pp. 7, 4. See also *Account of the Ordinary of Newgate*, 7 Nov. 1744, p. 5; Wilkinson, ed., *King of the Beggars*, pp. 151, 163; and the ballad 'Virginny'.

[2] Stevenson and Randolph to Cheston, Sept. 1773, CGP, Box 12; Alexander Walker to [Allason], 29 July 1765, Allason Papers, Box 4. See also Stevenson and Randolph to Cheston, 26 Apr. 1775, CGP, Box 15.

[3] Piper to Dixon & Littledale, 10 Aug. 1768, HPL, p. 52; Morgan, 'Convict Trade to Maryland', pp. 223-7. Quite uncommon was the petulant advertisement declaring that 'Seven Years Servants' would be sold 'as the Farmers, Planters, and others do their Wheat, for Ready Money only'. *Md. Gaz.* 18 Dec. 1766.

Board'.[1] In the meantime, expences mounted for food and medical care. Further, as at other stages of transportation, convicts were prone to escape. More than a few ran away almost as soon as vessels docked. In July 1772, for example, six prisoners fled from the *Thornton* shortly after it had reached Leedstown on the Rappahannock. Probably because of such dangers, a Virginia merchant believed that factors like himself merited higher commissions than traders ordinarily received in marketing slaves. 'Negroe Sales here has 10 per cent Commissions on them', wrote Thomas Cable to Jonathan Forward in 1724, 'and I am sure fellons deserves twice that Sum'.[2]

Due to the unsavoury reputation convicts had, some purchasers preferred buying other servants. 'I am in great Want of a Servant . . .', a person wrote to James Cheston, 'and would chuse an Indented Servant in Preference to a Convict'. A customer specially requested an indentured servant from the factor James Russell, instructing him, 'I would not have him unless he is a soberly orderly Fellow, such a one will be very happy with me.' Probably because others felt the same way, merchants sometimes smuggled convicts as indentured servants, or, as was more often the case, they advertised convicts either as 'servants' or as 'seven years servants'. While their real identities must have been known, such euphemisms created a more attractive impression than would have advertisements for 'convicts', 'felons', or 'gaolbirds'.[3]

Convicts did, however, offer buyers various advantages. Compared to slaves, they were significantly less costly. In the late colonial period, the average price of an adult male slave in the Chesapeake ranged between £35 and £44 sterling.[4] As shown in Table 10, most male convicts fetched less than £13 sterling. Periods of service, moreover, were longer than those for indentured servants, who generally contracted for fewer than five years. As a consequence,

---

[1] Piper to Dixon & Littledale, 9 Feb. 1768, HPL, p. 35. See also Schmidt, 'Convict Labor in Virginia', pp. 140-1, 149-50.

[2] Cable to Forward, 18 Jan. 1724, Cable Letterbook, p. 16; Purdie & Dixon's *Va. Gaz.*, 'William Nicholson', 'William Smith', 'Peter Knight', 'Patrick Burn', 'Joseph Wade', and 'Alexander Clubb', 23 July 1772.

[3] Turbutt Wright to Cheston, 11 Apr. 1773, CGP, Box 11; Joseph Mullan to James Russell, 25 June 1774, Russell Papers, Bundle 14, Coutts & Co., London (CW microfilm). See e.g. *Md. Gaz.* 14 June 1753, 15 July 1762, 8 Mar. 1764, 25 Apr., 4 July 1765, 18 Dec. 1766, 16 July 1767, 30 June 1768.

[4] Alice Hanson Jones, *Wealth of a Nation to Be: The American Colonies on the Eve of the Revolution* (New York, 1980), p. 117.

according to William Eddis, a young English visitor to Maryland, colonists viewed 'the convict as the more profitable servant'. Benjamin Franklin similarly noted that a number of buyers were 'tempted by the Lowness of the Price, and the Length of the Time'. Then, too, at least in Virginia after mid-century, convict servants did not have to be awarded freedom dues. For indentured servants, these consisted of an allowance of £3. 10s.[1]

Table 10. Convict Prices at Sales Conducted by Stevenson, Randolph, & Cheston in Maryland, 1767–1775[a] (percentages in parentheses)

Prices (£ sterling)	Male convicts	Female convicts
3–4	9 (2.7)	1 (1.0)
5–6	6 (1.8)	8 (8.0)
7–8	23 (6.8)	24 (24.0)
9–10	31 (9.2)	67 (67.0)
11–12	117 (34.6)	— —
13–14	78 (23.1)	— —
15–16	36 (10.7)	— —
17–18	17 (5.0)	— —
19–20	11 (3.3)	— —
21–22	3 (0.9)	— —
23–24	2 (0.6)	— —
25+	5 (1.5)	— —
Total	338 (100.2)	100 (100.0)

Note: a. Includes a small number of indentured servants. Convicts/servants sold in groups of six or more were not counted.

Sources: Factorage Book, 1767–75, and Account of Servants, 1774–75, Cheston-Galloway Papers, Boxes 5, 6.

Convicts with skilled trades fetched the highest prices. Because the economy was growing in diversity and artisans were in short supply, skilled labourers were always in great demand; besides

[1] Eddis, Letters from America, ed. Land, p. 38; [Franklin], 'A Conversation . . . on the Subject of Slavery', 26 Jan. 1770, in Leonard W. Labaree and William B. Willcox, eds., The Papers of Benjamin Franklin (New Haven, Conn., 1959–), XVII. 42, 'An Act for the better government of servants and slaves', 1753, Hening's Statutes, VI. 359; Smith, Colonists in Bondage, p. 239. In terms of profit, the difference could be substantial when it came to employing a convict rather than an indentured servant. Paul G. E. Clemens has concluded that during the early eighteenth century, 'a servant who [annually] produced 1,600 pounds of tobacco for seven years gave the planter an 11-per cent return, but if the harvest dropped to 1,200 pounds and the period of service to five years, the planter broke even'. 'The Operation of an Eighteenth-Century Chesapeake Tobacco Plantation', Agricultural History, XLIX (1975), 522. Obviously, there would still be a distinct difference in profit had the size of the annual harvest been the same.

giving masters the benefit of their trades, they could instruct
other servants. Whereas common and semi-skilled male labourers
normally cost from £7 to £14 sterling, the price of most tradesmen
ranged from £15 to £25 sterling.[1] Local factors, like Cheston,
received requests for particular varieties of tradesmen, sometimes
well before the arrival of incoming vessels. A buyer from Queen
Anne's requested not only a weaver but one 'who can Weave both
Woolen and Linnen, but certainly can weave Woolen well, especially
the coarser sorts of Kerseys or Serge'. Another person wrote to
Cheston that he was hoping for a blacksmith 'by your next ship'.[2]
Often, however, such requests could not be met, for the supply of
skilled convicts was limited. Following the arrival of one vessel,
Cheston had to tell a customer, 'There was None of the Servants
of the trades you mention left, . . . indeed the best of every kind
was gone off'. On one occasion, a local merchant, Thomas Smyth,
asked Cheston for a shoemaker and a house carpenter from aboard
his ship, the *Restoration*. Not only was a carpenter not to be had,
but Cheston was forced to inform Smyth, 'There is a shoemaker
onboard, but on Looking over my Memorandums I find I have
promised one to Mr Gittings here, who spoke to me for one several
Months ago.' Eight months later, with the arrival of another vessel,
Smyth repeated his request for a carpenter, only to be told that 'if
any comes in the next ship' he would be 'the first served'. Another
four months passed before Smyth finally received a carpenter.[3]

Other than tradesmen, servants with agricultural backgrounds
excited local interest. Benjamin Nicholson of Baltimore, in urging
Cheston to reserve three men 'used to Farming', specified reaping,
mowing, ploughing, and threshing as necessary qualifications.

[1] Testimony of Campbell, 1 Apr. 1779, *JHC* XXXVII. 310. See above, Chapter 2,
p. 53 n. 2, in addition to Table 10.

[2] John Chapple to Cheston, 28 Nov. 1774, Samuel Wickes to Cheston, 15 June
1773, CGP, Boxes 14, 12. See also, e.g., Abrose Barcroft to his Father, 1 Mar.
1723, in Harold B. Hancock, ed., 'Life in Bucks County in 1722/23', *Pennsylvania
History*, XXVII (1960), 399; Richard Gresham to Cheston or Capt. Spencer, 8 May
1771, Thomas Smyth to Cheston, 2 Apr., 25 Nov., 28 Dec. 1773, William Ringgold
to Cheston, 16 June 1773, Eleazer McOrmb to Cheston, 7 Jan. 1774, James Hodges
to Cheston, 27 Mar. 1774, CGP, Boxes, 10, 11, 12, 13; David Ross to John Hook,
22 May 1774, John Hook Papers, Duke University Library, Durham (CW microfilm);
Philip Richard Fendall to James Russell, 13, 26 Aug. 1774, John Augustine
Washington to Russell, 16 Aug. 1774, Russell Papers, Bundles 5, 18.

[3] Cheston to William Young, 6 Dec. 1772, Cheston to Smyth, 3 Apr., 24 Dec.
1773, 11 Apr. 1774, Smyth to Cheston, 2 Apr., 25 Nov., 3 Dec. 1773, CGP, Boxes
8, 11, 13.

Thomas Smyth desired a worker 'used to driving an Ox Team' who also understood 'cattle graising and mowing Grass'.[1] In addition, servants from England's West Country were favoured, though only partly because of their agricultural experience. Any number of requests, including appeals for tradesmen, expressed a preference for West Countrymen. Cheston told his Bristol partners that people in Maryland gave the 'preference to West Country Servants above all others'. In colonial eyes, the West Country had long compared favourably with London and other urban areas, due to their reputation as centres of idleness and vice. Thus in 1740, residents of Georgia requested servants who 'were strangers to London and used to hard labour in the country'. Some years later, an agent for George Washington explained the high price paid for a set of convicts and indentured servants by noting that they were 'country, likely people'.[2]

Only two sorts of convicts, other than those too lame, sick, or old to make proper servants, occasionally proved difficult for factors to sell. Women were not popular because they were considered less suited to either skilled or heavy labour and liable to become pregnant. Most sold for £7 to £10 sterling. 'The fewer women the better' was the refrain of one servant importer. A Glasgow contractor in 1763 informed the proprietor of a Virginia iron works: 'You need not expect any Servants or Convicts from this Country as there is not any to be got but women from the Correction house which I imagine will not answer your purpose'.[3] More problematic were convicts who gave signs of being especially troublesome, one reason perhaps why buyers routinely asked newly-imported transports to state their crimes. A Maryland factor in 1744 worried

[1] Nicholson to Cheston, 15 June 1773, Smyth to Cheston, 30 Mar. 1774, CGP, Boxes 12, 13. See also, e.g., John Page to Cheston, 19 Oct. 1773, Smyth to Cheston, 28 Dec. 1773, ibid.; Fendall to Russell, 13, 26 Aug. 1774, Russell Papers, Bundle 5.

[2] Cheston to Stevenson and Randolph, 17 June 1773, CGP, Box 8; Georgians quoted in Coldham, ed., *Bonded Passengers*, I. 143; Agent quoted in Worthington Chauncey Ford, ed., *Washington as an Employer and Importer of Labor* (1889; reprint edn., New York, 1971), p. 17. See also, e.g., Nicholson to Cheston, 15 June 1773, Smyth to Cheston, 3 Dec. 1773, 30 Mar., Nov. 1774, CGP, Boxes 12, 13, 14.

[3] Fendall to Russell, 13 Aug. 1774, Russell Papers, Bundle 5; James Lawson to John Semple, 3 Sept. 1763, James Lawson Letterbook, SRO (CW microfilm); Factorage Book, 1767–75, and Account of Servants, 1774–75, CGP, Boxes 5, 6. See also David Rosse v. James and William Donaldson, 20 June 1755, Fairfax County Order Book, 1754–56, pp. 323–4 (VSL microfilm); Salinger, 'Indentured Servants in Pennsylvania', pp. 275–7.

that 'no body' would buy a female convict because of 'her violent passions', and the Alexandria factor Harry Piper complained that 'good looking, half Gentleman sort' of convicts would 'not sell' because 'everyone are afraid of them'. On one occasion, Piper rejoiced after finally contracting to sell the last of a recent shipment. Included were an 'old Woman', two other women—'one [with] the Clap and one with Child'—and lastly 'a man that has been in the Country [i.e. previously transported] two or three times, a Consummate Villain'. 'I really was afraid', he confessed, 'no one would take him off my Hands.'[1]

Market conditions also affected sales. For one thing, the market sometimes became glutted with convicts and indentured servants, thereby driving down prices. This problem grew most acute in the early 1770s when, in response to deteriorating economic conditions at home, unusually large numbers of Irish servants arrived in the Chesapeake. From 1771 to 1775, Maryland alone took in nearly 3,500, along with more than 2,000 servants from England and Scotland and some 2,100 convicts. Upon the arrival of 121 convicts from Bristol in June 1773, Cheston warned his partners, 'As a Ship with near 200 being just arrived from London, one from Ireland with a considerable number, and another expected every day, these together with the number already disposed of here within these two months will affect the sale.' Later that summer, a Virginia factor advised the firm Dixon & Littledale, 'We have had a prodigious Importation of Servants this Year, if any should offer to you, do not be induced to take them, for they will scarce sell at any rate.'[2] In addition, market conditions for local staples influenced sales. If prices dropped for tobacco or, by the later colonial period, for corn and wheat (due to their growing importance by that time), planters were naturally less eager to acquire convicts or indentured servants. 'These low prices of Produce here,' Cheston wrote to Stevenson and Randolph in August 1774, 'will make it highly disadvantageous to us in the Sale of Servants. The high price which we have got heretofore, has in great Measure been owing to the

---

1 Reid quoted in Coldham, ed., *Bonded Passengers*, I. 50; Piper to Dixon & Littledale, 17 Sept. 1771, 15 June 1772, HPL, pp. 180, 206.
2 Cheston to Stevenson and Randolph, 13 June 1773, CGP, Box 8; Piper to Dixon & Littledale, 8 Sept. 1773, HPL, p. 263; Dickson, *Ulster Emigration*, pp. 76–81; Md. Shipping Returns, 1746-75. See also, e.g., Cheston to Stevenson and Randolph, 26 June 1773, 7 Jan., 30 Apr. 1774, 28 June 1775, CGP, Box 8; Piper to Dixon & Littledale, 25 July 1774, HPL, p. 281.

great demand for wheat, which, if the contrary takes place, cannot be any longer expected.'[1]

A majority of convicts were purchased in small quantities. For example, following the Maryland arrival of the *Margaret* in 1719, 109 convicts were sold to local buyers. Of the 109, 55, or just over half, were bought in single lots. All told, more than three-quarters were sold in groups of 5 or fewer convicts to a total of 64 individuals, whereas 2 purchasers, Patrick Sympson and William Black, jointly bought the remainder. This pattern stayed the same through the century. Maryland sales conducted by Stevenson, Randolph, & Cheston indicate a roughly similar breakdown, as shown in Table 11. Individual lots were larger, and on one occasion 55 convicts were sold to a single purchaser. None the less, out of 765 men and women, as many as 510 (66.7 per cent) were bought in parcels of 5 or fewer servants. Clearly factors, whenever possible, tried to sell transports in small groups. Unloading large numbers wholesale, called 'lumping', was generally a last resort that yielded smaller rewards. After the arrival of the *William* in December 1774, Cheston wrote to his partners, 'The Servants go off slower than I expected. . . . I shall try them a few days longer in the retail way and then Lump the remainder.'[2]

Large-scale purchasers generally retailed servants farther inland. Called 'soul drivers', they herded convict coffles from one town to another. On one such journey, the merchant David Ross proposed to take a quantity of servants from the Petersburg area in Southside Virginia to Charlotte County some seventy miles to the west. From there, they would continue on to New London, whereupon, after a day's rest, Ross planned to set out for Botetourt County in the upper Shenandoah Valley. The entire circuit would total well over 200 miles. 'They drive them through the Country like a parcell of Sheep untill they can sell them to advantage', wrote the servant John Harrower. Another noted, 'We were driven through the country like cattle to a Smithfield market and exposed to sale in public fairs as so many brute beasts'.[3]

---

[1] Cheston to Stevenson and Randolph, 31 Aug. 1774, CGP, Box 8.

[2] Cheston to Stevenson and Randolph, 11 Dec. 1774, CGP, Box 8; Provincial Court Deeds, 1719–23, pp. 18–21, MHR.

[3] Edward Miles Riley, ed., *The Journal of John Harrower: An Indentured Servant in the Colony of Virginia, 1773–1776* (Williamsburg, Va., 1963), p. 39; Williamson quoted in Coldham, ed., *Bonded Passengers*, p. 162; Ross to Hook, 23 Mar. 1772, John Hook Letters, VSL. See also Cheston to Stevenson and Randolph, 21 June

Table 11. Purchase of Convicts by Lot at Sales Conducted by Stevenson, Randolph, & Cheston in Maryland, 1767–1775[a] (percentages in parentheses)

Number of convicts per lot	Number of purchasers	Number of convicts
1	355 (81.4)	355 (46.4)
2	59 (13.5)	118 (15.4)
3	9 (2.1)	27 (3.5)
4	— —	— —
5	2 (0.5)	10 (1.3)
6	— —	— —
7	1 (0.2)	7 (0.9)
8	1 (0.2)	8 (1.1)[b]
9	— —	— —
10–19	4 (0.9)	51 (6.7)
20–29	2 (0.5)	51 (6.7)
30–39	1 (0.2)	39 (5.1)
40–49	1 (0.2)	44 (5.8)
50–59	1 (0.2)	55 (7.2)
Total	436 (99.9)	765 (100.1)[c]

Notes: a. Includes a small number of indentured servants.

    b. Corrected from 1.0 in the original.

    c. Corrected from 100.0 in the original.

Source: Kenneth Morgan, 'The Organization of the Convict Trade to Maryland: Stevenson, Randolph & Cheston, 1768–1775', WMQ, 3rd Ser. XLII (1985), 218. Since Morgan compiled his figures from surviving sales accounts, they do not include all the convicts imported by the firm between 1767 and 1775. The figures reflect individual purchases made at separate sales; thus, if a customer purchased convicts on two different occasions, the customer would be listed twice.

Retail buyers represented a broad social spectrum. All varieties of tradesmen purchased convicts, as did shopkeepers, merchants, shipbuilders, and iron manufacturers. Planter grandees who owned convicts included Charles Carroll of Carrollton and William Fitzhugh in Maryland, plus Virginians like Landon Carter, Alexander Spotswood, and George Washington. Ordinary planters, however, probably predominated among purchasers. In addition perhaps to a few slaves, they only could afford a short-term investment in servants. Especially during the first half of the century, many

1774, CGP, Box 8; Phineas Bond to Lord Carmathen, 16 Nov. 1788, in J. Franklin Jameson, ed., 'Letters of Phineas Bond, British Consul at Philadelphia, to the Foreign Office of Great Britain, 1787, 1788, 1789', *Annual Report of the American Historical Association for the Year 1896* (1897), p. 582; Schmidt, 'Convict Labor in Virginia', pp. 142-6, 153-61.

planters found themselves in that situation since expanding tobacco production in the Chesapeake often kept crop prices depressed and the capital planters had for acquiring slaves limited. A set of Virginians in 1749 referred to the common plight of the 'poorer Sort of Planters'. Having 'large Families to Support, and not Money enough to buy a Slave', they had instead 'been obliged to buy Convicts, who having a long Time to serve, and only the first Purchase to pay, came cheaper to them'. A recent study has found that in Kent County, Maryland middling planters worth from £100 to £500 owned nearly two-thirds of the white servants listed in estate inventories. Persons with estates worth less than £100 possessed just over one-fifth, and those with estates over £500 had about one-seventh of the servants. Due to the fact that the poor were less likely to have inventories compiled of their estates, these findings must be treated with caution, but it seems likely that most convicts were acquired by neither big nor small planters. For planters of modest means, they represented the most affordable source of bound labour.[1]

The convict trade was shaped by a combination of circumstances. Whereas British courts determined the volume and rhythm of the trade, factors peculiar to America affected where cargoes were sold, to whom, and at what prices. Less often did convicts, by absconding or staging shipboard rebellions, have any say. Supply was generally more steady than demand,[2] though most firms successfully adapted to fluctuating conditions. And so, after numerous weeks spent in prison and at sea, convicts embarked upon years in exile as bound labourers. Gone were loftier notions stressing rebirth and reformation to which public-minded men in Britain occasionally paid lipservice. Merchants boasted no such pretensions. Transportation, from the time ships left British harbours, became a

---

[1] Council Proceedings, 11 Apr. 1749, *LJC* II. 1035; Recognizance Bond for Henry White, 29 Sept. 1772, Anne Arundel County Convict Record, 1771–75, pp. 15–16; *Md. Gaz.* 21 Dec. 1752; Schmidt, 'Convict Labor in Virginia', p. 120; *Va. Gaz.* 11 Aug. 1738; Allan Kulikoff, *Tobacco and Slaves: The Development of Southern Cultures in the Chesapeake, 1680–1800* (Chapel Hill, N.C., 1986), pp. 78–85; Gary P. Secor, 'The Working Environment of White Servants in the Chesapeake, 1710–1750' (Unpublished undergraduate research paper, Virginia Polytechnic Institute and State University, 1984), pp. 6, 11. See also Eddis, *Letters from America*, ed. Land, p. 36; Gwenda Morgan, 'The Hegemony of the Law: Richmond County, 1692–1776' (Ph.D. diss., Johns Hopkins University, 1980), p. 206.

[2] Morgan, 'Convict Trade to Maryland', p. 220.

high-stakes enterprise, and as a consequence, involuntary servitude became a way of life for thousands of men and women. Profit, not penal policy, set the fate of British exiles. On colonial plantations not much would change.

5

EXILES IN THE PROMISED LAND

I

When large numbers of convicts started flowing into Virginia and Maryland, Chesapeake society had undergone a fundamental transformation. No longer did white servants dominate the ranks of plantation workers as they had during the preceding century; instead, black slaves afforded a more steady and profitable supply of field labour. Once merchants began carrying regular shipments from Africa and the West Indies in the late seventeenth century, planters turned to slavery on a sweeping scale. By 1720, the Chesapeake contained close to 40,000 slaves. The Virginia aristocrat William Byrd II rhapsodized in 1726, 'Like one of the patriarchs, I have my flocks and my herds, my bond-men, and bond-women'.[1]

For big planters in Virginia, times had been less happy when servants supplied most of the region's workforce. During the third quarter of the seventeenth century, impoverished white labourers had kept the province on the brink of civil war. Just as masterless men had plagued Mother England, the 'giddy multitude', a loose following of servants, landless freemen, and scattered slaves, threatened big planter dominance. A series of small uprisings erupted in the 1660s and early 1670s, followed by the explosion of Bacon's Rebellion in 1676. Across the tidewater, Virginia's lower orders took up arms against Governor William· Berkeley and provincial authorities. Battles were joined and plantations plundered before a lone group of 100 servants and slaves finally surrendered by the banks of the York River.[2]

In many British colonies during the seventeenth century where the labouring poor existed in sizable numbers, they posed a worrisome threat to social superiors. Maryland escaped serious

[1] Byrd to Charles Boyle, 5 July 1726, in Marion Tinling, ed., *The Correspondence of the Three William Byrds of Westover, Virginia, 1684-1776* (Charlottesville, Va., 1977), I. 355; US Bureau of Census, *Historical Statistics*, p. 1168.

[2] Morgan, *American Slavery, American Freedom*, pp. 235-70; T. H. Breen, 'A Changing Labor Force and Race Relations in Virginia, 1660-1710', *Journal of Social History*, VII (1973), 3-11.

turmoil, but indigent settlers staged occasional uprisings elsewhere, particularly in the West Indies. Barbados experienced a servant rebellion in the 1640s for which eighteen ringleaders were executed. The problem was much the same everywhere. Young males, lured across the Atlantic by false dreams, found few sources of consolation or grounds for hope. Ample supplies of firearms combined with shortages of land and women made them especially dangerous. In Virginia, Governor Berkeley despaired of ever subduing 'a People wher six parts of seaven at least are Poore Endebted Discontented and Armed'.[1]

But with the transition to slavery in the Chesapeake, social peace gradually arrived, according to several studies, as race, not class, separated the privileged from the unprivileged. Black Africans, associated in white eyes with savagery and sin, came to occupy positions of unremitting degradation. Differences in status still pervaded white society and rifts occasionally occurred, such as during the tobacco-cutting riots of the early 1730s. For the most part, however, race placed dirt farmers and other humble folk alongside aristocrats in the master class. Then, too, there were fewer white servants, and new lands were becoming available through removal of the Indians. With larger numbers of independent white landowners, colonists in the Chesapeake shared a growing commonality of interests rooted in plantation agriculture. Such were the prospects enjoyed by Virginians that the planter Robert Beverly II claimed in 1705, 'They live in so happy a Climate, and have so fertile a Soil, that no body is poor enough to beg, or want Food'. Likewise, a visiting French Protestant, Francis Louis Michel, reported, 'There is no other country, where it is possible with so few means and so easily to make an honest living and be in easy circumstances'.[2]

What a horrific shock, then, that the very 'Scum and Dregs' of

[1] Morris, *Government and Labor*, pp. 167–77, 181–2; Richard S. Dunn, 'Masters, Servants, and Slaves in the Colonial Chesapeake and the Caribbean', in David B. Quinn, ed., *Early Maryland in a Wider World* (Detroit, 1982), pp. 246–9; Berkeley quoted in Breen, 'Changing Labor Force', p. 4.

[2] Robert Beverly, *The History and Present State of Virginia*, ed. Louis B. Wright (Chapel Hill, NC, 1947), p. 275; William J. Hinke, trans. and ed., 'Report of the Journey of Francis Louis Michel from Berne, Switzerland, to Virginia, October 2, 1701–December 1, 1702', *VMHB* XXIV (1916), 124; Morgan, *American Slavery, American Freedom*, pp. 295–387; Breen, 'Changing Labor Force', pp. 13–18; Gary B. Nash, 'Social Development', in Greene and Pole, eds., *Colonial British America*, pp. 244–5.

Britain should be dumped on colonial shores.[1] The sudden spectre after 1718 of escalating numbers of convicts aroused deep apprehensions within the Chesapeake. Alarm arose partly because of the threat of disease convicts posed. Colonists became well-versed in the dangers of gaol fever and other maladies brought from aboard ships. In 1725, following the arrival of a vessel from London in the Rappahannock River, the local factor wrote to Jonathan Forward, 'I doubt not but I should have disposed of [the convicts] in this part of the River had it not been for a report spread abroad that the small pox raged among them so that none of the gentlemen in these parts would none of them go to the ship, nor suffer me to bring any of them up to their plantations.' Another Virginia factor noted of gaol fever, 'The people here are so much afraid of it.' Periodic panics erupted, during which it became difficult to separate fact from fiction. In 1767, reports of the deaths of an Eastern Shore widow and more than twenty of her slaves, allegedly from gaol fever, threw Marylanders into a frenzy. Charges and counter-charges as to the nature of the deaths were exchanged in the pages of the *Maryland Gazette* between alarmed citizens and an embattled defender of transportaion vainly protesting that convicts were not to blame. Several years later in Virginia, the wealthy Northern Neck planter Landon Carter recorded a similar episode in his diary:

We have been much alarmed in this house about a Jail disorder brought into the Neighbourhood by Colo. Frank Lee's servant bought of Somervill. The man has never been ill himself but only weak with imprisonment and a hard faring sea voyage. However every death that has happened in the neighbourhood has been imputed to that cause and many more that have not had it have been raised to strengthen the report from the frights and apprehensions of the women greatly cultivated by Bob Carter who brought one foolish story or another every time he went out and would not let me reason either to show the inconsistency or falsehood. I sent to Colo. Frank and it is all turned out a lie. There have been a few deaths but those owing to causes of another nature.[2]

Even more frightening, though, than the prospect of disease was

[1] Cecilius Calvert to Horatio Sharpe, 23 Dec. 1755, *Md. Archives*, VI. 329.
[2] James Horsenail to Forward, July 1725, quoted in Coldham, ed., *Bonded Passengers*, I. 43; Piper to Dixon & Littledale, 24 Oct. 1767, HPL, p. 62; Sharpe to Hamersley, 27 July 1767, *Md. Archives*, XIV. 412; Entry of 21 Apr. 1770, in Jack P. Greene, ed., *The Diary of Colonel Landon Carter of Sabine Hall, 1752-1778* (Charlottesville, Va., 1965), II. 391. Letters concerning the 1767 panic in Maryland appeared throughout the summer in the *Maryland Gazette*.

the menace transported felons posed not unlike that of earlier, more troubled times. Cast out of Britain for threatening social peace, they appeared to be neither able labourers nor industrious servants, and their transgressions were more serious than moral failings like debauchery and slothfulness traditionally ascribed to the British poor. They were not even local ruffians for whom colonial communities might have felt a special tolerance. As the 'abandoned Outcasts of the *British* Nation', convicts lay outside the customary networks that bound communities together. In the Chesapeake and other stretches of the colonial countryside, social harmony depended heavily upon the maintenance of face-to-face relationships and strong neighbourhood ties. 'It was a system', according to Rhys Isaac, 'in which networks of personal relationships had a functional—indeed structural—importance they no longer have in our urbanized scheme of things.'[1] Convicts were 'loose', 'untameable Persons' who were 'too idle to work' and 'wicked enough to murder and steal', 'wild Creatures' not 'brought to any civil Manners in England'. America would be deluged with 'wretches', 'Vermin', and 'Human Serpents'. Britain, complained a Bostonian who suffered no illusions about transportation's purpose, was 'emptying all' its gaols, and sending its 'Excrescences' abroad. 'What Advantage', asked a writer in New York's *Independent Reflector*, 'can we reap from a Colony of unrestrainable Renegadoes?' With lives and property no longer secure, 'many of the honest Inhabitants', predicted the Maryland Assembly in 1719, would 'quit their settlements'. America would fall victim, contemporaries warned, to droves of rampaging villains 'habituated upon the slightest Occasions, to cut a Man's Throat, for a small Part of his Property'.[2]

[1] 'Philanthropos', *Md. Gaz.* 20 Aug. 1767; Isaac, *The Transformation of Virginia, 1740–1790* (Chapel Hill, NC, 1982), p. 119; Morgan, *American Slavery, American Freedom*, pp. 320–6; Peter Charles Hoffer and William B. Scott, eds., *Criminal Proceedings in Colonial Virginia:* [*Records of*] *Fines, Examinations of Criminals, Trials of Slaves, etc., from March 1710* [*1711*] *to* [*1754*], [*Richmond County, Virginia*], American Legal Records, X (Athens, Ga., 1984), p. xxv; Lois Green Carr, 'Sources of Political Stability and Upheaval in Seventeenth-Century Maryland', *MHM* LXXIX (1984), 46–7.

[2] Lawes to Board of Trade, 10 Dec. 1722, in Sainsbury, ed., *Calendar of State Papers, Colonial Series*, XXXIII. 185; *American Weekly Mercury*, 14 Feb. 1721; Purdie & Dixon's *Va. Gaz.* 5 Feb. 1767; *Caribbeana ... Chiefly wrote by Several Hands in the West Indies ...* (London, 1741), II. 189; 'Americanus', *Pa. Gaz.* 9 May 1751; *Belfast News-Letter*, 14 Feb. 1766; 'Publicus', 15 Mar. 1753, in William Livingston *et al.*, *The Independent Reflector, or Weekly Essays on Sundry Important*

Convicts seemingly endangered the very foundations of society. Invariably their vicious habits would corrupt honest men and women, including servants and other members of the labouring poor. In Virginia, William Eddis encountered a widespread fear that 'the prevalence of bad example' among convicts 'might tend to universal depravity'. Benjamin Franklin noted claims that they threatened the 'Morals of the Servants and poorer People among whom they' were 'mixed'. 'What good mother . . .', he wrote in 1759, 'would introduce thieves and criminals into the company of her children, to corrupt and disgrace them'? Another Pennsylvanian urged that felons not be allowed to 'debauch the honest Natures and Manners of Mankind'.[1] So desperate were their characters, that convicts might make common cause with slaves. In Britain's plantation colonies, few prospects could be more chilling. As early as 1723, a Maryland grand jury worried that 'Servants and Slaves' would be led by convicts 'into the same Wicked Practices'. In Virginia, Governor William Gooch warned of 'intestine Insurrections of Slaves and Convicts'. Years later, a Maryland settler feared the alarming effect felons had upon 'other Servants and Negroes', whereas an anxious West Indian predicted 'Rioting, Maiming, Murdering, and every Kind of Villainy'. Caribbean planters especially harboured no doubts about convict loyalties. To guard against servile insurrection, island authorities commonly set population ratios between resident whites and blacks that slave imports could not exceed. Transportation, according to London merchant Duncan Campbell, was opposed by local planters because convicts were 'not considered among the Whites'. For the same reason, convicts were specially excluded when Jamaica in 1719 passed an act to encourage greater white immigration.[2]

Subjects More particularly adapted to the Province of New York, ed. Milton Klein (Cambridge, Mass., 1963), p. 165; Upper House Proceedings, 3 June 1719, *Md. Archives*, XXXIII. 345.

[1] Eddis, *Letters from America*, ed. Land, p. 36; Petition of Franklin to House of Commons, [12–15 Apr. 1766], in Labaree and Willcox, eds., *Franklin Papers*, XIII. 241; Franklin Letter of 9 May 1759 in *London Chronicle*, 12 May 1759, in ibid., VIII. 351; *American Weekly Mercury*, 14 Feb. 1721. See also Jones, *Present State of Virginia*, ed. Morton, p. 87.

[2] Presentment of the Maryland Grand Jury, Apr. 1723, Provincial Court Judgements, 1722–24, p. 132, MHR; Gooch to Board of Trade, 26 Mar. 1729, CO 5/1321/110–11; 'Extract of a Letter from Maryland', 26 Apr. 1751, *Pa. Gaz.* 9 May 1751; *Caribbeana*, II. 189; Testimony of Campbell, 15 Apr. 1778, *JHC* XXXVI. 928; Lawes to Board of Trade, received 14 June 1720, CO 137/13/255.

It was a pair of Virginians, however, who offered the most menacing forecast. In a sharply worded declaration before the colonial council in 1749, two Northern Neck councillors, William Fairfax and Thomas Lee, warned of increasing numbers of transported felons:

> As we have great Numbers of Negroes who are doomed as well as their Posterity to perpetual Slavery; and as it has been truly said that Freedom wears a Cap that can without a Tongue call together all those that long to shake off the Fetters of Slavery, when the Imports of Convicts . . . are sufficiently increased who are wicked enough to join our Slaves in any Mischief, it may, and in all Probability will bring sure and sudden Destruction on all his Majesty's good Subjects of this Colony.[1]

Alternative solutions to transportation urged by colonists included consigning felons in England to the galleys and coalpits. Colonists too favoured greater reliance upon capital punishment. 'I wish you would be so kind as to hang up all your felons at home', William Byrd II admonished an English acquaintance in 1736.[2] Colonial assemblies, meanwhile, voted restrictions to slow down importations. Fearing that the 'Peace of the Province' faced imminent peril, Maryland's lower house as early as 1719 tried to require purchasers to give security for the good behaviour of convicts. This maiden effort, however, was stymied when the upper house expressed fears about the bill's legality. Later attempts in the 1720s made by the assemblies of both Maryland and Virginia encountered stiff opposition from the crown, as did various efforts to impose trade duties, such as in 1754 when Maryland tried to levy a tax of 20*s.* on every imported felon. After first imposing a tax of £10 per head, Jamaica in 1731 raised its duty to £100, but it was quickly opposed by Whitehall. 'We did not imagine', the colony's council retorted, 'that [there] would be any objection to the bill, for [if] it be prudence in England to banish rogues; it must certainly be prudence here to endeavour to keep them out'. A tax

---

[1] Council Proceedings, 11 Apr. 1749, *LJC* II. 1035.

[2] Byrd to Benjamin Lynde, 20 Feb. 1736, Byrd to Mr Smyth, [6 Sept. 1740], in Tinling, ed., *Byrd Correspondence*, II. 474, 557; *American Weekly Mercury*, 14 Feb. 1721; Franklin Letter of 9 May 1759 in *London Chronicle*, 12 May 1759, in Labaree and Willcox, eds., *Franklin Papers*, VIII. 351. See also, e.g., Byrd to Boyle, 26 May 1729, in Tinling, ed., *Byrd Correspondence*, I. 396; 'Extract of a Letter from Maryland', 26 Apr. 1751, *Pa. Gaz.* 9 May 1751; 'Publicus', 15 Mar. 1753, in Livingston *et al.*, *Independent Reflector*, ed. Klein, p. 165; 'Thoughts concerning the French conduct in America concluded', *Boston Weekly News-Letter*, 17 Apr. 1755.

imposed by New Jersey fared no better. Just Pennsylvania, which enacted its first duty in 1722, successfully defied imperial authorities, chiefly by not submitting its laws for crown approval. Otherwise, the only acts normally permitted to stand were those requiring shipmasters to provide lists of any convicts aboard their vessels.[1]

Transportation provoked some of the most heated denunciations of imperial policy voiced by Americans before the Revolutionary era. Probably no other issue excited such hostility during the years of 'Salutary Neglect'. Franklin, who advocated exporting rattlesnakes to Mother England, called transportation 'an insult and contempt, the cruellest perhaps that ever one people offered another'.[2] Still, American protests, however strident, hardly had much chance of success. In London, colonial legislation almost always elicited angry complaints from merchants. English traders like Jonathan Forward and John Stewart denounced provincial regulations as assaults upon transportation itself. Forward claimed that an act passed by Virginia in 1722, requiring both shipmasters and purchasers of convicts to give security for their good behaviour, would 'disable' him 'from performing' his 'Contract with the Government'. Jamaica's 1731 import duty provoked appeals from merchants in London, Bristol, and Liverpool.[3] Not that ministry officials required much coaxing. England's stake remained too vital to suffer prohibitory restrictions. Preserving public peace at home took precedence over noisy protests from abroad.

How much of the success of transportation rested in American hands? To what extent did the system depend upon the colonies' need for cheap white labour? 'While we purchase[,] they will send

[1] Upper House Proceedings, 3, 5 June 1719, *Md. Archives*, XXXIII. 345, 349–50; Upper House Proceedings, 15 Oct. 1725, ibid., XXXV. 212; Board of Trade to Lords Justices, 5 July 1723, CO 5/1365/252–3; Board of Trade to Privy Council, 25 Aug. 1731, CO 138/17; Council of Jamaica to Governor Hunter, 14 Dec. 1731, enclosed in Hunter to Newcastle, 15 Dec. 1731, in Sainsbury, ed., *Calendar of State Papers, Colonial Series*, XXXVIII. 377; Mr Fane to Board of Trade, 15 Dec. 1731, in ibid., p. 379; Smith, *Colonists in Bondage*, pp. 119–22, 219; Herrick, *White Servitude in Pennsylvania*, pp. 123–7.

[2] Franklin Letter of 9 May 1759 in *London Chronicle*, 12 May 1759, in Labaree and Willcox, eds., *Franklin Papers*, VIII. 351; 'Americanus', *Pa. Gaz.* 9 May 1751.

[3] Forward to Allured Popple, received 26 June 1723, CO 5/1319/98; Smith, *Colonists in Bondage*, pp. 120–1; Board of Trade to Privy Council, 25 Aug. 1731, CO 138/17. Another reason import curbs in Pennsylvania were not disallowed was because so few English convicts were transported there. Consequently, the colony's laws escaped the ire of both merchants and ministry officials. Oldham, 'Transportation of British Convicts', p. 17.

them, and we bring the Evil upon our selves', the governor of Maryland claimed in 1725.[1] In fact, Britain in all likelihood would have sent them anyway, and arguably the choice colonists faced was not whether convicts came to America but whether they arrived as servants or freemen. On the other hand, colonists, through their purchases, did lighten the mother country's financial burden. Had merchants not been able to sell their cargoes, the crown would have been forced to pay them a larger subsidy. And while we should not minimize the anxiety that transportation caused in the colonies, many planters undoubtedly came to view convicts as a shrewd investment, thereby tempting them 'to run the Risque', as two Virginians observed. 'There are in all Societies', affirmed a person in Maryland, 'People that will run all Risks for the sake of making Profit'. Being young and male made convicts more dangerous, but it also enhanced their value as workers. Moreover, the fact that they were lawbreakers and ne'er-do-wells made them all the more exploitable. Planters had fewer qualms than did their cousins across the Atlantic about placing freeborn Englishmen in involuntary servitude. 'They are supposed to be receiving', wrote William Eddis, 'only the just reward which is due to repeated offenses'. Labouring men often suffered abusive treatment in the colonies, but transported felons made especially easy prey. Marked with the 'stamp of infamy', as Eddis put it, they were thought scarcely better than slaves. 'Worse than Negroes', in fact, was the verdict of a Jamaican governor. If convicts represented the dregs of British society, then numerous colonists became reconciled to making the most of them.[2]

II

During the mid-eighteenth century, areas within the Chesapeake with the greatest demand for cheap labour naturally received the

---

[1] Upper House Proceedings, 15 Oct. 1725, *Md. Archives*, XXXV. 212.

[2] Council Proceedings, 11 Apr. 1749, *LJC* II. 1035; Sharpe to Hamersley, 27 July 1767, *Md. Archives*, XIV. 413; Eddis, *Letters from America*, ed. Land, pp. 38, 36; Lawes to Board of Trade, received 14 June 1720, CO 137/13/255. It may be that in the Chesapeake opposition to transportation was limited largely to wealthy planters, fearful about the dangers convicts posed to social peace, and that transportation aroused less concern among planters of modest means who were dependent upon convict labour. There is no evidence, however, to suggest such a division in planter ranks, and, after all, convicts were also acquired by large planters.

bulk of the convict trade. In Virginia, most convicts inhabited the region north of the York River, with its growing tobacco and grain economy. There, slaves, though escalating in number, had not fully met local needs, particularly those of planters unable to afford more than just a few. The Northern Neck, a broad finger of land lying between the Rappahannock and Potomac Rivers, constituted the prime area. Governor Gooch described it in the 1730s as 'the Place of all this Dominion where most of the transported Convicts are sold and settled'. Comparatively few convicts, in contrast, were employed in less dynamic areas like the Eastern Shore or the lower James River Valley. 'That vile commodity', William Byrd II wrote in 1740, 'will not go off in York River', and the Alexandria merchant Harry Piper later claimed that servants would 'not sell in James River at any rate'.[1] Just how prevalent convicts were in the northern half of the colony is indicated by surviving shipping returns. For the period from 1725 to 1744, reasonably complete returns exist for Virginia's six naval districts where vessels were cleared through customs. Of a total of twenty-six vessels that I was able to ascertain were carrying convicts, eighteen arrived in the Rappahannock District, encompassing the area bordering the Rappahannock River, while all remaining eight arrived in the South Potomac District lying just to the north.[2]

[1] Gooch quoted in Fairfax Harrison, 'When the Convicts Came', *VMHB* XXX (1922), 255; Byrd to Smyth, [6 Sept. 1740], in Tinling, ed., *Byrd Correspondence*, II. 557; Piper to Dixon & Littledale, 6 Sept. 1769, HPL, p. 102; Schmidt, 'Convict Labor in Virginia', pp. 72–3. See also Piper to Dixon & Littledale, 25 Nov. 1767, HPL, p. 32.

[2] Virginia Shipping Returns, 1725–1753, CO 5/1442–6. The only district for which a reasonably good set of returns has not survived for this period is Accomack on the Eastern Shore, and there is no reason to suspect that many convicts ever were shipped there. Because Virginia returns generally listed convicts as 'passengers' or did not record them at all, I identified the twenty-six ships by searching for the names of convict vessels from London provided in the Treasury Money Books. See above, Chapter 4, p. 115 n. 4. Thus, the twenty-six do not include London vessels not in the Money Books or vessels from other British ports.

The fact that most convicts were transported to the area north of the York River is further illustrated by newspaper advertisements for runaway servants. Between 1736 and 1759, a period from which scattered issues of the *Virginia Gazette* have survived, there were ninety runaways for whom counties of origin can be determined. Seventy-nine came from the twenty counties lying north of the York, and of those, as many as thirty-seven runaways were from just the six counties making up the Northern Neck, depite the distance residents of those counties lay from Williamsburg where the *Gazette* was published and advertisements had to be placed. (In some instances, advertisements in the *Virginia Gazette* were supplemented by advertisements in the *Maryland Gazette* and the *Pennsylvania Gazette*).

So too, in Maryland, places with expanding economic horizons and a need for labour not fully met by slaves contained the most convicts. At the time of the colony's 1755 census, roughly three-quarters of the convict servant population of 1,981 resided in just four of fourteen counties: Baltimore, Charles, Queen Anne's, and Anne Arundel. Within these counties, they represented over 7 per cent of all labourers; hired and indentured servants constituted nearly 13 per cent and slaves some 80 per cent. If only productive adult workers are considered, then the proportions of convicts and other white labourers rise to 12 per cent and 22 per cent respectively, since just over half of the slaves, according to the census, were under 16 years of age or too infirm to work. All four of these counties produced large amounts of tobacco or, in some cases, growing quantities of wheat and corn. Poorer counties, like Dorchester, Somerset, and Worcester on the lower Eastern Shore, contained only a handful of convicts.[1]

Proximity to trading centres also affected the distribution of convicts. Because they represented a comparatively small investment, unlike imported slaves, felons did not normally draw retailers over long distances. Instead, they were sold to local residents, and areas close to ports employed the greatest numbers. Trade patterns were not so decisive in Virginia where four major rivers cut deep channels into the colony's interior and where innumerable plantation landings furnished docks for incoming vessels. In Maryland, however, counties that received the most convicts lay in close proximity to the colony's principal ports. The towns of Baltimore and Annapolis were the respective seats of Baltimore and Anne Arundel counties. Queen Anne's County was situated across the Bay from Annapolis and also lay between the Eastern shore ports of Oxford and Chestertown. Similarly, Charles County, besides being the site of Port Tobacco, lay across the Potomac not far from the key Virginia ports of Alexandria and Dumfries.

By the end of the colonial era, increasing numbers of convicts came to be employed in the Chesapeake's burgeoning backcountry. Rapid population growth and economic expansion created a strong demand for labour. Settlers naturally looked to white servants as well as slaves, especially once wholesalers began making regular trips from the tidewater. Already by 1755, Frederick County,

[1] 'Account of Number of Souls in Maryland', *Gentleman's Magazine*, 1764, p. 261.

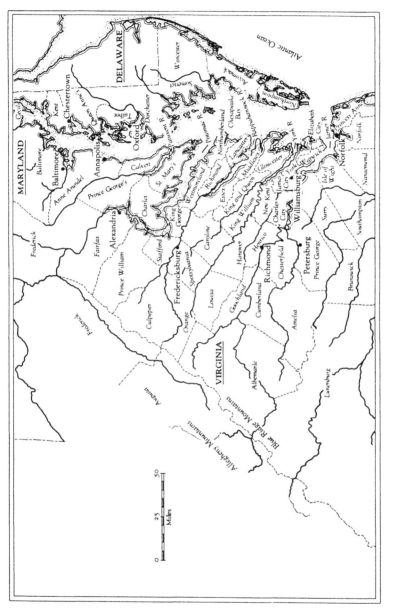

MAP 3. The Chesapeake, 1750

established in western Maryland seven years earlier, contained 136 convict servants out of some 14,000 inhabitants. Of thirty-nine convicts aboard the vessel *Hercules* when it arrived in Baltimore in 1773, thirty-two were bought by 'soul drivers', not only from Frederick but also from Augusta County in Virginia's Shenandoah Valley. The following year, the Baltimore merchant James Cheston wrote to his partners about several recent shipments of servants: 'An Indian War which has broke out on the back parts of this Province and Virginia will prevent their being sent there as usual'.[1] The growing diversity of economic activity in the Chesapeake, in manufacturing as well as agriculture, created a demand for servants with a wide range of skills. Convicts were employed as artisans and semi-skilled workers, both on plantations and in growing towns like Fredericksburg, Alexandria, Annapolis, and Baltimore. Convicts possessing skills were concentrated in a few trades. Especially numerous were shoemakers, blacksmiths, weavers, carpenters, bricklayers, and tailors. As a recent study has concluded of Chesapeake artisans, most practised 'crafts for whose products there existed widespread demand—clothing, shoes, and cloth—and those that could not be eliminated by import substitution—sawing, construction and barrel-making, repairs to tools and horse-shoeing'. Smaller numbers of convicts laboured as nailers, plasterers, and, among other things, as physicians, glassblowers, and horse jockeys.[2] Thomas Poney, a Maryland convict, was a county hangman, whereas another felon served as the childhood tutor of George

---

[1] Cheston to Stevenson and Randolph, 21 June 1774, CGP, Box 8; 'Account of Number of Souls in Maryland', *Gentleman's Magazine*, 1764, p. 261; 'List of Convicts Imported on the Ship *Hercules* ...', 23 Aug. 1773, Baltimore County Convict Record, 1770-74, pp. 368-9. See also 'Sales of Servants for Account of Mr Archibald Ritchie', [1766], Allason Papers, Box 4; *Md. Gaz.* 29 July 1773. Virginia traders seem to have marketed servants in the North Carolina backcountry. See John Hook to Robert Donald & Co., 30 July 1778, Hook Papers, Alderman Library. Another sign of the frontier's rising importance lies in the fact that of 198 Virginia runaways for the years 1760-75 whose place of origin can be determined, 42 absconded from the far western counties of Amherst, Augusta, Botetourt, Frederick, and Pittsylvania. No doubt the true proportion of runaways from the far west was even higher, since backcountry masters had less opportunity than those in the piedmont or tidewater to place advertisements in newspapers.

[2] Jean B. Russo, 'Occupational Diversification in a Rural Economy: Talbot County, Maryland, 1690-1759' (Unpublished paper presented at the 45th Conference on Early American History, Baltimore, 13-15 Sept. 1984), p. 22. See the varied range of skills and occupations contained in advertisements for runaway convicts in Table 14 in the Appendix. Some of these skills doubtless represented trades followed in Britain rather than in America.

Washington. Some convicts claimed crafts before they were transported, but occasionally they were trained on the spot. Samuel
Daniel of Middlesex County, Virginia 'learned' his servant 'to do
all Kinds of jobbing Smiths Work exceeding well'.[1] A few convicts,
particularly females, served as house servants and cooks. James
Cheston sent one customer a woman who 'says she has been used
to all kinds of household work and can sew plain work', and to
Anthony Stewart he sold a 'good tidy looking Girl named Sarah
Webster', who was 'examined by Captain McJacken who thinks
she will do for Mrs. Stewart'. On the other hand, household duties
required loyal servants with a smattering of manners. Thus, when
a person asked another Maryland factor for a servant for cooking
and washing, he specially requested a woman 'under Indenture for
Four years'. According to Harry Piper, Virginians were 'afraid of
Convicts as Waiting men'.[2]

The iron industry employed convicts as labourers along with
indentured servants and slaves. At one time or another before
the Revolution, upwards of sixty-five ironworks operated in the
Chesapeake. Major firms included John Tayloe's Neabsco Company
in Virginia and the Principio and Baltimore Companies in Maryland.
In 1770, Capt. Charles Ridgley purchased as many as fifty-five
convicts from a single shipload to work at his Northampton
ironworks in Baltimore County. Tasks were generally menial.
Although a few felons provided craftsmen like blacksmiths and
carpenters, most workers laboured as miners, woodcutters, and
wagon-drivers. Eddis described mining as the 'most laborious
employment allotted to worthless servants'.[3]

[1] Dixon & Hunter's *Va. Gaz.*, '?', 25 Mar. 1775; *Md. Gaz.*, 'Thomas Poney', 18
Sept. 1755; Jonathan Boucher, ed., *Reminiscences of an American Loyalist, 1738-
1789* (1925; reprint edn., Port Washington, NY, 1967), p. 49.

[2] Cheston to John Chapman, 5 Apr. 1773, Cheston to Anthony Stewart, 5 Apr.
1773, CGP, Box 8; Thomas Reeder to James Russell, 5 Aug. 1774, Russell Papers,
Bundle 16; Piper to John Dixon, 10 May 1769, HPL, p. 81. See also [Revel], *A
Transported Felon's Account*, p. 5; *Md. Gaz.* 28 Mar. 1765; Eddis, *Letters from
America*, ed. Land, p. 36.

[3] Eddis, *Letters from America*, ed. Land, p. 43; Cheston to Stevenson and
Randolph, 24 July 1770, CGP, Box 8; Charles G. Steffen, 'The Pre-Industrial Iron
Worker: Northampton Iron Works, 1780-1820', *Labor History*, XX (1979), 89-110;
Ronald L. Lewis, 'The Use and Extent of Slave Labor in the Chesapeake Iron
Industry: The Colonial Era', ibid. XVII (1976), 388-405. See also Lawson to Semple,
6 Feb. 1765, Lawson Letterbook; Clement Brooke to Charles Carroll &
Co., 4 Feb. 1774, Carroll-Maccubbins Papers, Box 7, MHS. For the occupational
hierarchy of one ironworks, see the 'Account of Persons employed at the Baltimore
Iron Works', 30 Apr. 1734, ibid., Box 6.

A majority of convicts were probably employed as field workers on plantations. Recent stress by historians on the growth of slavery in the Chesapeake should not blind us to the fact that convicts provided planters with a continued source of unskilled white labour.[1] Most transports arrived in the region with no discernible trades. For this reason, and because the local economy, despite its growing diversity, remained heavily agricultural, planters, from big to small, normally set them to field labour. Tobacco, wheat, and corn culture required strong backs, not highly skilled hands. According to one study, tending just a small plantation with approximately 30 acres under cultivation necessitated the equivalent of 400 10-hour days of labour. Tobacco was the dominant crop, even with the rising importance of grain after mid-century. In the late colonial period, tobacco accounted for three-quarters of all exports from the region.[2]

[1] For example, David Galenson in his excellent study, *White Servitude*, has speculated that 'unskilled servants may have virtually disappeared from the older areas of settlement on the lower Western Shore, where tobacco was grown on large plantations, relatively early in the eighteenth century' (p. 272 n. 51). And yet Charles County, according to the 1755 Maryland census, had the third largest convict servant population of any Maryland county, and Galenson himself notes that convicts after 1718 provided Maryland planters with 'cheap white labour' and that even 'some indentured servants' were used as 'field workers' (p. 157). In a recent article, Kenneth Morgan has concluded that a 'fair number of transports were either skilled or semi-skilled' and that many continued to serve in skilled or semi-skilled positions in the Chesapeake. Some clearly did, and perhaps Morgan meant to argue nothing more than that. The impression created by his article, however, is that scarcely any transports performed menial field labour. He cites Galenson's study by noting the region's widespread demand for skilled white labour and further observes that advertisements for runaway convict servants listed skilled or semi-skilled occupations. 'Convict Trade to Maryland', pp. 216–27. But not only does Morgan ignore the weight of literary evidence contrary to his principal points, he also neglects to explain how skilled and semi-skilled workers in Britain, in contrast to common labourers, could have been drawn to crime in such large numbers. Further, to assert that a demand for tradesmen existed in the Chesapeake does not prove that convicts normally met the demand. In fact they did not, as we have seen in Chapter 4. Moreover, runaway advertisements indicate the reverse of Morgan's point. Skills of any sort were listed in just over a third of all advertisements in Virginia, Maryland, and Pennsylvania newspapers during the mid-eighteenth century, despite the fact that masters were more likely to advertise for tradesmen because of their greater value (see below, Chapter 7, p. 196). Then, too, runaway advertisements overstate the proportion of convicts in skilled and semi-skilled positions because most advertisements appeared in newspapers printed after 1750, a period during which the economy was becoming more rapidly diversified.

[2] Beverly, *History and Present State of Virginia*, ed. Wright, p. 271; Irish House of Commons Proceedings, 3 Mar. 1736, in Leo Francis Stock, ed., *Proceedings and Debates of the British Parliaments respecting North America* (Washington, DC,

Some tradesmen were even forced to perform agricultural tasks, particularly if work for their talents happened to be scarce. In Queen Anne's County, Maryland, the convict Anthony Tucker was a weaver by trade, but ploughed and did 'other Plantation work'. In Virginia, Charles Speckman was given a hoe and ordered by his master to 'hill-up some corn' after first being informed there were no oportunities for 'milliners, watch-makers, or such trades' as Speckman had 'worked at in London'. So too, in Jamaica, Robert Perkins, a baker, discovered that 'his Trade' was 'nothing there'. Sold for about £10, he was 'put to Hoeing' and 'planting Tobacco'.[1]

Despite one historian's appraisal that convicts were 'put to a life of physical labour in the open air, with adequate food and careful supervision', they generally encountered a harsh lot as servants. The rise of black slavery resulted in fewer white workers on plantations, and prospects for small planters and other common folk had doubtless improved by the early eighteenth century. But rifts still existed in white society, and convicts and other servants remained subject to exploitation. As late as 1747 an Annapolis coroner noted the 'rigorous Usage and Ill-treatment of Masters to Servants'. By law, servants were entitled to adequate care and provisions, but observed a Maryland priest, 'These masters . . . are in general cruel, barbarous, and unmerciful'. Unlike in Britain where servitude was more paternalistic, masters more often considered servants to be property, not part of their families, and servant contracts could be transferred from one planter to another. In addition, American terms of servitude were longer, and servants encountered stiffer restrictions, such as being forced to carry passes when leaving the plantation. Affirmed a Baltimore resident in 1756, 'This is a very bad country for servants'.[2]

1937), IV. 856; *Pa. Gaz.* 2 Sept. 1742; Coldham, ed., *Bonded Passengers,* I. 86, 162-3; Thomas Hughes, *History of the Society of Jesus in North America, Colonial and Federal* (London, 1907), p. 342; Percy, 'Agricultural Labor', pp. 1-37; Richard B. Sheridan, 'The Domestic Economy', in Greene and Pole, eds., *Colonial British America,* p. 67. If they could be employed as house servants or in other positions, most female transports may have escaped field work due to traditional English attitudes against employing women in the fields, except during harvest. See Beverly, *History and Present State of Virginia,* ed. Wright, p. 271; Gloria L. Main, *Tobacco Colony: Life in Early Maryland, 1650-1720* (Princeton, NJ, 1982), pp. 108-9.

[1] *Md. Gaz.,* 'Anthony Tucker', 16 Sept. 1756; *The Life, Travels, Exploits, Frauds, and Robberies of Charles Speckman* . . . (London, 1763), pp. 14-15; *Account of the Ordinary of Newgate,* 5 July 1721, p. 3. See also *Pa. Gaz.,* 'Thomas Clark', 21 May 1761; Smyth to Cheston, 28 Dec. 1773, CGP, Box 13.

[2] Smith, *Colonists in Bondage,* pp. 128-9; *Md. Gaz.* 4 Aug. 1747; Father Mosley

Of any single group of convicts, tradesmen fared the best. Due to their skills, they held positions of privilege and responsibility. Working conditions were less regimented, and greater opportunities existed for travel beyond the plantation. A Charles County, Maryland convict, John Winter, was a 'very compleat House Painter' who could 'imitate Marble or Mahogany very exactly' and could 'paint Floor Cloths as neat as any imported from Britain'. He was hired out to several different Virginians, including to George Washington who in 1759 put Winter to work painting his newly enlarged home, Mount Vernon. Meanwhile, John Jones Van de Huville was permitted by his Alexandria master to practise medicine in nearby Prince George's County, Maryland and to keep some of his patients' fees. In fact, many convicts, hoping to gain special favours, claimed skills they did not possess. John Merry Tandy pretended to be a wheelwright, a carpenter, and a sawyer, but was 'Master' of none. Another convict, though really bred to farming, claimed a 'knowledge in many other Kinds of Business'. Probably the frequency of such claims led a skeptical purchaser in Maryland to write to the trader James Cheston, 'I have received the last Servant you sent me and if he can do what he says he will sute me very well.'[1]

Planter benevolence could also temper conditions of servitude, for a few convicts enjoyed reasonably close relationships with their owners. Transported for theft to Virginia, Richard Kebble was

quoted in Hughes, *History of the Society of Jesus*, p. 342; William Randal to Parents, 23 Sept. 1756, HCA 30/258; Morgan, *American Slavery, American Freedom*, pp. 126-7. See also John Campbell to William Sinclair, 26 July 1774, GD 136/416/1/13; William Moraley, *The Infortunate: or, the Voyage and Adventures of William Moraley* . . . (Newcastle, 1743), p. 33; Morris, *Government and Labor*, pp. 482-4, 488-91.

[1] *Md. Gaz.*, 'John Winter', 26 June 1760, 'John Jones Van de Huville', 1 Nov. 1764, 'John Merry Tandy', 29 Mar. 1770, 'Thomas Belcher', 16 Mar. 1769; Smyth to Cheston, 7 Apr. 1774, CGP, Box 13; Communication from W. W. Abbot, 14 May 1986. For opportunities for skilled convicts, see also *Md. Gaz.*, 'James Lowe', 27 July 1769; Purdie & Dixon's *Va. Gaz.*, 'William' and 'Hannah Daylies', 26 Mar. 1767. For the pretended skills of convicts, see also, e.g., *Md. Gaz.*, 'Henry Watts', 22 Nov. 1749, 'Edward Meacham', 26 Apr. 1753, 'John Hardie', 11 July 1754, 'James Hall', 19 Sept. 1754, 'John Ward', 26 June 1760, 'Richard Lelan', 26 May 1763, 'John Fricker', 21 June 1764, 'John Dobs', 2 May 1765, 'Edward Trickel', 25 Aug. 1768, 'William Perry', 28 Nov. 1771; *Pa. Gaz.*, 'Matthew Howard', 22 Jan. 1751, 'William Higgins', 16 June 1757, 'Joseph Penick', 1 June 1769, 'Joseph Pool', 30 May 1771, 'Edward Humphreys', 18 Aug. 1773; Purdie & Dixon's *Va. Gaz.*, 'Arundale Carness', 29 Aug. 1766, 'John Libiter', 21 June 1770; Rind's *Va. Gaz.*, 'Thomas Belcher', 16 Mar. 1769; Eddis, *Letters from America*, ed. Land, pp. 42-3.

given 'great Liberties' because his master 'looked upon him as a civil young Man'. Plain fear, too, loosened some servants' bonds. When a Virginia convict threatened his master with a knife and asked 'how long' he was to be 'his Servant', the poor man was put 'into such Consternations, that he never asked' the convict 'afterwards to go to work'. In Kent County, Maryland, Edward Davis signed a contract agreeing to keep his servant William Farrow for only five years if Farrow promised to 'behave himselfe'.[1]

Planter apprehensions, however, normally exacerbated conditions. Unlike other labourers, noted Benjamin Franklin, convicts 'must be ruled with a Rod of Iron'. Everyday fear together with a demand for labour and the convict's degraded status could result in especially harsh terms of servitude, even on small plantations where there were greater opportunities for intimacy between master and servant. Material conditions were extremely crude. Besides the danger of disease, arising not just from lingering ship'. board maladies but also from summer fevers to which arriving convicts had to become 'seasoned', days were long and hard, with Sundays providing the only respite. Food and clothing were scanty. According to the convict Edward Mires, his daily diet consisted of Indian corn, and skins furnished his only shoes. The lot of Elizabeth Sprigs was much the same: 'scarce any thing but Indian Corn and Salt to eat', and 'no shoes nor stockings to wear'. Many were forced to spend Sundays growing their own provisions, while even the servant-schoolmaster James Borthwick, enduring the 'meanest of Subsistance', had to supply his 'own Clothes and Linnen'.[2] In addition, convicts with a few shillings frequently lost them to masters, and numbers of workers experienced recurring abuse and hard usage. In the case of Joseph Lewin, he was 'transported to

[1] *A Genuine Account of the Behaviour, Confessions, and Dying Words, of the Malefactors* . . . (London, [1743]), p. 7; Servant Bond, 29 Apr. 1719, Kent County Bonds and Indentures, 1715–20, fo. 55, MHR; *Life of James Dalton*, p. 31. See also Servant Bond, 17 Apr. 1719, Kent County Bonds and Indentures, 1715–20, fo. 58–9. I am indebted to Lois Green Carr for directing me to the Kent records.

[2] [Franklin], 'Conversation on Slavery', 26 Jan. 1770, in Labaree and Willcox, eds., *Franklin Papers*, XVII. 42; *Account of the Ordinary of Newgate*, 24 Sept. 1722, p. 6; Sprigs to John Sprigs, 22 Sept. 1756, in Merrill Jensen, ed., *English Historical Documents: American Colonial Documents to 1776* (New York, 1955), p. 489; Borthwick to Drummond, 7 Aug. 1733, GD 24/1/464/N-0/545. See also *Account of the Ordinary of Newgate*, 5 July 1721, p. 3; [Revel], *A Transported Felon's Account*, p. 6; *Liberty Regain'd*, pp. 19–20; Green, *Sufferings of William Green*, p. 7.

Merryland, where a very rigid, severe Master purchased him, who beat him cruelly and unmercifully'. Banished for theft, John Read affirmed, 'No man knew the misery of such a state, but those who felt it'. Whippings were commonplace, especially for unruly servants, as were iron collars and chains. The Maryland convict Hannah Boyer was forced to wear a horse lock and chain on one of her legs. Another woman protested that if 'you Bitch', you are 'tied up and whipped to that Degree that you'd not serve an Animal'.[1]

As with other servants, convicts could petition county courts for relief from excessive abuse, and sometimes masters were admonished or fined. Only in a minority of instances, however, did courts discharge petitioners from service. Further, there was strong disincentive to bring complaints, for if a court thought a servant to be lying or otherwise sided with his master, a penalty would usually be imposed. In Westmoreland County, Virginia, a convict in 1724 received twenty lashes upon complaining of mistreatment, whereas in 1738 another Westmoreland convict, George Smith, received twenty-nine lashes and more than three years extra service.

[1] *Account of the Ordinary of Newgate*, 21 Oct. 1743, p. 9, 4 June 1770, p. 43; Sprigs to Sprigs, 22 Sept. 1756, in Jensen, ed., *American Colonial Documents*, p. 489; *Md. Gaz.*, 'Hannah Boyer', 28 May 1752; Stevenson and Randolph to Cheston, 25 Sept. 1773, CGP, Box 12. See also *Account of the Ordinary of Newgate*, 5 July 1721, p. 3, 3 Nov. 1725, p. 4, 7 Nov. 1744, p. 5; Petition of [?] to Charles Calvert, May 1726, Provincial Court Judgements, p. 399; Petition of Gabriel Tomkins to Walpole, [1733], SP 36/30/402; Randal to Uncle and Aunt, 23 Sept. 1756, HCA 30/258; *Old Bailey Sessions Papers*, 8-15 Sept. 1773, p. 397.

For references to whippings, iron collars, and chains, see *Md. Gaz.*, 'Henry Kirk', 27 May 1746, 'Thomas Butler', 14 Sept. 1748, 'Peter Ross', 20 Mar. 1751, 'Mary Burton', 2 May 1754, 'Robert Cox', 15 Aug. 1754, 'John Oulton', 5 Sept. 1754, 'John Morling', 11 Sept. 1755, 'Sarah Davis', 27 Apr. 1758, 'John Shunk', 21 May 1761, 'William Godden', 1 July 1762, 'George Seymour' and 'Stephan Hawkes', 16 Sept. 1762, 'John Child', 24 May 1764, 'Charles Campbell', 30 Apr. 1767, 'Hugh Clark', 12 Nov. 1767, 'Samuel Davenant' and 'Samuel Flood', 4 Aug. 1768, 'John Benhan' and 'John Miller', 8 Sept. 1768, 'Edward Hooper', 21 Dec. 1769, 'George Adams', 5 July 1770, 'Thomas Burn', 13 Dec. 1770, 'Thomas Williams', 9 May 1771, 'Joseph Dunn', 5 Sept. 1771, 'Edward Davy', 22 Oct. 1772, 'Anthony Jackson' and 'John Jones', 27 May 1773, 'William Walker', 22 July 1773, 'John Taylor', 8 June 1775, 'John Peacock', 30 Mar., 21 Sept. 1775, 'James Wilson' and 'Edmund Wells', 4 July 1776; *Pa. Gaz.*, 'Moses Long', 14 Aug. 1746, 'Robert Mulonic', 16 Feb. 1769, 'William Hatton', 6 July 1769, 'Thomas Price', 8 Nov. 1770, 'Charles Campbell', 6 Dec. 1770, 'Edward Williams', 25 Aug. 1773, 'Thomas Rogers' and 'Robert Collens', 15 Mar. 1775, 'William Manly', 15 May 1776; *Va. Gaz.*, 'Timothy Carpenter', 2 Sept. 1757; Purdie & Dixon's *Va. Gaz.*, 'Edmund Cooper', 14 Apr. 1768, 'William Stringer', 7 Sept. 1769, 'John Evrie', 18 Jan. 1770, 'Joseph Steel', 3 June 1773, 'Peter Robb' and 'John Farrell', 26 Aug. 1773; Rind's *Va. Gaz.*, 'Thomas Winthrop', 20 July 1769, 'Charles Sawyer', 2 June 1774.

After he had appealed to county justices that his master had 'beat and abused' him and 'starved him for want of Necessary victualls', the court accepted his master's explanation that Smith was a thief and a runaway.[1]

Convicts periodically compared their lot to 'slavery and bond-age'.[2] Significant differences, of course, distinguished any form of white servitude from black slavery—most obviously slaves and their offspring were doomed to perpetual servitude. Blacks, because of racial prejudice and their condition as slaves, also occupied positions of greater degradation. Still, material conditions for convicts and slaves, if contemporaries are to be believed, may not have differed very much. Some observers, in fact, held that convicts suffered harsher treatment. The complaint of a female felon—'Many Nea-groes are better used'—was echoed by Eddis, who noted that because slaves were a 'property for life', they were 'almost in every instance, under more comfortable circumstances than the miserable European, over whom the rigid planter exercises an inflexible severity'.[3]

Nor were differences in status as pronounced as might be expected. Colour mattered a great deal in eighteenth-century life, but convicts, in the eyes of fearful colonists, embodied the most repugnant features of human society. Poverty, violence, and immorality were all part of their world. If slaves appeared dull and inferior, Britain's criminal outcasts were clever and corrupt in ways that directly threatened the public good. Neither population, according to common thought, enjoyed any claim to 'virtue', that personal quality of self-control which freed individuals from evil habits and passions. Without virtue, men could never hope to achieve full civil status within society; instead they would remain

---

[1] Court Orders of 26 Nov. 1724 and 28 June 1738, Westmoreland County Orders, 1721-31, p. 77a, 1731-39, p. 272 (VSL microfilm); Morris, *Government and Labor*, p. 488. See also Moraley, *The Infortunate*, p 33; Kulikoff, *Tobacco and Slaves*, pp. 295-6.

[2] *Account of the Ordinary of Newgate*, 4 June 1770, p. 43. See also, e.g., ibid., 26 Oct. 1720, p. 3, 5 July 1721, p. 3; [Revel], *A Transported Felon's Account*, p. 6; Wilkinson, ed., *King of the Beggars*, pp. 168-9, 247; Coldham, *Bonded Passengers*, I. 107.

[3] Sprigs to Sprigs, 22 Sept. 1756, in Jensen, ed., *American Colonial Documents*, p. 489; Eddis, *Letters from America*, ed. Land, p. 38. See also Irish House of Commons Proceedings, 3 Mar. 1736, in Stock, ed., *Proceedings and Debates of British Parliaments*, IV. 856; *The Fortunate Transport, or, the Secret History of the Life and Adventures of the Celebrated Polly Haycock ... By a Creole* (London, [1750?]), p. 43.

subject to their own vicious lusts. 'They who begin with Thieving,' observed a West Indian, 'commonly go through the Catalogue of deadly Sins, if not prevented in Time by the Gallows.' Governor Gooch wrote of the 'impossibility of ever reclaiming' transported convicts. '*Old Transgressors*' will 'cease to Sin,' rhymed a Maryland resident in 1752, 'As well may *Ethiopian* Slaves, Wash out the Darkness of their Skin.'[1]

Convicts also suffered from being forced to work as common field hands, much like slaves. During the early generations of colonization when white servants dominated plantation forces, field work carried no special stigma. By the early eighteenth century, however, it was identified overwhelmingly with slaves. Indentured servants, who more and more consisted of skilled tradesmen as the century progressed, suffered less from this circumstance than unskilled felons. 'Among the Negroes to work at the Hoe' was how a Virginia convict described the latter's fate. Gooch noted derisively that working 'in the Field with the Slaves' was 'the common Usage of Convicts'.[2]

Not surprisingly, convicts and slaves were often vilified in the same breath. More than a few colonists viewed them as twin blots upon the commonweal, equally deserving of exclusion from the provinces. Both became objects of import duties and other attempted trade restrictions. In 1734, Governor William Cosby condemned New York's 'too great importation of Negroes and Convicts' while 'neighbouring provinces' were 'filled with honest usefull and labourious white people'. Echoed Lawrence Washington, George Washington's half-brother: 'We have increased by slow degrees except Negroes and convicts whilst our neighbouring Colonies . . . have become populous.' Similarly, in 1772 a writer in the *Virginia Gazette* indicted the convict and African trades as 'two *glorious* Importations of Corruption and Slavery to every civilized People'.[3]

---

[1] West Indian quoted in *Caribbeana*, II. 189; Gooch to Board of Trade, 22 Feb. 1739, CO 5/1324/156; *Md. Gaz.* 12 Oct. 1752; Jack P. Greene, *All Men Are Created Equal: Some Reflections on the Character of the American Revolution* (Oxford, 1976), pp. 23–4.

[2] [Revel], *A Transported Felon's Account*, p. 9; Gooch quoted in Schmidt, 'Convict Labor in Virginia', p. 102; Lois Green Carr and Russell R. Menard, 'Immigration and Opportunity: The Freedman in Early Colonial Maryland', in Tate and Ammerman, eds., *Chesapeake in the Seventeenth Century*, p. 231. See also John Dunmore Lang, *Transportation and Colonization . . .* (London, 1837), p. 39.

[3] Cosby quoted in Greenberg, *Crime and Law Enforcement in New York*, p. 29; Washington quoted in Duncan J. MacLeod, *Slavery, Race and the American*

Perhaps if convicts had appeared reclaimable, greater efforts might have been made to enhance their status and to segregate them from slaves. Prevailing fears of servile insurrection alone dictated that white and black workers should have been kept separate and unequal. In earlier years, racism had served as a valuable means of keeping unruly white labourers in Virginia from making common cause with slaves. The colony's legislature after Bacon's Rebellion passed a battery of laws designed to foster racial contempt in poor whites towards their darker-skinned compatriots.[1] But convicts were criminal outcasts with precious little stake in society; nor did colonists show much interest in giving them one. During wartime, authorities followed the same policy employed in Britain to remove the idle poor. Just as British vagrants were impressed into the royal navy and the army, convicts provided the colonies with cannon fodder against the Spanish, the French, and the Indians. In the English expedition against Cartagena in 1741 and again in the Seven Years War, they were impressed into military regiments. The Earl of Loudon, as commander-in-chief of British forces, claimed in 1757 that many of Virginia's recruits included felons 'bought out of the Ships before they landed'.[2] Otherwise, rather than encourage their assimilation within the white mainstream, colonists consigned felons to a nether class that was neither slave nor free. A European described them in 1766 as a 'special class of servants . . . between peasants and slaves'.[3]

Although convicts initially enjoyed many of the same legal privileges accorded to other servants, colonial legislatures began to strip away elementary rights—the Revd Hugh Jones even

Revolution (London, 1974), p. 70; Purdie & Dixon's *Va. Gaz.* 3 Dec. 1772. See also *Pa. Gaz.* 3 July 1732; Jones, *Present State of Virginia*, ed. Morton, p. 87.

[1] Morgan, *American Slavery, American Freedom*, pp. 328–37.

[2] Loudon to Duke of Cumberland, 8 Mar. 1757, in Stanley Pargellis, ed., *Military Affairs in North America, 1748–1765: Selected Documents from the Cumberland Papers in Windsor Castle* (New York, 1936), p. 319; Arthur N. Gilbert, 'Army Impressment during the War of the Spanish Succession', *The Historian*, XXXVIII. 696–701; Stephen F. Gradish, *The Manning of the British Navy during the Seven Years' War* (London, 1980), pp. 83–6; Morgan, *American Slavery, American Freedom*, p. 340; Hay, 'War, Dearth and Theft', p. 141. See also Sir William Johnson to Board of Trade, 28 May 1756, in *Documents Relative to the Colonial History of the State of New York* (Albany, 1853–87), VII. 87; Francis Fauquier to Board of Trade, 14 July, 2 Aug. 1759, CO 5/1329/148–50.

[3] Gottfried Achenwall, 'Some Observations on North America from Oral Information by Dr. Franklin', [July 1766], in Labaree and Willcox, eds., *Franklin Papers*, XIII. 356.

recommended making some criminals perpetual servants, whereas the Virginia legislature at one point considered keeping convicts confined in a separate county, thus preventing them 'from doing any hurt'. Neither alternative ever became a realistic possibility, but plainly, as the century progressed, convicts were meant to occupy a pariah class along with slaves, free blacks, and Indians. In Jamaica, for example, transports, by virtue of a 1728 act, were forced to forfeit all their possessions to the provincial government, even though in England the king had long since desisted from confiscating the goods or lands of felons. In Virginia, legislators steadily chipped away at the rights of convicts. In 1732, burgesses from Richmond and Westmoreland, two Northern Neck counties with large numbers of transported felons, petitioned to give local courts the right to try and condemn convicts in capital cases. Rather than be moved like normal criminals to the General Court in Williamsburg, the colony's highest tribunal, they would be tried and, if found guilty, executed on the spot like common slaves. Though this first bill failed to win approval, the assembly six years later passed an act depriving convicts of the customary right to be tried at the General Court by local jurors. Ordinary bystanders in Williamsburg, not men brought from the defendant's home county, were to hear capital cases. In both instances, reduced court costs were a key consideration, but equally clearly, the rights of convicts remained highly vulnerable. Indeed, in neither Virginia nor Maryland were convicts permitted to testify in courts of law, for, noted a 1748 Virginia statute, 'convicts, as well as negroes, mulattos, and Indians' were 'commonly of such base and corrupt principles'. By virtue of a 1762 statute, Virginia also denied convicts the right to vote during their banishment, even former servants who might have become freeholders.[1]

[1] 'An Act directing the method of trial of criminals for capital offences . . .', 1748, Hening's *Statutes*, V. 546–7; Jones, *Present State of Virginia*, ed. Morton, p. 135; Holdernesse to Attorney General, 14 Dec. 1753, SP 44/85/367–8; Beattie, *Crime and the Courts in England*, p. 338; Lower House Proceedings, 23 May 1732, *JHB* V. 123; 'An Act for directing and better regulating the elections of Burgesses . . .', 1762, Hening's *Statutes* VII. 519. Lawmakers in Virginia and Maryland stipulated that convicts could testify in cases involving other convicts, so that they would not be able to shield each other during criminal trials. Predicted one Annapolis resident: 'Our late Law . . . will, I dare say, occasion the Sale of many a Bed-cord, and the transporting many a Transport into the other World'. 'Extract of a letter from Annapolis', 15 Aug. 1751, *Pa. Gaz.* 5 Sept. 1751; 'An Act, for altering the method of Trial of certain Criminals therein mentioned', 1738, Hening's

Virginians left little doubt where transported felons stood when legislators took up the issue of freedom dues. Maryland and other provinces by and large left unresolved the question of whether convicts were entitled to the normal benefits accorded to indentured servants upon the completion of their terms. In Virginia, legislators debated the matter on several occasions before the assembly decided in 1749 that convicts were suitable recipients. Four years later, however, the assembly reversed its decision. In a 1753 statute, convicts were specifically excluded from the normal allowance of £3. 10*s*. Prevailing sentiment no doubt mirrored the views of Councillors Thomas Lee and William Fairfax who had strongly opposed the 1749 law. Although on that occasion they had objected to freedom dues on several grounds, including the likelihood that smaller planters would not be able to afford them, they also feared the double-edged effect the statute would have on the province's white workforce. 'Putting Volunteers and Convicts on the same Footing as to Rewards and Punishments,' they declared, 'is discouraging the Good and Encouraging the Bad; for what honest Man would chuse to serve in a Country where no Distinction is made?' Instead, the colony would be 'overwhelmed with a Inundation of all Sorts of Theives', ending ultimately, Lee and Fairfax predicted, in a bloody confrontation pitting convicts and slaves against the good subjects of Virginia. With social violence a growing possibility, it remained essential, they believed, to discourage the flow of felons to colonial shores. Far easier to make life more hellish for ex-servants than try to bleach their souls white.[1]

Statutes, V. 24-6; 'An Act to make the Testimony of Convicted Persons legal against Convicted Persons', 1751, *Md. Archives*, XLVI. 616.

[1] Council Proceedings, 11 Apr. 1749, *LJC* II. 1034-5; Lower House Proceedings, 8 Sept. 1736, 27 May 1740, *JHB* V. 291, 403; 'An Act for the better government of servants and slaves', 1753, Hening's *Statutes*, VI. 359. In so far as Lee and Fairfax were from counties north of the Rappahannock, their opposition to freedom dues has been viewed in a sectional context, whereby northern politicians were pitted against those from counties bordering the James and York rivers, an area less dependent upon convict labour. 'The large plantation owners of the James and York', Alonzo Thomas Dill has written, were less sensitive 'about raising the costs of small farmers through legislation affecting the supply of white labour'. 'Sectional Conflict in Colonial Virginia', *VMHB* LXXXVII (1979), 304-5. Dill's argument, however, is circumstantial, for the absence of division lists makes it impossible to ascertain in this case whether raising the costs of convict labour truly ignited sectional antagonisms in the assembly. In 1752, when the House of Burgesses debated whether to make 'owners of Convicts lyable for the costs attending any prosecution for felony', opposition to the bill came from such Northern Neck

Denying criminals customary rights and privileges would scarcely appear extraordinary if only a handful of men and women had been affected. But provincial legislation, piecemeal though it was, embraced an entire class of bound labour. Also, some planters seemingly began to view other servants in the same light as convicts due to their common association as labourers. Although convicts suffered from special legal restrictions, Eddis claimed that planters 'too generally conceive an opinion that the difference is merely nominal between the indented servant and the convicted felon'. 'Looked upon as in the *black* [my italics] class of convicts', was how a person at mid-century described the condition of ordinary servants, whereas another believed that they 'are obliged to Serve like slaves or Convicts, and are on the same footing'.[1] That, of course, could not have occurred in the case of highly skilled indentured servants, but such observations do afford tantalizing evidence that some servants were gradually becoming associated, in the public mind, with convicts, and, further, that many convicts were already viewed in much the same way as slaves. Certainly social arrangements in Virginia and Maryland, though drawn along racial lines, had not produced a striking improvement in the plight of many white labourers. By the late colonial period, thousands of convict servants and perhaps others toiled under debased conditions not altogether different from black slavery. At least for seven years' duration, convicts like slaves encountered rampant exploitation. For any set of labourers, such a prospect would be horrifying. For white Britons who gloried in their freedom, it seemed downright barbaric.

III

For a Maryland convict one March day in 1751, the early spring chores proved too taxing. Armed with an axe, he entered his master's home and descended upon the man's poor wife.

representatives as John Woodbridge and Robert Vaulx. On the other hand, the bill also attracted Northern Neck support from Landon Carter, Charles Carter, and Peter Hedgeman, despite the financial burden it threatened to create for convict owners. Landon Carter, 'Journal Privately Kept of the House of Burgesses', entries of 6, 10, 14 Mar. 1752, in Greene, ed., *Diary of Landon Carter*, I. 75, 79–80, 85–6; *JHB* VII. vii-viii.

[1] Eddis, *Letters from America*, ed. Land, p. 37; Williamson quoted in Coldham, ed., *Bonded Passengers*, I. 163; 'Journal of a French Traveller in the Colonies, 1765, II', *AHR* XXVII (1921), 84. See also *The Fortunate Transport*, p. 43.

Having no stomach for murder, however, the servant laid his hand upon a cutting block and chopped it off. 'Now make me work if you can', he shouted as he hurled her the severed hand. Fleeing to Pennsylvania, he never went back to the fields but turned to begging in Philadelphia streets. According to one local report, 'Nobody would give him any Relief', and within weeks he was dead from gangrene. Such was the penalty, related the report, for his 'fit of Laziness'.[1]

*

Physical descriptions printed in provincial newspaper advertisements for runaway servants provide an invaluable profile of colonial convicts. In many cases, they afford an unusual glimpse of their lives. More than a handful of runaways, for example, paraded tattoos, replete with crucifixes and the names of loved ones. William Roberts bore a darted heart on one arm and the name of his wife on the other.[2] Descriptions of bodily defects were particularly common in advertisements. Numerous convicts were badly scarred from smallpox or had physical afflictions like venereal disease. A Maryland convict had the 'King's Evil' (i.e. tuberculosis of the lymphatic glands) 'under his Chin'. Quite a few suffered from partial blindness.[3]

Many defects, in ways that diaries and letters never can, spoke

---

[1] *Md. Gaz.* 17 Apr., 1 May 1751.

[2] *Va. Gaz.*, 'William Roberts', 17 Nov. 1738. See also ibid., 'Samuel Tomlinson', 19 Nov. 1736, 'Winnifred Thomas', 5 Aug. 1737, 'John Coleman', 29 Sept. 1738, 'Richard Kibble', 6 July 1739, 'Charles Kenwell', 18 Sept. 1746; Rind's *Va. Gaz.*, 'John Abbott', 26 Jan. 1769; *Pa. Gaz.*, 'William Grace', 31 May 1750, 'Daniel Murphey', 25 June 1752, 'Walter Nicholls', 28 Nov. 1754, 'James Nisbet', 30 May 1765, 'Edward Ponting', 27 Apr. 1769, 'William Voice', 31 Aug. 1769, 'John Adams', 7 Sept. 1769; *Md. Gaz.*, 'John Bailey', 4 Mar. 1746, 'John Brookes', 30 Nov. 1748, 'John Raner', 31 Oct. 1754, 'Bartholomew Savage', 27 Aug. 1761, 'Thomas Preston', 17 June 1762, 'John Hubbard', 18 Oct. 1764, 'John Smith', 7 Aug. 1766, 'John Broughton', 2 July 1767, 'William Gafford', 10 Aug. 1769, 'Charles M'Donald', 7 Sept. 1769, 'James Wilson', 4 July 1776.

[3] *Md. Gaz.*, 'William Hutcheson', 5 Oct. 1758. References to smallpox scars were extremely common and too numerous to list here. For several instances of venereal disease, see *Md. Gaz.*, 'Patrick Clearly', 19 Apr. 1770; Rind's *Va. Gaz.*, 'William Griffith', 7 June 1770; Dixon & Hunter's *Va. Gaz.*, '? Walker', 11 Aug. 1775. For occurrences of blindness, see *Va. Gaz.*, 'William Cuddy', 26 Sept. 1745; Rind's *Va. Gaz.*, 'Israel Corwen', 16 June 1768; Purdie & Dixon's *Va. Gaz.*, 'David Jones', 2 Dec. 1773; *Pa. Gaz.*, 'James Courbet', 6 Mar. 1760, 'Edmund Collins', 22 Aug. 1765, 'Thomas Lockhart', 17 Aug. 1769, 'John Dawson', 1 Sept. 1773, 'James Lamberd', 10 Aug. 1774; *Md. Gaz.*, 'Thomas Parker', 5 July 1749, 'William Moulding', 28 May 1752, 'John Williams', 7 June 1753.

of unmistakably tough and violent conditions on both sides of the Atlantic. Bent backs, ugly burns, and crooked limbs reflected the common hardships encountered by the lower orders. Scars criss-crossed entire bodies. Many of these injuries were sustained during times of hard manual labour. Convicts bore marks from axes, scythes, and reaping hooks. A Baltimore County man had his legs broken by a cart, whereas John Jones of Botetourt, Virginia had a scar on his right leg from a 'wound when he followed the sea'.[1] Some men, like Dominick Hogan who was forced to wear a truss, suffered from badly protruding ruptures.[2] Thomas Winney, who served in Westmoreland County, Virginia, had lost part of his nose when he was kicked by a horse.[3] Often, however, the worst mutilations stemmed from human violence. Knife and sword wounds were common over all parts of the body. Besides a large mark on his forehead, William Rill bore two scars on the inside of a leg 'done with a Knife crosswise', while a Maryland convict had a 'scar on his throat cut by a sword'. Some idea of James Williams's childhood can be gathered from the fact that his mother had cut off two of his fingers.[4] James Andrews had lost the entire use of one hand after being shot through the wrist, and a Virginia convict bore scars from being shot in the neck.[5]

Among injuries received during servitude were marks left by whips, chains, and iron collars. Thomas Burns, for example, was

[1] Purdie & Dixon's *Va. Gaz.*, 'John Jones', 26 May 1772; *Pa. Gaz.*, 'John Robertson', 15 Aug. 1771. Scars and injuries of all varieties were very common. For a tiny sample, see *Md. Gaz.*, 'Edward Rose', 17 Aug. 1748, 'Jacob Parrot', 9 May 1750, 'Stephen Pane', 25 Sept. 1766; *Pa. Gaz.*, 'Thomas Dyer', 4 Apr. 1771, 'John Campbell', 7 Feb. 1771; Purdie's *Va. Gaz.*, 'Thomas Hall', 11 Oct. 1776. For injuries common among labourers in Britain, see John Rule, *The Experience of Labour in Eighteenth-Century Industry* (London, 1981), pp. 74–94; Malcolmson, *Life and Labour in England*, p. 77.

[2] *Pa. Gaz.*, 'Dominick Hogan', 11 July 1746. See also *Md. Gaz.*, 'Anthony Tucker', 16 Sept. 1756, 'James Griffiths', 30 June 1757, 'Edward Jean', 16 Apr. 1761, 'Robert Johnson', 15 June 1769; *Pa. Gaz.*, 'Edward Davis', 28 June 1764, 'Michael Kelly', 21 June 1770.

[3] *Md. Gaz.*, 'Thomas Winney', 23 Aug. 1749. See also Rind's *Va. Gaz.*, 'William Conoly', 23 July 1767; Purdie's *Va. Gaz.*, 'William Hipditch', 31 Jan. 1777.

[4] Purdie's *Va. Gaz.*, 'William Rill', 5 Sept. 1777; *Md. Gaz.*, 'James Williams', 26 June 1760; *Pa. Gaz.*, 'Thomas Morris', 10 Sept. 1747. See also, e.g., *Pa. Gaz.*, 'John Atkins', 25 June 1752, 'John Lollers', 24 July 1755, 'Benjamin Parkinson', 17 Aug. 1769, 'John Hickins', 28 July 1773; *Md. Gaz.*, 'William Lewis', 29 Aug. 1765, 'Charles Killeen', 2 July 1767.

[5] *Md. Gaz.*, 'James Andrews', 11 Aug. 1763, 'John Benham', 8 Sept. 1768. See also, e.g., Rind's *Va. Gaz.*, 'George Pitt', 25 Aug. 1768; Pinkney's *Va. Gaz.*, 'George Newton', 1 June 1775; *Pa. Gaz.*, 'Thomas Morgan', 14 June 1775.

'remarkably cut on the Buttocks by a Flogging' from his master, whereas Sarah Davis's whipping had left 'many Scars on her Back'.[1] Other wounds were self-inflicted. It is impossible to know how many labourers took their own lives, but some certainly tried. Thomas Goodwin in Cecil County, Maryland had a 'large Scar' where he had 'formerly cut his Throat', as did an Irishman who was otherwise described as looking 'very Fierce'. Though both men failed, enough others succeeded for the *Maryland Gazette* in 1747 to report mounting numbers of servant suicides. A former servant from Scotland noted how 'some of these poor deluded slaves, in order to put an end to their bondage, put a period to their lives'.[2]

Convict servants enjoyed few sources of solace. Those with trades may have received a measure of satisfaction from their work. Other than holding positions of preferment, some took considerable pride in their talents. The convict gardener John Adam Smith of Baltimore County, besides talking 'much of his Trade', commonly paraded a 'treatise on raising the pine apple', which he pretended was 'of his own writing'. Normally a shoemaker, Ricely Johnson possessed medical talents like bleeding and drawing teeth. 'When in Liquor', he bragged 'much of his Performance as a Doctor'. Elizabeth Berry was 'fond of boasting' that she was 'an excellent dairy maid', whereas William Cullimoor claimed 'to be a great Mower and Ditcher'. A Virginia convict, who was a 'Jack of all Trades', liked to talk about 'most Subjects of the Mechanicks'.[3] Still, expressions of pride like these usually lay in past accomplishments, not in the daily regimen of plantation labour. Some convicts seldom had opportunities to practise their skills. So desperate was the wool-

---

[1] *Md. Gaz.*, 'Thomas Burns', 13 Dec. 1770, 'Sarah Davis', 27 Apr. 1758. See also ibid., 'Henry Kirk', 27 May 1746, 'Thomas Butler', 14 Sept. 1748, 'Thomas Moore', 17 Aug. 1769, 'George Adams', 5 July 1770, 'William Walker', 22 July 1773; *Pa. Gaz.*, 'Moses Long', 14 Aug. 1746, 'John Shepard', 17 Oct. 1765, 'William Springate', 4 July 1771, 'Edward Williams', 25 Aug. 1773; *Va. Gaz.*, 'Timothy Carpenter', 2 Sept. 1757; Purdie & Dixon's *Va. Gaz.*, 'William Stringer', 7 Sept. 1769, 'John Evrie', 18 Jan. 1770, 'Joseph Steel', 3 June 1773, 'Peter Robb' and 'John Farrell', 26 Aug. 1773; Rind's *Va. Gaz.*, 'Charles Sawyer', 2 June 1774.

[2] *Pa. Gaz.*, 'Thomas Goodwin', 6 Sept. 1744; *Md. Gaz.*, 'John Garraughty', 25 Sept. 1766, 4 Aug. 1747; Williamson quoted in Coldham, ed., *Bonded Passengers*, I. 162. See also *Md. Gaz.*, 'Joseph Manyfold', 22 Apr. 1773; *Account of the Ordinary of Newgate*, 4 June 1770, p. 43.

[3] *Md. Gaz.*, 'John Adam Smith', 6 May 1773, 'Ricely Johnson', 23 Oct. 1766; Rind's *Va. Gaz.*, 'Elizabeth Berry', 20 July 1769; *Pa. Gaz.*, 'William Cullimoor', 12 Dec. 1765; *Va. Gaz.*, 'Joshua Dean', 11 Aug. 1738. See also *Md. Gaz.*, 'William Simmons', 10 Nov. 1769, 'John Peacock', 30 Mar. 1775.

comber and stocking weaver, Thomas Lamprey, that he often begged his Maryland master to sell him farther north 'so as he might be at his trade'.[1]

Work for men and women like Lamprey, plus countless others who were unskilled, afforded scant satisfaction. In the Chesapeake, the disciplined routine of planting, hoeing, and harvesting tobacco was more demanding than what most labourers were accustomed to in Britain, and the rewards were fewer. 'It would startle even an old planter,' commented a Virginian, 'to see an exact account of the labour devoured by an acre of tobacco, and the preparation of the crop for market.' In addition, corn and wheat needed tending on the typical plantation, along with other tasks like cutting firewood, weeding vegetable gardens, and erecting fences. In Britain, traditional work rhythms were more irregular, in part because of fluctuating employment but also, as E. P. Thompson has described, because many workers had long been accustomed to performing a prescribed set of tasks at their own pace—a pace marked by 'alternate bouts of intense labour and of idleness'. In the colonies, the drudgery of field labour, the lot of most convicts, invariably became a source of hardship and deep resentment. 'Like horses you must slave, and like galley-slaves will you be used', protested William Green. A Virginia convict, Jeffe Walden, later recalled, 'I was very much discontented, that I should work 7 Years for nothing', and Robert Perkins complained that his labours included 'all the Hardships that the Negro Slaves endured'. 'What we unfortunat English People suffer here', wrote a Maryland convict to her father in London, 'is beyond the probability of you in England to Conceive, let it suffice that I one of the unhappy Number, am toiling almost Day and Night.'[2]

Not only was plantation labour for convicts more demanding, but traditional institutions that might have tempered the worst

---

[1] *Pa. Gaz.*, 'Thomas Lamprey', 16 July 1767.

[2] John Taylor of Caroline quoted in Percy, 'Agricultural Labor', p. 3; Thompson, 'Time, Work-Discipline and Industrial Capitalism', *PP* 38 (1967), 73; Green, *Sufferings of William Green*, p. 15; *Account of the Ordinary of Newgate*, 7 Apr. 1742, p. 15, 5 July 1721, p. 3; Sprigs to Sprigs, 22 Sept. 1756, in Jensen, ed., *American Colonial Documents*, p. 489. See also *Life of James Dalton*, p. 31; [Revel], *A Transported Felon's Account*, p. 9; and the ballad 'Virginny'. For tobacco, see too T. H. Breen, 'The Culture of Agriculture: The Symbolic World of the Tidewater Planter, 1760-1790', in David D. Hall, John M. Murrin, and Thad W. Tate, eds., *Saints and Revolutionaries: Essays on Early American History* (New York, 1984), pp. 255-60.

effects of heavy exploitation were comparatively weak. Their world was not buffered by families, neighbours, and local parishes. However harsh the existence of Britain's poor, many at least drew some strength from community ties. As newcomers, convicts typically found themselves on plantations with scant opportunities for a settled social life. For one thing, other labourers with whom they might have shared a common identity were sparse. Whether the setting was a small or large plantation, there were probably no more than a handful of other white servants. A study has indicated that in Anne Arundel County, Maryland during the mid-eighteenth century the average plantation with bound labour did not contain a single servant. Instead, it normally contained around ten slaves, such was the heavy reliance upon black labour by that time. In Kent County, situated across the Bay, only 48.7 per cent of white servants named in their masters' estate inventories were listed with other white workers, and only 9.2 per cent were listed with more than two whites. In contrast, 55.4 per cent of the servants were listed with black workers, 34.9 per cent with more than two blacks, and 21.5 per cent with more than five blacks. In Virginia, black workers were even more prevalent. A plantation, the tutor at Robert Carter's Nomini Hall estate noted, was 'like a Town' where 'most of the Inhabitants are black'.[1] Convicts doubtless formed friendships with labourers on neighbouring plantations, but visiting was restricted not just by the need to carry passes but by the fact that white servants constituted such a small proportion of the general population. Otherwise, convicts were left to fraternize, when possible, with other persons on the fringes of rural society, such as sailors and pedlars. During the Seven Years War, one Virginia convict spent what time she could at an army camp 'with the Soldiers'.[2]

Establishing links, both on and off the plantation, was hampered

---

[1] Philip Vickers Fithian quoted in Ira Berlin, 'Time, Space, and the Evolution of Afro-American Society in British Mainland North America', *AHR* LXXXV (1980), 73; Carville Earle, *The Evolution of a Tidewater Settlement System: All Hallow's Parish, Maryland, 1650–1783* (Chicago, 1975), p. 46; Secor, 'Working Environment of White Servants', pp. 4–5, 9. See also Galenson, *White Servitude*, pp. 177–8.

[2] *Pa. Gaz.*, 'Susannah Day', 21 Sept. 1758. See also, e.g., *Pa. Gaz.*, 'Thomas Welch', 30 Aug. 1739, 'Catherine Davidson', 13 Feb. 1750, 'John Bottin', 21 Nov. 1771; *Md. Gaz.*, 'Richard Fish', 9 Aug. 1759, 'George Tucker' and 'Alexander Connell', 19 Sept. 1765, 'Richard Crouch', 28 Mar. 1771; Rind's *Va. Gaz.*, 'Susanna Ball' and 'Anne Ellis', 7 Apr. 1774.

by additional circumstances. Along with the deep stigma transports bore from being convicted criminals, there were significant cultural divisions that pervaded the ranks of white servants. Coming from the West Country, the Scottish Highlands, Ireland, or any of the other different parts of the British Isles, newly-arrived labourers, let alone servants from elsewhere in Europe, possessed dissimilar customs and values. Eating habits, dress, pastimes, and folklore were widely diverse. Even communication between natives of different regions was sometimes difficult. Not just distinctive accents but also varied dialects hampered understanding. In the newspaper advertisement for a fugitive Welsh servant from Harford County, Maryland, his master wrote that the servant's dialect was 'not very easy to be understood by a stranger'. The owner of an Irish runaway noted that he could not speak English. Likewise, when the convict Bampflyde-Moore Carew entered a colonial gaol, 'his Ears were confused with almost as many Dialects as put a Stop to the Building of *Babel*; . . . some were of *Kilkenny*, some *Limerick*, some *Dublin*, others of *Somerset, Dorset, Devon*, and *Cornwall*'. Eddis affirmed, 'In England, almost every county is distinguished by a peculiar dialect; even different habits, and different modes of thinking, evidently discriminate inhabitants, whose local situation is not far remote.'[1]

Nor was it likely that convicts would feel a common bond with many slaves in their midst. Language formed a critical barrier, at least in the case of newly imported Africans; and because they were less expensive than acculturated slaves, these 'salt-water' slaves were usually acquired by the same sort of persons that purchased convicts, planters who possessed estates worth from £100 to £500.[2] Racial prejudice, however, constituted the primary obstacle separating plantation labourers. British convicts no doubt shared the biases of a set of Gloucestershire iron workers who, when asked in 1725 to help 'teach Negroes' their trade, angrily declared that

---

[1] *Pa. Gaz.*, 'Thomas Jones', 12 June 1776; *Va. Gaz.*, 'Thomas Ryan', 18 June 1752; Wilkinson, ed., *King of the Beggars*, pp. 166–7; Eddis, *Letters from America*, ed. Land, p. 33; Malcolmson, *Life and Labour in England*, p. 94. In his study, 'Convict Labor in Virginia', Frederick Schmidt has contended that convicts possessed a wide range of social relations on and off the plantation (pp. 229–45, 281–2). His evidence, drawn almost entirely from scattered runaway advertisements, is, however, sparse and ultimately unpersuasive.

[2] Gerald W. Mullin, *Flight and Rebellion: Slave Resistance in Eighteenth-Century Virginia* (New York, 1972), p. 15.

'they were murdering Rogues', and they 'would have nothing to doe with them'. Noted a visitor to Philadelphia shortly after the Revolution: 'A white servant, no matter who, would consider it a dishonor to eat with colored people.'[1] There were always scattered instances where servants and slaves hunted together, traded together, and made love together, but racial divisions remained deep-seated.[2]

A few convicts, against heavy odds, managed to retain a semblance of family life. In isolated cases, family members, after being transported together, were sold to the same master. In the late 1760s, for example, three members of the Smith family, Joseph and two sons, laboured at the Patuxent Iron Works in Maryland. Farther north, in Cecil County, both Mary M'Creary and her son, John, worked at Bohemia Manor. Another mother, not herself a transport, followed her son from England. 'Having no other son, and not willing to have a separation from him for ever', she journeyed to Maryland with her young daughter.[3] Most labourers, however, remained bereft of close relations. Families left behind in Britain could not easily be replaced, principally since servants were predominantly male and also forbidden from marrying without the consent of their masters. Familial ties were probably weaker in the Chesapeake among convicts than among slaves, who by the mid-eighteenth century comprised nearly even numbers of males and females. For some convicts, romantic interludes may have afforded sexual and emotional satisfaction, but rarely for protracted periods of time. Brief trysts, not enduring bonds, probably typified the romantic habits of both John Sydenham, an Annapolis convict known for a 'very amorous Disposition', and Margaret Cane, who

---

[1] William Russell to William Chetwynd, 17 Apr. 1725, Additional MSS, 29600, British Library, London (Library of Congress photocopies); Kenneth Roberts and Anna M. Roberts, eds., *Moreau de St. Mery's American Journey [1793–1798]* (Garden City, NY, 1947), p. 302. See also below, Chapter 7, p. 198. For British racial attitudes in the eighteenth century, see Peter Fryer, *Staying Power: The History of Black People in Britain* (London, 1984), pp. 150–65. Perhaps, also, slaves were leary of associating with convicts, though I found no evidence of this.

[2] See e.g. 'An Act to prevent the mischiefs Arising From the Multiplicity of Useless Dogs . . .', 1765, *Md. Archives*, LIX. 276–7; Byrd to Lynde, 20 Feb. 1736, in Tinling, ed., *Byrd Correspondence*, II. 474; Gooch to Popple, 18 May 1736, CO 5/1324 (CW microfilm).

[3] 'Extract from a Revolutionary Journal by Hugh McDonald', in Walter Clark, ed., *The State Records of North Carolina* (1895; reprint edn., New York, 1970), XI. 836; *Md. Gaz.*, 'Joseph', 'William', and 'John Smith', 17 Sept. 1767; *Pa. Gaz.*, 'Mary' and 'John M'Creary', 19 July 1750. See also *Account of the Ordinary of Newgate*, 8 June 1744, p. 4; *Pa. Gaz.*, 'John' and 'Joseph Dudgen', 26 Oct. 1774.

reputedly was fond of 'the company of sailors'.[1] Even then, such unions were discouraged, particularly for women servants lest they become pregnant. Childrearing among servants, in contrast to that among slaves, brought added expences for masters, not potential profits. For bearing an illegitimate child, the mother faced a fine or whipping plus extra service, usually a period of one year, if she could not indemnify her master for her lost labour.[2]

Some escape from the grinding toil of plantation labour came with the onset of darkness and diversions like singing and card-playing. Fiddling provided occasional entertainment, and one Maryland convict, John Jackson, owned a set of bagpipes.[3] Drinking, however, became the predominant antidote. Large numbers spent their meagre resources on liquor, and alcoholism was commonplace. Fairly typical was Matthew Humphreys in Queen Anne's County, Maryland. According to his master, Humphreys was a 'great Lover of strong Liquor' and was 'subject to get drunk whenever' the chance arose. A Maryland planter advertised his convict servant for sale 'for no other fault than that of his being too much addicted to liquor'.[4]

Life within the quarters of convicts seems to have been combative. Physical descriptions periodically mentioned swollen eyes and bruised faces. Among angry young men and women, sharp words

---

[1] *Md. Gaz.*, 'John Swain Sydendam', 19 July 1753, 'Margaret Cane', 8 Nov. 1764. See also Lower House Proceedings, 5 June 1740, *JHB* V. 417; 'An Act for the relief of parishes from such charges as may arise from bastard children . . .', 1769, Hening's *Statutes*, VIII. 377. For the Chesapeake's black population, see Allan Kulikoff, 'A "Prolifick" People: Black Population Growth in the Chesapeake Colonies', *Southern Studies*, XVI (1977), 391–428.

[2] Morris, *Government and Labor*, pp. 350–1. For penalties given women servants for bearing illegitimate children, see e.g. Richmond County Order Books, 1739–46, pp. 263, 386, 427, 1746–52, pp. 67, 86, VSL.

[3] *Pa. Gaz.*, 'John Jackson', 15 June 1758. See e.g. *Va. Gaz.*, 'Bartholomew Fryet', 14 Dec. 1739; Purdie & Dixon's *Va. Gaz.*, 'Andrew Franks', 15 Aug. 1771, 'Thomas Scott', 28 July 1774; Pinkey's *Va. Gaz.*, 'Joseph Igrum', 3 Aug. 1775; *Md. Gaz.*, 'Elisha Bond', 21 Oct. 1747, 'John Fowler', 2 Aug. 1749, 'Thomas M'Clain', 1 Mar. 1753, 'Richard Brian', 29 Aug. 1762, 'Mortimer Soles', 25 Aug. 1763, 'Daniel Boot', 26 Aug. 1764, 'George Mitchell', 26 May 1774; *Pa. Gaz.*, 'William Grace', 31 May 1750, 'Jacob Parrott', 28 May 1752, 'Edward Bradshaw', 8 Apr. 1756, 'Jacob Silcoxe', 14 Mar. 1771, 'John Robertson', 15 Aug. 1771, 'Thomas Lovely', 2 July 1772.

[4] *Pa. Gaz.*, 'Matthew Humphreys', 26 Apr. 1764; *Md. Gaz.*, 24 July 1777. For a small sample of many such instances, see *Md. Gaz.*, 'Peter Lloyd', 4 June 1752, 'John Findley', 12 Sept. 1754, 'James Hardwick', 24 May 1764, 'George Tucker' and 'Alexander Connell', 19 Sept. 1765; Purdie & Dixon's *Va. Gaz.*, 'Dennis Shields', 17 Sept. 1767, 'Thomas Philips', 11 Mar. 1773.

and heated quarrels must have been fairly common. A Virginia convict, Richard Stevens, had two 'black Eyes' and his face was 'much bruised' from 'Fighting'. Besides being 'much addicted to Liquor', Henry Talbot of Annapolis was 'a quarrelsome Fellow' with 'a great Number of Scars on his Head'. Jacob Parrott, though given to 'cringe' before those he thought 'his superiors', was 'quarrelsome and abusive to others'.[1]

Boasts made by convicts typically recounted feats of daring, courage, and physical prowess. A servant in Baltimore County, Owen Coyl, claimed to have 'broke' as many as 'seven goals in Ireland'. Transported in 1772, Samuel Carter crowed that he had been banished once before, whereas a Virginia convict often recounted how in England he had 'petitioned his Majesty, after receiving sentence of transportation', to be 'hanged' instead. William Burns of Frederick County, Maryland bore a 'large Scar on his right Arm, which he often' showed 'when in Company'. Other convicts, like Robert Milby who had served in Flanders, recounted old military adventures. Daniel Rawson, according to his master in 1764, bragged 'much of having been on board of a Man of War'.[2] Not only did such feats bolster self-esteem under degrading conditions, but they also enhanced a convict's status in the eyes of compatriots. Thus, the habitual offender Charles Aires, a 'lusty', 'well-set' felon transported at least twice, was called 'My Lord' by other transports, and Joseph Wade, who had been transported as many as four times, was a reputed 'ringleader' among his friends.[3]

No wonder colonists agonized about thieves and hooligans in their

---

[1] *Md. Gaz.*, 'Richard Stevens', 30 Dec. 1762, 'Henry Talbot', 16 Aug. 1764; *Pa. Gaz.*, 'Jacob Parrott', 28 May 1752. See also, e.g., *Va. Gaz.*, 'William Nash', 9 May 1745; Rind's *Va. Gaz.*, 'John Steel', 27 May 1773; Pinkney's *Va. Gaz.*, 'Thomas Kelly', 18 Apr. 1777; *Md. Gaz.*, 'Anthony Harper', 30 Aug. 1753, 'Anthony Cayton', 31 Aug. 1769, 'Thomas Elton', 19 Oct. 1769.

[2] *Pa. Gaz.*, 'Owen Coyl', 16 June 1773; Rind's *Va. Gaz.*, 'Samuel Carter', 3 Dec. 1772, '?', 24 Dec. 1767; *Md. Gaz.*, 'William Burns', 10 Nov. 1768; *Md. Gaz.*, 'Robert Milby', 24 Aug. 1748, 'Daniel Rawson', 27 Sept. 1764. See also *Pa. Gaz.*, 'Henry Paiton', 28 May 1767, 'John Smith', 7 Sept. 1774; Rind's *Va. Gaz.*, '?', 24 Dec. 1767; *Md. Gaz.*, 'William Hall', 13 June 1776.

[3] *Md. Gaz.*, 'Charles Aires', 31 Oct. 1765; Purdie & Dixon's *Va. Gaz.*, 'Joseph Wade', 23 July 1772. The prisoner Revd William Dodd similarly noted of convicts in Newgate: 'Hear how with curses hoarse, and Vauntings bold, Each spirits up, encourages, and dares His desperate felow to more desperate proofs Of future hardy enterprize; to plans Of Death and Ruin.' Quoted in U. R. Q. Henriques, 'The Rise and Decline of the Separate System of Prison Discipline', *PP* 54 (1972), 64.

midst. Most British convicts were young, male, and experienced troublemakers. Past crimes and reports of shipboard uprisings furnished vivid evidence of their desperate tempers. Their bodies and their spirits reflected a tough, violent way of life that directly endangered the ordered harmony of colonial society. Who could say how many servants and slaves might be corrupted by their seemingly vicious habits? Nor were convicts insignificant in number. At least in the Chesapeake, upwards of 700 may have arrived in a typical year. Within four of Maryland's most populous counties, according to the 1755 census, convict servants represented an average of over 10 per cent of all adult white males. In the colony's most populous county, Baltimore, they comprised as much as 12.6 per cent of the adult white male population. Then, too, there were still other convicts in those counties, not counted in the census as servants because their terms had already expired. Equally large numbers of convicts almost certainly laboured in Virginia's Northern Neck.[1]

Worse still, servitude only appeared to make transported felons more rebellious. As free, white, and British, most felt deeply resentful about their lot as servile labourers. 'Work', one servant boldly informed his owner, 'was intended for Horses and not for Christians.'[2] Certainly if convicts, from their masters' viewpoint, had resembled either one, life and property would have seemed much more secure.

---

[1] 'Account of Number of Souls in Maryland', *Gentleman's Magazine*, 1764, p. 261.
[2] *Life of James Dalton*, p. 31.

6

TROUBLE IN THE CHESAPEAKE?

I

One cold Virginia evening in early 1729, fire swept the ancestral home of Col. Thomas Lee in Westmoreland County. In addition to the manor house, which contained a valuable library and large sums of cash, all the outbuildings on the estate were consumed by the flames. With barely their clothes on their backs, Lee, who was 'much scorched', and his family fled out of a window two minutes before the house collapsed. A young servant girl died in her bed. In later days, all sorts of rumours abounded, but, for Governor William Gooch, the reason for the blaze was obvious. Arson was the cause, and the culprits were convicts from England. Well before arrests could be made, Gooch for one was convinced that a 'pernicious Crew of transported Felons' had started the spectacular fire.[1]

*

If for much of the century the colonies furnished a dumping ground for British criminals, what sort of impact did they have upon provincial society? Did transportation make any difference, other than 1) providing an inexpensive supply of white labour, and 2) debasing the status of ordinary servants? Previous historians have claimed that transported felons caused widespread lawlessness. One study, for instance, has written of the 'well known fact' that in Virginia and Maryland 'convict labourers were responsible for much of the crime that was committed'. Another has even concluded that they caused a 'large proportion of the crimes recorded in eighteenth-century America'.[2] But was Britain's domestic crime problem simply exported across the Atlantic? Did the Chesapeake

---

[1] Gooch to Board of Trade, 26 Mar. 1729, CO 5/1321/110-11; Harrison, 'When the Convicts Came', pp. 253-4.

[2] Oldham, 'Transportation of British Convicts', p. 241; Clinton Rossiter, *Seedtime of the Republic: The Origins of the American Tradition of Political Liberty* (New York, 1953), p. 150. See also Morris, *Government and Labor*, pp. 329, 468-9; Smith, *Colonists in Bondage*, p. 129; Sollers, 'Convict Laborers in Maryland', p. 46; Herrick, *White Servitude in Pennsylvania*, pp. 138, 141.

fall victim, as anxious colonists feared, to rising waves of turbulence and disorder? Were these colonies becoming more like the mother country in its periodically high levels of lawlessness? Or did America's expansive wilderness forestall rampant crime, perhaps by providing destitute men and women with unprecedented economic opportunity?

In the eyes of most colonists, transportation produced little improvement in the moral character of felons. Convicts, according to common opinion, remained persons of evil fame who preyed upon honest men and women. Colonists typically held them responsible for sudden outbursts of crime. As early as 1721, Maryland's Provincial Court noted that 'Criminall prosecutions and felonys' had 'much Increased' since the 'late Importations of Convicts'. Governor Gooch blamed escalating lawlessness in Virginia on 'transported convicts . . . not discouraged from repeating the same Crimes' for 'which they were Sentenced at Home'. Their villainies, he charged in 1729, were 'yet more intollerable' than the dangers posed by restive slaves. Years later when counterfeit money began circulating in Annapolis, a writer in the *Pennsylvania Gazette* pointed to the recent arrival of felons transported for coining. Even for crimes committed by the local population, convicts were sometimes held to blame. After Philadelphia authorities in May 1751 arrested a forger, one person bitterly complained, 'No doubt he has had the Advantage of being improved by the Conversation of some of those Gentry, who are sent over "for the Improvement and well peopling of the Colonies." '[1]

Transported felons plainly committed some crimes, as revealed in the detailed coverage newspapers gave to serious offences when convicts were apprehended. According to the *Pennsylvania Gazette*, a Maryland convict, before he was finally hanged in Queen Anne's County, was whipped and pilloried on four separate occasions, once for stealing a bible. Elsewhere, a runaway, after receiving food

---

[1] Court Order, Apr. 1721, Provincial Court Judgements, 1719-22, p. 362; Gooch to Board of Trade, 16 July 1732, T 1/279/99; Gooch to Board of Trade, 26 Mar. 1729, CO 5/1321/110-11; *Va. Gaz.* 30 May 1751; *Pa. Gaz.* 13 Dec. 1770. See also, e.g., *Belfast News-Letter*, 14 Feb. 1766; Petition of Franklin to House of Commons, [12-15 Apr. 1766], in Labaree and Willcox, eds., *Franklin Papers*, XIII. 241. So, too, in Jamaica, convicts were blamed for an increase in crime. The governor in 1731 claimed that local merchants, 'who used to Sleep with their doors open', were 'obliged to keep Watches on their Counting and Store houses' because of incoming felons. Hunter to Board of Trade, 13 Nov. 1731, CO 137/19/110.

and shelter from a local planter, tried to murder him in his sleep with an axe. One of the most brutal crimes of the century was, in fact, perpetrated by a 21 year-old convict in Anne Arundel County, Maryland. As recounted in various papers, one March day in 1751 Jeremiah Swift, a field servant, was busy hoeing soil for tobacco hills along with two of his master's young sons while both the master, John Hatherly, and his wife were attending a funeral. Suddenly when Swift was asked by one of the boys 'if he thought he could make a Thousand Hills before Night', he flew into a blind rage and struck the lad repeatedly over the head with his hoe. Killing him on the spot, he chased the brother more than fifty yards, delivered several blows, and left him for dead. Swift then returned to his master's house and killed his 14 year-old daughter with an axe. Yet another child, in trying to save his sister, was stabbed with a knife but somehow escaped to see Swift later tried and executed. Afterwards, the body was hung in chains not far from the Hatherly plantation.[1]

Jeremiah Swift's bloody rampage was exceptional. Just how often did transported convicts commit ordinary felonies and misdemeanours? Were they responsible for a high proportion of Chesapeake crime? Newspaper accounts unfortunately fail to provide a clear answer. During the early 1750s, for example, when public opinion held that lawlessness was on the rise, papers in Virginia, Maryland, and Pennsylvania printed frequent denunciations of transportation. Benjamin Franklin, whose own house was burgled, wrote angrily in the *Pennsylvania Gazette*, 'When we see our papers filled so often with Accounts of the most audacious Robberies, the most cruel Murders, and infinite other Villanies perpetrated by Convicts transported from *Europe*, what terrible Reflections must it occasion! What will become of our Posterity!'[2] Still, specific cases involving convicts during the early 1750s only appeared occasionally in local papers. At other times, convicts rarely received even sporadic mention, though celebrated crimes

[1] *Pa. Gaz.* 9, 16 May, 27 June 1751, 11 Dec. 1755; Council Proceedings, 26 Apr. 1751, *Md. Archives*, XXVIII. 507. For other newspaper accounts of alleged crimes by convicts, see *Pa. Gaz.* 7 July 1737, 15 May 1746, 7 May 1752, 27 Feb. 1753, 11 July 1754, 1 Dec. 1763; *Va. Gaz.* 18 Aug. 1738; Rind's *Va. Gaz.* 11 Nov. 1773; Pinkney's *Va. Gaz.* 27 Oct. 1774; *Md. Gaz.* 17 Apr., 12 June, 6 Nov. 1751, 28 Mar. 1754, 13 Feb., 17 July, 27 Nov. 1755, 27 Nov. 1766, 29 July 1773.

[2] *Pa. Gaz.* 11 Apr. 1751, 1 Nov. 1750. For reports of widespread crime, see *Pa. Gaz.* 5 Mar. 1751; *Md. Gaz.* 17 July 1751, 12 Apr. 1753.

were still reported, as were the trials of suspected offenders.[1] If newspapers furnish a reliable index at all, convicts for the bulk of the mid-eighteenth century probably committed few offences.

Another source of information consists of pamphlets, published periodically during the eighteenth century, which contain biographies of criminals executed for especially serious offences. Aimed to instruct their readers in the perils of sin, these tracts usually appeared in the wake of public hangings. Local clergy composed some of the texts, while others were penned as last testaments by the condemned themselves, and, as in the case of execution tracts in Britain, they seem to have been accurate in their biographical detail. For the years 1718 to 1783, I found pamphlets describing the lives of thirty-two colonial criminals. While this number included a variety of British immigrants, only one of the thirty-two had been a transported felon: John Grimes, who was shipped to Maryland for a London robbery and was later convicted of burglary in New Jersey. Most of the immigrants instead came to America as soldiers, ordinary passengers, or as indentured servants. Before we jump to the conclusion that convicts were not well represented among the colonies' most dangerous offenders, it must be admitted that these pamphlets do raise a methodological problem, in that they were published overwhelmingly in northern cities like Philadelphia, New York, and Boston. Although they recount some offences committed in Virginia and Maryland, they ultimately throw little light upon crime in those provinces. The most we can conclude is that, however much crime convicts may have committed in the Chesapeake, probably they were not responsible for many serious offences outside the region.[2]

Fortunately, a surer perspective can be gleaned from court records. Legal documents pose problems of their own, but they remain a more accurate source than either newspapers or execution pamphlets. Chesapeake courts, for which there are minutes, left

---

[1] See above, p. 169 n. 1.

[2] Titles of the pamphlets can be found in Charles Evans, *The American Bibliography: A Chronological Dictionary of all Books, Pamphlets, and Periodical Publications Printed in the USA, 1639–1800*, 14 vols. (New York, 1903–59) and in Roger Bristol, *Supplement to Charles Evans' American Bibliography* (Charlottesville, Va., 1970). For a discussion of colonial execution literature, see Ronald A. Bosco, 'Lectures at the Pillory: The Early American Execution Sermon', *American Quarterly*, XXX (1978), 156–76; Greenberg, *Crime and Law Enforcement in New York*, pp. 100–7.

behind a reasonably systematic record of criminal activity. There was not much chance that many misdeeds committed by convicts would pass unnoticed, for the legal system operated with considerable effectiveness. Justices of the peace, grand juries, sheriffs, and constables helped to make local courts powerful agencies of law enforcement. Convicts especially were prosecuted with the full rigour of the law since they were widely feared.[1]

The records of Kent County, Maryland shed some light on patterns of criminal activity. In addition to court records, these include lists of convicts filed in county registers; of the few registers that still remain for Maryland counties, the most complete set has survived for Kent. Situated on the Eastern Shore, the county contained a population of around 6,000 by the mid-1730s and produced tobacco, wheat, and corn. More than a few of its inhabitants were convicts, for from 1732 to 1739 as many as 271 arrived from England and had their names recorded in the county. Originating in the south-western counties of Cornwall, Devon, Dorset, Hampshire, Somerset, and Wiltshire, about 80 per cent were men, and 75 per cent were non-capital offenders. Meanwhile, during the fifteen-year period from 1732 to 1746, bills of indictment were sought in the county court against 601 men and women, mainly for such crimes as assault, fornication, and non-violent property theft, including grand larceny. The court was empowered to try all offences not punishable by death or loss of member, in other words misdemeanours and less serious felonies. Not included were slave offences, which were heard by single magistrates and for which records have not survived.[2]

Remarkably few of the 601 were English convicts, given the suspicion that they typically aroused. Based upon local lists of

[1] For the Chesapeake criminal justice system, see Hoffer and Scott, eds., *Richmond County Criminal Proceedings*, pp. ix–lxxii; Peter C. Hoffer, 'Disorder and Deference: The Paradoxes of Criminal Justice in the Colonial Tidewater', in David J. Bodenhamer and James W. Ely, Jr., eds., *Ambivalent Legacy: A Legal History of the South* (Jackson, Miss., 1984), pp. 191–201; Douglas Greenberg, 'Crime, Law Enforcement, and Social Control in Colonial America', *American Journal of Legal History*, XXVI (1982), 309–11.

[2] Kent County Bonds and Indentures, 1732–39, Kent County Court Criminal Proceedings, 1732–46, MHR; 'Maryland in 1773', *MHM* II (1907), 362. In order to consider the largest number of possible offences, all indictment bills brought before the court were counted, including bills returned *ignoramus* as well as *bill vera*. Kent's population was estimated from figures in Clemens, *From Tobacco to Grain*, pp. 215–16.

felons imported not only into Kent but also into neighbouring Queen Anne's County, probably no more than forty-one men and women fell into that category.[1] As shown in Table 12, they accounted for less than 7 per cent of all Kent prosecutions, not including those involving slaves. If those also were counted, the proportion of convict prosecutions would be even lower. Some fifteen convicts were charged with morals offences, thirteen with assault, twelve with theft, and one with playing cards on the Sabbath. Of the forty-one, there were really only twenty-seven alleged offenders, since nine individuals were each charged with more than a single offence.[2] Though 'gentlemen' ostensibly committed nearly as many crimes, leading Kent offenders mostly comprised women charged with morals offences, planters charged with assault, and white servants and hired labourers charged principally with committing crimes against property.

Possibly convicts had a greater hand in more serious crimes. County courts, such as Kent's, did not hear offences like murder, robbery, and burglary. Unfortunately, higher court records are non-existent for Virginia and patchy for Maryland; nor are there adequate lists of imported felons to match against names given in surviving Maryland indictments.[3] On the other hand, some valuable records have survived for two counties in Virginia's Northern Neck, the area that contained the greatest number of the colony's convicts. During much of the eighteenth century, the counties of Westmoreland and Richmond, like others in Virginia, employed examining courts and oyer and terminer courts to handle instances of grand larceny and more serious felonies. Examining courts functioned as pre-trial hearings to determine whether suspected felons should be released, punished in the county on a lesser charge, or should instead

---

[1] Names of alleged offenders were checked against the names of the 271 Kent convicts, plus those of eighty-three brought into the county in earlier years and those of 187 imported into Queen Anne's. Kent County Bonds and Indentures, 1719-39, Queen Anne's County Land Records, 1727-42, MHR. In addition, there may have been some Irish or Scottish convicts among the 601, but they would have been comparatively few in number.

[2] Among the twenty-seven alleged offenders, twenty were originally listed among convicts imported into Kent, and seven were among those brought into Queen Anne's. Some of these, it should be emphasized, may not have been convicts at all. Several individuals with common names, such as 'John Jones', 'Thomas Jones', and 'John Smith', were included so that possible convicts would not go uncounted.

[3] Provincial Court judgements are reasonably complete for eighteenth-century Maryland, but beginning in the mid-1720s criminal cases were often heard by circuit courts, for which minutes have not survived.

Table 12. Distribution of Kent County Criminal Prosecutions by Social Standing or Occupation, 1732–1746 (percentages in parentheses)

	Assault		Morals offences		Property offences		Miscellaneous		Total	
Convicts	13	(5.8)	15	(6.7)	12	(8.8)	1	(6.3)	41	(6.8)
Free blacks	—	—	6	(2.7)	2	(1.5)	—	—	8	(1.3)
Labourers and servants	42	(18.8)	18	(8.0)	66	(48.5)	4	(25.0)	130	(21.6)
Women[a]	22	(9.8)	157	(69.8)	31	(22.8)	1	(6.3)	211	(35.1)
Planters	86	(38.4)	21	(9.3)	22	(16.2)	6	(37.5)	135	(22.5)
Gentlemen	31	(13.8)	1	(0.4)	1	(0.7)	—	—	33	(5.5)
Other	30	(13.4)	7	(3.1)	2	(1.5)	4	(25.0)	43	(7.2)
Total	224	(100.0)	225	(100.0)	136	(100.0)	16	(100.1)	601	(100.0)

Note: a. Women who were convicts or free blacks were included under those headings.

Source: Kent County Court Criminal Proceedings, 1732–46, Maryland Hall of Records.

stand trial at the General Court in Williamsburg. Oyer and terminer courts heard felony cases involving slaves, who were acquitted or convicted and punished on the spot. Reasonably complete sets of examining and oyer and terminer records exist for Westmoreland and Richmond. Each was a mixed tobacco, wheat, and corn county; Westmoreland was bounded by the Rappahannock and the Potomac Rivers, and Richmond lay on the Rappahannock. While Westmoreland had a population of nearly 7,000 by 1755, Richmond's was slightly smaller, about 5,500.[1]

Of any Virginia county, Westmoreland may well have received the greatest number of transported felons. Not only did its expansive economy generate a need for cheap labour, but its location between the two major arteries of the Northern Neck provided several prime spots for arriving vessels to unload their cargoes. Indeed, runaway advertisements suggest that Westmoreland planters commonly employed convicts. For example, of ninety Virginia runaways for whom there are advertisements in surviving issues of the *Virginia*

---

[1] For Richmond and a helpful discussion of Virginia's court system, see Hoffer and Scott, eds., *Richmond County Criminal Proceedings*, pp. ix–lii. See also Morgan, 'Hegemony of the Law'. A few slaves were tried by examining courts rather than by oyer and terminer courts. At mid-century, slaves comprised about 45% of each county's population. All population figures are taken from Table I in Robert E. and B. Katherine Brown, *Virginia, 1705–1786: Democracy or Aristocracy?* (East Lansing, Mich., 1964), p. 73a.

Gazette from 1736 to 1759, as many as eleven of them (12.2 per cent) originated in Westmoreland. The fact that such a high proportion was from Westmoreland becomes more striking when we consider that Virginia contained forty-two counties by mid-century, many of which were located closer than was Westmoreland to Williamsburg, where the *Gazette* was published and where advertisements had to be placed. If we assume that in an average year Virginia imported nearly 300 convicts and that runaway advertisements afford a rough index of how convicts were distributed in the colony, then Westmoreland may have annually received about 35 convicts—about the same number annually imported into Kent County, Maryland from 1732 to 1739.[1]

From 1731 to 1746, years during which the callings of white defendants were given in judicial records, Westmoreland courts heard thirty-eight cases involving fifty alleged felons. Of that number, only nine were convict servants, who were examined for a total of seven crimes. Twelve defendants were slaves, while planters, tradesmen, and indentured servants made up the rest. To put it another way, on average only once every 27 months was a convict servant examined for a felony in Westmoreland—scarcely a major crime wave. Not only were convict servants not responsible for most of the serious crime committed in Westmoreland, but the vast majority of those in the county never faced prosecution for felonious offences, particularly if we estimate that from 1731 to 1746 Westmoreland may have received more than 550 transports. Furthermore, some of the nine convicts that were examined probably never should have been brought to court. In all likelihood, local anxieties over transportation were especially strong during the 1730s, after the spectacular burning in Westmoreland of Thomas Lee's manor house in 1729; though convicts were alleged to have started the fire, none were ever convicted of the crime.[2]

---

[1] Extant issues of the *Virginia Gazette* are scattered for these years, so there were far more runaway advertisements than just the ninety that have survived. My estimate of the number of convicts imported into Virginia applies to the period 1718–45. See above, Chapter four, pp. 115–16.

[2] Westmoreland County Orders, 1731–46. There were actually eight different convicts since one of the nine, George Smith, was prosecuted twice. Anti-convict hysteria may have been further inflamed in the Northern Neck by the rioting that erupted there in 1732 when tenants and small planters burned public warehouses to protest the Inspection Act of 1730 and attempts by the provincial government and wealthy planters to regulate the quality of tobacco crops. Governor Gooch for one blamed convicts for some of the unrest. Gooch to Board of Trade, 30 Mar.

Then, also, Westmoreland probably contained an unusually large number of convicts, even for a Northern Neck county. More representative, in all likelihood, was Richmond. From 1736 to 1759, advertisements in surviving issues of the *Virginia Gazette* appeared for six Richmond runaways, not as many as those that appeared for Westmoreland convicts, but average by Northern Neck standards and still quite large when compared to the numbers of runaways that absconded from counties elsewhere in the colony. Moreover, Richmond affords a better testing ground than does Westmoreland in another respect: although 'convict servants' were identified in Westmoreland records, other convicts, who were not servants, may have been examined without being identified in the records as transported felons. It is impossible to know whether that may have happened. In Richmond, on the other hand, convicts, whether or not they were servants, were specially identified so that courts could be aware of 'previous convictions in weighing the likelihood of guilt'.[1]

According to records from 1720 to 1754, Richmond courts heard 103 cases of serious crime involving a total of 143 defendants. Of the 143, only eight, or less than 6 per cent, were convicts, and they were examined for eight separate offences. Twenty-seven defendants were slaves, with other whites forming the remainder. On average only once every fifty-two months was a convict examined for a felony in Richmond, even less often than in Westmoreland. Three

1732, CO 5/1323/12-13. The allegation, however, would seem to have been groundless. For the riots, see Kulikoff, *Tobacco and Slaves*, pp. 109-12. Of course, Irish and Scottish convicts having entered the colony as indentured servants might not have been indentified as convicts in examining records, but such instances would have been sparse.

[1] Hoffer and Scott, eds., *Richmond County Criminal Proceedings*, p. 82 n. 76. Among Virginia counties, Richmond ranked fifth, along with Frederick, in the number of convict runaways for whom advertisements appeared in the *Virginia Gazette* between 1736 and 1759. Extant court records were also examined for other Northern Neck counties: King George (1721-70), Lancaster (1718-75), and Northumberland (1719-66), as well as those for Prince William (1752-57, 1759-69) and Fairfax (1749-74) lying to the north of the Northern Neck (records for Stafford have not survived). Unfortunately, clerks in these counties did not regularly record the callings of criminal defendants. For the few references I was able to find to convict-related offences, see Fairfax County Order Books, 1754-56, p. 162; King George County Order Books, 1735-51, p. 315, 1751-65, p. 648, 1766-70, pp. 91-92, 95; Northumberland County Order Books, 1762-66, p. 346. All these records are available on microfilm at the VSL.

men were examined during the 1720s, two men in the 1730s, one woman during the 1740s, and two men during the early 1750s. Indeed, the infrequency of such offences is also suggested by the diary of the the wealthy Richmond planter, Landon Carter, which over the course of fifteen years mentions occasional crimes, but none committed by convicts.[1]

The preponderance of the offences allegedly committed by Northern Neck convicts involved crimes against property—both those offences committed in Virginia and those committed originally in Britain. In the case of four Richmond convicts whose offences in Britain can be determined, two were transported for horse-stealing, one for 'theft', and one for stealing two gamecocks. In Virginia, all seventeen convicts were charged with property offences, such as housebreaking, horse-stealing, and grand larceny. The worst crime involved John Hesrock, who was charged in Richmond not only with housebreaking but also with murdering his master with an axe and throwing his mistress into a 'potatoe hole'. Asked what reason he might have had, Hesrock replied only, 'None att all that I knew of.' More fortunate was the defendant William Sherring, who was recommended for mercy by the court that examined him. Though he had reputedly stolen most of the vestments out of a church to sell for food, the court ruled that his crime resulted not from 'any Surreptitious or thievish Intention' but 'from an impaired Understanding and dispair Occasioned by the Dread of returning to his masters Service'.[2]

If patterns of criminality in Kent County, Maryland and in the Northern Neck afford an accurate index, and there seems no reason to suspect they do not, two points are reasonably clear: first, very few convicts of all those transported to the Chesapeake were ever prosecuted for committing felonies or misdemeanours; and second, the large majority of criminal acts were committed by other, 'more

[1] Richmond County Criminal Trials, 1710-54 (VSL microfilm); Hoffer and Scott, eds., *Richmond County Criminal Proceedings*, pp. 37-249; Greene, ed., *Landon Carter Diary*. The diary covers the years 1757-58, 1763-64, and 1770-78. Peter Hoffer has written that 'runaways and transported convicts' appeared 'frequently in the criminal record' of Richmond and that, along with slaves, convicts 'swelled the dockets' in the 1730s. Hoffer, 'Disorder and Deference', pp. 194, 189. However, he offers no evidence to support these assertions, and, in fact, only two convicts were brought before examining courts during the 1730s.

[2] Examination of John Hesrock, 24 Jan. 1727, Examination of William Sherring, 20 May 1754, Richmond County Criminal Trials, 1710-54, pp. 117, 352-3.

respectable' segments of the colonial population, even in areas where convict concentrations were heaviest. Colonists' apprehensions that transportation would produce waves of theft and violence were widely exaggerated. As at least one Virginian noted during a session of the House of Burgesses, it was a 'Seeming Falshood' that 'most of the Felonies' in the colony were 'perpetrated by Convicts'.[1] Contrary to prevailing fears, coffers were not emptied and throats were not slashed—not, at least, by many transported felons. Men and women, who in numerous cases bore long and chequered pasts, followed a different course in the American wilderness. Probably only the Elizabethan visionary Richard Hakluyt, in his more optimistic moments, could have predicted such a happy outcome.

II

Could economic conditions have permitted convicts to escape their criminal pasts? Away from the harsh world of Britain's labouring poor, might they have had less reason to commit property offences? As Defoe described in *Moll Flanders* and the *Life of Colonel Jack*, could they have found opportunities for material advancement—at least those convicts who were no longer servants or those fortunate enough to have escaped servitude altogether? Certainly America never had Britain's vast extremes in wealth and its large class of dependent white poor. Food shortages rarely arose, and only small segments of the colonial population were normally eligible for poor relief. In 1734, a Scottish immigrant to Virginia claimed, 'A great many who have been transported, for a punishment, have found pleasure, profit, and ease'. Echoed the French traveller Hector St John de Crèvecoeur, 'Many of those who have been transported as felons are now rich, and strangers to the stings of those wants that urged them to violations of the laws'. Earlier historians in their studies of transportation have devoted scant attention to the prospects faced by convicts. Surprisingly little light has been shed since Abbot Emerson Smith concluded that 'their ultimate fate'

---

[1] John Martin quoted in Carter, 'Journal Privately Kept of the House of Burgesses', entry of 10 Mar. 1752, in Greene, ed., *Landon Carter Diary*, I. 79.

was 'shrouded in mystery, where it is perhaps as well that it should remain'.[1]

Although cases of quick wealth were unusual, some individuals enjoyed modest success. Particularly fortunate were those that brought private funds over from Britain. Buying themselves out of servitude, they fared better than ordinary convicts. The felon George Sutton left England 'well provided of every Thing'. 'Having carried Money out with him', he arrived in Virginia and journeyed to Philadelphia where, he later recalled, he 'could have lived very well'. Son of a baronet, William Parsons received an annuity of £30 sterling, whereas the perjurer Elizabeth Canning, whose controversial London conviction in 1754 netted several hundred pounds sterling in donations from well-wishers, also enjoyed a comfortable life in exile. Transported to New England, she was reputably married and lived another twenty years until her death in Wethersfield, Connecticut.[2]

Marriage, in its own right, provided a pathway of upward mobility, for at least a few convicts profited from wedding well-to-do provincials. One woman, after being transported to Jamaica, married a local planter and later ran a tavern after his death. The thief Joseph Lewin, after first labouring for a brutal master in Maryland, was sold to an affluent widow in Pennsylvania whom he eventually married. Lewin received both land and slaves before he squandered large sums of cash in Philadelphia alehouses. On the other hand, a young Scottish servant in Charles County, Maryland noted, 'I have heard of several people by marrying advantageously ... come from nothing to something but I have heard two [*sic*] of more whose predecessors have been along while in the Country and yet are in straiting enough circumstances.'[3]

---

[1] Roderick Gordon to [?], 27 June 1734, RH 15/1/95/31, SRO; Crèvecoeur, *Letters from an American Farmer* (1782; reprint edn., New York, 1963), p. 82; Smith, *Colonists in Bondage*, p. 303. For like-minded accounts stressing the opportunities available to convict servants, see 'Eighteenth Century Maryland as Portrayed in the "Itinerant Observations" of Edward Kimber', *MHM* LI (1956), 329; Colquhoun, *Treatise on Police*, pp. 454–5; Watson, *Annals of Philadelphia*, II. 267.

[2] *Account of the Ordinary of Newgate*, 3 Mar. 1737, pp. 13–14; *Genuine Account of W. Parsons*, p. 7; *Malefactor's Register*, IV. 69; Purdie & Dixon's *Va. Gaz.* 5 Aug. 1773.

[3] Quoted in David Curtis Skaggs, *Roots of Maryland Democracy, 1753–1776* (Westport, Conn., 1973), p. 51; Knapp and Baldwin, eds., *Newgate Calendar*, I. 168; *Account of the Ordinary of Newgate*, 21 Oct. 1743, pp. 9–10.

Convicts with skilled trades generally enjoyed the best prospects. Because of economic diversification, attractive opportunities existed for craftsmen in the Chesapeake and neighbouring colonies. 'This part of the World . . .', an English visitor to America wrote in 1758, '[is] one of the Best Cuntrys I ever see for a Tradsman'. The fate of David Benfield, a thief from Oxford, was one such success story. Banished in 1771 to Maryland, he began a medical practice in Baltimore County after managing to avoid seven years of servitude. In a rambling, semi-literate letter, he informed his former Oxford gaoler, 'I have had very Great Success in My undertakings. I have folloed nothing but physick and Surgorey since I have been heare. I have Don many Good and famus Cures in old wounds.' Recounting that he had 'bisness a nuf for 2', Benfield hoped 'this yeare' to 'yearn upwards of a hundred pound'. Another convict, Anthony Lamb, upon serving out his sentence in Virginia, moved to New York where he reportedly became America's 'most celebrated and skilful optician, and maker of mathematical instruments', trades that he 'carried on' with 'great success'.[1]

But these were isolated cases. Prospects for most convicts, especially former servants without skills, were less cheering. While available opportunities may have represented an improvement over the destitution suffered by Britain's lower orders, freemen still experienced hard times. 'I Believe i was Born under a Bad planet', a former indentured servant struggling in Maryland complained, 'or Else i mite had a Trade two [*sic*] and not suffered the heate of Sun from day Break tell dark'. Benjamin Franklin, in contrast to more optimistic observers, believed that 'instances of transported thieves advancing their fortunes in the colonies' were 'extreamly rare'.[2] Some indication of how rare can be seen from a group of 145 male felons imported into Kent County, Maryland from 1732 to 1735. Of this number, only 5 men could be traced with reasonable certainty in property records for *all* of Maryland, including wills,

---

[1] Barker, Jr., to Palmer, 16 Dec. 1758, Prentis Papers; Benfield to David Whitton, 20 July 1772, in Philip Babcock Gove, 'An Oxford Convict in Maryland', *MHM* XXXVII (1942), 194; Isaac Q. Leake, *Memoir of the Life and Times of General John Lamb . . .* (1850; reprint edn., New York, 1971), p. 9; Richard Hofstader, *America at 1750: A Social Portrait* (New York, 1973), p. 63. See also Jones, *Present State of Virginia*, ed. Morton, pp. 87–8.

[2] William Roberts to John Broughton, 9 Aug. 1769, in James P. Horn, 'The Letters of William Roberts of All Hollows Parish, Anne Arundel County Maryland, 1756-1769', *MHM* LXXIV (1979), 128; Franklin Letter of 9 May 1759 in *London Chronicle*, 12 May 1759, in Labaree and Willcox, eds., *Franklin Papers*, VIII. 351.

estate inventories, and debt books, which were compilations of landholdings. Some extremely common names had to be discarded from the 145, and doubtless many individuals could not be found because of early death or emigration from the colony. Still, a good number of men probably led such obscure lives that they effectively disappeared from public records, the poor being less likely to leave wills or have inventories compiled of their estates. For obvious reasons, their names also would not have appeared among landholders in county debt books.[1]

Among the five convicts whom I was able to trace, none was well-to-do. Landholdings were found for three: John Pascoe from Cornwall, who owned at varying times from 132 to 370 acres, George Carter from Dorset, with from 50 to 175 acres, and George Batt also from Dorset, with 100. Within the Chesapeake, such men qualified as small planters.[2] Inventories have survived for three of the five convicts. James Case from Dorset, whose effects were valued at £7. 12s. 10d., owned only some clothes and a quantity of tobacco nearly ten years after his Maryland arrival. The largest estate, £71. 8s. 10d., was left by James Chubb of Cornwall, but probably John Pascoe was better off because of his landholdings. Even so, Pascoe, with possessions valued at £47. 5s. 3d., hardly lived in comfort. A non-capital felon transported in 1732, he probably never laboured as a servant, for at least as early as 1736 he owned 132 acres. At the time of his death in 1748, he was a struggling, illiterate planter with no slaves or servants and only a few livestock. Nearly half the value of his inventoried estate consisted of tobacco. Apparently Pascoe spent his years in America without family or many friends, for he bequeathed a brother in

[1] The five were George Batt, George Carter, James Case, John Chubb, and John Pascoe. Kent County Bonds and Indentures, 1732-35. For two useful analyses of probate records, see Gloria L. Main, 'Probate Records as a Source for Early American History', *WMQ*, 3rd Ser., XXXII (1975), 89-99; Daniel Scott Smith, 'Underregistration and Bias in Probate Records: An Analysis of Data from Eighteenth-Century Hingham, Massachusetts', ibid., 100-10. Female convicts were not included in the sample because the possibility of marriage, once their terms had been completed, would make them much more difficult to trace. Indeed, marriage probably represented the best opportunity open to many of them. See Carr and Menard, 'Immigration and Opportunity', p. 233 n. 59.

[2] For Pascoe, see Kent County Debt Books, 1736, fo. 49, 1743, fo. 57, 1747, fo. 83; for Carter, Kent County Debt Books, 1754, fo. 25, 1757, fo. 25; for Batt, Baltimore County Debt Book, 1754, fo. 33. Unless otherwise noted, all probate records cited in this chapter are located at the MHR.

Cornwall all of his property, including 150 acres of dubious worth named 'Pasco's Poor lot'.[1]

Maryland inventories found for scattered other convicts, besides the 145 men in the Kent sample, confirm that very few felons enjoyed even modest success. Of 395 additional males imported into Kent and Queen Anne's Counties between 1719 and 1750, inventories were located for eight who could reasonably be identified as convicts. Just one person, Peter Manley, a Devon offender transported in 1720, boasted an estate in excess of £100. A middling tobacco planter, Manley had possessions worth £190. 12s. 9d. after having been in Maryland for twenty-five years. He had one servant but no slaves.[2] More typical were John and William Pugsley, whose estates, like those of three others, were each valued at less than £40. As brothers, both came from Somerset, but John was transported to Queen Anne's in March 1736 and William to Kent later that August. When William died thirteen years later, he left a paltry estate of £29. 15s. 6d., in addition to some clothing that he willed to his brother. For his part, John, who had moved by then across the Bay to Anne Arundel County, died less than a year afterwards with an estate of about £37 to his name. Included among other items were ten and a half barrels of Indian corn (£4. 14s. 6d.), one 'old Gun much out of Repair' (10s.), six cows and other assorted livestock (£18. 9s. 0d.), some old carpentry tools (10s.), and one 'Old feather Bed, One old Rug, one Blankett, [and] one Bolster Truckle Bedstead and Cord' (£4. 10s. 0d.).[3] Men like the

---

[1] Inventory of James Case, 12 Oct. 1743, Maryland Inventories and Accounts, 28, p. 18; Inventory of John Chubb, 10 Jan. 1745, ibid., 30, pp. 293-5; Inventory of John Pascoe, 22 May 1749, ibid., 41, pp. 265-7; Kent County Bonds and Indentures, 1731-35, pp. 14-16; Kent County Debt Book, 1736, fo. 49; Will of John Pascoe, 30 Aug. 1747, Maryland Wills, 26, pp. 86-7, MHR.

[2] Inventory of Peter Manley, 10 Sept. 1745, Maryland Inventories, 32, pp. 9-11; Kent County Bonds and Indentures, 1719-44; Queen Anne's County Land Records, 1727-50.

[3] Queen Anne's County Land Records, 1729-36, p. 461; Kent County Bonds and Indentures, 1735-40, pp. 52-4; Inventory of William Pugsley, 1749, Maryland Inventories, 43, pp. 452-3; Will of William Pugsley, 10 Apr. 1749, Maryland Wills, 26, pp. 87-8; Inventory of John Pugsley, 19 May 1750, Maryland Inventories, 43, pp. 77-8. For the five remaining convicts, see Inventory of William Legg, 2 July 1722, ibid., 8, pp. 118-20; Inventory of John Grantlett, 16 Feb. [1743?], ibid., 27, p. 307; Inventory of John Hickman, 26 July 1745, ibid., 32, pp. 14-15; Inventory of Barnard Purse, 4 Apr. 1768, ibid., 104, pp. 97-8. No inventory was found for the convict Walter Freestone, but except for 600 pounds of tobacco to pay for his burial, he willed all his property to his wife, who died soon after Walter's death and for whom an inventory has survived. Will of Walter Freestone, 3 Dec. 1741,

Pugsleys did not face imminent starvation, but they enjoyed at best a coarse subsistence, marked by estates in which crops and livestock predominated to the exclusion of many personal possessions or items of furniture. The Pugsleys also represented the privileged few, better off than ordinary convicts for whom no traces can be found of their later lives.

Overcrowding and a shortage of land lay at the heart of the problem. In the mid-eighteenth century, newly freed servants trying to enter the ranks of small planters encountered severe obstacles. Besides lacking capital to buy tools, seed, livestock, and servants or slaves, few of them could afford the cost of land. Over the years, population growth, soil exhaustion, rising tobacco prices, and the spread of large plantations with increasing numbers of slaves had resulted in steadily rising property values. In Talbot County, Maryland, land prices rose from 5*s*. 5*d*. per acre at the start of the century to 9*s*. 3*d*. in the 1730s to £1. 4*s*. 5*d*. by the 1760s. The 'part of this province lying contiguous to trade and navigation, being already well peopled . . .', a Virginian observed, 'the value of Lands [is] pretty high'. A study of All Hallow's Parish, Maryland has shown that whereas one-third of adult white males did not own land around 1700, nearly half were non-landowners by the middle of the century, while in Virginia's Northern Neck, tenancy by the 1780s claimed at least half of the families. Leasing property, however, also exceeded the financial capabilities of most freemen. Father Mosley, a Maryland priest, commented in 1772, 'It has been a fine poor man's country; but now it is well peopled; the lands are all secured; and the harvest for such is now all over.'[1]

Maryland Wills, 22, pp. 460-1; Inventory of Mary Freestone, Jan. [1744?], Kent County Inventories, Box 12, folder 46.

[1] Campbell to Sinclair, 26 July 1774, GD 136/416/1/9; Mosley quoted in Hughes, *Society of Jesus in North America*, p. 342; Clemens, *From Tobacco to Grain*, pp. 231, 97-105; Earle, *Evolution of a Tidewater Settlement System*, p. 209; Kulikoff, *Tobacco and Slaves*, pp. 134-5. See also Bond to Leeds, 22 Sept. 1789, in Jameson, ed., 'Letters of Phineas Bond', p. 619; Darrett B. and Anita H. Rutman, *A Place in Time: Middlesex County, Virginia, 1650-1750* (New York, 1984), pp. 238-40; Russell R. Menard, 'From Servant to Freeholder: Status Mobility and Property Accumulation in Seventeenth-Century Maryland', *WMQ*, 3rd Ser., XXX (1973), 57-64; Carr and Menard, 'Immigration and Opportunity', pp. 233-5; Lorena S. Walsh, 'Servitude and Opportunity in Charles County, Maryland, 1658-1705', in Aubrey C. Land, Lois Green Carr, and Edward C. Papenfuse, eds., *Law, Society, and Politics in Early Maryland* (Baltimore, 1977), pp. 122-8; Main, *Tobacco Colony*, pp. 118-23; Allan Lee Kulikoff, 'Tobacco and Slaves: Population, Economy and Society in Eighteenth-Century Prince George's County, Maryland (Ph.D. diss.,

Existing conditions were kind to convicts with skilled trades, but others probably became wage labourers or, in some cases, sharecroppers by working on someone else's plantation for a part of the crop. Even then, opportunities for employment were not numerous. Years of servitude so ruined some convicts' health that no one would hire them. After the servant Henry Mainwaring was 'disabled to Work by Sickness', he was unable to 'maintain himself in the Plantations by his Labour'. Then, too, slave labour on plantations restricted opportunities for white workers. 'The lands', noted Mosley, 'are mostly worked by the landlords' negroes; and, of consequence, white servants, after their terms of bondage is out, are stroling about the country without bread.'[1] In fact, some convicts, out of indebtedness, were forced once more to become servants. In Maryland, by virtue of a 1744 act, debtors could be indentured to their creditors, which, according to a recent study, 'may only have given official sanction to an existing practice'. John Harris was originally a transported felon who 'served his time out', only to 'become a servant again' in Kent County.[2]

Compared to other white labourers, convict freemen had an especially rough lot. If an examination of discrimination towards immigrants is correct, convicts may have suffered, like indentured servants, from being outsiders without local ties and firm roots in the community.[3] Mostly, however, they were handicapped by their chequered pasts. Hence in Virginia, large numbers never received freedom dues, and, noted a contemporary, well-to-do transports, fortunate enough to purchase their liberty, were still 'looked on in a scandalous Manner'. In 1736, three such felons, including two former attornies, were 'routed out' of Philadelphia. As an exploitable source of labour, convicts were appealing to colonists, but as free labourers, unbound by the constraints of servitude, they became much less employable. In New England, the sailor John Thomson

Brandeis University, 1976), pp. 100–72; Skaggs, *Roots of Maryland Democracy*, pp. 46–7, 57–60; Hoffer and Scott, eds., *Richmond County Criminal Proceedings*, p. xiv.

[1] Report of Justice Parker, 30 Apr. 1742, SP 36/58/191; Mosley quoted in Hughes, *Society of Jesus in North America*, I. 342.

[2] Margaret M. R. Kellow, 'Indentured Servitude in Eighteenth-Century Maryland', *Histoire Sociale–Social History*, XVII (1984), 253; *Pa. Gaz.*, 'John Harris', 20 Sept. 1770. See also ibid., 'John Christie', 16 May 1771.

[3] Carr and Menard, 'Immigration and Opportunity', p. 235. See also Greenberg, *Crime and Law Enforcement in New York*, p. 104, and the suggestive runaway advertisement for Matthew Savage in Rind's *Va. Gaz.* 17 Dec. 1772.

was careful not to inform anyone that he had once been transported, for 'it would have deprived' him of his 'livelihood'.[1] Even skilled tradesmen were sometimes unable to earn a living if their origins were known. The watchmaker James Hancock, for instance, travelled to Philadelphia after 'not getting any work' in Leedstown, Virginia, where he was first transported. A free man, he found employment within days but was pointed out as a convict by a former acquaintance. As he later recalled, 'I was then drove to the necessity [to leave Pennsylvania] . . ., having no money nor friends.'[2]

*

Few convicts faced such happy prospects as William Riddlesden upon reaching America. Transported once before for stealing the communion plate out of a Whitehall chapel, he was banished a second time in the autumn of 1720. As a lawyer, he was no ordinary felon, nor did he live like one. From England, he brought a 'great Cargo of Cutlets Ware to Traffick' and an elegant mistress who reputedly possessed 'rich Silk Cloaths and a Gold Striking Watch'. Upon marrying, they resided in Annapolis, Maryland in 'great Splendor'. By one account, he was as 'famous a Convict as any in Maryland'. But Riddlesden's life of ease suddenly soured. Needing a livelihood, he petitioned for an attorney's licence, only to have his request denied. 'Twas' reported he was a Convict', a friend later recalled. His day in court came, but as a defendant charged with forging an attorney's commission from the king. Acquitted of the crime, Riddlesden next hoped for better luck in Philadelphia, where he set up shop as a tallow chandler and 'pretended to give learned Advice in the Law'. Still in need of a licence, he offered the governor's secretary 'a considerable Reward', but was rebuffed. He then pushed on to Boston but fared little better there. Further, his wife by then had left him for England. Finally in the summer of 1722, Riddlesden also sailed home, hoping, as he put it, 'to gett his bread'. After marrying a second time, he was arrested in Cambridge for returning early from transportation. Calling himself 'Corn-

---

[1] *Genuine Account of W. Parsons*, p. 7; Extract from *Whitehall Evening-Post*, 11 Dec. 1736, in *Caribbeana*, II. 189; *Old Bailey Sessions Papers*, 18–23 May 1774, p. 214. See also Eddis, *Letters from America*, ed. Land, pp. 36–7.

[2] *Old Bailey Sessions Papers*, 3–9 June 1772, pp. 226–7. See also ibid., 15–21 Feb. 1775, p. 148.

wallis', he was only discovered after trying to solicit a pardon for 'William Riddlesden'. None the less, he enjoyed a measure of good fortune. Saved from the gallows, he was again ordered for transportation in May 1723.[1]

III

While many freemen may not have experienced the economic distress that plagued Britain's poor, with some even achieving respectable livelihoods, economic opportunity does not explain ultimately why convicts committed so little crime. Not only did most freemen, at least in the Chesapeake, still have a harsh lot, but other convicts, those that remained servants, fared even worse. Despite having to endure miserable living conditions, including bad food and scanty clothing, they, too, committed surprisingly few crimes.

Perhaps the labour required by servitude provided a means of 'rehabilitation', much as some of transportation's proponents in Britain hoped. That seems unlikely, however, for, even by eighteenth-century standards, colonial work conditions were scarcely calculated to instil habits of thrift and industry. While some convicts suffered harsh, at times brutalizing treatment as servants, others, notably skilled workers and those fortunate enough to be house servants, experienced comparatively little discipline. In the absence of supervision by penal authorities, convict labour in the colonies, as the reformer Jeremy Bentham later observed, was administered not 'under regulations concerted by the united wisdom of the nation' but 'under the uncertain and variable direction of a private master, whose object was his own profit'.[2]

More important were several factors fundamental to the nature of crime in the Chesapeake and much of America. For one thing,

---

[1] *American Weekly Mercury*, 7, 14 Feb. 1721, 23 Feb. 1723; Philemon Lloyd to [?], 30 July 1722, in *The Calvert Papers: Selections from Correspondence* (Baltimore, 1894), p. 43; Deposition of James Perkins, 14 Aug. [1723], SP 35/45/33; *His Lordship* v. *William Riddlesden*, Apr. 1721, Provincial Court Judgements, 1719–22, pp. 403–5, 417–19; Deposition of George Barclay, [1723], SP 35/45/33; Petition of William Riddlesden to Lords Justices, [1723], SP 35/45/33; Report of Justice Cracherode, 28 Aug. 1723, SP 35/45/33; *The Newgate Calendar*, p. 72; Howson, *Thief-Taker General*, pp. 136–7.

[2] Bentham quoted in James Heath, *Eighteenth Century Penal Theory* (London, 1963), p. 226. See also Merivale, *Lectures on Colonization*, pp. 370–1.

though convicts were mostly exiled for crimes against property, opportunities for theft were doubtless fewer, as evidenced by the lower incidence of property offences in the Chesapeake. In 1710, the Virginia governor, Alexander Spotswood, pointed to a general absence of crime in informing the Bishop of London, 'I have observed here less swearing and Prophaneness, less Drunkeness and Debauchery, less uncharitable feuds and animositys, and less Knaverys and Villanys than in any part of the world where my Lot has been'. While in later years many colonists grew alarmed over the dangers posed by transportation, crime never became a major social problem before the Revolution. Indeed, William Byrd II, an opponent of transportation, claimed that although 'pilfering convicts [are] sent over amongst us', 'we have no such trades carried on . . . as that of house-breakers, highway-men, or beggers. We can rest securely in our own beds, with all our doors and windows open, and yet find every thing exactly in place the next morning. We can travel all over the country, by night and by day, unguarded and unarmed, and never meet with any person so rude as to bid us stand.'[1]

---

[1] Spotswood to Bishop of London, 4 Oct. 1710, in R. A. Brock, ed., *The Official Letters of Alexander Spotswood* . . . (Richmond, 1882-85), I. 28; Byrd to Boyle, 5 July 1726, in Tinling, ed., *Byrd Correspondence*, I. 355. See also *An Essay upon the Government of the English Plantations on the Continent of America–by an American* (London, 1701), p. 46; Byrd to Peter Beckford, 6 Dec. 1735, in Tinling, ed., *Byrd Correspondence*, I. 464; J. P. Brissot de Warville, *New Travels in the United States of America, 1788*, ed. Durand Echeverria, trans. Mara Soceanu Vamos and Durand Echeverria (Cambridge, Mass., 1964), p. 297; 'A Native of Philadelphia', *Pennsylvania Packet, and Daily Advertiser*, Philadelphia, 17 Nov. 1785.

To date, the most comprehensive examination of criminal prosecutions in Virginia court records has concluded that 'property was fairly safe'. 'From the viewpoint of any one locality', Arthur P. Scott has written, 'it cannot be said that crimes against property were ever alarmingly frequent.' Scott, *Criminal Law in Colonial Virgina* (Chicago, 1930), p. 238. Indeed, in an average year in Richmond County between 1720 and 1754, courts heard fewer than 3 cases involving serious property offences (i.e. grand larceny, horse-stealing, burglary, arson, robbery, etc.); in Westmoreland, between 1731 and 1746, the annual average was roughly 2. Ideally, one could show more conclusively that the incidence of theft and other property offences was generally lower in the Chesapeake than it was in Britain. Unfortunately, it would be extremely difficult to establish a workable comparison. Even if one could ascertain accurate population figures on which to base crime rates, surviving court records only measure prosecuted crime, not real crime. In the Chesapeake, where the criminal justice system operated effectively, the discrepancy between real and prosecuted crime was probably not very great, but in Britain, which had such a lax system of law enforcement, the 'dark figure' of unknown crime was considerable.

Although Byrd was prone to exaggerate, it is clear that high levels of theft normally require intensive settlement, since sufficient concentrations of moveable wealth are needed to attract criminals. Thus, London and other British cities, with their dense populations, were natural breeding grounds during the eighteenth century. They were also centres of Britain's commercial revolution. As John Beattie has written of London:

There was a huge development of commercial activity in London after 1660, a rapid increase in river traffic, in the number of warehouses and docks and in the amount of goods being transported in and out of the capital by road and water. Shops became more numerous and began to display their goods in a way that made them attractive and accessible to thieves as well as customers.[1]

In his analysis of such property offences as robbery, burglary, and shop-lifting, Beattie has found that rates in England were much higher in urban rather than rural areas. So, too, in the colonies, property offences were most common in cities, such as Philadelphia and New York. But in the Chesapeake, where a majority of convicts were transported, population density remained reasonably low throughout the eighteenth century. Whereas by mid-century 23 per cent of England's population lived in settlements of 2,500 or more people, Virginia and Maryland did not then contain a single town with 2,500 or more inhabitants. Further, levels of private opulence and commercial activity were not comparable to the wealth found in London and other cities. In the countryside by mid-century, there was a growing network of small stores, mostly Scots-operated, but their number was limited by the fact that large planters received

Prosecuted offences represented only the 'tip of an iceberg'. Ignatieff, 'State, Civil Society, and Total Institutions', p. 186. John Beattie has hypothesized that 'Sir John Fielding's rhetorical estimate that "not one in a hundred of these robbers are taken in the fact" may well have been close to the mark in some years.' *Crime and the Courts in England*, p. 149. There is also a growing body of evidence to suggest that many offences in England were dealt with, not by regular assize and quarter sessions courts, but by single magistrates and other local officials. It would be impossible to include such offences in estimates of English crime. See above, Chapter 1, pp. 29-30, and the discussion in Hoffer, 'Disorder and Deference', pp. 187-201. Yet a final problem, at least in terms of measuring serious crime, stems from the fact that figures based on British indictments are not strictly comparable with figures from Virginia examining courts, since those courts represented a pre-indictment phase in the colony's legal system.

[1] Beattie, 'Pattern of Crime in England', pp. 92-3; Greenberg, *Crime and Law Enforcement in New York*, p. 143. See also McMullan, *Canting Crew*.

most of their luxury goods directly from abroad. With fewer towns, shops, and warehouses, pickpockets, shop-lifters, and burglars were more scarce. Less commercial traffic on roads and rivers furnished fewer targets for robbers. No doubt consumer activity and commercial horizons in the Chesapeake were expanding, but there was still an element of truth in the comment of a visitor to Virginia in 1702: 'Much evil is absent there, because there is no opportunity for it.' Britain's dregs, affirmed a Maryland resident in 1770, were 'precluded' the 'Practice of those Vices' common to 'their native Country'.[1]

Nor in the Chesapeake was there a nascent criminal subculture, in itself often a product of urbanization. There were 'disorderly houses' frequented by members of the lower orders, prompting occasional criminal prosecutions to curb these and similar places of entertainment for servants and slaves.[2] But nowhere in the Chesapeake was there a growing network of night-houses, brothels, and flash pubs, such as made an important contribution to property crime on the other side of the Atlantic. Gangs remained fewer, as did receivers of stolen goods, upon whom in Britain ordinary felons, and not just professional criminals, were often forced to depend. 'In the Colonies,' claimed an English magistrate in 1754, 'where a great part of the white Tenants are Transports, Thieving is never heard of . . . . The Reason is plain, there are no Receivers.'[3]

[1] Hinke, ed., 'Journey of Michel', p. 124; Observations by Bennet Allen, 26 Sept. 1770, *Md. Gaz.* 27 Sept. 1770; Beattie, *Crime and the Courts in England*, pp. 140-264, passim; Corfield, *Impact of English Towns*, p. 9; Lorena S. Walsh, 'Urban Amenities and Rural Sufficiency: Living Standards and Consumer Behavior in the Colonial Chesapeake, 1643-1777', *Journal of Economic History*, XLIII (1983), 109-17; Greenberg, *Crime and Law Enforcement in New York*, pp. 57, 115-18, 142-5. See also King, 'Crime, Law and Society in Essex', pp. 43-53.

[2] See e.g. entry of 3 Feb. 1772, in Greene, ed., *Landon Carter Diary*, II. 649; Morris, *Government and Labor*, p. 429.

[3] Thomas Lediard, *A Charge Delivered to the Grand Jury* . . . (London, 1754), p. 24. See also *Essay upon Government of the English Plantations*, p. 46; Byrd to Beckford, 6 Dec. 1735, in Tinling, ed., *Byrd Correspondence*, I. 464; Lenman and Parker, 'State, the Community and the Criminal Law', p. 38. What gangs there were in the Chesapeake and other rural areas usually specialized in horse-stealing. Hugh F. Rankin, *Criminal Trial Proceedings in the General Court of Colonial Virginia* (Williamsburg, Va., 1965), pp. 167-9; Scott, *Criminal Law in Virginia*, pp. 222-5. Not only were horses more easily stolen than household items or store goods, but they did not require marketing by receivers. Not that receivers did not exist at all, at least in more urban areas. Of two Annapolis receivers and their involvement with a local convict, the *Maryland Gazette* reported on 17 Oct. 1765: 'Several very considerable Traders (in the Way of Receiving Stolen Goods) have lately been found out in this Town, and removed from their Lodgings to the Prison.

Moreover, theft in many parts of Britain was safer as well as easier. Law enforcement was extremely weak. Forest regions and other parts of the countryside outside the reach of constables and justices of the peace were notorious as rural rookeries and thieves' dens. Even more so, London and other large cities assured criminals of a valuable cloak of anonymity. As Adam Smith remarked, in a city a man was 'sunk in obscurity and darkness'. His 'conduct', Smith wrote, 'is observed and attended to by nobody and he is therefore very likely to neglect it himself, and to abandon himself to every sort of low profligacy and vice'. Similarly, the philosopher William Paley noted that England's 'great cities' experienced high levels of crime not only by 'presenting easier opportunities and more incentive to libertinism' but 'principally by the refuge' they afforded 'to villainy, in means of concealment, and of subsisting in secrecy'.[1]

Despite the standard British view of America as a lawless land, personal conduct in most colonial communities was more tightly regulated. Counties and towns in the Chesapeake were less populated and much smaller than those in Britain, so that courts and other agencies of law enforcement were able to operate with greater effectiveness. Also, unlike parts of Britain undergoing rapid urbanization, the Chesapeake remained a society characterized by face-to-face relationships and close neighbourhood ties. According to William Byrd II, one of the reasons for Virginia's lack of crime was 'because we have no great citys to shelter the thief'. Moral behaviour was a matter of vital community concern. The conduct

A Man and his Wife of the Name of *Burt*, were discovered to have followed that Business for a good while, by a Convict Servant Woman, who lay at the Point of Death, but being very uneasy in her Mind, she sent for her Mistress, and confessed, that she had often wronged her Master and her, by the Persuasion of those People, by Stealing of Pewter, Candle sticks, Pillows, Sheets, Pillow-Cases, etc., and that they wanted her to Steal a Bed, but she told them she could not get it out of the Window.'

[1] Smith quoted in Beattie, 'Pattern of Crime in England', p. 93; Paley quoted in Philips, 'Law-Enforcement in England', p. 162; Malcolmson, *Life and Labour in England*, pp. 111–12. See also McMullan, *Canting Crew*. In 1754, the high constable Saunders Welch, alarmed by the numbers of people who flocked to London to 'practice' their 'Knavery' after finding their 'continuance in the Country unsafe', vainly proposed that itinerant labourers be forced to carry certificates stating their name, age, previous employers, and purpose in travelling to the city. Should they not then be able to produce a certificate, any justice of the peace could 'pass such parties back to their Settlement as Rogues and Vagabonds are passed'. Welch to Lord [?], 18 Feb. 1754, SP 36/153/26.

of slaves, servants, and other 'disorderly persons' prompted special scrutiny within a neighbourhood. Constables, sheriffs, militia patrols, grand juries, and justices of the peace all were expected to help control the idle and dissolute, as, of course, was the institution of servitude, an important means of social supervision in its own right. Probably only in that way did the labour enforced on convicts help to discourage crime. Former Governor Spotswood commented in regard to a refractory convict, 'The utmost Care will be taken to keep him closely to honest Labour, to prevent so dangerous a Fellow from injuring the Publick.'[1]

Partly because of the intensity of local surveillance, convicts and other servants were more likely to commit thefts as fugitives on the run, rather than as workers employed on plantations. After absconding from their masters, they not only had greater reason to steal, but they had less to lose since they were already 'wanted' by local authorities as runaways. Indeed, of the eight convicts brought before Richmond County examining courts between 1720 and 1754, five were runaway servants. Otherwise, theft was too dangerous. When the transported felon, Charles Speckman, boldly proposed to his Virginia master that they 'go halves' in 'thieving', he was told that he had 'come into a wrong country for that'. 'Practicing theft', advised the master, 'would soon bring him to ruin'.[2]

IV

Although convicts committed little crime, given the traditional

---

[1] Byrd to Beckford, 6 Dec. 1735, in Tinling, ed., *Byrd Correspondence*, I. 464; Isaac, *Transformation of Virginia*, p. 106; *Pa. Gaz.*, 'Joshua Dean', 15 June 1738. See also Greenberg, 'Crime, Law Enforcement, and Social Control', *American Journal of Legal History*, XXVI (1982), 309–11; David H. Flaherty, 'Crime and Social Control in Provincial Massachusetts', *HJ* XXIV (1981), 339–60; Philips, 'Law-Enforcement in England', pp. 176–8.

[2] *Life of Charles Speckman*, p. 14; Richmond County Criminal Trials, 1710–54. In Richmond County, according to Gwenda Morgan, 'Most of the servants selected to appear before the examining courts were taken up in the process of escaping from their masters.' Morgan, 'Hegemony of the Law', p. 202. Westmoreland court records do not give as full a description of convict crimes as do Richmond records, so it cannot be determined how many of the nine Westmoreland convicts prosecuted between 1731 and 1746 were runaways. At least one convict, Michael Ward, was apprehended in the process of absconding from his master. Westmoreland County Orders, 1731–39, p. 175. See also the discussion below in Chapter 7 and advertisements in colonial newspapers for scattered references to crimes by runaways.

nature of colonial society, did they pose a more dangerous threat to social peace? Were fears of insurrection and mass violence in the Chesapeake ever justified? Certainly seeds of discontent were as rife among convicts as they had been among servants and other angry young men who rose up during Bacon's Rebellion and lesser seventeenth-century disturbances. Exploitation of white labourers never fully ceased with the introduction of black slavery. Further, convicts, compared to ordinary servants, had especially turbulent spirits. Mostly young and male, and boldly defiant of authority, they were neither easily cowed nor strangers to violence.

Two insurrections nearly took place. The first involved a conspiracy among a small band of Annapolis convicts in early 1721 to seize the town's arms and magazine. Whether they intended to launch a full-scale rebellion is unknown; local magistrates uncovered the plot before a single shot was fired.[1] The following decade, a slightly larger group of Irish convicts hatched an uprising in the fledgeling colony of Georgia. Plans called for setting Savannah afire and murdering scores of fleeing townspeople. Nicknamed the 'Red String Conspiracy', the uprising was quashed just as plotters identified by red strings about their wrists were beginning to assemble.[2] However unsuccessful, these conspiracies showed that convicts were prepared to rebel against local authorities and that the risk of organized resistance could never be discounted.

Chances for success, however, were extremely slim. Not only were convicts often widely dispersed, but serious divisions pervaded their ranks. Transportation brought together people of considerable diversity. In addition to their disparate cultural origins, differences in status kept convicts from forming a cohesive group with common grievances. For transports with skills or those able to buy their freedom, there was little incentive to consort with field servants. Prospects for personal success lay in achieving respectability and earning an honest living. The convict-physician David Benfield noted in 1772, 'All my old a quaintans Livs neare me but are all Sarvants which I Dont Ceep cumpany with, for I Keep the best

---

[1] Annapolis Mayor's Court Proceedings, 17 Jan., 3 Mar. 1721, pp. 26-32.
[2] Samuel Quincy to Peter Gordon, 3 Mar. 1735, Thomas Causton to Georgia Trustees, 10 Mar. 1735, Thomas Christie to Georgia Trustees, 19 Mar. 1735, Quincy to Harman Verelst, 28 Aug. 1735, in Allen D. Candler, *et al.*, eds., *The Colonial Records of the State of Georgia* (Atlanta and Athens, Ga., 1904-82), XX. 246-7, 258-9, 269-72, 462-3.

Cumpany as near as I Can.'[1] Even among the majority of men
and women consigned to servitude, strong wills and combative
personalities probably hindered internal cohesion. Convict loyalties
extended to family, community, region, country, and in some
instances, to professional gangs, but expressions of group con-
sciousness seem to have been notably faint.

A successful insurrection would also have required the support
of large numbers of slaves. Without aid from the Chesapeake's
heavily black labour force, convicts and other white servants
remained too few to mount a major uprising. Chiefly because of
racial prejudice, however, convicts rarely crossed the colour line,
and popular fears of a servile rebellion were never realized. White
and black labourers shared much in common, but gone were earlier
days when they had occasionally made common cause. White
convicts, at least in their own eyes, belonged to the master race.

There is a final explanation for why uprisings were rare and, indeed,
why convicts committed few crimes in the Chesapeake. After their
terms of servitude had expired, large numbers of them migrated to
new localities, thereby diffusing any potential threat to social peace.
Were it not for this exodus, observed a Maryland resident, 'we
should be over-run with them'. Lacking families or many friends,
they had little reason to remain in original haunts. According to
William Eddis, few convicts stayed behind since the stigma of
past crimes was 'too strong upon them to be easily erased'.
Worsening economic prospects also produced a steady stream of
migrants to other provinces and the colonial frontier. Only in new
localities did they and other poor whites perhaps find a measure
of opportunity as leaseholders and small planters. As early as 1717,
Governor Spotswood of Virginia observed, 'The inhabitants of our
Frontiers are composed generally of such as have been transported
hither as Servants, and being out of their time, settle themselves
where Land is to be taken up'. Even then, however, there were
substantial costs associated with moving and starting a plantation,
including outlays for transportation, livestock, food, equipment,
and the land itself, no matter how cheap the rent or patent price.
Probably most freemen instead became labourers, hunters, and

---

[1] Benfield to Whitton, 20 July 1772, in Gove, 'Oxford Convict in Maryland', p.
194. See also Roberts and Roberts, eds., *Moreau de St. Mery's American Journey*,
p. 297.

itinerant traders. The Pennsylvania assembly noted in 1754, 'Our Indian trade is carried on (some few excepted), by the vilest of our own Inhabitants and by convicts imported from Great Britain and Ireland.'[1]

Then, also, many convicts ran away as servants before the expiration of their terms. Plainly one reason why few convicts appeared before examining courts in Westmoreland and Richmond Counties was that large numbers of them fled the Northern Neck, as shown by the numerous runaway advertisements that appeared in the *Virginia Gazette*. Some runaways travelled to the frontier, while others headed north to urban areas such as Philadelphia and New York. Probably most, however, returned to Britain. The Atlantic, much like the frontier, afforded a critical safety valve. Almost as soon as Britain first began to transport large quantities of criminals, multitudes started returning home. 'There are great Numbers of . . . Street Robbers', London magistrates shortly complained, 'who are Felons convict returned from Transportation'.[2] Transportation was coming full circle, with a vengeance.

---

[1] 'Extract of a Letter From Maryland', 26 Apr. 1751, *Pa. Gaz.* 9 May 1751; Eddis, *Letters from America*, ed. Land, pp. 36–7; Spotswood quoted in Smith, *Colonists in Bondage*, p. 297; Pennsylvania assembly quoted in Walter Hart Blumenthal, *Brides from Bridewell: Female Felons sent to Colonial America* (Rutland, Vt., 1962), p. 41. A loyalist refugee from Georgia wrote in 1783: 'The Southern Colonies are overrun with a swarm of men from the western parts of Virginia and North Carolina, distinguished by the name of Crackers. Many of these people are descended from convicts that were transported from Great Britain to Virginia at different times, and inherit so much profligacy from their ancestors, that they are the most abandoned set of men on earth, few of them having the least sense of religion. . . . During the King's Government these Crackers were very troublesome in the settlements, by driving off gangs of horses and cattle to Virginia, and committing other enormities; they also occasioned frequent disputes with the Indians, whom they robbed, and sometimes murdered'. Anthony Stokes, *A View of the Constitution of the British Colonies . . .* (London, 1783), pp. 140–1. See also Johnson to Board of Trade, 28 May 1756, in *Documents Relative to Colonial New York*, VII. 87. For the general movement of poor whites from the Chesapeake to new areas, see Kulikoff, *Tobacco and Slaves*, pp. 52–3, 74–7, 92–9, 141–53; Rutman and Rutman, *Place in Time*, pp. 239–40; Clemens, *From Tobacco to Grain*, pp. 162–3.

[2] Westminster and Middlesex Justices to Townshend, [1720s], SP 35/67/8.

7

COMING HOME

I

During the eighteenth century, great numbers of convicts fled from their masters. Despite the harsh punishments given to runaways, escapes grew very common. A Pennsylvania farmer in 1723 remarked about a favourite servant, 'If I were sure he would stay with me, I would not part with him on any account, but being a convict for 7 years I am afraid he'll run.' Years later, William Eddis noted that for 'real or imaginary causes', they 'frequently attempt to escape'. 'Many' convicts, affirmed Benjamin Franklin, 'escape from the Servitude to which they were destined'.[1]

How often convicts absconded is difficult to gauge. Unfortunately, newspaper advertisements for runaways only furnish an incomplete guide. Probably advertisements were placed for just a small fraction of fugitive convicts. Some owners may not have thought their servants worth the price of an advertisement; for others, the inconvenience may have been too great, particularly if they did not reside near Williamsburg, Annapolis, or Philadelphia, where papers were printed. Instead, they may simply have posted notices on public buildings. Then, too, the long period of time that often elapsed between a convict's disappearance and the date of his master's notice suggests that many colonists viewed newspaper advertising as a last resort; the names of runaways caught quickly may never have appeared in print. Conversely, some owners may have avoided advertising if their servants had clearly succeeded in escaping. Finally, even when advertisements were placed, some

[1] Barcroft to his Father, 1 Mar. 1723, in Hancock, ed., 'Life in Bucks County', p. 399; Eddis, *Letters from America*, ed. Land, p. 38; Petition of Franklin to House of Commons, [12–15 Apr. 1766], in Labaree and Willcox, eds., *Franklin Papers*, XIII. 241. Of indentured servants, a North Carolinian wrote in 1716: 'White servants are seldom worth keeping and never stay out the time indented for'. John Urmstone to Secretary of the Society for the Propagation of the Gospel in Foreign Parts, 15 Dec. 1716, in William L. Saunders, ed., *Colonial Records of North Carolina* (1886; reprint edn., New York, 1968), II. 261. For similar comments, see Patrick Tailfer *et al.* to Georgia Trustees, received 27 Aug. 1735, in Candler *et al.*, eds., *Georgia Colonial Records*, XX. 366; Warville, *New Travels in the United States*, ed. Echeverria, trans. Vamos and Echeverria, p. 206.

convicts probably were identified as 'servants' rather than as 'convicts', thus making proper identification today impossible.

Even so, newspapers printed large quantities of advertisements for fugitive convicts. Papers in Virginia, Maryland, and Pennsylvania were frequently filled with notices urging their capture.[1] For the period from 1746 to 1775, for instance, when issues of the *Maryland Gazette* are reasonably complete, advertisements appeared for as many as 993 separate Maryland convicts—an average of just over 33 runaways per year.[2] If we estimate that Maryland received at least 12,000 convicts during that same period, then perhaps 9 per cent of the colony's imported felons appeared in runaway notices, particularly if we allow for those improperly identified in the advertisements as 'servants'. Clearly sizable numbers of convicts attempted to escape from Chesapeake plantations and towns.

In most respects, runaways differed little from the general convict population. A high proportion, as one might expect, were males. Of 1,401 Maryland and Virginia runaways of known gender who were listed in notices during the mid-eighteenth century, 1,328, or nearly 95 per cent, were men and boys. In so far as males composed roughly 80 per cent of all convicts, their proportion among runaways was especially high. Masters, of course, were more likely to advertise for males due to their greater value, but it is also possible that female convicts were less willing to hazard the wilderness. Not all resembled the Annapolis servant Hannah Boyer. Described as a 'very strong, fresh coloured, robust, masculine Wench' with a scar over one eye, Boyer ran off by herself in the spring of 1752.[3]

Runaways also tended to be young, though they were naturally a bit older than convicts just arriving in the colonies. Fully 580, or 59.4 per cent, of 976 fugitives with known ages were under 30 years

---

[1] All statistical compilations relating to Maryland and Virginia runaways are based on advertisements in the *Maryland Gazette* (1746–75), the *Pennsylvania Gazette* (1736–75), and the *Virginia Gazette* (1736–40, 1745–46, 1751–59, 1761–63, 1765–75). Issues of the *Virginia Gazette*, even for the years that are listed, are generally sparse, especially before 1766.

[2] Notices printed in the *Maryland Gazette* were supplemented by advertisements for Maryland runaways in the *Pennsylvania Gazette* and the *Virginia Gazette*.

[3] *Md. Gaz.*, 'Hannah Boyer', 18 May 1752. Seven runaways were not included among the 1,401 because their gender could not be determined from the notices. Runaways who absconded two or more times were only counted once.

of age, while another 253, or 25.9 per cent, were between 30 and 39 years.[1] In addition, most runaways were English, followed by a sizable proportion that were Irish. Among those whose native origins were specified, 68.3 per cent were English or Welsh, 25.1 per cent were Irish, and 3.4 per cent were Scottish, with various others making up the remainder.[2] Nor did fugitives differ significantly from other felons in their callings. Probably the large majority were common labourers, for skills of any sort were listed in just over a third of advertisements, despite the fact that masters were more likely to advertise for convicts with skills because of their greater value.[3]

In one regard, runaways were atypical. In all likelihood, they encompassed the most daring men and women in the convict population. Taking flight was an act of resistance that required uncommon boldness. In addition to the dangers of the wilds, runaways risked severe penalties if they were caught. As in the case of fugitive slaves, these included a stiff whipping and being forced to wear a heavy iron collar called a 'pot-hook' around the neck. In Maryland, runaway servants had to give ten days service for every one day they were absent; in Virginia, twice the time was required, plus extra service to help compensate masters for the costs of their recapture. Notwithstanding such penalties, an Annapolis felon, Jonathan Emyson, stoutly warned his master in 1721 that he would run away if not permitted to purchase his freedom for £10. When the master threatened to haul him before a constable, Emyson replied that 'he had been before thousands and that he did not Care'.[4]

Newspaper advertisements testified to the defiant character of fugitive convicts. 'Bold', 'forward', and 'impudent' were particularly

---

[1] Of the remainder, 116 (11.9%) were in their forties, 24 (2.5%) were in their fifties, and 3 (0.3%) were 60 years or older. See Table 15, Appendix.

[2] Native origins were given for a total of 802 runaways. See Table 16, Appendix.

[3] See Table 14, Appendix. Of course, it is possible that skilled and semi-skilled convicts, because of their privileged positions, had less reason to escape, but other factors than just mistreatment propelled runaways. See the discussion below, pp. 204-6. Moreover, tradesmen may have been more likely to flee than other servants, because their freedom of movement would have given them unique opportunities for flight. See Gerald Mullin's discussion of skilled slaves who became runaways. *Flight and Rebellion*, pp. 89-98.

[4] Annapolis Mayor's Court Proceedings, 3 Mar. 1721, p. 27; Wilkinson, ed., *King of the Beggars*, p. 170; Morris, *Government and Labor*, pp. 450-8.

common descriptions.[1] A few runaways resembled William Barrow, who reputedly bore a 'bashful Look' and was 'apt to cry if sharply examined', and a small number suffered from speech impediments, perhaps induced by fright.[2] Far more typical, however, was John Robinson, a 'hard looking man', or Sarah Robbins, who had a 'bold staring' countenance. The Maryland convict Edward Elliot was known for his fiercely 'wild Look' when 'taxed with any Thing', as was James Cole, who 'when provoked' had an 'insolent daring Aspect'. A Virginia convict 'of a very proud bold behaviour' reportedly 'set his hands on his sides when speaking' and took 'long steps with a proud air'. William Hatton, with a scar running from the corner of his mouth to his chin, had a 'very remarkable way of staring any body in the face' who spoke to him. Indeed, a Maryland resident was probably not far wrong in commenting in 1767, 'The wicked and bad of them that come into this Province, mostly run away to the Northward.'[3]

[1] See *Pa. Gaz.*, 'James Daley', 9 June 1748, 'Owen M'Vey', 7 Mar. 1753, 'John Adams', 7 Sept. 1769, 'William Manly', 15 May 1776; *Md. Gaz.*, 'Thomas Butler', 14 Sept. 1748, 'John Sergenson', 18 Apr. 1750, 'Elizabeth Hawkins', 19 July 1753, 'Thomas Ross', 9 Aug. 1753, 'James Samples', 23 Oct. 1755, 'John Jackson', 15 June 1758, 'John Smith', 17 Aug. 1758, 'Richard Fish', 9 Aug. 1759, 'John Simmons', 23 Apr. 1761, 'Robert Chant', 3 Nov. 1763, 'John Williams', 10 May 1764, 'William Bostock', 5 Sept. 1765, 'William Harriss', 22 May 1766, 'Francis Wingle', 19 June 1766, 'Stephen Pane', 25 Sept. 1766, 'Thomas Raven', 11 Dec. 1766, 'William Daniel Angess', 11 June 1767, 'John Miller' and 'John Humphries', 24 May 1770, 'John Taylor', 8 June 1775; *Va. Gaz.*, 'Robert Shiels' and 'William Roberts', 17 Nov. 1738, 'William Ferrell', 17 July 1752; Purdie & Dixon's *Va. Gaz.*, 'Edmund Cooper', 14 Apr. 1768; Rind's *Va. Gaz.*, 'Charles Sawyer', 2 June 1774; Purdie's *Va. Gaz.*, 'John Thrift', 26 May 1775, 'Thomas Hall', 11 Oct. 1776, 'Dennis Connoly', 5 June 1778. For the use of similar adjectives, like 'impudent', 'pert', 'saucy', 'impertinent', 'proud', and 'resolute', see *Pa. Gaz.*, 'James Cavanach', 16 June 1748, 'Thomas Atkins', 25 June 1752, 'Benjamin Shotton', 22 July 1756, 'Benjamin Archer', 3 May 1764, 'Edward Thompson', 29 Aug. 1765, 'Isaac Pinkeney', 17 Oct. 1771, 'Thomas Ager', 7 July 1773, 'William Manly', 8 Nov. 1775; *Md. Gaz.*, 'William Logan', 22 Sept. 1757, 'John Rodd', 5 Jan. 1758, 'Thomas Read', 7 June 1759, 'George Westall', 12 July 1759, 'Cornelius O'Neil', 1 May 1760, 'John Winter', 26 June 1760, 'Robert Miller', 15 July 1762, 'William Kneller', 28 May 1767, 'Timothy Linch', 4 June 1767, 'James Collis', 15 Sept. 1768, 'Thomas James', 18 June 1769, 'John Hickey', 2 Aug. 1770, 'Joseph Coltman', 15 Dec. 1774; Dixon & Hunter's *Va. Gaz.*, 'William Wells', 10 June 1775; Purdie's *Va. Gaz.*, 'William Armstrong', 28 July 1775.

[2] 'William Barrow', *Pa. Gaz.*, 8 Nov. 1759. For speech impediments, see *Va. Gaz.*, 'Anne Wheatley', 27 Jan. 1737; Rind's *Va. Gaz.*, 'Philip Helenford' and 'John Gonnion', 14 Apr. 1768; *Md. Gaz.*, 'Samuel Coleman', 7 Oct. 1747, 'Thomas Poney', 18 Sept. 1755, 'John Ware', 11 Sept. 1760, 'Benjamin Saltee', 18 Sept. 1760, 'Giles Truelock', 3 June 1762, 'Evan Morris', 10 July 1766, 'John Evans', 4 Sept. 1766, 'Charles Campbell', 30 Apr. 1767, 'John Barrot', 4 June 1767.

[3] Purdie & Dixon's *Va. Gaz.*, 'John Robinson', 23 June 1768; *Pa. Gaz.*, 'Sarah

Less than half of all fugitives absconded without the aid of other runaways, and, either by choice or necessity, they travelled by themselves. For a majority of runaways, however, who fled in small groups, compatriots provided practical assistance and moral support. William Neilson, for instance, the 'ringleader' and spokesman for several Scottish runaways, was literate enough to forge passes for the entire band. Similarly, when the Maryland felon John Thomas escaped with another servant in 1769, he reportedly planned to 'rig his Companion, as well as he' could with 'spare Cloathing' that he had carried off.[1] Significantly, convicts seldom escaped with persons outside their own ranks. Of 836 with companions, as many as 685, or 81.9 per cent, fled with fellow convicts. Eighty-seven absconded with indentured servants, while especially few, only thirty-nine fugitives, joined up with slaves or free blacks, despite the preponderance of black labourers in the Chesapeake. Racial and cultural divisions remained deep-seated among plantation workers. Blacks with whom convicts did abscond were often acculturated and reasonably fluent in English. Sometimes they had valuable skills or possessed special knowledge of the surrounding countryside. The slave who fled with two Maryland convicts in a sloop during the spring of 1754 spoke passing English and was a 'good Hand by Water'. Another slave who ran off with a Maryland felon was 'supposed to be conducting him' along 'back Roads' with which he was well 'acquainted'.[2]

Robbins', 14 Apr. 1773; *Md. Gaz.*, 'Edward Elliot', 17 Dec. 1772, 'James Cole', 16 Oct. 1751; Rind's *Va. Gaz.*, 'Christopher Fiddes', 19 Oct. 1769; *Pa. Gaz.*, 'William Hatton', 15 Sept. 1768; 'A. B.', *Md. Gaz.*, 30 July 1767.

[1] *Md. Gaz.*, 'William Neilson', 18 June 1767, 'John Thomas' and '?', 2 Mar. 1769. Of 1,479 Maryland and Virginia runaways, 643 absconded by themselves, while 836 were in league with one or more persons.

[2] *Md. Gaz.*, 'John Wright' and 'John Smith', 4 Apr. 1754, '?', 2 May 1754. See also *Pa. Gaz.*, 2 Oct. 1729, 'Thomas Overton', 9 June 1743, 'John Parsons', 3 Nov. 1743, '?' and '?', 30 May 1751, 'John Child' and 'John Penmore', 8 Mar. 1764; *Va. Gaz.*, 'Edward Ormsby', 3 Feb. 1738, 'Daniel Young', 11 May 1739, 'Thomas Waters', 9 May 1745; Rind's *Va. Gaz.*, 'James Penticost', 21 Sept. 1769; Pinkney's *Va. Gaz.*, 'Charles White' and 'James Leighton', 23 Nov. 1775; *Md. Gaz.*, 'Robert Harrison', 20 Sept. 1749, 'Richard Cox', 21 Oct. 1756, 'William Bostock' and 'Richard Purchase', 5 Sept. 1765. Servants and slaves might have been slightly deterred from running away together in Virginia because there servants who absconded with slaves were, if caught, 'required to serve additional time technically owed by the black' (Rutman and Rutman, *Place in Time*, p. 264 n. 13); however, in Maryland, which does not seem to have had such a penalty, servants and slaves ran away together with no greater frequency.

Runaways absconded during every month of the year, but, as one might suspect, most ran while the weather was relatively warm. Of 963 men and women for whom months of flight are known, 691, or 71.8 per cent, ran off from April to September.[1] Travelling by foot represented the most common mode of escape, but ample numbers, if they were good riders, stole horses. For fugitives with access to boats, the Chesapeake's broad inlets and numerous estuaries furnished paths of flight. The Virginia convict Richard Kebble escaped down the Rappahannock River during a make-believe fishing expedition. After sailing 60 miles, he went ashore and fled into the woods. More ambitious was the flight of six felons who similarly absconded by means of the Rappahannock. Upon reaching the Chesapeake and the mouth of the York River, they left their boat and stole a small sloop from an elderly man and his son. The fugitives set out towards New York, but contrary winds kept the vessel adrift until it was overtaken by an English man-of-war.[2]

On land, runaways normally hid in the woods and rested by day and travelled by night.[3] Possessions were kept to a minimum, extending mostly to clothing, blankets, and food. Tools were sometimes taken, at least by craftsmen hoping to ply their trades as freemen.[4] Occasionally, more personal belongings were included. Three felons from Baltimore County took with them a 'large black spaniel dog', while a runaway from nearby Anne Arundel County carried along a razor and an 'old day-book'.[5] Some took firearms, swords, or other weapons for hunting and self-defence. In 1768, when the fugitive Michael Conaway was threatened with capture, he 'pulled out of his Bosom' an 'old rusty Bayonet'. One runaway,

---

[1] Table 17, Appendix. Two related reasons why so many ran off between April and September are that convicts often absconded soon after arriving in the Chesapeake, normally in late spring and summer, and the work regimen on plantations was the most severe at that time. See below, pp. 205–6.

[2] *Genuine Account of the Malefactors*, p. 7; *Pa. Gaz.*, 2 Oct. 1729.

[3] *Account of the Ordinary of Newgate*, 7 Apr. 1742, p. 15, 8 June 1744, pp. 3–5; *Genuine Account of the Malefactors*, p. 7; *Discoveries of John Poulter*, p. 28; *Pa. Gaz.*, 'William Manly' and 'Thomas Pearson', 15 May 1776.

[4] See e.g. *Va. Gaz.*, 'Thomas Rennolds', 24 Sept. 1736; *Md. Gaz.*, 'David Rawl', 9 Sept. 1746, 'John Swain Sydenham', 19 July 1753, 'William Gafford', 10 Aug. 1769, 'Jessee Jordan', 2 Nov. 1769; *Pa. Gaz.*, 'Edward Houlton', 13 Mar. 1750, 'William Voice', 31 Aug. 1769, 'John Dudgen', 26 Oct. 1774.

[5] *Pa. Gaz.*, 'John Clark', 'James Wood', and 'John Ancell', 21 Aug. 1766; *Md. Gaz.*, 'George Holt', 31 July 1777.

before fleeing from a copper works in western Maryland, armed himself with a stick of explosives.[1]

In some instances, runaways took the opportunity to pilfer goods from surrounding towns and plantations. Besides stealing horses and boats for quick escapes, they carried off clothes and provisions. Before running from Baltimore County, the Irishman Michael Kelly told a fellow servant that having 'no money', he planned to 'plunder' and 'change his apparel the first opportunity'. A Virginia convict heading for the Rappahannock pilfered from milk-houses along the way. From these, he obtained bacon, greens, and bread to supplement a chicken stolen out of a hen-house. At least a few convicts indulged heartier appetites. In 1770, John Chambers stole as much as £150 in cash from his Baltimore master. The Williamsburg servant of two wigmakers, by contrast, filched a parcel of wigs which he later sold on his way up the James River. The master of two convicts from Prince George's County, Maryland warned that being 'great villains' they would 'steal any thing that is in their way'.[2]

Often the unwitting victims of runaways happened to be fellow workers. Access was easy enough to servant belongings, and convicts evidently felt few binding ties to other labourers. In late 1768, four Virginia convicts allegedly 'robbed the rest' of their master's 'servants' of various items before fleeing. Similarly, the runaway Absalom Spruce stole numerous 'clothes from his fellow servants' when he absconded one summer. Prized articles included servant indentures by which fugitives hoped to disguise their identities. If indentures included service discharges or temporary passes, runaways were even more fortunate. When Francis Irwin fled in 1759, law-abiding colonists were warned that he would try

---

[1] *Md. Gaz.*, 'Michael Conaway', 23 June 1768, 'John Raner', 31 Oct. 1754. See also *Va. Gaz.*, 'William Kitchingman', 9 Mar. 1739; Purdie & Dixon's *Va. Gaz.*, 'Thomas Kerr', 22 Dec. 1768; Rind's *Va. Gaz.*, 'Richard Hatton', 23 July 1767; *Md. Gaz.*, 'Francis Murray', 24 June 1746, 'Robert Milby', 24 Aug. 1748, 'Robert Harrison', 20 Sept. 1749, 'Thomas Butler', 12 Sept. 1750; 'Joseph Rainbird' and 'James Cole', 16 Oct. 1751, 'Richard Fish', 9 Aug. 1759, 'Benjamin Archer', 26 Apr. 1764, 'William Robertson', 30 Aug. 1764; *Pa. Gaz.*, 'John Malone', 26 Sept. 1765, 'Michael Hayne' and 'Nathaniel Powell', 14 Dec. 1769.

[2] *Pa. Gaz.*, 'Michael Kelly', 14 Sept. 1769; *Account of the Ordinary of Newgate*, 8 June 1744, pp. 3-5; Purdie & Dixon's *Va. Gaz.*, 'John Chambers', 22 Mar. 1770; *Va. Gaz.*, 'William Byrn', 10 Nov. 1752; Pinkney's *Va. Gaz.*, 'Francis Matthews' and 'Michael Conroy', 21 Sept. 1775.

to pass for 'Stephen Stiffert', having 'Stole his Indentures with a Discharge thereon'.[1]

To increase their prospects for success, runaways employed all sorts of masquerades. Adopting aliases was an elementary ruse, as was forging passes, for the small minority that was literate. A Maryland convict, for that purpose, took 'Pen, Ink, and Paper with him'. Fugitives also shaved their heads and switched clothes. For evening camouflage, a pair of Virginia convicts 'blacked' themselves with coal and tallow carried off in a kettle. In 1758, the Maryland owner of a runaway named 'Elizabeth' thought she would 'probably pass for a Soldier's Wife' or might even 'dress herself in Man's Apparel'. Some tried to pass as paupers or cripples, such as the runaway who pretended he was a beggar whose tongue had been 'cut out by the Indians'. Yet more ingenious was Sarah Wilson, a former servant in the queen's household who was transported to Maryland in 1771. After about a year, Wilson fled to South Carolina where she masqueraded as Princess Matilda, sister of the queen. Her Maryland master belatedly recalled that she had made 'a common practice' of marking 'her cloaths with a crown'. Another report recounted:

She travelled from one gentleman's house to another under these pretensions, and made astonishing impressions in many places, affecting the mode of royalty so inimitably, that many had the honour to kiss her hand; to some she promised governments, to others regiments, with promulgations of all kinds, in the Treasury, Army, and in the Royal Navy.[2]

[1] Purdie & Dixon's *Va. Gaz.*, 'William Alexander', 'Edward Williams', 'Henry Johnson', and 'George M'Key', 28 Jan. 1768, 'Absalom Spruce', 16 Aug. 1770; *Md. Gaz.*, 'Francis Irwin', 8 Mar. 1759. See also *Pa. Gaz.*, 'John Wilson', 20 June 1744, 'Joseph Holmes', 13 June 1754, 'Joseph Fisher', 6 Sept. 1759, 'Joseph Holland', 8 Oct. 1761, 'William Blake', 7 July 1768, 'John London', 7 Sept. 1769, 'John Fowler', 7 Dec. 1769, 'William Smart' and 'John Brown', 2 Aug. 1771, 'John Collier', 7 July 1773; *Va. Gaz.*, 'Isabella Pierce', 9 May 1745; Rind's *Va. Gaz.*, 'John Abbott', 'Philip Clerk', and 'Thomas Conner', 26 Jan. 1769; *Md. Gaz.*, 'William Jefferies', 10 June 1756, 'William Mansfield', 9 Mar. 1758, 'James Griffitts', 11 May 1758, 'William Collett', 20 Sept. 1759, 'Benjamin Williams', 14 Aug. 1760, 'James Groves', 20 Sept. 1764, 'Joseph Clark', 16 May 1765, 'William Lewis', 29 Aug. 1765, 'Henry Glover', 3 Apr. 1766, 'John Sandels', 'John Hawkerday', and 'Edward Thompson', 17 Apr. 1766, 'John Tink', 11 June 1772, 'Joseph Lamb', 10 Dec. 1772.

[2] *Md. Gaz.*, 'Joseph Green', 23 Apr. 1767, 'John Benhan' and 'John Miller', 5 May 1768; *Pa. Gaz.*, 'Elizabeth', 21 Sept. 1758, 'John Williams', 3 Nov. 1763, 'Sarah Wilson', 19 May 1773. For Wilson, see also the separate news report in ibid. Of 1,408 runaways mentioned in ads, there were references either to forgery or to the ability to write for 156.

Fugitives were forced to rely mostly upon their own wits. In contrast to the extended networks of friends and relatives that harboured runaway slaves in many areas of the plantation South, places of refuge were extremely scarce. Popular apprehensions about transported criminals and an absence of close relations both worked against broad-based support among the lower orders. Exceptions were infrequent, such as when the Irish convict Mary Floyd was 'harboured and entertained a considerable Time' in Annapolis. Similarly, in 1745 two runaways from Caroline County, Virginia were reportedly concealed in Norfolk by a 'lame Shoemaker, and a Woman of Evil Fame', both of whom also had once lived in Caroline.[1] Otherwise, convicts were left to depend upon fellow runaways, though even then bonds of friendship sometimes fell victim to ruthless self-interest. In 1758, the Maryland servant John Syms, soon after absconding with a 'drunken school-master', stole his compatriot's clothing and books.[2]

Despite problems of food and shelter that fugitives faced in the wilderness, chances for escape were probably good. For one thing, convicts, as opposed to slaves, could more easily blend into the free population. A person in 1735 noted the problem of determining 'whether they were Servants or not', whereas 'Negroes' could 'always be known and taken into Custody'. Moreover, because of their smaller value, there was less incentive to try to retrieve convicts, ordinarily a long and costly undertaking if one advertised in newspapers or sent out a party of searchers. 'It is very expensive to find them and bring them back', a person observed of runaway servants. Small planters, for whom convicts represented a significant investment, were likely hampered by limited resources. The Maryland planter Thomas Saunders lost practically everything except for his land when his 'irich Convict servant' robbed him of his horse and the 'Chief' of his and his wife's 'Cloaths'. Saunders, who was forced to mortgage the land in order to get by, later lamented

---

[1] *Md. Gaz.*, 'Mary Floyd', 21 Jan. 1768; *Va. Gaz.*, 'Thomas Butler' and 'Thomas Proby', 23 May 1745. For slave networks, see Philip D. Morgan, 'Colonial South Carolina Runaways: Their Significance for Slave Culture', in Gad Heuman, ed., *Out of the House of Bondage: Runaways, Resistance, and Marronage in Africa and the New World* (London, 1986), pp. 57–78; Mullin, *Flight and Rebellion*, pp. 106–12, 117–21; Peter H. Wood, *Black Majority: Negroes in Colonial South Carolina from 1670 through the Stono Rebellion* (New York, 1974), pp. 248–9, 263–8.

[2] *Md. Gaz.*, 'John Syms', 7 Sept. 1758. See also, e.g., ibid., 'Matthew Jolly', 'Henry Kirk', and 'Terrence Flanagan', 27 May 1746; *Life of James Dalton*, p. 32.

to a friend, 'I never heard of him since'.[1] Newspaper notices announcing the capture of runaways were sparse, as were county court hearings during which masters petitioned to have the service of apprehended fugitives extended. Of seventeen convicts from Westmoreland and Richmond Counties who appeared in surviving runaway advertisements between 1737 and 1757, I only found hearings in the court records of those counties for two: Bryan Kelly and William Barber, who ran off together from Richmond in August 1737 and were captured twenty-five days later.[2]

Certainly runaways were fiercely determined. The fugitive Jeffe Walden, when threatened with capture by his master's blacksmith, proclaimed that he 'was upon hasty Business' and 'no Man should stop' him. 'Chusing rather to suffer Death than to go back', Walden struck the smith with a 'Hedging Bill' and fled. Similarly, John Oulton, after being overtaken by an overseer in Baltimore County, grabbed a knife and stabbed his pursuer in the chest.[3] When at first unsuccessful, convicts made repeated attempts to escape. References in newspaper advertisements to iron collars and fresh whippings attested to their dogged persistence. The master of fugitive convict Moses Long alerted readers, 'The fellow maybe easily known, being cut on his back and Arms from a late whipping he had, on his attempting to run away, the night before.' One convict, reputed to be a 'notorious villain', ran away as many as four times within his first eight weeks in Maryland. Just as

---

[1] Tailfer *et al.* to Georgia Trustees, received 27 Aug. 1735, in Candler *et al.*, eds., *Georgia Colonial Records*, XX. 366; Warville, *New Travels in the United States*, ed. Echeverria, trans. Vamos and Echeverria, p. 206; Saunders to Theadosia Saunders, 9 Oct. 1756, quoted in Isabel M. Calder, ed., *Colonial Captivities, Marches and Journeys* (1935; reprint edn., Port Washington, N.Y., 1967), p. 153.

[2] Richmond County Order Books, 1732-39, pp. 551-2. See also Smith, *Colonists in Bondage*, p. 269; Morris, *Government and Labor*, pp. 453-8. I also looked for the names of the seventeen in claims filed before courts by individuals who may have sought legal restitution for retaking them. Records were checked not only for Westmoreland and Richmond but also for the other Northern Neck counties of King George, Northumberland, and Lancaster (records for Stafford have not survived). The name of only one fugitive was found, and that is a questionable case since the claim may have stemmed from an earlier incident in which the convict, John Berry, absconded and was caught. Northumberland County Order Books, 1737-43, p. 72. Of course, some of the seventeen may have been apprehended elsewhere, for claims were filed in counties where runaways were caught. Some runaways may also have been retaken by their masters, who would not have filed claims to be compensated.

[3] *Account of the Ordinary of Newgate*, 7 Apr. 1742, p. 15; *Pa. Gaz.*, 11 Apr. 1754.

determined was Edward Houlton, transported from London in 1743. Sold to a baker, he shortly absconded. After being caught and purchased by a ferry boat operator, he again ran away. Three masters and three flights later, it would seem that he was at last successful.[1]

Convicts absconded for many reasons. There were always scattered numbers, for example, who fled because of the sudden dislocation resulting from a change in owners. The Maryland felon David Hughes ran away soon after the death of his Charles County master. Upon being retaken and sold to a Virginian, he escaped again.[2] Crime by convicts sometimes prompted sudden departures, such as when George Washington's house painter 'Stole a good deal' of 'Paint and Oyl' and 'apprehensive of Justice ran off' from Mount Vernon.[3] Strife within servant quarters was a cause, for among fugitives described with bruised eyes from boxing, no doubt some were attempting to flee from local ruffians.[4] And, too, a few runaways absconded in search of loved-ones. When a fugitive woman from the Fredericksburg area fled in 1774, she supposedly hoped to rejoin a former lover labouring as a silversmith in Norfolk. According to her disgruntled master, the smith would originally 'have married her if her temper had not been too disagreeable'. Another runaway tried to travel as far as New York, where he had an uncle. On the other hand, very few convicts possessed wives, kin, or close friends to encourage even local jaunts. Unlike slaves, who often absconded to nearby towns and plantations to visit blood relatives, felons rarely fled from plantations with thoughts of ever returning.[5] Hopes were tied instead to speedy flight and escape.

[1] *Pa. Gaz.*, 'Moses Long', 21 Aug. 1746, 'Edward Williams', 25 Aug. 1773, 'Edward Houlton', 13 Mar. 1750. See also above, Chapter 5, p. 150 n. 1.

[2] *Md. Gaz.*, 'David Hughes', 18 May 1748.

[3] Washington quoted in Abbot communication, 14 May 1986. See also, e.g., *Va. Gaz.*, 'Daniel Whealan', 12 Dec. 1745; *Pa. Gaz.*, 'James Spencer' and 'Patrick Byrne', 13 Aug. 1747; *Md. Gaz.*, 'Edward Hooper', 21 Dec. 1769.

[4] See e.g. above, Chapter 5, pp. 164–5.

[5] Rind's *Va. Gaz.*, 'Susanna Ball', 7 Apr. 1774; *Md. Gaz.*, 'William Newcomb', 19 Mar. 1767. See also, e.g., *Va. Gaz.*, 'Thomas Lee', 5 May 1738; Rind's *Va. Gaz.*, 'Anne Ellis', 7 Apr. 1774; *Pa. Gaz.*, 'Jacob Parrot', 27 Mar. 1753; 'Richard Delany', 17 July 1776; *Md. Gaz.*, 'John Tongue', 29 Mar. 1764, 'Thomas Moore', 17 Aug. 1769; Rind's *Va. Gaz.*, 'Philip Vaughan', 1 June 1769. For visiting by slaves, see Morgan, 'Colonial South Carolina Runaways', in Heuman, ed., *Out of the House of Bondage*, pp. 57–78; Mullin, *Flight and Rebellion*, pp. 106–10, 129; Wood, *Black Majority*, pp. 248–9; Kulikoff, *Tobacco and Slaves*, pp. 343–4, 379–80.

Many runaways sought to flee the grinding regimen on plantations. While loose supervision by careless owners spurred occasional flights,[1] brutal and degrading conditions of servitude
constituted a far more common cause. John Read's despair resulted
in 'several efforts' to 'escape from his slavery and bondage'. After
repeated failures, he planned to hang himself, which, he later
recounted, he was 'fully determined to do, had he not succeeded
in his last escape'. Jeffe Walden, who was 'very much discontented'
with his work, commented after his flight, 'My Thoughts were
always taken up in meditating my Escape'. Similarly, Samuel Ellard,
after being sold to a planter who 'used him very cruel', became
'determined if possible, to run away; and accordingly, the very first
Opportunity he had, he embraced'. Nor did convicts have much
incentive to stay where they were, inasmuch as many of them never
had the opportunity to learn a trade or even to receive freedom
dues once their terms expired.[2] Without a prospective stake in
society, they had less reason to invest years of hard labour under
the Chesapeake sun.

Above all, convicts were unable to re-create a world that might
have lent greater meaning to their lives. Without families and other
institutions that helped to ameliorate everyday life in Britain,
grounds for discontent grew even greater. Separation from home
and family invariably became a source of despair, in many cases
more pressing than physical mistreatment. Consequently, owners
such as Thomas Smyth of Kent County, Maryland expressed
genuine bewilderment over the flight of their servants. 'This is the
third time', wrote Smyth of his servant, 'he has run away without
the least reason.' Ten years later, another master bemoaned how
three convicts, having 'lived extremely well', had 'gone off, without
any Cause of Complaint'.[3] In fact, most convicts first tried to

---

[1] See e.g. *Md. Gaz.*, 'John Winter', 26 June 1760, 'James Lowe', 27 July 1769;
Purdie & Dixon's *Va. Gaz.*, 'William and Hannah Daylies', 26 Mar. 1767.

[2] *Account of the Ordinary of Newgate*, 4 June 1770, p. 43, 7 Apr. 1742, p. 15, 7
Nov. 1744, p. 5. See also ibid., 5 July 1721, p. 3, 3 Nov. 1725, p. 4; *Life of Charles
Speckman*, p. 15; *Old Bailey Sessions Papers*, 8–15 Sept. 1773, p. 397. To help
ensure that his servant John Barton, an 'Outlawed Smuggler', served him 'faithfully
Seven Years', Charles Carter, a King George County, Virginia justice of the peace,
took the highly unusual step of agreeing to pay Barton the sum of ten pounds for
each of the 'two last years of his Servitude' once they were completed. Servant
Bond, 3 Mar. 1750, King George County Orders, 1735–51, p. 658.

[3] *Pa. Gaz.*, 'Benjamin Shotton', 22 July 1756, 'John Sandels', 'John Hawkerday',
and 'Edward Thompson', 17 Apr. 1766. See also Purdie & Dixon's *Va. Gaz.*, 'John
Booker', 13 Aug. 1772.

abscond, not after years of wearying labour, but soon after their arrival in the Chesapeake. Of 188 runaways for whom dates of landing in the colonies were given in newspaper advertisements, over half fled within the first four months, and over three-quarters ran away during the first year. In contrast, only eleven of the 188 fled after having been in America for more than three years.[1]

Favourite destinations included crowded urban areas like Philadelphia and New York, which offered anonymity and the chance of employment. 'In which Places no Questions are asked', an English criminal noted of colonial cities. Lodging could easily be had at taverns, notorious in northern cities for concealing servants and apprentices. 'The environs of this city very much abound' with 'abominable [tavern] houses', a Philadelphian complained in 1772.[2] Cities also offered better prospects for thieving than did the Chesapeake countryside. Benjamin Franklin believed that runaways often wandered 'at large from one populous Town to another' committing 'many Burglaries Robberies and Murders'. Another person claimed that convicts 'did not rob' in Virginia and Maryland but 'in the neighbouring' provinces. The Maryland runaway Levy Barnett, after first fleeing to Philadelphia, was apprehended for robbing the cabins of five vessels in New York harbour.[3] Still other runaways travelled to western Pennsylvania, the North Carolina frontier, and other sections of the backcountry. Prospects of being

[1] See Table 18, Appendix. These figures are slightly biased because masters were not as likely to advertise for more 'senior' servants with fewer years of service to perform.

[2] *Discoveries of John Poulter*, p. 28; Philadelphian quoted in John K. Alexander, *Render Them Submissive: Responses to Poverty in Philadelphia, 1760–1800* (Amherst, Mass., 1980), p. 62; Morris, *Government and Labor*, p. 424; Greenberg, *Crime and Law Enforcement in New York*, pp. 97, 198.

[3] Petition of Franklin to House of Commons, [12–15 Apr. 1766], in Labaree and Willcox, eds., *Franklin Papers*, XIII. 241; Testimony of Campbell, 15 Apr. 1778, *JHC* XXXVI. 928; *Pa. Gaz.*, 'Levy Barnett', 18 June 1767, and report of his New York arrest, 24 Sept. 1767. A person observed in 1753, 'It is remarked at *Philadelphia*, that of the great Number of Criminals, for several Years past executed there, scarce any of them were Children of *America*, or honestly came over for a Settlement in the Country.' 'Publicus', 15 Mar. 1753, in Livingston *et al.*, *Independent Reflector*, ed. Klein, p. 168. Shortly after the Revolution, another claimed, 'Philadelphia is to be considered as the harbour and the refuge of numerous criminals, whom detection has driven from other states'. 'Native of Philadelphia', *Pa. Packet and Daily Advertiser*, 17 Nov. 1785. See also, e.g., *Pa. Gaz.* 1 Dec. 1763; Herrick, *White Servitude in Pennsylvania*, p. 227. On the other hand, it seems unlikely that convicts were ever responsible for more than a small fraction of urban crime in northern colonies. See above, Chapter 6, p. 170.

caught were not as likely farther west, and opportunities were better for acquiring land. At least a few runaways reportedly absconded to western Maryland hoping to find jobs at iron forges.[1]

For the vast majority of convicts, however, passage home was always the paramount hope. Even before he was transported, the convicted robber John Smith vowed that 'America should not hold him fourteen years, nor two neither.' Of a convict in Maryland whom no one would buy, a factor predicted, 'If I turn her about her business . . . she will certainly come home'. Newspaper notices frequently alerted readers that runaways would attempt to board vessels bound for Britain, and shipmasters were strictly warned from admitting suspicious passengers. 'It is more than presumeable', declared an advertisement for a Virginia runaway, 'he will endeavour to pass as a sailor, and get on board some ship or vessel, which all masters of such are hereby forewarned, at their peril, from indulging him in.' As shown in Table 13, there were 294 runaways with discernible destinations given in newspaper advertisments. Of this number, as many as 198, just over two-thirds, were thought to be planning ultimately to board ships. In addition, some of those heading for such seaports as New York, Philadelphia, Baltimore, Annapolis, and Norfolk doubtless had similar intentions. By contrast, very few runaways expected to remain in the Chesapeake. 'I will soon bid farewell to Virginny', affirmed a convict ballad.[2]

With such a thriving trans-Atlantic trade in the mid-eighteenth century, vessels regularly embarked for British ports. Only during wartime were shipping opportunities restricted. Along with major seaports, river towns and private landings afforded spots for boarding. In 1768, two runaways from Frederick County, Maryland were thought to be headed down the Patuxent River 'offering themselves to man any Vessel going to Sea'. A few years later, a pair of Fredericksburg convicts were 'observed' on the banks of the Rappahannock, 'hailing two schooners bound down the river'.

[1] Purdie & Dixon's *Va. Gaz.*, 'Joseph Loveday', 8 July 1773; *Pa. Gaz.*, 'Stephen Richards', 24 July 1776; *Md. Gaz.*, 'Samuel Woolridge', 15 Apr. 1773.
[2] *Old Bailey Sessions Papers*, 15–21 Feb. 1775, p. 144; Factor quoted in Coldham, ed., *Bonded Passengers*, I. 50; Purdie & Dixon's *Va. Gaz.*, 'Arundale Carness', 29 Aug. 1766. In the case of runaway slaves for whom newspaper notices could be found reporting their capture, Gerald Mullin found a 'high correlation between the subscribers' estimates of their runaways' destinations and the jailers' publication of where the runaways were intercepted'. *Flight and Rebellion*, p. 188. For 'Virginny', see above, Chapter 2, p. 64 n. 2.

Table 13. Destinations of Maryland and Virginia Runaways[a] (percentages in parentheses)

Destination	Runaways	
Boarding a ship[b]	198	(67.4)
Philadelphia	29	(9.9)
New York City	13	(4.4)
Backcountry[c]	10	(3.4)
Virginia sites	10	(3.4)
Maryland sites	7	(2.4)
Carolinas	6	(2.0)
Other[d]	21	(7.1)
Total	294 (100.0)	

Notes: a. Fugitives who ran away more than once were included as many times as they absconded. In addition to the 294, there were 28 other runaways who were not counted because two or more possible destinations were given for each of them. Their destinations, however, largely resembled the ones given above.

b. Includes runaways whose masters warned shipmasters not to take them aboard their vessels. Not included, however, were runaways reputed to be trying to pass as sailors.

c. Includes the Chesapeake backcountry in addition to other frontier areas.

d. Thirteen runaways travelling to northern colonies; 4 looking for work; 2 heading for 'seaports'; and 2 intending to enlist in the army.

Likewise, the owner of Mary Davis predicted that she would 'make toward Rappahanock, as she was often inquiring whether many Vessels lay there'.[1]

Chances for escape improved dramatically once runaways reached ocean-going vessels. In all likelihood, passage across the Atlantic was easier and cheaper than flight overland to the backcountry. For those without funds, there was always the possibility that they could steal or earn the passage price. In 1764, a Maryland master believed that his servant, William Dove, having 'no Money with him', had 'got into Business, in order to get Money to pay his Passage home'.[2] Occasionally, a vessel's crew smuggled runaways aboard, though more frequently, convicts enlisted as sailors to work

---

[1] *Md. Gaz.*, 'William Simmons' and 'William Burns', 10 Nov. 1768; Purdie & Dixon's *Va. Gaz.*, 'John Booker' and 'John Libiter', 21 June 1770, 'Mary Davis', 21 Jan. 1773. See also, e.g., *Md. Gaz.*, 'Bartholomew Savage', 27 Aug. 1761; ibid., 13 Oct. 1774; Dixon & Hunter's *Va. Gaz.*, 'William Wells', 10 June 1775; *Account of the Ordinary of Newgate*, 5 July 1721, p. 3. Douglas Hay has drawn attention to the fact that transports were more likely to return during peacetime, because of the disruption wars caused to shipping, in 'War, Dearth and Theft', pp. 142-3.

[2] *Pa. Gaz.*, 'William Dove', 2 Aug. 1764.

their way back to Britain. Shipmasters, despite repeated warnings from irate planters, commonly signed fugitives aboard, in some cases paying them for their labour.[1] Ships that helped to rid Britain of dangerous criminals returned home with mounting numbers of desperate runaways. As in the convict trade to America, commercial priorities loomed large in the illicit traffic home. Pressed to bolster their crews, captains showed far more interest in stout bodies than in pure hearts.

II

Runaways began returning to Britain almost as soon as the first shiploads of felons started to arrive in the Chesapeake. Within a decade of the Transportation Act, a steady flow had commenced to London, Bristol, and other ports. 'Great Numbers have been come back', Bernard Mandeville noted in 1725, 'before half their Time was expired'.[2] Helping to fuel this exodus were still other convicts who never laboured as colonial servants. As we have seen, they escaped the gruelling lot of plantation workers by purchasing their freedom. Other sources of discontent in the colonies, ranging from poor economic opportunities to social ostracism, drove them home before the end of their terms. Transported for theft, Thomas 'Handy' Johnson, for example, only returned to England after failing to find work. Because he was a convict and had a withered right hand, 'Nobody there', he subsequently lamented, 'would employ or give him any Thing.' Similarly, John Oney, was 'so aged'

[1] *Md. Gaz.*, 'Bartholomew Savage', 27 Aug. 1761, 'William Simmons' and 'William Burns', 10 Nov. 1768, 'James Holmes', 7 Sept. 1775; ibid., 13 Oct. 1774; Purdie & Dixon's *Va. Gaz.*, 'John Booker' and 'John Libiter', 21 June 1770; Dixon & Hunter's *Va. Gaz.*, 'William Wells', 10 June 1775; *Discoveries of John Poulter*, p. 28; *Account of the Ordinary of Newgate*, 8 June 1744, p. 6; *Malefactor's Register*, III. 99; Thomas Molland, *Special Grace Uninterrupted, in its Egress . . .* (n.p., 1775), p. 23.

[2] Mandeville, *Enquiry into the Frequent Executions at Tyburn*, p. 47. See also [Defoe], *Applebee's Weekly Journal*, London, 26 Jan. 1723, in Michael F. Shugrae, ed., *Selected Poetry and Prose of Daniel Defoe* (New York, 1968), p. 214; Westminster and Middlesex Justices to Townshend, [1720s], SP 35/67/8; Townshend to [?], 8 Oct. 1728, PC 1/4/86; Ollyffe, *Essay Offer'd for an Act of Parliament*, pp. 11–12; Hare, *Sermon Preached to the Societies for the Reformation of Manners*, pp. 29–30; *Va. Gaz.* 28 Jan., 30 Dec. 1737, 13 July 1739; *London Evening Post*, 4 Nov. 1738; 'Heads of a Bill for the more effectual and easy Prosecuting . . . Felons Returned from Transportation', 31 Jan. 1739, SP 36/152/111; Newcastle to Attorney and Sollicitor Generals, 6 Mar. 1752, SP 44/134/116–17; [Shebbeare], *Letters on the English Nation*, I. 146; *Discoveries of John Poulter*, pp. 28, 44.

and 'infirm' that 'no one would buy, or employ him'. After having 'rambled' and 'begged about the Country, for a considerable Time', he was placed aboard a ship to England, reportedly 'against his Will'.[1]

Like fugitive servants, other felons also felt pulled by ties of family and country. Familiar people and surroundings exerted a powerful attraction. Banished for life, John Pringle, a Scotsman, travelled home 'to his Native Country in order to see his parents'. The robber Thomas Butler, though he 'was not unmindful of his Sentence of Banishment', felt 'a strong Desire to see *London*, and know whether his old Friends and Companions were yet in Being'.[2] Some men also worried about the ability of their families to make ends meet without their help. John Meff returned to England in 1721 because he was 'over desirous to see how' his 'Wife and Children fared'. 'I was resolved', he observed afterwards, 'to return at all Adventures'. Hearing that 'his wife and children were in the parish work-house', the Londoner John Creamer returned to 'work in the country' and 'send for' his family. Another convict, transported for smuggling, came home because his wife and seven children were 'destitute of Bread'.[3]

Just as strong, in many instances, were loyalties to organized gangs. Among returning felons, members of British gangs were amply represented. They also enjoyed advantages not shared by ordinary convicts. By the mid-eighteenth century, bands possessed a rudimentary network of contacts spanning both sides of the Atlantic. 'It is well known', complained a set of Virginians in 1749,

[1] *Account of the Ordinary of Newgate*, 18 Sept. 1727, p. 3; *Old Bailey Sessions Papers*, 16–21 Oct. 1728, p. 3. See also, e.g., Petition of Riddlesden to Lords Justices, [1723], SP 35/45/78; *Old Bailey Sessions Papers*, 3–9 June 1772, pp. 226–7. In addition, there were always a few convicts who returned to Britain against their will. Thomas Huddle and James Goswell were carried home after being impressed aboard British ships, whereas the pilot William Lee, after being court-martialled in America for the loss of a vessel, was sentenced to imprisonment in London's Marshalsea prison. *Old Bailey Sessions Papers*, 3–5 Sept. 1746, p. 260, 13–16 Sept. 1758, pp. 309–10; Report of Justice Abney, 15 Apr. 1749, SP 36/110/188. See also Petition of John Grayling to King, n.d., SP 36/150/83.

[2] Petition of John Pringle, [1720?], JC 3/10/281; *Account of the Ordinary of Newgate*, 11 Oct. 1752, p. 138. See also Petition of Blewitt to Townshend, n.d., SP 36/150/137; *Account of the Ordinary of Newgate*, 10 Mar. 1735, p. 13, 3 Mar. 1737, p. 6, 18 Mar. 1740, p. 20.

[3] *Select Trials . . . at the Sessions-House in the Old Bailey . . .* (London, 1734), I. 56; *Account of the Ordinary of Newgate*, 5 Aug., 14 Oct. 1772, p. 13; Petition of John Harvey to Newcastle, n.d., SP 36/150/163. See also Petition of Hugh Kelly to Townshend, n.d., SP 36/154/142.

'that they [i.e. convicts] hold a Correspondence with the Gangs of Theives they came from'.[1] Gang connections in the colonies at times consisted of nothing more than informal reunions, such as when Joseph Gillard and William Burk, two hardened British felons who happened to be travelling in America, took a detour through Maryland to 'see some of their old acquaintances, who had been transported thither from England'. Similarly, William Riddlesden, after being transported to Maryland in 1720, spent much of his time in Annapolis 'jollily carrowsing with some of his Associates', who had recently bought 'off their Servitude'.[2]

But often gang associations were more purposeful. In most cases, their primary design was to funnel transported members home as quickly as possible. Before convict vessels left British ports for America, some bands paid shipmasters to guarantee that compatriots were not sold in the colonies as servants. According to John Poulter, a former gang member, the normal fee was 'about ten Pounds Sterling', though 'some give more and some less'. Once they had crossed the Atlantic, passage home was easily arranged. 'As there are Ships coming home every Week, if they can pay their Passage they are refused in no ship', commented Poulter. The notorious thief and receiver of stolen goods Mary Young returned early on two occasions with the aid of funds received from her gang. One-tenth of the band's 'great Booty' had been 'laid up to support any of them that fell into Trouble'; so that when she was twice transported, she was 'plentifully provided with Necessaries'.[3] Some gangs even had agents in colonial ports to speed the safe return of comrades. The English alderman John Hewitt protested in 1763 that a Coventry band had 'Friends ready as soon landed in America to purchase their Liberty, and a Fund established to defray the Expence of their Return'. Indeed, when ten years earlier Capt. John Fall, a leader of the 'Coventry Gang', and his wife returned to Britain after less than a year in exile, they 'brought over with them' as many as 'fourteen other transports'. On another occasion, two gang members named Richardson and Douglass happened to arrive in Annapolis on separate ships. Richardson,

[1] Council Proceedings, 11 Apr. 1749, *LJC* II. 1035.

[2] *Account of the Ordinary of Newgate*, 17 Mar. 1755, pp. 38, 41; *American Weekly Mercury*, 14 Feb. 1721.

[3] *Discoveries of John Poulter*, p. 28; *Gentleman's Magazine*, 1741, p. 162. For further details about Young, who was hanged in 1741, see Linebaugh, 'Ordinary of Newgate', pp. 265-6.

having purchased his freedom, boarded Douglass's vessel and carried off two of his best suits. By selling them on shore and adding some of his own funds, he was able to secure his friend's liberty for £10.[1]

Significantly, perhaps, gangs never showed much interest in extending illicit activities to the colonies. Some English bands maintained connections in Ireland and on the Continent,[2] but, despite the presence of numerous transported felons, attempts were not made to organize criminal ventures across the Atlantic. Maybe no need existed to expand their operations, or perhaps communications problems would have proven too immense. Incentive, however, must also have been lacking because America seemed backward and provincial. Mary Young, after being transported to Virginia in 1738, reportedly returned early to England upon discovering that 'Business in her Way [i.e. as a receiver of stolen goods] could not be transacted there'. According to one account, she 'soon found that America was a country where she could expect but little emolument from the practices she had so successfully followed in England'.[3]

Whatever the precise reasons, gang members rarely spent prolonged periods of time in the colonies. Along with hundreds of fugitive servants, they routinely boarded ships bound for British ports. While less menacing malefactors remained securely in America, the 'most desperate and audacious' criminals, as a set of London magistrates pointed out, crossed the Atlantic in worrisome numbers.[4] Like prodigal sons, wastrels and thieves returned home freed from the wilderness. Whether many had been redeemed by it remained less certain.

III

America held little interest for the likes of James Dalton. Born

[1] Hewitt to Halifax, 17 July 1763, SP 44/139/253; Hewitt to Halifax, 22 Nov. 1764, Deposition of John Smith, 31 July 1763, Deposition of Patrick Reif, 8 July 1763, in [Hewitt], *Journal of J. Hewitt*, pp. 207, 143, 130.

[2] See e.g. Knapp and Baldwin, eds., *Newgate Calendar*, I. 367; Howson, *Thief-Taker General*, pp. 142–4, 173–4; Beattie, *Crime and the Courts in England*, p. 164; Hay, 'Crime, Authority and the Criminal Law', p. 162.

[3] *Account of the Ordinary of Newgate*, 18 Mar. 1741, p. 7; *The Newgate Calendar*, p. 18.

[4] Westminster and Middlesex Justices to Townshend, [1720s], SP 35/67/8.

in St Sepulchres parish in London, at the age of 5 he had seen his father hanged at Tyburn. Not that the experience afforded much of a deterrent, for by his eleventh birthday, he, too, had started thieving, and after numerous robberies he found himself in 1720 sentenced at the Old Bailey to transportation. Placed aboard the *Honour* for Virginia, Dalton and fifteen other prisoners mounted an uprising during a fierce storm. Seizing the ship, they sailed for two weeks until they reached the Spanish coast, where they scrambled ashore. Supplied with money and provisions off the vessel, they made their way to Amsterdam and successfully got shipping back to England. Committing new crimes, Dalton was arrested and sentenced to hang for returning early. Due to a royal pardon, however, he avoided the gallows and again was transported, though he first tried to escape by smuggling a file inside a gingerbread cake. Arriving safely in Virginia, he was sold to an Irishman, from whom he soon attempted to abscond. On a second try he succeeded and signed aboard a vessel bound for Bristol. There Dalton was apprehended once more, though only for housebreaking because court officers knew nothing of his background. After being transported a third time, he remained a servant in Virginia long enough to threaten his master with a knife and to be caught after escaping first to North Carolina and later to New York. Not surprisingly, his master agreed to discharge him for £10—'he finding me not to be ruled', Dalton later observed. During the next few years in America, he worked for a boat pilot, fathered an illegitimate son, and was sold back into servitude for a fresh theft. Upon running away, he returned to London and committed yet new robberies. Convicted at the Old Bailey, Dalton was hanged in 1730. If America could not keep him, Britain would.[1]

*

Capital punishment was the penalty normally reserved for returning fugitives. Although offenders could hope to be pardoned, royal mercy was shown only in a minority of cases. Fewer than one-third of convicted offenders at the Old Bailey between 1749 and 1771 received pardons. To ensure the effectiveness of transportation,

[1] *Life of James Dalton*; Howson, *Thief-Taker General*, pp. 139–40, 310.

crown officials were determined to punish offenders harshly in the hope of deterring additional convicts from re-crossing the Atlantic. Towards the same end, rewards were offered by proclamation and later by statute for the conviction of fugitives. 'If once such Criminals', warned Sir John Fielding, 'could flatter themselves that they might return Home before their Time with a Possibility of Safety it would immediately fill our Streets with Pickpockets and Housebreakers, and our Roads with Footpads and Highwaymen'.[1]

In most cases, however, prospects were surprisingly good for remaining at large without being caught, and very few fugitives were ever captured and hanged. At the Old Bailey from 1749 to 1771, only thirty-one people were sentenced to death for returning early from transportation. On the Midland assize circuit, even fewer, six, received the death penalty during roughly the same period, while on the Home circuit, from 1755 to 1775, seventeen were sentenced to hang. Some fugitives, of course, were apprehended and convicted for other capital crimes and, as a consequence, were not prosecuted for returning early, but probably a great majority of fugitives succeeded in escaping detection. A London resident complained in 1737 that though large numbers returned 'when they please', there was 'no Notice taken of them'.[2]

Much of the problem stemmed from Britain's traditionally weak system of law enforcement. At a time when watchmen and other amateur guardians laboured under a heavy administrative and judicial workload, it was not difficult for clever fugitives to avoid detection, particularly those that did not return to their original neighbourhoods. Since criminal information was not routinely circulated between different jurisdictions, magistrates had little way of knowing the identity of returned convicts if brought before them for other offences. Then, too, watchmen were notoriously susceptible to bribery. 'There are some Watchmen in the City of *London*', a

---

[1] Fielding to Suffolk, 1 Feb. 1773, SP 37/10/11; Howard, *Account of the Principal Lazarettos*, p. 255; Radzinowicz, *History of English Criminal Law*, II. 63; Beattie, *Crime and the Courts in England*, p. 52. See also Report of Justice Parker, 30 Apr. 1742, SP 36/58/191. Only Scotland mandated a different punishment, by which means convicted felons were to be kept in prison and subjected to monthly whippings until they could be successfully re-transported. See Gilbert Hutcheson, *Treatise on the Offices of Justices of the Peace . . . in . . . Scotland . . .* (Edinburgh, 1806), I. 181.

[2] *Va. Gaz.* 30 Dec. 1737; Howard, *Account of the Principal Lazarettos*, pp. 255, 253; *British Parliamentary Papers: Report from the Select Committee on Criminal Laws . . . 8 July 1819* (Shannon, Ireland, 1968), Appendix 7, pp. 168-9. See also *London Evening Post*, 23 Dec. 1738.

convicted burglar declared in 1744, 'as great Rogues as any living'. More than a few London magistrates, or 'trading justices' as some were called for living by their judicial income, also were known for illegal dealings. 'Some of whom', remarked Edmund Burke, 'were notoriously men of such infamous characters that they were unworthy of any employ whatsoever'.[1]

Prosecuting returned felons posed further problems. To guarantee successful convictions, former trial records and transportation certificates needed to be produced, along with witnesses willing to confirm the identity of suspected offenders. At the Old Bailey, fugitives were often acquitted due to insufficient evidence. Although Thomas Floyd remained in exile less than seven years, he was freed because the record of his original conviction was missing. A convict in 1747 escaped the gallows when court officials discovered that the wording in his transportation order had been irregular. Indeed, a London resident observed: 'It is certain Numbers do return from Transportation; but it being so much Trouble to bring them down to the Old Bailey, prove them to be the Persons transported, and that did the Fact transported for, that People don't care for the Trouble of it'. A Parliamentary committee in 1739 noted how 'Justices find themselves under great difficulties how to Act under any Informations laid before them against such Felons with regard to the Evidence to Justify a Commitment and compelling proper Persons to Prosecute'.[2] Largely because of bureaucratic obstacles, watchmen were even slower than they might have been to apprehend fugitives. Rather than place them in custody, warnings were usually given not to remain in public. In 1772, when John Law was arrested by a London watchman, he had already received repeated admonitions to stay in hiding. 'I have seen him several times in

---

[1] *Account of the Ordinary of Newgate*, 8 June 1744, pp. 9-10; Burke quoted in Philips, 'Law-Enforcement in England', p. 163; Styles, 'Problem of Criminal Investigation', pp 132-5; Landau, *Justices of the Peace*, pp. 184-5. See also, e.g., *Old Bailey Sessions Papers*, 18-24 Sept. 1765, p. 318, 12-18 Jan. 1774, p. 61.

[2] *Va. Gaz.* 28 Jan. 1737; 'Bill for Prosecuting Felons Returned from Transportation', 31 Jan. 1739, SP 36/152/111; *Old Bailey Sessions Papers*, 15 Jan. 1777, p. 81, 29 Apr.-1 May 1747, p. 140. See also, e.g., ibid., 12-15 Oct. 1726, p. 8, 4-7 Dec. 1728, p. 7, 10-12 Oct. 1733, p. 208, 17-22 Apr. 1751, p. 157, 11-18 Sept. 1751, p. 250, 17-20 Apr. 1765, p. 133, 8-15 Sept. 1773, p. 430, 16-26 Feb. 1774, p. 126; *London Evening Post*, 4 Nov., 23 Dec. 1738; Newcastle to Solicitor-General, 15 Dec. 1739, SP 44/131/222; 'An act for the more easy and effectual conviction of offenders found at large within the kingdom of Great Britain, after they have been ordered for transportation', 1743, 16 George II, c. 15; *Annual Register*, 1765, p. 81; Knapp and Baldwin, eds., *Newgate Calendar*, II. 359.

Smithfield since he returned from transportation,' the watchman later observed, 'and have begged of him to get out of the way, for fear I should have charge of him.'[1]

To be sure, fugitives risked capture if they carelessly returned to their original haunts and consorted freely in public. One thief was arrested in London after openly threatening to kill all the city's watchmen. Another, upon hearing that the man who had prosecuted him for robbery had been placed in Newgate for debt, boldly went to see him at the prison gate. 'You are in the Inside, but I am Without', he taunted the man. During a second visit, the fugitive was arrested after the debtor grabbed him through the bars. The thief Richard Hutton, after spending only a few months abroad, came home to the very London neighbourhood where local officials had known him well. A turnkey, James Aylomer, later testified that he had 'locked him up' in past years a 'great many times'. Enough rumours spread of Hutton's whereabouts for him shortly to have found himself in the hands of two watchmen. At a cost of thirteen and a half guineas to his humble father, Hutton kept his freedom and the watchmen left in peace. Unhappily, though, he pressed his luck. Captured once again, he was told that if he 'would raise a friend', he would be set free. 'My father', Hutton explained afterwards, 'had not money to give them, so they took me to gaol'. Convicted at the Old Bailey, he received the death penalty.[2]

Fugitives also had to fear informants and snitches, or old neighbours wishing to settle private scores. In 1726, a London watchman captured the thief Benjamin Aldridge, only because a quarrel between Aldridge and a woman caused her to charge him with returning from transportation. Another fugitive lived for two years with his aged mother 'in good Reputation' until 'some Evill disposed person thro' Envye Caused him to be taken up'. Equally unfortunate was the fate of John Steele. After coming home to England to see his wife, Steele found that she had forsaken him to remarry. Worse still, the new husband, Isaac Ely, had him arrested and placed in gaol. Ely, protested Steele at his trial, 'now swears against me only to get rid of me, that he may have my wife to

[1] *Old Bailey Sessions Papers*, 9–16 Dec. 1772, p. 33.

[2] *Pa. Gaz.* 17 Feb. 1742; *Old Bailey Sessions Papers*, 5–10 Dec. 1753, pp. 11–12, 11–14 Sept. 1754, p. 297; Md. Shipping Returns, 1746–75; Coldham, ed., *Bonded Passengers*, III. 78. See also, e.g., *Account of the Ordinary of Newgate*, 6 Nov. 1723, p. 4, 11 Oct. 1752, pp. 138–9.

himself'.¹ Otherwise, returned felons stood a good chance of being arrested if they were seen committing new crimes. After apprehending a convict with a bag of stolen goods, the watchman William Godfrey told him, 'Had I seen you without any thing about you, I should have taken no notice of you, but I fear you are got to your old trade again, and I think it is my duty to stop you'. Similarly, though the former burglar Thomas Peak had 'often been desired to keep out of the way', he was arrested when found in the home of a receiver of stolen goods.²

For some men and women, returning home brought new opportunities for respectability and honest labour. Convicts with ready means of employment stood the best chance of becoming law-abiding citizens. Samuel Ellard, who earned upwards of 30*s.* a week as a porter in a London fruit market, 'behaved himself very honestly and industriously'. He later recalled, 'Tho' several knew of his former Misfortune, yet did he work in this manner for two Years together, and none offered to molest him'. The Hampshire convict James Brown travelled to Buckinghamshire, 'where he thought no body would know him' and 'where he lived honestly, and his Master liked him well'. Another convict, who through the aid of his brother succeeded in becoming a tailor's apprentice, was reputed to be 'very industrious and assiduous in his Business'.³

What proportion of felons, after returning home, attained honest livelihoods is impossible to calculate. Probably, however, there were as many, if not more, who turned once again to crime. Many contemporaries, in fact, were convinced that fugitive convicts constituted a major cause of spiralling crime rates. Typical was Lord Townshend's belief in 1728 that a recent spate of London robberies was 'greatly to be imputed to the unlawfull return of Felons Convict, who have been transported to his Majesty's

¹ Petition of Elizabeth and Rachell Witham to King, [7 Sept. 1720], SP 35/23/44; *Old Bailey Sessions Papers*, 13–15 Oct. 1725, p. 7, 31 Aug.-3 Sept. 1726, p. 8. See also Petition for William Morton, 8 Dec. 1772, JC 3/37.
² *Old Bailey Sessions Papers*, 12–15 Sept. 1764, p. 285, 20–7 Feb. 1771, p. 119. See also, e.g., Petition for Pringle, [1720?], JC 3/10/281; Thomas Gisborne *et al.* to [Newcastle], 23 July 1735, SP 44/128/415–16; Lord Rochford to Lady St Leger, 22 Aug. 1771, SP 37/8/188; *Account of the Ordinary of Newgate*, 7 Apr. 1742, p. 16; *Old Bailey Sessions Papers*, 2–7 May 1764, pp. 189–90, 21–8 Oct. 1772, p. 439.
³ *Account of the Ordinary of Newgate*, 7 Nov. 1744, p. 6; *Va. Gaz.* 30 June 1738; *Account of the Ordinary of Newgate*, 1 June 1752, p. 75. See also, e.g., *Gentleman's* Magazine, 1763, p. 410; Petition of Liskerett Officials and Inhabitants to [?], n.d., SP 36/150/8.

Plantations'. Ten years later, a newspaper report affirmed: 'Robberies are become very frequent, which it's reckoned to be in great Measure owing to the Numbers that get off yearly, (after Conviction) by Transportation'.[1]

Instances were legion of convicts who became workaday criminals. A few like William Burk, who 'stole many things in the voyage' from America, did not wait until they had reached Britain.[2] Henry Cole, after returning to London from Virginia, committed upwards of twenty burglaries before he was finally caught, whereas Joseph Johnson, working in league with four compatriots, travelled for many years throughout the English countryside filching money from unsuspecting farmers.[3] Such was the high rate of recidivism that felons not uncommonly found themselves transported more than once during their lifetimes, at least those who managed to escape being hanged for returning early. Some were transported two or three times, while one receiver of stolen goods in London was transported on four occasions. By the middle decades of the eighteenth century, some felons comprised a floating population of criminals that travelled back and forth across the Atlantic.[4]

[1] Townshend to [?], 8 Oct. 1728, PC 1/4/86; *Va. Gaz.* 30 Dec. 1737. See also, e.g., Hare, *Sermon Preached to the Societies for the Reformation of Manners*, pp. 29-30; *London Evening Post*, 4 Nov. 1738; 'Bill for Prosecuting Felons Returned from Transportation', 31 Jan. 1739, SP 36/152/111.

[2] *Account of the Ordinary of Newgate*, 17 Mar. 1755, p. 41. See also *Old Bailey Sessions Papers*, 20-2 Oct. 1756, p. 344.

[3] *Account of the Ordinary of Newgate*, 8 June 1744, pp. 6-8, 19 July 1738, pp. 14-15. See also, e.g., Gisborne *et al.* to Newcastle, 23 July 1735, SP 44/128/415-16; Lord Harrington to John Baille *et al.*, 7 Dec. 1738, SP 44/83/267-8; Fielding to Mr. Porten, 19 Aug. 1771, SP 37/8/182-3; *Old Bailey Sessions Papers*, 25-7 May 1721, p. 1, 6-13 Dec. 1721, p. 9, 10-12 May 1744, pp. 129-30, 17-19 Oct. 1750, p. 178, 2-7 May 1764, pp. 189-90, 12-15 Sept. 1764, p. 285, 19-22 Oct. 1768, p. 379, 7-10 Dec. 1768, pp. 36-7, 20-7 Feb. 1771, p. 119, 9-16 Dec. 1772, pp. 35-6, 11-16 Jan. 1775, p. 93, 15-21 Feb. 1775, pp. 147-8, 31 May-6 June 1775, p. 215; *American Weekly Mercury*, 8 June 1721; *Account of the Ordinary of Newgate*, 14 Mar. 1722, p. 4, 18 Sept. 1727, p. 3, 20 Nov. 1727, p. 3, 2 Oct. 1734, p. 8, 10 Mar. 1735, p. 13, 3 Mar. 1737, p. 6., 7 Apr. 1742, p. 16, 18 Oct. 1749, p. 84, 11 Feb. 1751, p. 53, 23 Mar. 1752, p. 48, 1 June 1752, pp. 80-1, 16 Apr. 1753, pp. 43-7, 12 Oct. 1763, pp. 71-3, 4 June 1770, p. 43; *A True and Genuine Account of the Behaviour, Confessions, and Dying Words of the Four Malefactors . . . Executed at Kennington-Common, 12 Apr. 1765* (London, [1766]), p. 4; *Gentleman's Magazine*, 1767, p. 92; Molland, *Special Grace Uninterrupted*, p. 23; Knapp and Baldwin, eds., *Newgate Calendar*, II. 125-6, 482, 493.

[4] *Life of Charles Speckman*, p. 6. See also, e.g., *Account of the Ordinary of Newgate*, 14 Mar. 1726, p. 4, 3 Aug. 1726, p. 4, 12 Oct. 1763, pp. 72-3; *Va. Gaz.,* 'Richard Kibble', 6 July 1739; Purdie & Dixon's *Va. Gaz.*, 'Joseph Wade', 23 July 1772; *Md. Gaz.*, 'Thomas Butler', 14 Sept. 1748, 'Samuel Gasford', 22 Oct. 1772,

Considerable disagreement existed among contemporaries over the motives that induced convicts to commit new crimes. Authorities concurred that their plight as fugitives made them all the more prone to resort to violence to avoid detection and capture. A Parliamentary committee pointed to the 'great Numbers' of 'Felons Returned From Transportation' who became 'more desperate than others as their Case' was 'worse'.[1] Otherwise, explanations varied greatly. Of one felon, a person concluded that 'like a dog returning to his vomit' he 'became as wicked as ever'. Daniel Defoe believed that 'Infatuation' and 'Impudence' led many to 'fall into the same Channel of Crime'. The thief John Meff, who claimed that an 'evil Genius' helped drive him to his 'former wicked Practices', later bemoaned that he had not followed the advice of his wife and led a 'regular and sober Life'. Less charitable was another convict who blamed his wife's alcoholism for his misbegotten ways. Though his 'decent and sober Behavior' had gained him the 'Esteem of his Neighbourhood', he allegedly turned to robbery to support her daily consumption of gin.[2]

Genuine poverty most commonly revived old habits. If numerous convicts first gravitated to crime out of material necessity, then returning felons were even more poverty-stricken and more prone to crime. Though numbers may have acquired honest employment, many fugitives incurred new hardships, particularly those fugitives that returned to earlier haunts where they were known. They

'William Inkley', 13 June 1776; *Pa. Gaz.*, 'George Williams', 17 Sept. 1767, 'Edward Holder', 18 Oct. 1770; *Gentleman's Magazine*, 1741, p. 162, 1750, p. 339; Hewitt to Halifax, 22 Nov. 1764, in [Hewitt], *Journal of J. Hewitt*, p. 207; Knapp and Baldwin, eds., *Newgate Calendar*, II. 125, 359, 491; *The Newgate Calendar*, pp. 17–19; Howson, *Thief-Taker General*, pp. 310–11. On occasion, troublesome situations for colonial factors arose when planters discovered former runaways among newly arrived transports. After the arrival of a vessel in the summer of 1768, Harry Piper recounted, 'I had in this Ship one or two which I sold in the Hicks, which I wish had been hanged (as they were before Transported) and probably will put me to some trouble and expence, as the person to whom they were first sold has since been with me'. Piper to Dixon & Littledale, 10 Aug. 1768, HPL, p. 50. See also *Colonists in Bondage*, p. 367 n. 55.

[1] 'Bill for Prosecuting Felons Returned from Transportation', 31 Jan. 1739, SP 36/152/111. See also Nathaniel Blackerby to Charles Delafaye, 7 Mar. 1726, SP 35/61/52; Hare, *Sermon Preached to the Societies for the Reformation of Manners*, p. 30; *London Evening Post*, 4 Nov. 1738.

[2] *True Account of the Four Malefactors*, p. 4; [Defoe], *Applebee's Weekly Journal*, 26 Jan. 1723, in Shugrae, ed., *Poetry and Prose of Defoe*, p. 217; *Select Trials at the Old Bailey* (1742), I. 72; *Account of the Ordinary of Newgate*, 18 Oct. 1749, pp. 83–4.

resembled the former horse thief Thomas Ashby, who could not
'go about his business for fear of being taken up'. Much the same
fate awaited Gabriel Tomkins upon coming home. Transported in
1722 to Providence Island in the western Caribbean, he returned
to England two years later. Unable to 'Settle in any lawfull way
of business', Tomkins was 'obliged to Sculk about the Country and
carry on the Smuggling trade to get Bread'. Caught for returning
early with his convict wife, Joseph Lucas wrote to her shortly
before his execution: 'You know very well that, ever since our
return from Virginia, we have neither rest nor peace. ... It is a
sad thing to always be in fear, it is living a dog's life.' The thief
Robert Perkins later recounted that he was 'always uneasy and
afraid'.[1]

Even after transportation terms had expired and convicts no
longer feared for their lives, economic hardships were common. On
top of the normal problems faced by the lower orders, many former
criminals suffered from unsavoury reputations. Of a convicted
robber in 1732, William Thomson, the Recorder of London,
remarked, 'Tis a greate hazard if any one will employ him here,
and then he will be in danger of returning to the same course.'[2]
Further, transports bore a special stigma since, unlike offenders
who were branded, whipped, or briefly imprisoned, they had been
removed for several years, if not longer, from community life.
Upon returning, most of them probably encountered some measure
of ostracism; no longer exiles, they none the less remained social
outcasts.

In the meantime, scores of convicts rejoined organized gangs. If
contemporaries are to be believed, criminal bands, both in London
and the provinces, included large numbers of felons returned from
transportation. Sheltered by a network of inns and night houses,
they committed frequent burglaries and highway robberies. The
fabled 'Coventry Gang' contained numerous convicts who had
'returned before the Expiration of their Sentence', including the
notorious pickpocket and shop-lifter, 'Long Peg', who had been
transported five times. Magistrates that tried to arrest them had

---

[1] Petition of Ashby to King, 1743, SP 36/60/190; Petition of Tomkins to King,
[1733], SP 36/30/403; Lucas quoted in Coldham, ed., *Bonded Passengers*, I. 107;
Account of the Ordinary of Newgate, 5 July 1721, p. 3.

[2] Thomson to [?], 16 June 1732, SP 36/27/34. See also [?], 'In Holy Writ ...',
[1785?], HO 42/7.

their lives threatened. There were also the so-called 'Hastings Outlaws', a band of smugglers transported in the late 1730s who returned shortly afterwards to ply their trade along the Sussex Coast. In Devon, fugitives made up a gang in the early 1750s that terrorized the surrounding countryside, whereas years earlier the foremost crime chieftain in London, Jonathan Wild, relied heavily upon fugitive convicts. According to one of the many criminal charges filed against him in 1725, Wild made them his 'Agents' because they could not incriminate him and because they were always at his mercy. The following year, a Westminster magistrate noted how returned felons did 'more mischief in the Streets' because they were both 'more Desperate' and were 'more trusted by Robbers' since convicts could not be 'Evidence against them'.[1] So alarmed at the time was George II by gang crime, that he ordered the Treasury to pay a reward of £40 for every felon convicted of returning early from transportation. Still, the problem remained acute, and convicts continued to come home in threatening numbers. As late as 1773, Alderman John Hewitt, the nemesis of the 'Coventry Gang', fretted, 'There are more returned transports at this time in the Kingdom than known before'.[2]

Banishing convicts to America remained a leading weapon for many years in British efforts to combat crime. If only by expelling droves of dangerous malefactors, transportation helped to counter rising lawlessness. Moreover, once in the colonies, convicts committed few new offences. For most of the eighteenth century, as we have seen, traditional society in America was unsuited to concentrated criminal activity, despite the British view of the colonies as a lawless land. Inasmuch as chances for theft and other property crimes were fewer, probably the great bulk of transported felons

---

[1] Hewitt to Halifax, 17 July 1763, SP 44/139/253; Hewitt to Halifax, 22 Nov. 1764, in [Hewitt], *Journal of J. Hewitt*, p. 207, *passim*; Hay, 'Crime, Authority and the Criminal Law', pp. 167–73; *London Evening Post*, 23 Dec. 1738; Cal Winslow, 'Sussex Smugglers', in Hay *et al.*, eds., *Albion's Fatal Tree*, p. 124 n. 2; Sidney Stafford Smythe to Earl of Holdernesse, 28 Sept. 1753, SP 36/123/94; Howson, *Thief-Taker General*, pp. 92, 239; Blackerby to Delafaye, 7 Mar. 1726, SP 35/61/52; Townshend to [?], 8 Oct. 1728, PC 1/4/86. See also *American Weekly Mercury*, 17 Jan. 1727; 'Bill for Prosecuting Felons Returned from Transportation', 31 Jan. 1739, SP 36/152/111; Newcastle to Recorder of Chester, 10 Apr. 1739, SP 44/131/118; *Account of the Ordinary of Newgate*, 18 Oct. 1749, p. 84.

[2] Hewitt quoted in Hay, 'War, Dearth and Theft', p. 143; Townshend to [?], 8 Oct. 1728, PC 1/4/86.

never ran foul of the law, at least in the colonial countryside. Contrary, however, to the hopes of some proponents, transportation did not save many souls. Performing penance on tobacco plantations held out little hope for personal improvement, especially once convicts began returning home. Desperate straits and economic distress together with greater opportunities for larceny made fugitives in Britain more dangerous than ever. As criminals arrived in deepwater ports, thieves reverted to old tricks, gangs received fresh recruits, and government authorities began to search for a better solution to the problem of crime.

8

EPILOGUE

I

Britain's foremost punishment after 1718, transportation represented a major innovation in the administration of justice. As an intermediate penalty between capital punishment and lesser sanctions such as whipping and branding, it became a vital alternative to the existing structure of punishment. It afforded a means of removing threatening offenders from the social mainstream, and without heavy reliance upon either the death penalty or imprisonment, thereby avoiding not only a bloodbath but the creation of a massive corrections system and a coercive force to staff it. The ultimate beauty of transportation, in the public mind, was that it promised to restore social peace without endangering traditional freedoms. No matter that convicts experienced hard usage across the Atlantic (or that they engendered widespread fear among colonists), so long as Britons were spared prisons and the spectre of hard labour at home.

In the long run, ironically, transportation probably facilitated the growth of prisons. For one thing, by removing convicted offenders from public view, it shifted the focus of penal policy away from deterrence and exhibitions of physical suffering. Though public confidence in traditional penalties was already waning by the time of the Transportation Act, authorities still fashioned frightening spectacles out of executions; and even lesser punishments, such as whipping and pillorying, were administered before crowds of onlookers. But banishment, as one observer noted in 1751, lacked the 'example or the shame' that characterized other penalties; only when transports were led to vessels for boarding were they publicly humiliated.[1] Otherwise, they were segregated, as prison inmates would be later. Transportation ultimately may have made hard labour more acceptable as well. During the eighteenth century, it was sometimes argued that putting criminals to work at home was no worse fate than what convicts endured in America. While public

---

[1] 'Extract from an Essay on Punishment of Felony . . .', 1751, SP 36/117/382.

sentiment over hard labour remained sharply divided for many years, transportation probably led growing numbers to ask, as did a London writer in 1776, 'Where is the difference, whether' a convict 'is a slave for a term of years in Britain or America?'[1]

Of related importance, transportation signalled the beginning of greater government efforts to curb crime, resulting in a commitment of resources unparalleled in the history of Britain's criminal justice system. Although government assumed no responsibility for the care of transports once they left British shores, authorities willingly expended large sums of money to ensure their expulsion, perhaps more than £200,000 if along with Treasury subsidies we include county expenditures in England and Ireland.[2] In that respect, transportation helped to pave the way for later government support, not just for prison construction, but also for the creation of professional police forces.

Not that transportation and the changes it wrought always enjoyed public favour. In addition to irate Americans, others, too, periodically attacked the wisdom of banishing malefactors. Few objections ever were voiced about the harsh conditions aboard convict vessels or the abuses suffered in the colonies by convict servants; nor did gross inequities in their treatment prompt many protests. More pressing, in the view of citizens and government officials alike, were concerns closer to home. High rates of lawlessness alone guaranteed that transportation would be faulted as an imperfect solution to the nation's crime problem. '*Transportation* has too long been indulged to those Crimes', affirmed 'Verus' in 1738 in the *Gentleman's Magazine*, 'to which the Lenity

---

[1] 'Candidus', *London Magazine*, 1776, p. 425. See also Eboranos, *Considerations for Rendering the Punishment of Criminals more Effectual*, p. 48; *Gentleman's Magazine*, 1750, p. 533; 'Extract from an Essay on Punishment', 1751, SP 36/117/382.

[2] This estimate seems reasonable, in so far as (1) Treasury subsidies from 1718 to 1772 totalled more than £86,000; (2) provincial counties in England generally paid contractors from £3 to £5 per head; (3) roughly the same number of transports came from those counties as the number subsidized by the Treasury before 1772 when the subsidy ended; and (4) Ireland transported more than 13,000 people at a likely cost of over £50,000. Merchants in Scotland received no fees until after 1766. For a more detailed discussion of these points, see above, Chapter 3. My estimate only considers merchant fees paid by government authorities. It does not include the ancillary costs of (1) gaoling prisoners awaiting transportation; (2) paying in some cases for their transportation to ships in port; and (3) poor relief for many families left without breadwinners.

of our Laws has allowed the Benefit of the Clergy; Experience has convinced us, that it is ineffectual'.[1]

Transportation was invariably criticized by those who believed that deterrence should remain the prime purpose of punishment. The mere threat of banishment as a deterrent, they claimed, was a hopelessly poor substitute for more public penalties. By the late colonial era, America no longer resembled a primitive wilderness, and foreign exile there, asserted opponents, had lost much of its original terror. The jurist Daines Barrington urged that felons be carried to more desolate sites, whereas in 1773 a magistrate in Scotland lamented, 'In this part of the Kingdom, Transportation to America, begins to lose every Characteristick of punishment'.[2] In the meantime, transportation, claimed some foes, drained Britain of potential labourers. In so far as population, by the eighteenth century, was considered a valuable national asset, it was feared that the country was depriving itself of a vital source of manpower.[3]

Still, the gravest problem, government officials realized as early as the 1720s, arose from the number of convicts who found their way back across the Atlantic. After all, transportation's chief value lay in keeping threatening malefactors safely exiled abroad. In the midst of seemingly high crime rates, anxious contemporaries commonly lamented the numbers of desperate fugitives who returned home to menace honest men and women. A newspaper correspondent in 1738 complained, '*Transportation* does not answer the End proposed, the Convicts are continually returning, and are made more desperate than before.' Measures taken to curb the problem included not only government rewards for criminal arrests

[1] 'Verus', *Gentleman's Magazine*, 1738, p. 286. For an exception that questioned the legality of selling convicts as 'slaves', see *Malefactor's Register*, III. 99.

[2] Thomas Miller to Suffolk, 25 Oct. 1773, SP 54/46/250; [Barrington], *Observations upon the Statutes*, pp. 352-3. See also 'Verus', *Gentleman's Magazine*, 1738, pp. 286-7; 'Extract from an Essay on Punishment of Felony', 1751, SP 36/117/382; *Proposals to the Legislature, For Preventing the Frequent Executions and Exportations of Convicts* . . . (London, 1754), pp. 26, 39; *Thoughts on Capital Punishments* . . . (London, 1770), p. 2; Purdie & Dixon's *Va. Gaz.* 8 Oct. 1772; A. G. L. Shaw, *Convicts and the Colonies: A Study of Penal Transportation from Great Britain and Ireland to Australia and Other Parts of the British Empire* (Carlton, Victoria, 1977), p. 42.

[3] See Eboranos, *Considerations for Rendering the Punishment of Criminals more Effectual*, pp. 44-5; 'Verus', *Gentleman's Magazine*, 1738, p. 287; Fielding, *Proposal for Making an Effectual Provision for the Poor*, p. 72; *Proposals to the Legislature*, pp. 26, 39; Radzinowicz, *History of English Criminal Law*, I. 263 n. 11; Appleby, *Economic Thought and Ideology*, pp. 135-57.

but also more rigid shipping procedures to restrict the return of felons. In 1731, one Englishman urged that transports have slits burnt in their ears to ensure easy identification should they return to Britain.[1] Others proposed that new dumping grounds be substituted for Maryland and Virginia. Suggested locations ranged from Nova Scotia, at a time when its commercial traffic with Britain was infrequent, to Algeria and Morocco, where felons might be exchanged for British subjects kidnapped by North African pirates. 'That Punishment ... would rid without Slaughter, or Probability of Return, the Country of the Vermin of Society', Bernard Mandeville affirmed in 1725.[2]

Not until a major crime wave in the early 1750s, however, was a serious challenge to transportation mounted. Alarmed by growing lawlessness following the War of the Austrian Succession, lawmakers hunted for new remedies. In January and February 1752, Parliament considered a bill designed to supplement transportation with the novel penalty of hard labour in the royal dockyards. The bill would not have eliminated transportation; instead it would have granted the king the right to sentence offenders to hard labour as a substitute. Noting the failure of past punishments to suppress crime, the preamble called attention to transportation's principal weakness. 'The Punishment of Transportation ...', it observed, 'hath frequently been evaded, by the Offenders returning ... before the Expiration of the Terms for which they have been transported'. None the less, though the House of Commons voted its approval, the bill died in the House of Lords. According to the penal reformer Jonas Hanway, one objection had been the likelihood that putting convicts to work in England would have caused 'such dangers and difficulties, as would render it a very improper experiment'. Even more criminals might have escaped from confinement than were continually coming home from the colonies.[3] Another objection

[1] *London Evening Post*, 4 Nov. 1738; 16 George II, c. 15; Newcastle to Attorney- and Solicitor-Generals, 6 Mar. 1752, SP 44/134/116–17; 8 George III, c.15; Radzinowicz, *History of English Criminal Law*, II. 63; Ollyffe, *Essay Offer'd for an Act of Parliament*, p. 12.

[2] Mandeville, *Enquiry into the Frequent Executions at Tyburn*, p. 52; Petition of Forward to King, n.d., CO 217/37/1; *Gentleman's Magazine*, 1752, p. 326.

[3] 'A Bill for the Better preventing Thefts and Robberies ...', 1752, in Sheila Lambert, ed., *House of Commons Sessional Papers of the Eighteenth Century* (Wilmington, Del., 1975), IX. 357–67; Jonas Hanway, *Defects of Police*, p. 221. See also Charles Jones, *Some Methods Proposed Towards Putting a Stop to the Flagrant Crimes of Murder, Robbery, and Perjury ...* (London, 1752), p. 11.

arose from the public's traditional opposition to hard labour. Held to be synonymous with slavery, it was thought an improper punishment for freeborn Englishmen, no matter how lowly and degraded their condition. In 1751, an essayist complained that 'multitudes of Silly People' opposed hard labour from the belief that 'the English are free, and should never be Slaves' nor 'accustomed to the sight of Chains', even though, he noted, a transported felon was already a 'slave in America'. Another person remarked sarcastically, 'This is a Sort of Breach of English liberty, to make People Work, who can live by Stealing'.[1]

With Parliament's defeat of the hard labour bill, government authorities remained alarmed by the spectre of returning felons, and transportation still provoked opposition. But because practical options were so few, courts continued to depend heavily upon it. During the 1760s, the Old Bailey banished nearly three-quarters of its convicted felons. At the same time, steps were actually taken to increase the flow of transported convicts. Hence, Parliament's passage in 1766 of a law placing transportation procedures in Scotland on a firmer footing, while two years later plans were formulated to banish hardened prostitutes along with more serious offenders. At one point, the Board of Trade was even instructed to prepare a report on the feasibility of banishing greater numbers of convicts as a means of reducing the reliance of the state on capital punishment. Whatever the flaws in the system of transportation, officials resorted to it in the absence of viable alternatives. As an intermediate sanction between corporal punishment and the death penalty, it commanded persistent support. Transportation, concluded Sir John Fielding in early 1773, was the 'most humane and effectual Punishment we have'.[2]

II

Few officials by then could have suspected that within a matter of years transportation would be abruptly halted by the American

[1] 'Extract from an Essay on Punishment', 1751, SP 36/117/382; *Pa. Gaz.* 14 May 1752. See also *Gentleman's Magazine*, 1750, p. 533, 1752, pp. 82, 326; *Proposals to the Legislature*, pp. 32-6; 'Philanthropos', *London Magazine*, 1768, p. 640; Hanway, *Defects of Police*, p. 221.

[2] Fielding to Suffolk, 1 Feb. 1773, SP 37/10/11; *Old Bailey Sessions Papers*, 1760-69; 6 George III, c. 32; Purdie & Dixon's *Va. Gaz.* 21 Apr. 1768; Halifax to Board of Trade, 5 Nov. 1763, CO 5/65/281.

Revolution. By curtailing Britain's leading punishment, the war threw the criminal justice system into chaos. It is difficult to imagine how any other single event could have so disrupted the punishment of criminals.

In retrospect, there were early signs to give officials warning of impending trouble. By the 1770s, angry protests in the colonies against the Stamp Act and the Townshend duties had signalled a growing mood of defiance against imperial authority. While convict shipments had not been affected by the non-importation movement of 1768–70, and American independence appeared an unlikely prospect, it was probably more than coincidental that some English courts shortly began to banish fewer criminals. At the Old Bailey between 1770 and 1775, offenders cast for transportation fell to fewer than two-thirds of all convicted felons. About the same time, according to recent studies, there was a similar trend in both Essex and Surrey away from banishment, whereas in Middlesex, observed a contemporary in 1772, local magistrates unanimously decided to 'exert their utmost endeavours to substitute actual hard labour as a punishment, instead of transportation'.[1]

To some degree, declining reliance by these courts upon transportation may have stemmed from the government's decision to cease subsidizing the removal of convicts from London, Middlesex, Buckinghamshire, and the Home Counties. In 1772, upon the death of John Stewart, who along with Duncan Campbell had served as government contractor, the Treasury opted to leave shipping arrangements entirely in the hands of local magistrates. On the other hand, the reason subsidies were no longer thought necessary appears to have been because merchant competition was great for the right to carry transports, even 'without any premium'. As a consequence, loss of the subsidy may not have created a heavy new burden for localities to assume.[2] Evidence also suggests that for other than financial reasons government officials by the early 1770s were trying to lessen their traditional dependence upon transportation, at least until a site other than America could be found. Already in 1769, the crown had briefly experimented with

[1] John Hawkins to Lord [?], 13 Oct. 1772, SP 37/9/271; King, 'Crime, Law and Society in Essex', pp. 340–3; Beattie, *Crime and the Courts in England*, pp. 560–4; *Old Bailey Sessions Papers*, 1770–75.

[2] 'Treasury Minutes relating to Duncan Campbell's loss on Mr. Stewart's Contract for transporting Felons . . .', 3 Nov. 1772, T 1/514/296.

stationing a small group of convicts at a British garrison on the West African coast. The following year, Parliament openly debated the wisdom of transporting felons to either Africa or the East Indies, and by 1773 Lord Mansfield was rumoured to be preparing a bill ordering that felons either be shipped to the East Indies or be imprisoned. A London report claimed, 'This Regulation is said to be in consequence of a remonstrance from the provinces of Virginia, Maryland, and Connecticut, complaining of the inundation of vagabonds from Great-Britain and Ireland.'[1] The bill was never introduced, but newspapers continued to print reports about government plans to transport criminals to Africa or to the South Pacific. Although the reputed purpose behind these schemes was usually to keep transported felons from easily returning home, the government may also have been seeking to appease American opinion.[2]

Whatever the exact thinking of officials on the eve of American independence, the war had a crippling impact upon the administration of justice. Though reliance upon transportation had been declining, just how important it remained to the nation's penal armoury rapidly became clear. With the outbreak of hostilities in the spring of 1775, vessels were abruptly refused entry into colonial ports. Most officials expected that the rebellion would be short-lived, and the Solicitor-General declared in Parliament that 'when tranquility was restored to America, the usual mode of transportation might be again adopted'.[3] But with the escalating fighting, lawmakers were forced to devise makeshift measures for housing

---

[1] *Pa. Gaz.* 18 Aug. 1773; Earl of Rochford to Secretary at War, 19 May [1769], WO 1/874/65, PRO; Robert Browne to Rochford, [1769], WO 1/874/69; Lang, *Transportation and Colonization*, pp. 14–15. I have not been able to find a copy of the remonstrance.

[2] Purdie & Dixon's *Va. Gaz.* 9 June, 15 Sept 1774; Pinkney's *Va. Gaz.* 29 Sept. 1774. A less likely motive was suggested by an Essex magistrate. Noting that 'an insurrection' in the 'Northern provinces may be justly apprehended', he warned against supplying the 'malcontents' with potential recruits from British gaols. *Chelmsford Chronicle*, 11 May 1770. Nor would it appear that growing government anxiety over the loss of population to America played a role. Those fears were confined in the early 1770s to the emigration of labouring families from Scotland and Ireland. Bernard Bailyn, 'The Challenge of Modern Historiography', *AHR* LXXXVII (1982), 15–16.

[3] *Parliamentary Register* . . ., IV, 9 May 1776, p. 106; Dixon's *Va. Gaz.* 16 Sept. 1775. After the summer of 1775, the only known appearance of a vessel with convicts occurred in April 1776 when the *Jenny* arrived in the James River with a cargo of convicts and servants from Newcastle. Evidently they were allowed to disembark. Oldham, 'Transportation of British Convicts', p. 91.

hundreds of criminals. Parliament in the spring of 1776 passed the 'Hulks' Act, though not without strong objections against its plan for consigning criminals to hard labour. 'The sight of an Englishman, transformed into a galley slave,' lamented a writer in the *London Magazine*, 'is humiliating. . . . Englishmen, in their most degenerate condition, are designed for a better fate.' A member of Parliament complained that 'the people having slavery daily before their eyes, it would at length become familiar to them'. Still others protested that the act was 'one of the many schemes of the crown for subverting the liberties of the people, and destroying the essence of the constitution'.[1]

Beginning that August, however, convicts were crowded aboard weather-beaten warships moored on the Thames near Woolwich. Not long afterwards, additional hulks were anchored in the harbours of Plymouth and Portsmouth. During the day, prisoners were put to such tasks as raising ballast and constructing new dockyards. By night, they were secured aboard ships in cramped and disease-ridden quarters. The mortality rate ran as high as 1 in 4 during the first three years. Furthermore, though prisoners were kept in chains, they posed a major security risk by often trying to escape. In 1778, 150 convicts attempted an uprising in which two men were killed and ten more were wounded.[2]

Keeping felons imprisoned in provincial gaols offered an alternative to the hulks, but those, too, became sickly and overcrowded. Edmund Burke described them as 'nests of pestilence'. A penitentiary act was passed in 1779, calling for the construction of two new prisons where inmates would be kept at hard labour for a maximum of two years. The act, however, was never executed, due to constitutional objections about government involvement in prison management, fears about returning inmates so soon to society, and disagreements over building costs. In the ten years after 1776, the nation's already cramped prison population, according to one estimate, swelled by 73 per cent. By 1783, Whitehall was being barraged with reports of overcrowded gaols throughout the country. The following autumn, the Home Secretary observed, 'The great

---

[1] 'Remarks on the Convict Act', *London Magazine*, 1776, p. 369; 'Candidus', ibid., p. 425; 'Remarks on the Convict Act', ibid., 1777, p. 265; *Parliamentary Register*, IV, 9 May 1776, p. 106. See also ibid., p. 104.

[2] Ignatieff, *Just Measure of Pain*, pp. 80–1; Campbell to Suffolk, 1 Oct. 1778, DCBL, II. 248–50.

Number of Felons under sentence of Transportation, who are now in confinement in this Kingdom, have rendered the condition of the Gaols extremely alarming'. 'All our gaols are overglutted,' affirmed a contemporary, 'and half the British navy, converted into justitia galleys, would scarce suffice to contain all our English penitents.'[1]

What made matters worse was the sudden upsurge in domestic theft and violence Britain faced in the early 1780s. On top of the bloody Gordon riots of 1780, a crime epidemic erupted. Escalating unemployment caused by a trade depression and the demobilization of thousands of young men, combined with a sharp rise in food prices and a decline in real wages, sparked a crisis of fearsome proportions. 'Allmost all Peoples minds are more occupied about the Depredatory Cruelties and Robberies that are continually carrying on,' claimed a London resident in late 1782, 'than they are about the fate of Gibraltar or the Event of Our Arms.' Nor were areas spared outside the capital. 'The kingdom is infested', wrote one person, 'with the most formidable and dreadful number of abandoned wretches, that for a Series of Years have committed their depradations on the publick.' An inhabitant of rural Wales complained in 1786, 'We are not more Secure in our property of every kind than if we were Savages.'[2]

Greater reliance upon capital punishment was one consequence of Britain's crime crisis. The mid-1780s witnessed a sharp increase in the use of the death penalty. Whereas in the ten years before 1782, nearly two-thirds of all capital convicts in London and nearby counties had received clemency, in 1785 slightly more than one-third of them were granted royal pardons. That year in London and Middlesex as many as ninety-seven persons were executed. Rising numbers of hangings also occurred in other parts of England. Capital punishment, however, scarcely afforded a permanent solution. Not even hardened public officials believed that hundreds of

[1] Burke quoted in *The Parliamentary History of England* (London, 1814), XXV. 431; Sydney to Lt. Gov. Clarke, 5 Oct. 1784, CO 137/84/146; *The Means of Effectually Preventing Theft and Robbery . . .* (London, 1783), p. 82; Ignatieff, *Just Measure of Pain*, pp. 84–5, 93–6.

[2] John Bindley to Mr Townshend, 16 Sept. 1782, HO 42/1/138; Thomas Robertson, Jr., to [?], 30 Nov. 1782, HO 42/1/409; Mr Davies to Lord [?], 15 Apr. 1786, HO 42/8; Ignatieff, *Just Measure of Pain*, pp. 82–4; Beattie, *Crime and the Courts in England*, pp. 223–5; Hay, 'War, Dearth and Theft', p. 145; David Mackay, *A Place of Exile: The European Settlement of New South Wales* (Melbourne, 1985), pp. 14–15.

men and women could routinely be sent to the gallows, if only because courts would never tolerate such loss of life. One person observed, 'If this evil of Executions . . . increases in the proportion it of late has done, it is to be feared that if the Judges would continue to pass Sentences it may become difficult to find Juries to condemn'.[1] In the meantime, a variety of remedies were proposed to Whitehall authorities. Included were plans for licensing pistols and for enlisting convicts in the royal navy.[2] Some men urged that more strenuous efforts be made to reform the moral character of criminals. By the 1780s, despite traditional opposition, imprisonment and hard labour had continued to gain favour. John Howard, a Bedfordshire philanthropist, and William Eden, the prominent politician, became particularly strong proponents of new and better prison facilities, to provide not just incarceration but a genuine means of rehabilitation.[3]

Rehabilitation, however, had never been a principal aim of government penal policy, nor was it now. As shown by the ill-fated penitentiary act of 1779, the crisis of the 1780s encouraged only limited experimentation. Instead, most authorities remained committed to furthering social peace at home by exporting criminals abroad. Removing malefactors was much easier than attempting to reclaim them or, for that matter, trying to remedy the root causes of crime. 'The grand consideration', the British governor of Cape Coast Castle in Africa noted of convicts in 1783, 'seems to be, *to get them out of Europe at all Events*'.[4] Banishment, of course, continued to provoke sharp debate. Opponents remained alarmed about the possibility of felons returning home early from exile,[5]

---

[1] 'Propositions relating to the Causes and Prevention of Robberies', [1781], SP 37/15/475–6; *British Parliamentary Papers: Report from the Select Committee on Criminal Laws*, Appendices 5, 7, and 2, pp. 155–7, 168–9, 137; Hay, 'Crime, Authority and the Criminal Law', pp. 520–1; King, 'Decision-Makers and Decision-Making', p. 50.

[2] John Diston to Lord [?], 8 Sept. 1783, HO 42/3/128; Robertson, Jr., to [?], 10 Dec. 1782, HO 42/1/428.

[3] Ignatieff, *Just Measure of Pain*, pp. 47–79, 93–8.

[4] Richard Miles to [?], 1 Feb. 1783, T 70/33/53. The penitentiary act itself kept transportation alive by giving courts the authority to order criminals to be transported to any place beyond the seas.

[5] 'On the Convict Act', *London Magazine*, 1776, p. 369; 'Abstract of Mr. Thomas Robertson's Plan for the employment in his Majesty's Royal Navy of Convicts . . .', 10 Dec. 1782, HO 42/1/430; [M. Madan], *Thoughts on Executive Justice . . .* (London, 1785), p. 75.

while others continued to question the value of transportation as a deterrent. In addition, critics like the London philanthropist Jonas Hanway and the philosopher William Paley strongly criticized the loss of valuable labourers to foreign lands.[1] But majority sentiment overwhelmingly favoured a return to transportation. As crime rates soared and prisons overflowed with hundreds of diseased and dangerous offenders, leading officials saw no other solution. Affirmed the London magistrate Sampson Wright, 'The Public will be happy to get rid of them at any Rate'.[2]

III

Surely it was an act of desperation when government authorities, even before the signing of the Treaty of Paris in September 1783, decided to reopen the convict trade to America. While prospects for peace may have encouraged hopes of success, ministers could not have forgotten American hostility towards transportation. Alternatives, however, were few, and by early 1783 crown officials, particularly the Treasury, were resigned to a resumption of the trade. Some courts were already ordering criminals to be transported to 'his Majesty's Colonies and Plantations in America'. For the time being, these sentences could not be enforced, but on 12 July, in response to a proposal from Lord North, then home secretary, George III wrote, 'Undoubtedly the Americans cannot expect nor ever will receive any favour from Me, but the permitting them to obtain Men unworthy to remain in this Island I shall certainly consent to.' By then, North had enlisted George Moore, a London merchant eager to sell transported felons for their labour, and within weeks his vessel, the *George*, was ready to sail for Maryland with an initial cargo of 143 prisoners. Moore was promised £500

---

[1] Hanway, *Defects of Police* (London, 1775), pp. 199–200, and *Distributive Justice and Mercy* . . . (London, 1781), pp. 18–19, 135–6, 151–3; Paley, *The Principles of Moral and Political Philosophy* (London, 1785), pp. 26–9, 543. See also 'On the Convict Act', Aug. 1776, *London Magazine*, 1776, pp. 424–7; William Eden, 'An Introductory Discourse on Banishment', in [D. Barrington], *The History of New Holland* . . . (London, 1787), pp. xvii–xx; [Hewitt], *Journal of J. Hewitt*, pp. 63–4.

[2] Wright to [?], 24 Aug. 1782, HO 42/1/290. See also, e.g., Bindley to Townshend, 16 Sept. 1782, HO 42/1/139; Mollie Gillen, 'The Botany Bay Decision, 1786: Convicts, not Empire', *English Historical Review*, XCVII (1982), 740–66.

from the Treasury besides whatever profits the convicts fetched as servants.[1]

No one could later fault George Moore's diligence. Before the *George* got underway, he made careful preparations for its arrival in Baltimore. Ready to assist in the marketing of the vessel's cargo was George Salmon, a prominent Whig merchant with an eye for the main chance. 'I don't know any thing would bring more money here', Salmon had assured Moore, 'than a parcel [of] Servants or Convicts which was formerly a good business.' Together the men agreed to disguise the ship's passengers as indentured servants. 'Servants is the word', Salmon reminded Moore at one point, 'and they may be imported every Day in the Year.' As an added precaution, the vessel was to be given a new name, and Nova Scotia was to be announced in London as its destination. Once at sea, the captain would sail for Maryland. Though American independence had meant the end of transportation, who would refuse refuge to a wayward vessel in distress, even if the true identity of its passengers should be discovered?[2]

Disaster struck early. Hardly had the ship, newly rechristened the *Swift*, cleared the Thames in late August when the convicts rebelled and ran the vessel aground off the Sussex coast. More than a quarter of them escaped, so that when later that year the ship finally reached Maryland, just over a hundred prisoners remained aboard. Upon it being anchored off Baltimore, unusually heavy snows and frigid temperatures ruined any chance for quick sales by keeping most buyers confined to home; in the meantime, the

---

[1] George III to Lord North, 12 July 1783, North to George III, 11 July 1783, in Sir John Fortescue, ed., *The Correspondence of King George the Third* ... (London, 1928), VI. 415–16; North to Lords of Treasury, 5 Nov. 1783, SP 44/330/313; Baltimore County Convict Record, 1770–74, pp. 388–9; Oldham, 'Transportation of British Convicts', p. 225; Beattie, *Crime and the Courts in England*, p. 594. North and George III were aware that convicts might not be welcome in America; they agreed that Moore would 'land them in Nova Scotia' if they could not be 'landed in any part of the United States'. North to George III, [18 July 1783], in Fortescue, ed., *Correspondence of George III*, p. 418. For a detailed account of this entire episode, see A. Roger Ekirch, 'Great Britain's Secret Convict Trade to America, 1783–1784', *AHR* LXXXIX (1984), 1285–91.

[2] Salmon to Moore, 30 Apr., 22 Nov., 3 Oct. 1783, Woolsey & Salmon Letterbook, pp. 478, 503–4, 494; Joshua Johnson to John Jay, 22 Aug. 1783, in Richard B. Morris, ed., *John Jay: The Winning of the Peace* (New York, 1980), II. 572–3; Matthew Ridley to William Paca, 12 Sept. 1783, Ridley Collection, Case 8, Massachusetts Historical Society, Boston; Cheston to Randolph, 23 Feb. 1784, CGP, Box 8.

Swift became trapped by ice 'thick enough to bear a hogshed [of] Tobacco'. With prisoners daily threatening to escape and costs mounting for food, clothing, and medical care, a clearly disgusted Salmon wrote to Moore in early February 1784, 'I [have] thought several times it would be almost as good to let the Villains go on shore and so have done without them. . . . If I find I Cannot sell them for some price or other, I will turn them adrift'. By the following month, many of the convicts purchased locally had already run away from their masters, while others, still on board, were gravely ill and nearing death. To make matters worse, angry state politicians, who had learned of the hoax, were preparing a ban against all incoming felons in spite of Salmon's best efforts to distribute 'Porter and Cheese' among his 'friends' in the legislature. 'I have been plagued beyond expression', the weary merchant wrote to Moore that March.[1]

Most of the convicts were finally sold, but both men suffered heavy losses. Besides having to shoulder the expence of boarding so many prisoners, they received little from purchasers. A shortage of hard currency had forced Salmon to extend credit, and once large numbers of convicts had begun to abscond, buyers stubbornly refused to honour their debts. Not surprisingly, as early as February Salmon flatly advised Moore to 'send no more'. By then, however, Moore was already preparing for a second voyage. In early April, with backing from Whitehall, his vessel, the *Mercury*, set sail with 179 convicts. But again prisoners rebelled, and when the vessel, after a long and harrowing passage, reached the American coast, no port would permit its entry. The convicts were finally unloaded in British Honduras, much to the anger of local settlers. 'We are the only nation on earth', protested the Honduran agent in London, 'who seem not to know How to dispose of our Criminals'.[2]

Such then was the end of transportation to Britain's former

---

[1] Salmon to Moore, 15 Jan., 4 Feb., 15 Mar. 1784, 31 Dec. 1783, Woolsey & Salmon Letterbook, pp. 512–14, 517–22, 510–11; Knapp and Baldwin, eds., *Newgate Calendar*, III. 124.

[2] Salmon to Moore, 4 Feb., 15 Mar. 1784, Woolsey & Salmon Letterbook, pp. 517–22; Robert White to Secretary Evan Nepean, 25 Jan. 1785, CO 123/3/86; Nepean to Lords of Treasury, 12 Apr. 1784, HO 36/4/48–9; Moore to Lords of Treasury, 13 July [1786?], HO 42/9/565; Examination of Nepean, Minutes of Parliamentary Committee on Convicts, 27 Apr. 1785, HO 7/1/23–24; Oldham, 'Transportation of British Convicts', pp. 234–49. For a second failed attempt by Moore to transport convicts to British Honduras, see Gillen, 'Botany Bay Decision', p. 748.

colonies. Never again did government oficials try to export convicts to the United States. Local opposition was too widespread, and prospective schemes to smuggle felons clearly impractical. In 1785, a parliamentary committee assigned to resolve the country's worsening penal crisis concluded, 'with regret', that the 'Ports of the United States have been shut against the Importation of Convicts'. 'The old System of transporting to America', rhapsodized the committee, 'answered every good purpose which could be expected from it'.[1] Desperate men often seek remedies in the past, and in the turbulent years after American independence fearful Englishmen were no exception.

Following these abortive efforts to revive transportation to America, new spots were considered as possible sites, including the coast of West Africa. Army companies stationed along the Gold Coast had received criminal recruits in earlier years, and in 1785 Parliament discussed government plans to carry 200 felons to the island of Lemaine, 400 miles up the Gambia River. The scheme, however, was strongly opposed and defeated. Some critics like Edmund Burke predicted that untold numbers would perish from the region's unhealthy climate, while others feared that landing dangerous criminals among African natives would precipitate a massacre. The veteran naval commander Sir George Young declared before a parliamentary committee, 'If the Convicts were armed they would probably kill and rob the Natives, or if unarmed, the Natives would rob and kill them'. A proposal later that year to locate criminals farther south near the mouth of the Das Voltas

---

[1] On a slightly more hopeful note, the committee observed, 'It does not appear . . . whether such Prohibitions are intended to operate perpetually or whether they may be removed in consequence of some future Arrangement'. Report of Parliamentary Committee on Convicts, June 1785, HO 42/6. In later years, only scattered shipments of British convicts, in defiance of both English and United States authorities, were unloaded on American shores. The principal culprits were Irish merchants, who with the backing of their government, nominally independent since 1782, transported several hundred Irish felons up until the late 1780s. *Salem Mercury*, 15 July 1788; Lord Fitz-Gibbon to W. W. Grenville, 2 Dec. 1789, in *Fortescue Manuscripts*, Historical Manuscripts Commission, *Thirteenth Report*, Appendix, Part III (London, 1892), I. 546-8; 'An Account of the Sums paid in the Treasury Office for the Transportation of Convicts within the four last Years', [*c.* 1790], *JHCI* XIII, Appendix, p. cccli. In 1788, the US Congress officially urged states to 'pass proper laws for preventing the transportation of convicted malefactors from foreign countries into the United States'. Entry of 16 Sept. 1788, in W. C. Ford, ed., *Journals of the Continental Congress, 1774-1789* (Washington, DC, 1937), XXXIV. 528.

River fared no better. 'Every Plan, which the Kings Servants have proposed, for transporting the Convicts out of the Kingdom,' Lord Sydney, the current home secretary, despaired, 'has met with such Opposition, that it has been almost impossible to carry any of them into Execution'.[1]

Only in August 1786, after months of study and debate, did authorities finally decide upon the site of Botany Bay, lying on the eastern coast of Australia. Explored by Capt. Cook in 1770, it was first recommended in 1779 as a possible location by Sir Joseph Banks, a member of the Cook expedition. Not before disillusionment with America and Africa, however, did Botany Bay become the government's choice. Although the greater distance to Australia meant much higher shipping costs, establishing a colony in such a sparsely inhabited country was less likely to disturb local natives. The climate was healthy enough, and agricultural conditions were reputedly good. Moreover, there was little likelihood that many felons would ever return home, for Botany Bay was separated from Britain by some 15,000 miles. A proponent noted that there was not 'even the most distant probability of their return'. Banks himself attested that 'Escape would be very difficult'. Amidst wild animals and occasional 'savages', transported convicts would be far removed, he emphasized, 'from any Part of the Globe inhabited by Europeans'.[2]

Domestic tranquillity never comes cheaply, but by 1786 most Englishmen were happy to pay the cost of founding a penal colony half-way around the world. Over the next eighty years, courts would banish more than 150,000 felons to Australia. Not until the later decades of the nineteenth century would Britain resort to punishing all of its criminals at home. By then, the country possessed a far-flung prison system, capable of confining dangerous malefactors for lengthy periods of time. Much as in earlier years, however, rehabilitation continued to be an elusive goal. Contrary

[1] *Parliamentary History*, XXV. 391-2, 431; First Report of Parliamentary Committee on Convicts, 9 May 1785, HO 42/6; Sydney to Sir John Wrottesley, 6 Nov. 1785, HO 13/3/239; Oldham, 'Transportation of British Convicts', pp. 186-224, 254-85.

[2] Sir George Young quoted in Ged Martin, ed., *The Founding of Australia: The Argument about Australia's Origins* (Sydney, 1978), p. 21; Testimony of Banks, 1 Apr. 1779, *JHC* XXXVII. 311; Shaw, *Convicts and the Colonies*, 43-57; Gillen, 'Botany Bay Decision', pp. 740-66; Mackay, *Place of Exile*, pp. 38-70.

to the hopes of reformers who favoured prisons as a means of moral regeneration, isolating convicted offenders, not reintegrating them into the social mainstream, remained the guiding premiss of government policy. With the final demise of transportation, walls of mortar and brick, rather than deepwater seas, marked the boundaries between crime and society in the years ahead.

APPENDIX

Table 14. Skills of Maryland and Virginia Runaways

Skills[a]

Tradesmen: 335 (64.7%)

Baker	5	Millwright	2(2)
Basketmaker	1	Nailer	7(1)
Blacksmith	43(4)	Painter	4(1)
Brazier	1(1)	Plasterer	6(1)
Bricklayer	22(4)	Quilter	1
Brickmaker	4(1)	Sailmaker	2
Buckelmaker	1	Shipwright	4(1)
Butcher	8	Shoemaker	52
Carter	2	Silversmith	4(1)
Carver	1	Soapboiler	1(1)
Clothier	1	Tailor	24
Coachmaker	1	Tanner	2
Currier	1(1)	Tinker	3
Fuller	1	Tinplate worker	1
Glassblower	1	Watchmaker	2
Glazier	1(1)	Weaver	42(6)
Gunstocker	1	Wheelwright	5(2)
Harnessmaker	3	Wigmaker	3(1)
Hatter	7	Woodworkers	
Hempdresser	2	Cabinetmaker	5(1)
Jeweller	3(1)	Carpenter	32(7)
Knitter	2	Cooper	6
Miller	9	Sawyer	5(2)
		Wool-comber	1(1)

Table 14.—*cont.*

Skills[a]			
House Servants: 40 (7.7%)		**Miscellaneous: 79 (15.3%)**	
Barber	12	Apothecary	1
Cook	2(2)	Army Drummer	1(1)
Dairymaid	1	Chimney Sweeper	1
Gardener	17(2)	Clerk	2(1)
Groom	1(1)	Doctor	1
Jockey	3(1)	Fiddler	2
Maid	1	Grocer	1
Waitingman	3(2)	Malster	1
		Sailor	48(8)
		Schoolmaster	7
		Soldier	13(5)
		Tavernkeeper	1

Agricultural Workers: 55 (10.6%)	
Ditcher	2(1)
Farmer	53(12)

Industrial Workers: 9 (1.7%)	
Miners	4
Ropemakers	2(1)
Wagoners	3
Total for all skills	518

Note: a. In the event that a servant possessed more than a single skill, the skill given first in the runaway advertisement was listed. Figures in parentheses represent those servants who had multiple skills. Fugitives who ran away two or more times were counted only once.

Table 15. Age of Maryland and Virginia Runaways (percentages in parentheses)

Age	Runaways[a]	
10–14	2	(0.2)
15–19	57	(5.8)
20–24	253	(25.9)
25–29	268	(27.5)
30–34	170	(17.4)
35–39	83	(8.5)
40–44	85	(8.7)
45–49	31	(3.2)
50–54	21	(2.2)
55–59	3	(0.3)
60+	3	(0.3)
Total	976 (100.0)	

Note: a. Fugitives who ran away two or more times were included as many times as they absconded, since their ages would have changed between escape attempts.

Table 16. Native Origins of Maryland and Virginia Runaways (percentages in parentheses)

Birthplace	Runaways[a]	
England and Wales	548	(68.3)
Ireland	201	(25.1)
Scotland	27	(3.4)
Other	26	(3.2)
Total	802 (100.0)	

Note: a. Fugitives who ran away two or more times were counted only once.

Table 17. Flight by Month of Maryland and Virginia Runaways (percentages in parentheses)

Month	Runaways[a]
January	23 (2.4)
February	35 (3.6)
March	70 (7.3)
April	85 (8.8)
May	129 (13.4)
June	127 (13.2)
July	132 (13.7)
August	145 (15.1)
September	73 (7.6)
October	69 (7.2)
November	48 (5.0)
December	27 (2.8)
Total	963 (100.1)

Note: a. Fugitives who ran away two or more times were included as many times as they absconded.

Table 18. Length of Servitude of Maryland and Virginia Runaways (percentages in parentheses)

Servitude	Runaways[a]
0–1.9 Months	79 (42.0)
2–3.9 ,,	22 (11.7)
4–5.9 ,,	16 (8.5)
6–11.9 ,,	27 (14.4)
1–1.9 Years	19 (10.1)
2–2.9 ,,	14 (7.5)
3–3.9 ,,	5 (2.7)
4–4.9 ,,	4 (2.1)
5–5.9 ,,	2 (1.1)
6+— ,,	— —
Total	188 (100.1)

Note: a. Only the first flight was counted for fugitives who ran away two or more times.

BIBLIOGRAPHY

I. PRIMARY SOURCES

A. MANUSCRIPTS: GREAT BRITAIN

Brecknock Museum, Brecon
  Transportation Bonds, 1727-74
British Library, London
  Additional Manuscripts, 27826
City Record Office, Coventry
  Transportation Records, 1741-66
Cumbria Record Office, Carlisle
  Transportation Certificates, 1768-69
Derbyshire Record Office, Matlock
  Transportation Records, 1720-72
Devon Record Office, Exeter
  Transportation Records, 1729-64
Gloucestershire Record Office, Gloucester
  Treasurers' Books, 1727-73
Guildhall Records Office, London
  Miscellaneous Mansucripts
Leicestershire Record Office, Leicester
  Quarter Sessions Bonds and Orders, 1720-83
Public Record Office, London
  Chancery Papers
    C 11/1223   Judicial Proceedings, 1725
  Colonial Office Papers
    CO 5/65 America and West Indies: Original Correspondence, 1760-64
    CO 5/1319, 1321, 1329 Virginia: Original Correspondence, 1720-26, 1727-29, 1756-60
    CO 5/1365   Virginia: Entry Books, 1717-27
    CO 5/1442-6   Virginia: Shipping Returns, 1725-53
    CO 37/36   Bermuda: Original Correspondence, 1772-77
    CO 123/3   British Honduras: Original Correspondence, 1784-85
    CO 137/13, 19, 84   Jamaica: Original Correspondence, 1718-21, 1730-32, 1783-84
    CO 138/17   Jamaica: Entry Books, 1725-34
    CO 201/2   British New Guinea: Original Correspondence, 1790
    CO 217/37   Nova Scotia and Cape Breton: Original Correspondence, c. 1720-1817

High Court of Admiralty Papers
    HCA 1/19, 57   Criminal Papers, 1735-44, 1736-49
    HCA 30/258   Intercepted Mails and Papers, 1756
Home Office Papers
    HO 7/1   Convicts: Miscellaneous, 1785
    HO 42/1-9   Domestic: Letters and Papers, 1782-86
    HO 104/1   Criminal: Letter Book, 1762-86
Privy Council Papers
    PC 1/4   Unbound Papers, 1728
State Papers, Domestic
    SP 35/5-78   Letters and Papers, 1716-27
    SP 36/1-161   Letters and Papers, 1727-60
    SP 37/1-15   Letters and Papers, 1760-82
    SP 44/80-96   Criminal Papers, 1715-82
    SP 44/119-43   Domestic Papers, 1716-82
    SP 44/232   Naval Papers, 1766-84
    SP 44/330   Treasury and Accounts, 1775-83
    SP 54/16, 46   Scotland: Letters and Papers, 1725, 1771-76
    SP 63/402   Ireland: Letters and Papers, 1739
Treasury Office Papers
    T 1/279, 514   Original Correspondence, 1732, 1775
    T 47/10   Register of Emigrants, 1774-75
    T 53/42-52   Money Books, 1744-72
    T 70/33   Expired Commissions, 1781-99
War Office Papers
    WO 1/874   Public Offices: In-Letters, 1767-69
Scottish Record Office, Edinburgh
  High Court of Justiciary Records
    JC 3/8-39   Books of Adjournal, 1718-75
    JC 11/7-14, 22-7   North Circuit Minute Books, 1730-49, 1758-70
    JC 27   Small Papers: Supplementary Series [1537-1891]
  Private Papers
    GD 14   Campbell of Stonefield Muniments
    GD 24   Abercairny Muniments
    GD 214   Hannay Papers
    RH 15   Miscellaneous Bundles

B. MANUSCRIPTS: UNITED STATES

Alderman Library, University of Virginia, Charlottesville
  John Hook Papers
  Harry Piper Letter Book
  Prentis Papers, Documents, 1743-1858
Colonial Williamsburg Inc., Research Center, Williamsburg
  John Hook Papers, Duke University Library, Durham (microfilm)

James Lawson Letterbook, Scottish Record Office, Edinburgh (microfilm)

Russell Papers, Coutts & Co., London (microfilm)

Library of Congress, Washington, DC

Additional Manuscripts, 29600, British Library, London (photocopies)

Landing Certificates, 1718–36, Guildhall Records Office, London (photocopies)

Woolsey & Salmon Letterbook

Maryland Hall of Records, Annapolis

Annapolis Mayor's Court Proceedings

Anne Arundel County Convict Record

Baltimore County Convict Record

Baltimore County Debt Books

Kent County Bonds and Indentures

Kent County Court Criminal Proceedings

Kent County Debt Books

Kent County Inventories

Maryland Inventories and Accounts

Maryland Shipping Returns

Maryland Wills

Provincial Court Judgements

Queen Anne's County Land Records

Maryland Historical Society, Baltimore

Thomas Cable Letterbook

Carroll-Maccubbin Papers

Cheston-Galloway Papers

Maryland Shipping Returns

Massachusetts Historical Society, Boston

Matthew Ridley Collection

Virginia State Library, Richmond

Fairfax County Order Books (microfilm)

John Hook Letters

King George County Order Books (mircrofilm)

Lancaster County Orders (microfilm)

Northumberland County Order Books (microfilm)

Prince William County Order Books (microfilm)

Richmond County Criminal Trials (microfilm)

Richmond County Order Books (microfilm)

Westmoreland County Orders (microfilm)

William Allason Papers

C. MANUSCRIPTS: AUSTRALIA

Mitchell Library, Sydney

Duncan Campbell Business Letter Book

Duncan Campbell Private Letter Book

D. NEWSPAPERS AND PERIODICALS

American Weekly Mercury, Philadelphia.
Annual Register, London.
Belfast News-Letter.
Boston Weekly News-Letter.
Chelmsford Chronicle.
Daily Universal Register, London.
Gentleman's Magazine, London.
Georgia Gazette, Savannah.
London Evening Post.
London Magazine.
Maryland Gazette, Annapolis.
Pennsylvania Gazette, Philadelphia.
Pennsylvania Packet, and Daily Advertiser, Philadelphia.
Salem Mercury.
South Carolina Gazette, Charleston.
Virginia Gazette, Williamsburg.
Dixon & Hunter's *Virginia Gazette*, Williamsburg.
Pinkney's *Virginia Gazette*, Williamsburg.
Purdie's *Virginia Gazette*, Williamsburg.
Purdie & Dixon's *Virginia Gazette*, Williamsburg.
Rind's *Virginia Gazette*, Williamsburg.

E. PRINTED WORKS

An Account of the Endeavours That have been Used to Suppress Gaming-Houses . . . (London, 1722).
Atkinson, J. C., ed., *The North Riding Record Society* . . ., 9 vols. (London, 1883-92).
[Barrington, D.], *The History of New Holland* . . . (London, 1787).
[——], *Observations upon the Statutes, Chiefly the More Ancient* . . . (London, 1766).
Bell, Jr., Whitfield, J., 'Adam Cunningham's Atlantic Crossing, 1728', *Maryland Historical Magazine*, L (1955), pp. 195-202.
Beverly, Robert, *The History and Present State of Virginia*, ed. Louis B. Wright (Chapel Hill, NC, 1947).
Blackstone, William, *Commentaries on the Laws of England*, 4 vols. (Oxford, 1765-69).
Blizard, William, *An Essay on the Means of Preventing Crimes and Amending Criminals* (London, 1785).
Bond, Carroll T., ed., *Proceedings of the Maryland Court of Appeals, 1695-1729*, American Legal Records, I (Washington, DC, 1933).
Boucher, Jonathan, ed., *Reminiscences of an American Loyalist, 1738-1789* (1925; reprint edn., Port Washington, NY, 1967).

Bristol, Roger, *Supplement to Charles Evans' American Bibliography* (Charlottesville, Va., 1970).

British Parliamentary Papers: Report from the Select Committee on Criminal Laws . . . 8 July 1819 (Shannon, Ireland, 1968).

Brock, R. A., *The Official Letters of Alexander Spotswood . . .*, 2 vols. (Richmond, 1882).

Browne, William Hand *et al.*, eds., *Archives of Maryland* (Baltimore, 1883-).

Buckinghamshire Manuscripts, Historical Manuscripts Commission, *Fourteenth Report*, Appendix, Part IX (London, 1895).

[Burt, Edward], *Letters From a Gentleman in the North of Scotland . . .*, 2 vols. (London, 1754).

Bush, Bernard, comp., *Laws of the Royal Colony of New Jersey, 1703-1745* (Trenton, 1977).

Calder, Isabel M., ed., *Colonial Captivities, Marches and Journeys* (1935; reprint edn., Port Washington, NY, 1967).

Callander, John, ed., *Terra Australis Cognita: or, Voyages to the Terra Australis . . .*, 3 vols. (Edinburgh, 1766-68).

The Calvert Papers: Selections from Correspondence (Baltimore, 1894).

Cameron, John, and Imrie, John, eds., *The Justiciary Records of Argyll and the Isles, 1664-1772*, 2 vols. (Edinburgh, 1949, 1969).

Candler, Allen D., *et al.*, eds., *The Colonial Records of the State of Georgia*, 28 vols. (Atlanta and Athens, Ga., 1904-82).

Carribbeana . . . Chiefly wrote by Several Hands in the West Indies . . ., 2 vols. (London, 1741).

Clark, Walter, ed., *The State Records of North Carolina*, 16 vols. (1895-1907; reprint edn., New York, 1970).

Colquhoun, P., *A Treatise on the Police of the Metropolis . . .* (London, 1800).

'Convicts for Transportation', Massachusetts Historical Society, *Proceedings*, XLIX (Oct. 1915-June 1916), 328-9.

Cox, J. Charles, *Three Centuries of Derbyshire Annals . . .*, 2 vols. (London, 1890).

Crèvecoeur, Hector St John de, *Letters from an American Farmer* (1782; reprint edn., New York, 1963).

Crittal, Elizabeth, ed., *The Justicing Notebook of William Hunt 1744-1749* (Devizes, 1982).

Defoe, Daniel, *The Fortunes and Misfortunes of the Famous Moll Flanders . . .*, ed. G. A. Starr (London, 1971).

——, *A Tour Thro' the Whole Island of Great Britain . . .*, 3 vols. (1724-26; reprint edn., London, 1968).

The Discoveries of John Poulter . . . (London, 1761).

Dobson, David, comp., *Directory of Scots Banished to the American Plantations, 1650-1775* (Baltimore, 1984).

Documents Relative to the Colonial History of the State of New York 15 vols. (Albany, 1853–87).

Eboranos [Thomas Robe], *Some Considerations for Rendering the Punishment of Criminals more Effectual* ... (1733, reprinted in his *A Collection of Political Tracts* [London, 1735]).

Eddis, William, *Letters from America*, ed. Aubrey C. Land (Cambridge, Mass., 1969).

'Eighteenth Century Maryland as Portrayed in the "Itinerant Observations" of Edward Kimber', *Maryland Historical Magazine*, LI (1956), 315–36.

An Essay upon the Government of the English Plantations on the Continent of America-by an American (London, 1701).

Evans, Charles, *The American Bibliography: A Chronological Dictionary of all Books, Pamphlets and Periodical Publications Printed in the USA, 1639–1800*, 14 vols. (New York, 1903–59).

Fielding, Henry, *A Proposal for Making an Effectual Provision for the Poor* ... (London, 1753).

Fielding, Sir John, *An Account of the Origins and Effects of a Police* ... (London, 1758).

Fitzsimmonds, Joshua, *Free and Candid Disquisitions, on the Nature and Execution of the Laws of England* ... (London, 1751).

Ford, W. C., ed., *Journals of the Continental Congress, 1774–1789*, 34 vols. (Washington, DC, 1904–37).

Fortescue Manuscripts, Historical Manuscripts Commission, *Thirteenth Report*, Appendix, Part III (London, 1892).

Fortescue, Sir John, ed., *The Correspondence of King George the Third* ..., 6 vols. (London, 1927–28).

The Fortunate Transport; or, the Secret History of the Life and Adventures of the Celebrated Polly Haycock ... *By a Creole* (London, [1750?]).

Fowle, J. P. M., ed., *Wiltshire Quarter Sessions and Assizes, 1736* (London, 1955).

Gee, Joshua, *The Trade and Navigation of Great-Britain Considered* (1738; reprint edn., New York, 1969).

A Genuine Account of the Behaviour, Confessions, and Dying Words, of the Malefactors ... (London, [1743]).

A Genuine ... *Account of the Life and Transactions of W. Parsons, Esq.* ... (*London, 1751*).

Gove, Philip Babcock, 'An Oxford Convict in Maryland', *Maryland Historical Magazine*, XXXVII (1942), 193–8.

Green, William, *The Sufferings of William Green* ... (London, [1775?]).

Greene, Jack P., ed., *The Diary of Colonel Landon Carter of Sabine Hall, 1752–1778*, 2 vols. (Charlottesville, Va., 1965).

Hakluyt, Richard, *A Discourse Concerning Western Planting*, ed. Charles

Deane, Collections of the Maine Historical Society, 2nd Ser. (Cambridge, Mass., 1877).

Hamer, Philip M., and Rogers, Jr., George C., eds., *The Papers of Henry Laurens* (Columbia, SC, 1968-).

Hancock, Harold B., ed., 'Life in Bucks County in 1722/23', *Pennsylvania History*, XXVII (1960), 397-402.

Hanway, Jonas, *The Defects of Police* ... (London, 1775).

——, *Distributive Justice and Mercy* ... (London, 1781).

Hening, William Waller, ed., *The Statutes at Large; Being a Collection of All the Laws of Virginia from the First Session of the Legislature in the Year 1619*, 13 vols. (Richmond and Philadelphia, 1809-23).

[Hewitt, John], *A Journal of the Proceedings of J. Hewitt* ... (n.p., 1790).

Hinke, William J., trans. and ed., 'Report of the Journey of Francis Louis Michel from Berne, Switzerland, to Virginia, October 2, 1701-December 1, 1702', *Virginia Magazine of History and Biography*, XXIV (1916), 1-43, 113-41, 275-303.

Historical Manuscripts Commission, *Report on the Records of the City of Exeter* (London, 1916).

Hoffer, Peter Charles, and Scott, William B., eds., *Criminal Proceedings in Colonial Virginia:[Records of] Fines, Examinations of Criminals, Trials of Slaves, etc., from March 1710 [1711] to [1754], [Richmond County Virginia]*, American Legal Records, X (Athens, Ga., 1984).

Howard, John, *An Account of the Principal Lazarettos in Europe* (Warrington, 1789).

——, *The State of the Prisons in England and Wales* (Warrington, 1777).

Hume, David, *Commentaries on the Law of Scotland, Respecting the Description and Punishment of Crimes*, 2 vols. (Edinburgh, 1797).

Hutcheson, Gilbert, *Treatise on the Offices of Justices of the Peace* ... *in* ... *Scotland* ..., 2 vols. (Edinburgh, 1806).

Jameson, J. Franklin, ed., 'Letters of Phineas Bond, British Consul at Philadelphia, to the Foreign Office of Great Britain, 1787, 1788, 1789', *Annual Report of the American Historical Association for the Year 1896* (1897), 513-659.

Jennings, John Melville, ed., 'The Poor Unhappy Transported Felons Sorrowful Account of His Fourteen Years Transportation at Virginia in America', *Virginia Magazine of History and Biography*, LVI (1948), 180-94.

Jensen, Merrill, ed., *English Historical Documents: American Colonial Documents to 1776* (New York, 1955).

Jones, Charles, *Some Methods Proposed Towards Putting a Stop to the Flagrant Crimes of Murder, Robbery, and Perjury* ... (London, 1752).

Jones, Hugh, *The Present State of Virginia*, ed. Richard L. Morton (Chapel Hill, NC, 1956).

'Journal of a French Traveller in the Colonies, 1765', *American Historical Review*, XXVI (1920-21), 726-47, XXVII (1921-22), 70-89.

Journals of the House of Commons, 155 vols. (London, 1547-1900).

Journals of the House of Commons of the Kingdom of Ireland, 19 vols. (Dublin, 1796-1800).

Kaminkow, Marion and Jack, eds., *Original Lists of Emigrants in Bondage from London to the American Colonies, 1719-1744* (Baltimore, 1967).

Knapp, Andrew, and Baldwin, William, eds., *The Newgate Calendar . . .*, 4 vols. (London, 1824-28).

Labaree, Leonard W., and Willcox, William B., eds., *The Papers of Benjamin Franklin* (New Haven, Conn., 1959-).

Lambert, Sheila, ed., *House of Commons Sessional Papers of the Eighteenth Century* (Wilmington, Del., 1975-).

Leake, Isaac Q., *Memoir of the Life and Times of General John Lamb . . .* (1850; reprint edn., New York, 1971).

Lediard, Thomas, *A Charge Delivered to the Grand Jury . . .* (London, 1754).

Le Hardy, William, ed., *Hertfordshire County Records: Calendar to the Sessions Books . . .* (Hertford, 1931).

Liberty Regain'd: Set Forth in the Remarkable Life and Actions of W*** S***, Esq. . . . (London, 1755).

The Life and Actions of James Dalton . . . (London, [1730]).

The Life, Travels, Exploits, Frauds, and Robberies of Charles Speckman . . . (London, 1763).

Livingston, William, *et al.*, *The Independent Reflector, or Weekly Essays on Sundry Important Subjects More particularly adapted to the Province of New York*, ed. Milton Klein (Cambridge, Mass., 1963).

[Madan, M.], *Thoughts on Executive Justice . . .* (London, 1785).

The Malefactor's Register . . ., 5 vols. (London, [1779?]).

Mandeville, B., *An Enquiry into the Causes of the Frequent Executions at Tyburn . . .*, (1725; reprint edn., Millwood, NY, 1975).

The Manuscripts of the House of Lords, New Ser., (London, 1964-).

'Maryland in 1773', *Maryland Historical Magazine*, II (1907), 354-62.

'Maryland in 1720', *Maryland Historical Magazine*, XXIX (1934), 252-5.

McIlwaine, H. R., ed., *Legislative Journals of the Council of Colonial Virginia, 1680-1776*, 3 vols. (Richmond, 1918-19).

——, and Kennedy, J. P., eds., *Journals of the House of Burgesses of Virginia, 1619-1777*, 13 vols. (Richmond, 1905-15).

Meaby, K. Tweedale, *Nottinghamshire: Extracts from the County Records of the Eighteenth Century* (Nottingham, 1947).

The Means of Effectually Preventing Theft and Robbery . . . (London, 1783).

Molland, Thomas, *Special Grace Uninterrupted, in its Egress . . .* (n.p., 1775).

Moraley, William, *The Infortunate: or, the Voyage and Adventures of William Moraley* . . . (Newcastle, 1743).

The Newgate Calendar (New York, 1962).

Nourse, Timothy, *Campania Foelix. Or, a Discourse of the Benefits and Improvements of Husbandry* (1700; reprint edn., New York, 1982).

O'Callaghan, E. B., ed., *Calendar of Historical Manuscripts in the Office of the Secretary of State, Part II, English Manuscripts* (Albany, 1866).

Ollyffe, George, *An Essay Humbly Offer'd for an Act of Parliament to Prevent Capital Crimes* (London, [1731]).

The Ordinary of Newgate, His Account of the Behaviour, Confession and Dying Words, of the Malefactors who were Executed at Tyburn (London, 1720–72).

Paley, William, *The Principles of Moral and Political Philosophy* (London, 1785).

Pargellis, Stanley, ed., *Military Affairs in North America, 1748–1765: Selected Documents from the Cumberland Papers in Windsor Castle* (New York, 1936).

The Parliamentary History of England . . ., 24 vols. (London, 1812–20).

Parliamentary Register . . ., 112 vols. (London, 1775–1813).

Perry, J., ed., 'The Transportation of Felons to America, 1717–1775: Some North Riding Quarter Sessions Records', *North Yorkshire County Record Office Journal*, VIII (1981), 65–117.

The Proceedings on the King's Commissions of the Peace, Oyer and Terminer, and Gaol Delivery for the City of London; and also the Gaol Delivery for the County of Middlesex, Held at Justice-Hall in the Old Bailey (London, 1718–77).

Proposals to the Legislature, For Preventing the Frequent Executions and Exportations of Convicts . . . (London, 1754).

R., J., *Hanging, Not Punishment Enough, For Murtherers, High-way Men, and House-Breakers* . . . (London, 1701).

Redington, Joseph, ed., *Calendar of Treasury Papers*, 6 vols. (1868–89; reprint edn., Nendeln, Liechtenstein, 1974).

——, and Roberts, R. A., eds., *Calendar of Home Office Papers of the Reign of George III*, 4 vols. (1878–99; reprint edn., Nendeln, Liechtenstein, 1967).

[Revel, James], *A Sorrowfull Account of a Transported Felon, That Suffered Fourteen Years Transportation at Virginia, in America* . . . (n.p., n.d.).

Riley, Edward Miles, ed., *The Journal of John Harrower: An Indentured Servant in the Colony of Virginia, 1773–1776* (Williamsburg, Va., 1963).

Roberts, Kenneth and Anna M., eds., *Moreau de St Mery's American Journey [1793–1798]* (Garden City, NY, 1947).

Sainsbury, W. Noel, ed., *Calendar of State Papers, Colonial Series* (1860–; reprint edn., Nendeln, Liechtenstein, 1964–).

Saunders, William L., ed., *The Colonial Records of North Carolina*, 10 vols. (1886–90; reprint edn., New York, 1968).

Select Trials . . . at the Sessions-House in the Old Bailey . . ., 2 vols. (London, 1734–35).

Select Trials at the Sessions-House in the Old Bailey, 4 vols. (London, 1742).

Serious Thoughts in Regard to the Publick Disorders . . . (London, [1751]).

A Sermon Preached to the Societies for the Reformation of Manners . . . (London, 1731).

Shaw, William A., ed., *Calendar of Treasury Books*, 32 vols. (London, 1904–57).

——, ed., *Calendar of Treasury Books and Papers*, 5 vols. (1897–1903; reprint edn. Nendeln, Liechtenstein, 1974).

[Shebbeare, John], *Letters on the English Nation by Batista Angeloni, a Jesuit who Resided Many Years in London*, 2 vols. (London, 1756).

Shugrae, Michael F., ed., *Selected Poetry and Prose of Daniel Defoe* (New York, 1968).

Silverthorne, Elizabeth, ed., *Deposition Book of Richard Wyatt, JP, 1767–1776* (Guilford, 1978).

Smith, Alexander, *A Compleat History of the Lives and Robberies of the Most Notorious Highway-men, Foot-pads, Shop-lifts, and Cheats . . .*, 3 vols. (London, 1719–20).

Some Reasons Humbly Offer'd, Why the Castration of Persons Found Guilty of Robbery and Theft . . . (Dublin, 1725).

The Statutes at Large, Passed in the Parliaments Held in Ireland . . ., 20 vols. (Dublin, 1786–1801).

Stephen, Leslie, and Lee, Sidney, eds., *Dictionary of National Biography*, 63 vols. (London, 1885–1900).

Stevenson, W. H. *et al.*, eds., *Records of the Borough of Nottingham . . .* (London and Nottingham, 1882–).

Stock, Leo Francis, ed., *Proceedings and Debates of the British Parliaments respecting North America*, 5 vols. (Washington, DC, 1924–41).

Stokes, Anthony, *A View of the Constitution of the British Colonies . . .* (London, 1783).

The Third Charge of Sir Daniel Dolins . . . (London, 1726).

Thoughts on Capital Punishments . . . (London, 1770).

Tinling, Marion, ed., *The Correspondence of the Three William Byrds of Westover, Virginia, 1684–1776*, 2 vols. (Charlottesville, Va., 1977).

A True and Genuine Account of the Behaviour, Confessions, and Dying Words of the Four Malefactors . . . Executed at Kennington-Common, 12 Apr. 1765 (London, [1766]).

US Bureau of Census, *Historical Statistics of the United States, Colonial Times to 1970: Part 2* (Washington, DC, 1975).

Warville, J. P. Brissot de, *New Travels in the United States of America, 1788*, ed. Durand Echeverria, trans. Mara Soceanu Vamos and Durand Echeverria (Cambridge, Mass., 1964).

The Whole Genuine Proceedings at the Assize of Peace, Oyer and Terminer, for the County of Kent . . ., (n.p., 1766).

Wilkinson, C. H., ed., *The King of the Beggars, Bampflyde-Moore Carew* (Oxford, 1931).

William-Jones, K., ed., *A Calendar of the Merioneth Quarter Sessions Rolls*, I, *1733-1765* (Aberystwyth, 1965).

II. SECONDARY SOURCES

Alexander, John K., *Render Them Submissive: Responses to Poverty in Philadelphia, 1760-1800* (Amherst, Mass., 1980).

Anderson, Fred, *A People's Army: Massachusetts Soldiers and Society in the Seven Years' War* (Chapel Hill, NC, 1984).

Anstey, Roger, *The Atlantic Slave Trade and British Abolition, 1760-1810* (London, 1975).

Appleby, Joyce Oldham, *Economic Thought and Ideology in Seventeenth-Century England* (Princeton, NJ, 1978).

Bailyn, Bernard, 'The Challenge of Modern Historiography', *American Historical Review*, LXXXVII (1982), 1-24.

Barlow, Derek, *Dick Turpin and the Gregory Gang* (Chichester, 1973).

Beattie, J. M., 'Administering Justice without Police: Criminal Trial Procedure in Eighteenth-Century England', in Rita Donelan, ed., *The Maintenance of Order in Society* (Ottawa, 1982), 12-22.

——, *Crime and the Courts in England, 1660-1800* (Princeton, NJ, 1986).

——, 'Crime and the Courts in Surrey, 1736-1753', in J. S. Cockburn, ed., *Crime in England, 1550-1800* (Princeton, NJ, 1977), 155-86.

——, 'Judicial Records and the Measurement of Crime in Eighteenth-Century England', in Louis A. Knafla, ed., *Crime and Criminal Justice in Europe and Canada* (Waterloo, Ontario, 1981), 127-45.

——, 'The Criminality of Women in Eighteenth-Century England', *Journal of Social History*, VIII (1975), 80-116.

——, 'The Pattern of Crime in England, 1660-1800', *Past and Present*, 62 (1974), 47-95.

——, 'Towards a Study of Crime in 18th-Century England: A Note on Indictments', in Paul Fritz and David Williams, eds., *The Triumph of Culture: Eighteenth-Century Perspectives* (Toronto, 1972), 299-314.

Berlin, Ira, 'Time, Space, and the Evolution of Afro-American Society in British Mainland North America', *American Historical Review*, LXXXV (1980), 44-78.

Blumenthal, Walter Hart, *Brides from Bridewell: Female Felons sent to Colonial America* (Rutland, Vt., 1962).

Breen, T. H., 'A Changing Labor Force and Race Relations in Virginia, 1660-1710', *Journal of Social History*, VII (1973), 3-25.

——, 'The Culture of Agriculture: The Symbolic World of the Tidewater Planter, 1760-1790', in David D. Hall, John M. Murrin, and Thad W. Tate, eds., *Saints & Revolutionaries: Essays on Early American History* (New York, 1984), 247-84.

Brewer, John, 'An Ungovernable People? Law and Disorder in Stuart and Hanoverian England', *History Today*, XXX (1980), 18-27.

Brown, Robert E., and Brown, B. Katherine, *Virginia, 1705-1786: Democracy or Aristocracy?* (East Lansing, Mich., 1964).

Butler, James Davie, 'British Convicts Shipped to American Colonies', *American Historical Review*, II (1896), 12-33.

Cameron, Joy, *Prisons and Punishment in Scotland: From the Middle Ages to the Present* (Edinburgh, 1983).

Cappon, Lester J., ed., *Atlas of Early American History: The Revolutionary Era, 1760-1790* (Princeton, NJ, 1976).

Carr, Lois Green, and Menard, Russell R., 'Immigration and Opportunity: The Freedman in Early Colonial Maryland', in Thad W. Tate and David L. Ammerman, eds., *The Chesapeake in the Seventeenth Century: Essays on Anglo-American Society* (Chapel Hill, NC, 1979), 206-42.

Clemens, Paul G. E., *The Atlantic Economy and Colonial Maryland's Eastern Shore: From Tobacco to Grain* (Ithaca, NY, 1980).

——, 'The Operation of an Eighteenth-Century Chesapeake Tobacco Plantation', *Agricultural History*, XLIX (1975), 517-31.

——, 'The Rise of Liverpool, 1665-1750', *Economic History Review*, 2nd Ser., XXIX (1976), 211-25.

Coldham, Peter Wilson, ed., *Bonded Passengers to America*, 9 vols. (Baltimore, 1983).

——, 'Transportation of English Felons', *National Genealogical Society Quarterly*, LXIII (1975), 172-5.

Coleman, Kenneth, *Colonial Georgia: A History* (New York, 1976).

Corfield, P. J., *The Impact of English Towns, 1700-1800* (Oxford, 1982).

Daultrey, Stuart, Dickson, David, and Ó Gráda, Cormac, 'Eighteenth-Century Irish Population: New Perspectives from Old Sources', *Journal of Economic History*, XLI (1981), 601-28.

Davies, Stephen J., 'The Courts and the Scottish Legal System, 1600-1747: The Case of Stirlingshire', in V.A.C. Gatrell, Bruce Lenman, and Geoffrey Parker, eds., *Crime and the Law: The Social History of Crime in Western Europe Since 1500* (London, 1980), 120-54.

Deane, Phyllis, and Cole, W. A., *British Economic Growth, 1688-1959: Trends and Structure* (Cambridge, 1967).

Dickson, R. J., *Ulster Emigration to Colonial America, 1718-1775* (London, 1966).

Doyle, David Noel, *Ireland, Irishmen and Revolutionary America, 1760-1820* (Dublin, 1981).

Dunn, Richard S., 'Masters, Servants, and Slaves in the Colonial Chesapeake and the Caribbean', in David B. Quinn, ed., *Early Maryland in a Wider World* (Detroit, 1982), 242-66.

——, 'Servants and Slaves: The Recruitment and Employment of Labor', in Jack P. Greene and J. R. Pole, eds., *Colonial British America: Essays in the New History of the Early Modern Era* (Baltimore, 1984), 157-94.

Earle, Carville, *The Evolution of a Tidewater Settlement System: All Hallow's Parish, Maryland, 1650-1783* (Chicago, 1975).

Ekirch, A. Roger, 'Bound for America: A Profile of British Convicts Transported to the Colonies, 1718-1775', *William and Mary Quarterly*, 3rd Ser., XLII (1985), 184-200.

——, 'Great Britain's Secret Convict Trade to America, 1783-1784', *American Historical Review*, LXXXIX (1984), 1285-91.

——, *'Poor Carolina': Politics and Society in Colonial North Carolina, 1729-1776* (Chapel Hill, NC, 1981).

——, 'The Transportation of Scottish Criminals to America during the Eighteenth Century', *Journal of British Studies*, XXIV (1985), 366-74.

Ensminger, Audrey H., *et al.*, eds., *Foods and Nutrition Encyclopedia*, 2 vols. (Clovis, Calif., 1983).

Fassbach, Scott, 'The Convict Trade to the Late Eighteenth Century Chesapeake' (Unpublished seminar paper, Johns Hopkins University, 1981).

Flaherty, David H., 'Crime and Social Control in Provincial Massachusetts', *Historical Journal*, XXIV (1981), 339-60.

Ford, Worthington Chauncey, ed., *Washington as an Employer and Importer of Labor* (1889; reprint edn., New York, 1971).

French, Christopher J., 'Eighteenth-Century Shipping Tonnage Measurements', *Journal of Economic History*, XXXIII (1973), 434-43.

Fryer, Peter, *Staying Power: The History of Black People in Britain* (London, 1984).

Galenson, David W., *White Servitude in Colonial America* (Cambridge, 1981).

George, M. Dorothy, *London Life in the 18th Century* (New York, 1965).

Gilbert, Arthur N., 'Army Impressment during the War of the Spanish Succession', *The Historian*, XXXVIII, 689-708.

Gillen, Mollie, 'The Botany Bay Decision, 1786: Convicts, not Empire', *English Historical Review*, XCVII (1982), 740-66.

Gradish, Stephen F., *The Manning of the British Navy during the Seven Years' War* (London, 1980).

Graham, Henry Grey, *The Social Life of Scotland in the Eighteenth Century* (London, 1937).

Greenberg, Douglas, *Crime and Law Enforcement in the Colony of New York, 1691–1776* (Ithaca, NY, 1976).

Greene, Jack P., *All Men Are Created Equal: Some Reflections on the Character of the American Revolution* (Oxford, 1976).

Grubb, Farley, 'Immigration and Servitude in the Colony and Commonwealth of Pennsylvania: A Quantitative and Economic Analysis' (Ph.D. diss., University of Chicago, 1984).

——, 'Morbidity and Mortality on the North Atlantic Passage: Evidence from Eighteenth-Century German Immigration to Pennsylvania', *Journal of Interdisciplinary History*, forthcoming.

Hanawalt, Barbara A., *Crime and Conflict in English Communities, 1300–1348* (Cambridge, Mass., 1979).

Harris, Michael, 'Trials and Criminal Biographies: A Case Study in Distribution', in Robin Myers and Michael Harris, eds., *Sale and Distribution of Books from 1700* (Oxford, 1982), 1–36.

Harrison, Fairfax, 'When the Convicts Came', *Virginia Magazine of History and Biography*, XXX (1922), 250–60.

Hay, Douglas, 'Crime, Authority and the Criminal Law: Staffordshire, 1750–1800' (Ph.D. diss., University of Warwick, 1975).

——, 'Property, Authority and the Criminal Law', in Douglas Hay *et al.*, eds., *Albion's Fatal Tree: Crime and Society in Eighteenth-Century England* (New York, 1975), 17–63.

——, 'War, Dearth and Theft in the Eighteenth Century: The Record of the English Courts', *Past and Present*, 95 (1982), 117–60.

Heath, James, *Eighteenth Century Penal Theory* (London, 1963).

Henriques, U. R. Q., 'The Rise and Decline of the Separate System of Prison Discipline', *Past and Present*, 54 (1972), 61–93.

Herrick, Cheesman A., *White Servitude in Pennsylvania: Indentured and Redemption Labor in Colony and Commonwealth* (New York, 1969).

Hoffer, Peter C., 'Disorder and Deference: The Paradoxes of Criminal Justice in the Colonial Tidewater', in David J. Bodenhamer and James W. Ely, Jr., eds., *Ambivalent Legacy: A Legal History of the South* (Jackson, Miss., 1984), 187–201.

Hofstader, Richard, *America at 1750: A Social Portrait* (New York, 1973).

Horn, James, 'Servant Emigration to the Chesapeake in the Seventeenth Century', in Thad W. Tate and David L. Ammerman, eds., *The Chesapeake in the Seventeenth Century: Essays on Anglo-American Society* (Chapel Hill, NC, 1979), 51–95.

——, 'The Letters of William Roberts of All Hollows Parish, Anne Arundel County Maryland, 1756–1769', *Maryland Historical Magazine*, *LXXIV* (1979), 117–32.

Howson, Gerald, *Thief-Taker General: The Rise and Fall of Jonathan Wild* (London, 1970).

Hughes, Thomas, *History of the Society of Jesus in North America, Colonial and Federal* (London, 1907).

Ignatieff, Michael, *A Just Measure of Pain: The Penitentiary in the Industrial Revolution, 1750–1850* (New York, 1978).

——, 'State, Civil Society, and Total Institutions: A Critique of Recent Social Histories of Punishment', *Crime and Justice: An Annual Review of Research*, III (1981), 153–92.

Innes, Joanna, 'Social Problems: Poverty and Marginality in Eighteenth-Century England' (Unpublished paper presented at a conference on 'The Social World of Britain and America, 1600–1820', Williamsburg, Va., 4–7 Sept. 1985).

Isaac, Rhys, *The Transformation of Virginia, 1740–1790* (Chapel Hill, NC, 1982).

Jervey, Theo D., 'The White Indentured Servants of South Carolina', *South Carolina Historical and Genealogical Magazine*, XII (1911), 163–71.

Jones, Alice Hanson, *Wealth of a Nation to Be: The American Colonies on the Eve of the Revolution* (New York, 1980).

Kellow, Margaret M. R., 'Indentured Servitude in Eighteenth-Century Maryland', *Histoire Sociale–Social History*, XVII (1984), 229–55.

King, Peter, 'Crime, Law and Society in Essex, 1740–1820' (Ph.D. diss., University of Cambridge, 1984).

——, 'Decision-Makers and Decision-Making in the English Criminal Law, 1750–1800', *Historical Journal*, XXVII (1984), 25–58.

Klein, Herbert S., *The Middle Passage: Comparative Studies in the Atlantic Slave Trade* (Princeton, NJ, 1978).

Kulikoff, Allan, 'A "Prolifick" People: Black Population Growth in the Chesapeake Colonies', *Southern Studies*, XVI (1977), 391–428.

——, 'Tobacco and Slaves: Population, Economy and Society in Eighteenth-Century Prince George's County, Maryland' (Ph.D. diss., Brandeis University, 1976).

——, *Tobacco and Slaves: The Development of Southern Cultures in the Chesapeake, 1680–1800* (Chapel Hill, NC, 1986).

Landau, Norma, *The Justices of the Peace, 1679–1760* (Berkeley, Calif., 1984).

Lang, John Dunmore, *Transportation and Colonization . . .* (London, 1837).

Langbein, John H., '*Albion's* Fatal Flaws', *Past and Present*, 98 (1983), 96–120.

——, 'Shaping the Eighteenth-Century Criminal Trial: A View from the Ryder Sources', *University of Chicago Law Review*, L (1983), 1–136.

Lenman, Bruce, and Parker, Geoffrey, 'The State, the Community and the Criminal Law in Early Modern Europe', in V.A.C. Gatrell, Bruce Lenman, and Geoffrey Parker, eds., *Crime and the Law: The Social*

History of Crime in Western Europe Since 1500 (London, 1980), 11-48.

Lewis, Ronald L., 'The Use and Extent of Slave Labor in the Chesapeake Iron Industry: The Colonial Era', *Labor History*, XVII (1976), 388-405.

Linebaugh, P., 'The Ordinary of Newgate and His *Account*', in J. S. Cockburn, ed., *Crime in England, 1550-1800* (Princeton, NJ, 1977), 246-69.

——, 'Tyburn: A Study of Crime and the Labouring Poor in London during the First Half of the Eighteenth Century' (Ph.D. diss., University of Warwick, 1975).

Lockhart, Audrey, 'Some Aspects of Emigration from Ireland to the North American Colonies between 1660 and 1775' (M.Litt. thesis, Trinity College, Dublin, 1971).

Mackay, David, *A Place of Exile: The European Settlement of New South Wales* (Melbourne, 1985).

Mackenzie, W. C., *The Western Isles: Their History, Traditions and Place-Names* (Paisley, 1932).

Main, Gloria L., 'Probate Records as a Source for Early American History', *William and Mary Quarterly*, 3rd Ser., XXXII (1975), 89-99.

——, *Tobacco Colony: Life in Early Maryland, 1650-1720* (Princeton, NJ, 1982).

Malcolmson, Robert W., *Life and Labour in England, 1700-1780* (New York, 1981).

Martin, Ged, ed., *The Founding of Australia: The Argument about Australia's Origins* (Sydney, 1978).

McCusker, John J., 'Colonial Tonnage Measurement: Five Philadelphia Merchant Ships as a Sample', *Journal of Economic History*, XXVII (1967), 82-91.

McMullan, John L., *The Canting Crew: London's Criminal Underworld, 1550-1700* (New Brunswick, NJ, 1984).

Menard, Russell R., 'From Servant to Freeholder: Status Mobility and Property Accumulation in Seventeenth-Century Maryland', *William and Mary Quarterly*, 3d Ser., XXX (1973), 37-64.

——, 'From Servants to Slaves: The Transformation of the Chesapeake Labor System', *Southern Studies*, XVI (1977), 355-90.

Merivale, Herman, *Lectures on Colonization and Colonies* (1861; reprint edn., New York, 1967).

Minchinton, W. E., 'Bristol-Metropolis of the West in the Eighteenth Century', *Transactions of the Royal Historical Society*, 5th Ser., IV (1954), 69-89.

——, King, Celia, and Waite, Peter, eds., *Virginia Slave-Trade Statistics, 1698-1775* (Richmond, 1984).

Morgan, Edmund S., *American Slavery, American Freedom: The Ordeal of Colonial Virginia* (New York, 1975).

Morgan, Gwenda, 'The Hegemony of the Law: Richmond County, 1692–1776' (Ph.D. diss., Johns Hopkins University, 1980).

Morgan, Kenneth, 'The Organization of the Convict Trade to Maryland: Stevenson, Randolph & Cheston, 1768–1775', *William and Mary Quarterly*, 3rd Ser., XLII (1985), 201–27.

Morgan, Philip D., 'Colonial South Carolina Runaways: Their Significance for Slave Culture', in Gad Heuman, ed., *Out of the House of Bondage: Runaways, Resistance, and Marronage in Africa and the New World* (London, 1986), 57–78.

Morris, Richard B., *Government and Labor in Early America* (New York, 1946).

Mullin, Gerald W., *Flight and Rebellion: Slave Resistance in Eighteenth-Century Virginia* (New York, 1972).

Munroe, John A., *Colonial Delaware: A History* (Millwood, NY, 1978).

Nash, Gary B., 'Social Development', in Jack P. Greene and J. R. Pole, eds., *Colonial British America: Essays in the New History of the Early Modern Era* (Baltimore, 1984), 233–61.

Nettles, Curtis P., *The Roots of American Civilization: A History of American Colonial Life* (New York, 1938).

O'Brien, Eris, *The Foundation of Australia* (London, 1937).

Oldham, Wilfrid, 'The Administration of the System of Transportation of British Convicts, 1763–1793' (Ph.D. diss., University of London, 1933).

Percy, David O., 'Agricultural Labor on an Eighteenth-Century Chesapeake Plantation' (Unpublished paper presented at the 45th Conference on Early American History, Baltimore, 13–15 Sept. 1984).

Philips, David, '"A New Engine of Power and Authority": The Institutionalization of Law-Enforcement in England, 1780–1830', in V. A. C. Gatrell, Bruce Lenman, and Geoffrey Parker, eds., *Crime and the Law: The Social History of Crime in Western Europe Since 1500* (London, 1980), 155–89.

Price, Jacob M., 'The Rise of Glasgow in the Chesapeake Tobacco Trade, 1707–1775', *William and Mary Quarterly*, 3rd Ser., XI (1954), 179–99.

Radzinowicz, Leon, *A History of English Criminal Law and its Administration from 1750*, 4 vols. (London, 1948–68).

Rankin, Hugh F., *Criminal Trial Proceedings in the General Court of Colonial Virginia* (Williamsburg, Va., 1965).

Rawley, James A., *The Transatlantic Slave Trade: A History* (New York, 1981).

Rees, Gareth, 'Copper Sheathing, An Example of Technical Diffusion in the English Merchant Fleet', *Journal of Transport History*, New Ser., I (1971), 85–94.

Robson, L. L., *The Convict Settlers of Australia, an Enquiry into the*

Origins and Character of the Convicts Transported to New South Wales and Van Diemen's Land, 1787–1852 (Carlton, Victoria, 1965).

Rogers, Nicholas, 'Popular Protest in Early Hanoverian London', *Past and Present*, 79 (1978), 70–100.

Rossiter, Clinton, *Seedtime of the Republic: The Origins of the American Tradition of Political Liberty* (New York, 1953).

Rule, John, *The Experience of Labour in Eighteenth-Century Industry* (London, 1981).

——, 'The Manifold Causes of Rural Crime: Sheep-Stealing in England, c 1740–1840', in John Rule, ed., *Outside the Law: Studies in Crime and Order, 1650–1850* (Exeter, 1982), 102–29.

Russo, Jean B., 'Occupational Diversification in a Rural Economy: Talbot County, Maryland, 1690–1759' (Unpublished paper presented at the 45th Conference on Early American History, Baltimore, 13–15 Sept. 1984).

Rutman, Darret B. and Anita, *A Place in Time: Middlesex County, Virginia, 1650–1750* (New York, 1984).

Salinger, Sharon Vineberg, 'Labor and Indentured Servants in Colonial Pennsylvania' (Ph.D. diss., University of California, Los Angeles, 1980).

Schmidt, Frederick Hall, 'British Convict Servant Labor in Colonial Virginia' (Ph.D. diss., College of William and Mary, 1976).

Scott, Arthur P., *Criminal Law in Virginia* (Chicago, 1930).

Secor, Gary P., 'The Working Environment of White Servants in the Chesapeake, 1710–1750' (Unpublished undergraduate research paper, Virginia Polytechnic Institute and State University, 1984).

Sharpe, J. A., *Crime in Early Modern England* (London, 1984).

——, *Crime in Seventeenth-Century England: A County Study* (Cambridge, 1983).

——, 'The History of Crime in Late Medieval and Early Modern England: A Review of the Field', *Social History*, VII (1982), 187–203.

Shaw, A. G. L., *Convicts and the Colonies: A Study of Penal Transportation from Great Britain and Ireland to Australia and other parts of the British Empire* (Carlton, Victoria, 1977).

Sheehan, W. J., 'Finding Solace in Eighteenth-Century Newgate', in J. S. Cockburn, ed., *Crime in England, 1550–1800* (Princeton, NJ, 1977), 229–45.

Sheridan, Richard B., 'The Domestic Economy', in Jack P. Greene and J. R. Pole, eds., *Colonial British America: Essays in the New History of the Early Modern Era* (Baltimore, 1984), 43–85.

Skaggs, David Curtis, *Roots of Maryland Democracy, 1753–1776* (Westport, Conn., 1973).

Smith, Abbot Emerson, *Colonists in Bondage: White Servitude and Convict Labor in America, 1607–1776* (Chapel Hill, NC, 1947).

Smith, Daniel Scott, 'Underregistration and Bias in Probate Records: An Analysis of Data from Eighteenth-Century Hingham, Massachusetts', *William and Mary Quarterly*, 3rd Ser., XXXII (1975), 100–10.

Sollers, Basil, 'Transported Convict Laborers in Maryland during the Colonial Period', *Maryland Historical Magazine*, II (1907), 17–47.

Souden, David, ' "Rogues, Whores and Vagabonds"? Indentured Servant Emigrants to North America and the Case of Mid-Seventeenth-Century Bristol', *Social History*, III (1978), 23–41.

Speck, W. A., *Stability and Strife: England, 1714–1760* (Cambridge, Mass., 1977).

Spierenburg, Pieter, *The Spectacle of Suffering: Executions and the Evolution of Repression: From a Preindustrial Metropolis to the European Experience* (Cambridge, 1984).

Steffen, Charles G., 'The Pre-Industrial Iron Worker: Northampton Iron Works, 1780–1820', *Labor History*, XX (1979), 89–110.

Styles, John, 'Criminal Records', *Historical Journal*, XX (1977), 977–81.

——, 'Sir John Fielding and the Problem of Criminal Investigation in Eighteenth-Century England', *Transactions of the Royal Historical Society*, 5th Ser., XXXIII (1983), 127–49.

Temple, Sarah B. Gober, and Coleman, Kenneth, *Georgia Journeys . . .* (Athens, Ga., 1961).

Thompson, E. P., 'Time, Work-Discipline and Industrial Capitalism', *Past and Present*, 38 (1967), 56–97.

——, *Whigs and Hunters: The Origins of the Black Act* (London, 1975).

Walsh, Lorena S., 'Servitude and Opportunity in Charles County, Maryland, 1658–1705', in Aubrey C. Land, Lois Green Carr, and Edward C. Papenfuse, eds., *Law, Society, and Politics in Early Maryland* (Baltimore, 1977), 111–33.

——, 'Urban Amenities and Rural Sufficiency: Living Standards and Consumer Behavior in the Colonial Chesapeake, 1643–1777', *Journal of Economic History*, XLIII (1983), 109–17.

Walton, Gary M., 'Colonial Tonnage Measurement: a Comment', *Journal of Economic History*, XXVII (1967), 392–7.

Watson, John F., *Annals of Philadelphia, and Pennsylvania, in the Olden Time . . .*, 3 vols. (Philadelphia, 1884).

Wood, Peter H., *Black Majority: Negroes in Colonial South Carolina from 1670 through the Stono Rebellion* (New York, 1974).

Wrightson, Keith, *English Society, 1580–1680* (London, 1982).

Wrigley, E. A., 'A Simple Model of London's Importance in Changing English Society and Economy, 1650–1750', *Past and Present*, 37 (1967), 44–70.

——, and Schofield, R. S., *The Population History of England, 1541–1871: A Reconstruction* (London, 1981).

INDEX

medical experiments, as alternative to
 transportation 62–3
merchants, convict 139
 aims of 3, 77, 97–8, 118–19, 131–2
 and early trade 18, 70
 fees charged by 70–1, 78–82, 84–5, 86
 legal obligations of 71, 88, 97
 and English trade 72–82
 in London 73–5, 78, 139
 social origins of 74–5
 in Bristol 74–5, 78, 139
 competition among 81–2
 and Irish trade 83–6
 and Scottish trade 85–6, 88–90
 and Atlantic crossing 97–8, 101
 efforts of, to reduce mortality 97–8,
  107–8
 fear convict rebellion 110
 see also trade, convict
merchants, indentured servant 75, 85,
 89
merchants, slave 74, 75
Mercury (ship) 235
Michel, Francis Louis 134
Middlesex 17, 24 n.
 and transportation subsidy 18
 convicts from 22, 23, 47, 49, 228
 trade fees in 80
 capital punishment in 231
Midland assize circuit 23, 34, 48, 49, 214
military service 62, 153
Mohawks 52
Moll Flanders 4, 59–60, 63, 177
Montrose 89
Moore, George 233–5
Morgan, Gwenda 190 n.
Morgan, Kenneth 117 n., 146 n.
Morgan, Thomas 93
Morice, Humphrey 37
Morocco 226
Morris, Richard B. 2
mortality:
 of convicts: in British gaols 34, 82,
  106–7; during Atlantic crossing
  49–50, 97–8, 103–8, 111; aboard
  hulks 230
 in slave and servant trades 105–6, 108

native origins:
 of convicts 46–8
 of convict runaways 196, 241
Neabsco Company 145
Nevis 113

Newcastle 73
New England 32, 112–13
Newgate (Dublin) 90
Newgate (London) 82, 90, 92
New Jersey 115, 138–9
Newry 83
newspapers:
 crime reports in 11, 169–70
 runaway advertisements in 141 n.,
  144 n., 146 n., 157, 173–4, 175,
  194–5
 notices of runaway capture in 203
New York 187
 receives convicts 112–13, 152
 and convict runaways 193, 206, 207,
  208
Nicholson, Benjamin 126
Norfolk 207
Norfolk assize circuit 28, 34, 48, 49
North, Lord 233
Northampton ironworks 145
North Carolina 117
Northern assize circuit 48, 49
Northern Neck (Va.):
 convicts in 141, 154, 166, 173–4, 175
 and sectionalism 155 n.
 crime in 172–6
 tenancy in 182
Northumberland, Duke of 52
Nottinghamshire 54
Nourse, Timothy 29
Nova Scotia 112–13, 117, 226, 234

occupations:
 of convicts 46, 52–55, 56, 58, 125–7
 of criminals generally 54, 172, 173,
  174
 see also skills
Old Bailey 33
 sentencing at 21, 31, 34–5, 38, 214,
  227, 228
 and pardons 34–5, 38, 213
 'Black Session' at 106
 and returned convicts 213, 214
Old Bailey Sessions Papers 5
Owners Goodwill (ship) 103
Oxford, Md. 122, 142
Oxford assize circuit 48, 49
oyer and terminer courts 172–3, 1⁻
 175–6

Paley, William 15, 189, 233
pardon process:
 importance of 33–4, 40, 44